The Child's Curriculum

The Child's Curriculum
Working with the natural values of young children

Edited by

Colwyn Trevarthen

Jonathan Delafield-Butt

Aline-Wendy Dunlop

OXFORD
UNIVERSITY PRESS

Great Clarendon Street, Oxford, OX2 6DP,
United Kingdom

Oxford University Press is a department of the University of Oxford.
It furthers the University's objective of excellence in research, scholarship,
and education by publishing worldwide. Oxford is a registered trade mark of
Oxford University Press in the UK and in certain other countries

First Edition published in 2018

Impression: 1

Published in the United States of America by Oxford University Press
198 Madison Avenue, New York, NY 10016, United States of America

British Library Cataloguing in Publication Data
Data available

Library of Congress Control Number: 2018955018

ISBN 978–0–19–874710–9

Printed and bound by
CPI Group (UK) Ltd, Croydon, CR0 4YY

Table of Contents

Abbreviations

ACEs	adverse childhood experiences		OLJ	online learning journal
ADHD	attention deficit hyperactivity disorder		PHSE	personal health and social education
BTC	Brazelton Touchpoints Center		PICL	Parents Involved in their Children's Learning (study groups)
CfE	Curriculum for Excellence			
DAP	developmentally appropriate practice		PISA	Programme for International Student Assessment
ECE	early childhood education		PND	postnatal depression
ECEC	early childhood education and care		POET	Scottish Pedagogies of Educational Transitions (project)
EDN	evolved developmental niche			
EEA	evolutionary adaptedness		QTS	Qualified Teacher Status
EEL	Effective Early Learning (project)		RE	religious education
ELC	Early Learning and Childcare		RIE	Resources for Infant Educarers®
ELiN	Early Learning in Nature (project)		SBHG	small-band hunter-gatherer
EOC	Equal Opportunities Commission		SPIN	Stichting Promotie Intensieve Thuisbehandeling Nederland (or 'Association for the Promotion of Intensive Home Training in the Netherlands')
EPPE	Effective Provision of Pre-School Education (Project)			
EYITT	Early Years Initial Teacher Training			
HCZ	Harlem Children's Zone		TLRI	Teaching and Learning Research Initiative
HNC	Higher National Certificate			
IMF	International Monetary Fund		UNCRC	United Nations Convention on the Rights of the Child
IMP	intrinsic motive pulse			
LTBS	'Learning to be Strong' (assertiveness programme)		UNICEF	United Nations International Children's Emergency Fund, now named the United Nations Children's Fund
LOS	learning operating system			
MIC	Men in Childcare			
NAEYC	National Association for the Education of Young Children		VIG	Video Interaction Guidance
			WHO	World Health Organization
OECD	Organisation for Economic Co-operation and Development			

List of Contributors

Dr. Cath Arnold
Early Years Consultant and Associate of
the Pen Green Research,
Development and Training Centre,
Corby, Northants, UK

Mr. Tam Baillie
Former Scotland's Commissioner for
Children and Young People, Scotland

Professor Tina Bruce
University of Roehampton, London,
England

Dr. Gary Clapton
School of Social and Political Science,
University of Edinburgh, Scotland

Ms. Keryn Davis
CORE Education, Christchurch,
New Zealand

Dr. Jonathan Delafield-Butt
University of Strathclyde, Glasgow,
Scotland

Mr. Robin Duckett
Sightlines Initiative, Newcastle, England

Professor Aline-Wendy Dunlop
School of Education, University of
Strathclyde, Glasgow, Scotland

Ms. Tracy Gallagher
Joint Head of the Pen Green Centre for
Under Fives and Their Families,
Corby, Northants, UK

Ms. Angela M. Kurth
Department of Psychology,
University of Notre Dame, USA

Ms. Ruta McKenzie
CORE Education, Christchurch,
New Zealand

Ms. Chris Miles, MBE
Former Pre School Education
Co-ordinator, Fife Council Education
Service, Scotland and former chair of
the Forest Schools Group of the Forestry
Commission, Scotland

Professor Darcia Narvaez
University of Notre Dame, USA

Dr. Ingela K. Naumann
School of Social and Political Science,
University of Edinburgh, Scotland

Dr. Rebecca Nye
The Open University, England

Assistant Professor Sally Peters
University of Waikato, New Zealand

Ms. Catherine Reding
Sightlines Initiative, Newcastle, England

Mr. Alan Sinclair
Centre for Confidence, Scotland

Professor Joshua Sparrow
Harvard Medical School, USA

Mr. Kenny Spence
Men In Childcare,
Edinburgh, Scotland

Professor Colwyn Trevarthen
University of Edinburgh, Scotland

Professor Pauline von Bonsdorff
University of Jyväskylä, Finland

Chapter 1

Defining the child's curriculum, and its role in the life of the community

Colwyn Trevarthen, Aline-Wendy Dunlop, and Jonathan Delafield-Butt

From being a person-in-relations to sharing in the knowledge and skills of a culture with its customs and laws

We share the philosopher John Macmurray's understanding of *The Form of the Personal*—his conviction that all experience comes from the 'self as a purposeful agent', and that all achievements of our societies come from 'persons in relations', acting and working together (Macmurray 1959, 1961).

Guided by inspiring educators such as Froebel, we are particularly concerned with the needs of the young child, hopefully growing from infancy in intimate trust with an affectionate and playful family into an active participant in a collaborative social world, seeking the supportive company of teachers who welcome the strengths of early years. We learn from the findings of Clyde Hertzman, a doctor concerned with public health, and his collaborators of the consequences, through all stages of a person's life, of poor support in this 'biological embedding' of the human spirit (Hertzman 2000, 2013; Heymann et al. 2006). Angela Kurth and Darcia Narvaez, in Chapter 6, identify the same environment as the 'evolved developmental niche' for a moral development, and which Ingela Naumann in Chapter 13 concludes must be the moral and practical foundation for just policies of early childhood education and care of ambitious modern states competing in a global economy. There is a need to protect the spirit of the child in a hostile world (Arnold 2014).

Young children's need is not just for an environment that supports strong growth of their individual abilities. Children play their part in the vitality of the human social engagement system (Porges and Daniel 2017), which guides the well-being and confidence of the whole community. Chapter 9, by Alan Sinclair and Tam Baillie, relates early childhood education and care (ECEC) policies to the United Nations Convention on the Rights of the Child (UNCRC 1989), and to what is happening in Scotland now. The primary source of 'the wealth of nations' is the playful creativity of children in affectionate relations with companions in understanding, at home with the family and in places provided for care and education. There are great inequalities in provision for the right to this shared life in early years that must be addressed by political will and ambition if society is to benefit and improve its efficiencies in health and well-being, together with its wealth.

In Chapter 12, Aline-Wendy Dunlop, of the School of Education at the University of Strathclyde, and Coordinator of the Scottish Pedagogies of Educational Transitions (POET) project, considers the care and education of young children in Scotland over time, drawing from Enlightenment thinking through to the present time. She emphasizes that, 'relationships and interactions with others form the natural core of children's experience and shape their futures. The ways in which children step in and out of the world outside the family, forming new relationships with people, places and in their thinking, is the substance of any child's curriculum'—sentiments in keeping with the master of the Scottish Enlightenment, Francis Hutcheson, who defined 'innate sympathy' as the foundation for human moral and intellectual achievements.

Scottish early humanist thinking, and the work of four universities—St Andrews, Glasgow, Aberdeen, and Edinburgh—established in the fifteenth and sixteenth centuries, can guide us in a transformed world ambitious in new technologies and the accumulation of wealth through trade. We need to foster the natural agency of the young child, with a focus on the support of a shared sense of well-being in relational pedagogies. Aline-Wendy calls this 'the child's gift' to educational policy and practice. To understand this primary stage of education in cultural knowledge and skills, a multidisciplinary approach is essential, and one that respects the wisdom of the past in planning for the future. That is what we have invited our authors to achieve.

Education—how to bridge between the spirit of a child and ambitious policies of state rule

This is both a difficult and a promising moment in the history of early education, with animated debate about plans to reform and regulate teaching practice, taking note of a changing science of the living human mind with its *autopoietic*, or 'self-making', powers and *consensual* or collaborative creativity (Maturana, Mpodozis, and Carlos Letelier 1995), its playfulness, not just its ability to learn new skills and symbols.

At the same time there have been extensive elaborations of the artificial environments we inhabit, with powerful tools for communication and for storing of knowledge, and new machines for representing facts along with ways to use them. These changes bring both new freedoms and new rules of collaboration, which may become restricted to benefit a few in positions of power.

Traditional communities and their adaptations are being dismantled and blended by migration, separating family members and placing them in different, unfamiliar worlds. Intimacy of work and understanding is changed, and traditional values are questioned. In consequence, the inborn powers of the human spirit for mastery of experience and cooperation in enterprises are both given more responsibility and frequently overlooked. We have to investigate carefully what can be developed to benefit learning of new ways of life in modern cultures, and what must be preserved for the sake of well-being of young children, for their intuitive intelligence, and for self-confidence in a lifetime of growth in understanding. We endorse the opinion of the New Zealand Ministry of Education, as quoted by Sally Peters, Keryn Davis, and Ruta McKenzie in Chapter 16:

> As global citizens in a rapidly changing and increasingly connected world, children need to be adaptive, creative and resilient. They need to 'learn how to learn' so that they can engage with new contexts, opportunities and challenges with optimism and resourcefulness.

(Ministry of Education 2017, p.7)

Accepting the innocent curiosity and affection of the story-telling child

Early childhood has become an important field of research in its own right. It should be, for we have all travelled and remembered those early years—personally as adventurous children, as Chris Miles reminds us in Chapter 5, or participating with them intimately as parents, and as practitioners and carers ... or as grandparents:

> There is no more joyful time. What a delight when visiting grandchildren staying for a week are asked, 'What shall we do today?', and then to hear the possibilities, the stories, the 'tell us about you when you were little', the memories of their parents, and the long drawn out days of playing, imagining, inventing, scripting each other's adventures. This time of making dressing-up clothes— clowns, pirates, wizards, and knights—led to a wonderful circus show with a sharing of roles and a very admiring family audience.

This spirit of the young child lifts us and takes us into new possibilities and new life stories. Early childhood serves a wealth of enthusiasm for the family and community well before school, and this enthusiasm carries into school, but there, often, schools' strong emphasis on classroom learning and achieving a list of learning objectives depresses the child's spirit of curiosity and enthusiasm for learning. Improved policy needs to follow the child's energy for learning in play and to think about what we offer children in school practice to capture this inventive, happy spirit in cooperation with them. In Chapter 3, Tina Bruce describes how careful observation of the spontaneous inventiveness of children by Friedrich Froebel led him to appreciate that play or 'free work' leads naturally to obedience for hard work with vocabulary and arithmetic. A child aged two to seven years in kindergarten is exploring rules and techniques, as well as using and discovering aesthetic and spiritual principles, as defined by Pauline von Bonsdorff in Chapter 7 and Rebecca Nye in Chapter 8. A sense of beauty in actions of the body that are creative of memorable experiences, and a respect for the spirit that inspires both making and sharing joy in graceful and moral behaviours in 'relational consciousness', are the two guiding principles of human vitality at every stage of development. They seek protection from anxiety of ugliness, and shame for bad actions and loneliness.

In Chapter 16, Sally Peters, Keryn Davis, and Ruta McKenzie confirm the observations of Froebel—that the young child's play is generative of skills for work, 'making sense of life in the world' with 'working theories' of what it is that makes sense to other people, and what they know to do with it. The development of 'common sense' and cooperation in all sorts of artificial beliefs and skills depends on mutual understanding for the co-construction of learning. This is the principal theme of Elwyn Richardson's experience, in a small New Zealand primary school, of how, *In the Early World* (the title of his first book), children's artful talents may thrive and enrich their learning of formalities of language or mathematics (Richardson 1964). Since this researcher in teaching practice developed his work with the older children, the renowned early years curriculum of New Zealand, *Te Whāriki* (Ministry of Education 2017), has been developed to attend to the pre-school period. It is inspired by the Maori belief that the child must 'lead the way', seeking support and new ideas for play from experienced companions. It forms the basis of early education policy for the New Zealand government, taking into account evidence from many 'developed' countries that weak response to, or neglect of, the young child's needs and wishes can lead to serious problems regarding social understanding and responsibility in later life. This evidence supports special training of nursery teachers in the practice of responsive education as described by Guy Claxton (2015)—an education that 'builds learning power' by recognizing the experience-testing initiatives of the 'learning operating system' of the playful child.

The psychology of such a bio-ecological relationship, and its story-making or 'mini-theories' co-constructed with the impulses of the child, is addressed in Chapter 2 by Colwyn Trevarthen, and in Chapter 4 by Jonathan Delafield-Butt. Jonathan focuses on the pleasure of constructive and adventurous projects of activity for a developing body and mind. He illustrates the nature of children's actions as intentional at all levels of expression to convey the drama of felt lives in shared actions. These actions follow a plan to guide the movements of the body—conscious of its feelings—through bold and careful steps to proud completion that makes sense of the endeavour in units, or parcels. These are early narratives evident before words on which knowledge of facts and rules of knowledge can be learned later. But the foundation for this learning is first relational and emotional. Jonathan observes that 'the joy at the conclusion of the project, with those motivations and bodily feelings, ensures it will be remembered and repeated'. Jerome Bruner names this a 'narrative intelligence' that serves and enables the logic of rational intelligence. We are story-making creatures, and our stories develop on a base of interpersonal relations to become more sophisticated in technical complexity over time (Bruner 2003).

In Chapter 2, Colwyn Trevarthen defines the innate impulse of children to engage with others emotionally and meaningfully in a natural spirit of shared belonging, and creative meaning-making. This zest for 'an adventure of ideas' co-created with others is the substance teachers and early years practitioners work with each day. Colwyn reminds us that before children can learn the rational skills of literacy and numeracy with a store of remembered facts that education policy typically attends to, a child must first belong to a community of affectionate and caring others that altogether serve as the bedrock for confident curiosity and risk-taking in the adventure of learning that delivers those political goals: 'a child in any human world shares the joy of a curious and clever life with companions, within and outside the family'. By tracing the development of skills for learning from infancy into early childhood, Colwyn recalls over a half-century of research that demonstrates children's appetite for learning their culture, and the detail of the sensitive affective relations that make this possible. Insights for training and professional care have been directly translated from this work to improve the ways in which teachers and caregivers can engage with children to be aware of, attend to, and support the emotional lives of our youngest citizens.

Peters, Davis, and McKenzie report on several studies investigating the benefits and challenges of teaching that cultivates and records working theories, including their ideas about belonging to a community and its culture. The sensitivity even toddlers with little language have for belonging to a particular collaborative group or community that they appreciate as 'special' leads to interest in the value of community-centred education projects for very young children and their parents, including the development of teaching in a minority language. They conclude their account of assisting the growth of children's' working theories as follows: 'This work is interesting and challenging. It requires skilled adults who can respond appropriately, and a context that supports the complexity of teachers' work and encourages a sense of wonder and curiosity for all'.

An outstanding example of community-affirming education for early years is Loris Malaguzzi's Reggio Emilia approach to sharing the enthusiasm in creativity and celebration of 'the hundred languages of childhood', responsive to their habitat, town, and culture. This is the philosophy adopted in Chapter 11 by Robin Duckett and Cath Reding of Sightlines, in Newcastle, in an exploration of how groups of children can create artful, exciting, and memorable accounts of their purposeful minds in a rich and challenging environment inside and outside school. Making and riding motorbikes in the litter of the forest gives fun to a group of primary reception class boys, and then it becomes an inspiring encounter with an imagined bear that smashed their work. In another Sightlines project, Cath Reding inspired a group of five-year-old girls to create a dance performance for their parents and their teacher, which they called 'Awakening Beauty' (described by Trevarthen and Panksepp 2016). It tells the story of how Beauty was saved from the spell of an evil fairy by good fairies and a brave prince.

The achievement of the Reggio Emilia model of early education is also appreciated by a study comparing different models of early education, reviewed by Kurth and Narvaez in Chapter 6. Here, they identify community-centred approaches that support young children's initiatives to 'grow into cooperative, agile moral actors'.

The wonderful transformation of a large, impoverished ethnic community by the 'place-based' work of educator Geoffrey Canada in the Harlem Children's Zone (HCZ) of New York, aided by Dr. T. Berry Brazelton and his Touchpoints project to support development from birth, is described by Josh Sparrow in Chapter 14. The HCZ was created to protect children's development in a very difficult world, using 'a relational, developmental, strengths-based, and culturally grounded approach'. Geoffrey Canada's project, by reclaiming supportive environments by collaboration between parents and teachers, ensured educational achievement for thousands of young people in an area of poverty and neglect, aiming 'to activate their community's collective problem-solving capacity, to share their dreams for their children, and to provide emotional support and concrete resources for each other'. The success of groups such the Harlem Gems—to encourage observation of children's abilities as discoverers, learners, and teachers—and Baby College—for young infants and their parents to meet and share life experiences in Harlem—led President Obama's administration to create federally funded place-based initiatives called 'Promise Neighborhoods' across the United States.

The present politics of early, 'pre-school' education must understand the need for providing an ECEC that is supportive of care by parents at home, and complementary to their care when there are hardships for the family—for example, low socioeconomic status, poor parenting, stress, and lack of stimulation, as identified by Hertzman. The provision must work with the needs and hopes of parents, as richly described by Josh Sparrow, and also by Cath Arnold and Tracy Gallagher of Pen Green in Corby in Chapter 15. There, a teacher, Margy Whalley, who had worked in Brazil and Papua, New Guinea, was assisted by the mayor of the town in making a world-renowned transformation of a community impoverished by closure of a large steel industry that had been the sole place of employment for most fathers. These stories from Harlem and Corby make clear that the spirit of the child, which animates discovery and learning, is adapted not just to receive 'support' from the community, but also to be an active 'inspiration' that can stimulate community leaders to work towards collaborative well-being and the overcoming of hardships for families.

Moral principles for a rich life of learning in a modern world

We have planned our book to address three aspects of early learning and responsive education. In Chapters 2–6, authors describe the primary motives and feelings for playful discovery of meaning in young life stories, and the nature of supportive parenting for building their scope of creative application and their morality in social projects. In Chapters 7–11 they clarify the deep aesthetic and spiritual feelings of human beings which give value to learning, and how these are supported by an investment in an early education that recognizes differences, including sex differences, in the personality of learners and teachers, listening to the hundred languages of the child. Finally, in Chapters 12–16, with particular attention to changes of services in Scotland, we examine the policies and achievements for educational provision in wealthy countries, and how an assistance of personal development and learning by the educational establishment must respect the imaginative and moral powers of young children, cooperate with and assist in parental care, and enable a community in which the children are raised as participants.

In Chapter 13, Ingela Naumann, Senior Lecturer in Social Policy at the School of Social and Political Science, University of Edinburgh, reviews the conflicted history of state provision for care and education in early childhood over the past two centuries, leading, in Europe, to the Organisation for Economic Co-operation and Development (OECD). She observes that, with the United Nations Children's Fund (UNICEF) and the World Bank, 'governments are spending more money than ever on 'early interventions', and in particular, early childhood education and care (ECEC).' 'For the first time in history there exists universal, or near-universal, access to ECEC for preschool children in most OECD countries.'

But, this care for early childhood reflects practical and ideological differences in state governance. In Denmark and Sweden, 60%–80% of children aged zero to three receive care from the state, whereas in the other countries percentages are below 40%, and in the UK are around 30% and falling. Recently developed early years curricula for three- to five-year-olds aim to improve, and test, cognitive development in pre-school children with attention to 'human capital development'. At the same time scientific evidence on early postnatal development of the human brain has led to the idea that a 'teaching' of rational practices and media of communication is important from infancy, but these ideas about a readiness for 'instruction' misunderstand the nature of children and their creative initiative. Popularization of these two topics has 'led to an oversimplification of the positive link between ECEC and child outcomes'. Ingela concludes that we need 'a renewed moral debate about the forms and content of state intervention into children's lives, and in particular, a critical discussion about the role of ECEC to support the development and flourishing of the "whole child", alongside the child's integration and participation in their cultural community'. These are the principles of moral development advocated by Kurth and Narvaez.

Responses of dedicated teachers to the closure of nursery schools

We draw on our experience of ten years of change and controversy in the communities of Scotland we know best. Events that radically reduced the provision of care and learning for young children inspired a group of teachers to oppose economic policies that were leading to the closure of established nursery schools with long records of excellent service in disadvantaged parts of the community in Glasgow and Edinburgh, to make education work.

We established a Child's Curriculum Group in 2006, and have organized conferences and publications to develop and disseminate knowledge and aims in order to save established nursery schools we value, and to inform those who determine policies and provide facilities for early years about the needs of pre-primary children and their families in relation to support from experienced teacher and carers (http://www.childscurriculum. org.uk/).

Encouraged by Enid Whitham, former chair at the British Association For Early Childhood Education (now Early Education) and advisor for Lothian Region for nursery education, teacher Barbara Robertson brought together Gill MacKinnon, Head of High School Yards, which was also under threat of closure, and teachers Kate Frame, Judy Goodier, Kitty Renton, and Moira Small, who met to lead and inform opposition to local authority closures of valued model nursery schools in Glasgow, Edinburgh, and the Lothians.

Measures by local administrators were intended to save money, to transfer trained teachers to primary schools, and in one case to make space for a housing development. Barbara Robertson invited Colwyn Trevarthen to assist with insights from developmental psychology on the natural gifts active children, from infancy, show for learning from a rich and varied environment as they express themselves in intimate communication with family, friends, and attentive teachers. Moira, Colwyn, and Aline-Wendy, whose former nursery school, Westfield Court, was also threatened with closure, went to meet with Adam Ingram, the Scottish Government's Minister for Children and Early Years.

Enid Whitham, as an energetic leader of nursery education who encouraged practice of the creative and expressive arts in early learning, knew that community projects for early childcare and education must value the well-being of the child as a contribution to society as a whole, and she backed the Pre-School Home Visiting project instigated by the Lothian Regional Council in the 1970s was independently evaluated by John Raven and Gail McCall. After the evaluation had been completed and published, Enid, as an advisor in early education, supported the continuing development of the teachers involved until her retirement. These teachers worked with families in their own homes and communities to encourage and support a rich home learning environment. Simultaneously, within schools, they worked to advance a climate of recognition and sharing of parental and professional skills and knowledge. Enid also supported the work of Forest Schools which led learning into the natural world where children aged three to five years can greatly benefit from independent exploration and building, and which also led to children sharing with their teachers their appreciation of stories and pictures relating to what they already knew from books about nature.

The need to distinguish learning in creative and convivial play from instruction about knowing and doing in 'proper' ways

Sarah Boyak, elected Convenor of the Scottish Parliament's Environment and Rural Development Committee in 2003, became Deputy Minister for the Environment and Rural Development in 2007. She was aided by Ros Marshall, Liberton Nursery Teacher, married to Andy Burns, who was the former leader of Edinburgh City Council working to improve the environment, transport, and education.

Early in 2006, Sarah Boyak responded to concerns expressed by Ros Marshall about reductions in nursery school support for communities. She confirmed that, with no statutory requirement for qualified teachers to be in nursery schools, the Glasgow City Council intended to transfer nursery teachers to primary schools, to reduce class sizes. This policy led to an intense debate after Fred Forrester, an English schoolteacher and Deputy General Secretary of the Educational Institute of Scotland, had an article published in *The Scotsman* on 13 September 2006, presenting his judgement that, 'as the primary sector needs more qualified teachers, taking them from nurseries is a sensible move', and, 'the pretence that pre-school provision should contain an element of formal education should be abandoned'.

There were many responses. Retired teacher Kitty Renton wrote,

> Yes, indeed, Fred Forrester, nurseries are for play, … where children have opportunities to develop physically, socially, emotionally and intellectually in a carefully planned environment. Play provides the adult with opportunities to observe and assess the child's level of development so that, in all areas, appropriate learning experiences can be planned. The nursery setting should be well resourced, with a trained staff team led by a teacher with specialist early education training. Longitudinal research by Kathy Sylva et al. reveals that if we wish our young children to get off to the best possible start in life, they will be placed in nurseries in which the staff team is led by an enthusiastic, highly qualified teacher. Furthermore, should entry to primary school be delayed to age 6 or 7, then the quality of INFORMAL pre-primary education is even more crucially important.

The Council had decided that nursery schools were too expensive, and they could not understand why they were necessary. They required too many staff, including those with degrees in early education who earned high wages. Such staff could be transferred to primary schools to improve the teacher–pupil ratio. The nursery schools would become nursery classes attached to a primary school and there would no longer be a head teacher in charge. Instead, the primary school head teacher or a promoted member of the primary school staff took on overall responsibility, with early years practitioners remaining in the class. Often, the promoted staff had little or no specialist early years training. Thus the autonomy of the nursery school was lost and wider work with parents and the community was problematic or seriously compromised

Retired teacher Moira Small recalls,

> Our arguments were that the Nursery School often became a special oasis where not only the children came to play in a safe place with stimulating and challenging things to experience but where parents could make friends and enjoy company at a time when they were often isolated from the immediate families and friends, either as migrants newly arrived in the UK with a language problem, or as families in Craigmillar and Wester Hailes separated from the people they know well. By inviting them into the Nursery they could often learn about how to help their children develop and learn and enjoy the Nursery community.

High-profile conferences that record the work of the Child's Curriculum Group

The wisdom of the child learner in early years animated our work and led to our first conference in 2010, opened by Adam Ingram and with presentations by many of the contributors to this book (http://www.childscurriculum.org.uk/previous-events/conf2010.php). Sadly, Enid was unwell and unable to attend the conference, and she died that year.

In spite of our writing to the press, taking part in protest meetings, and engaging the help of sympathetic politicians at the Scottish Parliament, local governments continued with plans to close nursery schools. We were determined to develop our efforts into a collaboration of people from many different disciplines and occupations united in their knowledge that the abilities shown by young children in a receptive environment are a primary resource for recovering a secure and productive way of life for themselves, and for the community.

In 2010, nursery schools assessed as 'excellent' were closed while the population of children under primary school age was rising, and one building which the community wanted to buy for use as a school was demolished to make space for housing, and more children. All the arguments for closure were based on economics, or provision for health and safety.

It is clear that more conservative, industry-related politics and concern for prosperity in production and sale of material possessions can lead to neglect of the contribution of young children, and of institutions that are adapted in practical ways to the natural needs of the children and their families in terms of support in their immediate social worlds. As Alan Sinclair and Tam Baillie report in Chapter 9, the findings of responsible research in economics do not support the narrower focus on immediate productivity and profits, and especially the privilege it gives to the wealthier parts of society who promote it. An important theme is the discovery that focusing on meeting the needs of the youngest, and of the neediest parts of the community, can lead to broad benefits for the whole population, provided that the practices, policies, and beliefs are coherent, and sufficiently sensitive to sustain basic values in a life of learning. These are the main conclusions of Chapters 6, 9, and 13–16.

We are pleased to see that at the time of writing, both the UK and Scottish governments have pledged and put into action ambitious plans to secure increased early childhood care provision for all three- to four-year-olds, with some support for younger children whose parents struggle to meet the cost. But we caution that while this is a welcome move to be commended, in the UK we have more work to do to ensure that early education and care accepts the nature of the child as an innately curiously learner, dependent for confidence and well-being on trusting and enduring sensitive relations with caregivers. Training of this workforce requires attention to ensure these professionals follow the needs and interests of the child, and can support them over time with robust relationships. And high turnover of staff and management with abrupt changes to key workers and caregivers will not meet the emotional needs of the children these policies seek to support, and can be disruptive rather than supportive. More care and attention are required in policy and governance if we are to 'get it right' for every child.

Foundations of human imagination, and its cooperation in the cultural achievements of the community

Scientific research on the role of emotion as life-controlling actions of the brain has led to a view that the intentions and states of awareness of our animate selves are not only excited by the senses and built by learning, but also created 'imaginatively' from within by vitality-sustaining 'affective consciousness'. We guide our actions by feelings that anticipate the level of effort and the pleasure or fear that will accompany any impulse to move, that direct rational cognitive achievements, and that also guide communication and learning in social groups.

Leading researchers in the study of emotions and their adaptation for cooperative social life give complex aesthetic and moral emotions—such as those described by Tina Bruce, Pauline von Bonsdorff, and Rebecca Nye in their respective chapters—a primary place in

Figure 1.1 A skilled teacher in Cameron House Nursery School appreciating a child's story, while his friends attend, sharing his feelings.

the construction of rational comprehension and meaningful communication, as well as in building a confident place in relationships of family and community. The emotions that appreciate graceful execution of actions and inspire gracious communication, with pride in achievement or shame at failure, have a directive function in the experience of a human life from infancy (Stern et al. 1998; Damasio 2003; Panksepp and Biven 2012; Narvaez 2014; Meares 2016; Porges and Daniel 2017).

The authors of this book focus, with their special expertise, on how the flourishing of a child's creative impulses and convivial feelings contribute to the development of meaningful life with companions, as in the spontaneous attention of the group to a child's story illustrated in Figure 1.1. In addition, they were invited to assess the benefits and constraints of administrative and political actions of those in official positions of power, and the interpretations of the motives of young children and their parents by science and academic psychology.

References

Arnold, J.C. (2014). *Their Name Is Today: Reclaiming Childhood in a Hostile World*. Robertsbridge: Plough Publishing House.

Bruner, J.S. (2003). *Making Stories: Law, Literature, Life*. Cambridge, MA: Harvard University Press.

Claxton, G. (2015). The development of learning power. A new perspective on child development and early education. In: S. Robson and S. Quinn (eds.) *International Handbook of Young Children's Thinking and Understanding*. UK: Routledge, pp. 367–76.

Damasio, A.R. (2003). *Looking for Spinoza: Joy, Sorrow, and the Feeling Brain.* Orlando, FL: Harcourt.

Hertzman, C. (2000). The case for an early childhood development strategy. *Isuma,* Autumn 2000, 1(2), 11–18, http://www.peelearlyyears.com/pdf/The%20Case%20for%20an%20Early%20Childhood%20 Development%20Strategy,%20Canada.pdf, accessed 28 Feb 2018.

Hertzman, C. (2013). Social inequalities in health, early child development and biological embedding. *Revue d'Epidémiologie et de Santé Publique,* **61**(Suppl. 2), S39–46. http://europepmc.org/abstract/ MED/23684106/reload=0;jsessionid=m7Et04EDaEySrO0VF, accessed 28 Feb 2018.

Heymann, J., Hertzman, C., Barer, M.L., and Evans, R.G. (eds.) (2006). *Healthier Societies: From Analysis to Action.* Oxford: Oxford University Press.

Macmurray, J. (1959). *The Self as Agent* (Volume I of *The Form of the Personal*) (paperback edition, 1969). London: Faber and Faber.

Macmurray, J. (1961). *Persons in Relation* (Volume II of *The Form of the Personal*) (paperback edition, 1970; new edition, with introduction by F.G. Fitzpatrick, Humanities Press International, 1991; reissued by Faber and Faber, 1995). London: Faber and Faber,

Maturana, H., Mpodozis, J., and Carlos Letelier, J. (1995). Brain, language and the origin of human mental functions. *Biological Research,* **28**(1), 15–26.

Meares, R. (2016). *The Poet's Voice in the Making of Mind.* London/New York: Routledge.

Ministry of Education. (2017). *Te Whāriki He whāriki mātauranga mō ngā mokopuna o Aotearoa. Early Childhood Curriculum.* Update. Wellington, NZ: Ministry of Education.

Narvaez, D. (2014). *Neurobiology and the Development of Human Morality: Evolution, Culture and Wisdom.* New York: Norton.

Panksepp, J. and Biven, L. (2012). *The Archaeology of Mind: Neuroevolutionary Origins of Human Emotions.* New York: Norton.

Porges, S., and Daniel, S. (2017). Play and dynamics of treating pediatric medical trauma. Insights from polyvagal theory. In: S. Daniel and C. Trevarthen (eds.) *Rhythms of Relating in Children's Therapies: Connecting Creatively with Vulnerable Children.* London: Jessica Kingsley, pp. 113–25.

Richardson, E. (1964). *In the Early World* (3rd edn published in 2012). Wellington, NZ: New Zealand Council for Educational Research.

Stern, D.N., Sander, L.W., Nahum, J.P., Harrison, A.M., Lyons-Ruth, K., Morgan, A.C., Bruschweiler-Stern, N. and Tronick, E.Z. (1998). Non-interpretive mechanisms in psychoanalytic therapy: The 'something more' than interpretation. *International Journal of Psycho-Analysis,* 79, 903–21.

Trevarthen, C. and Panksepp, J. (2016). In tune with feeling: Musical play with emotions of creativity, inspiring neuroaffective development and self-confidence for learning in company. In: S. Hart (ed.) *Inclusion, Play and Empathy: Neuroaffective Development in Children's Groups.* London: Jessica Kingsley, pp. 29–54.

UNCRC (1989). United Nations Convention on the Rights of the Child, https://www.unicef.org.uk/ what-we-do/un-convention-child-rights/, accessed 28 Feb 2018.

Chapter 2

What young children give to our learning

Colwyn Trevarthen

Why are we so intellectually dismissive towards narrative? ... Storytelling performs the dual cultural functions of making the strange familiar and ourselves private and distinctive. If pupils are encouraged to think about the different outcomes that could have resulted from a set of circumstances, they are demonstrating useability of knowledge about a subject. Rather than just retaining knowledge and facts, they ... use their imaginations to think about other outcomes ... This helps them to think about facing the future, and it stimulates the teacher too.
(Bruner 1996, pp. 39–42, on the role of narrative in the development of culture)

Our purpose

All contributors to this book appreciate the creative vitality of children—how ready they are to learn life-enriching stories in a kind and convivial environment of teachers and caregivers who are affectionate friends conscious of their pupils' needs. As parents, teachers, or casual playmates, we have been inspired by participating in childish vitality, responding to the special sensibilities that emerge at different ages from birth in ways that may be assisted by education, as long as it is motivated by shared understanding.

We also know the difficulties a teacher may confront in a regulated service of instruction at school, which requires tests of 'output' or 'progress' in specified tasks deemed essential for intelligent participation in the conventional practices of culture. And we know the unhappiness of a child who fails to understand prescribed lessons. We are concerned that a one-sided belief in instruction, with institutional rules of practice and definitions of meaning and thinking, may cause shame that blocks learning, especially in early years—that crucial adventurous stage of a young person's development.

We have agreed to work on this problem—to seek principles of practice that defend the natural vitality and conviviality of the embodied and growing child's mind before, and into, school. We combine our experience to oppose any curriculum of training of intelligence and obedience that has been conceived only to help the privileged gain wealth and power, and to protect their rank and possessions.

In the final words of her masterpiece on *Children's Minds*, Margaret Donaldson summarizes the risk of insensitive teaching as follows:

> In the life of a child, joy in the immediate involvement of the body in skilled activity comes early and spontaneously. As we have seen already, this is by no means an unthinking joy, but it is not reflective. The later exercise of the reflective capacities can bring joy too—but this is a joy that does not come unaided....
>
> Thus if at last we become really good at helping large numbers of people to the experience of intellectual satisfaction, we should have more freedom to turn to the development of human potentials of other kinds. Certainly it should not then be too hard—or too dangerous—to reinstate the human band. And the probable result would be a vast release of creative energy.
>
> Beyond this, I leave speculation to the futurologists. But if we are not willing to try and to keep trying, in the light of knowledge attained, to help our children meet the demands which we impose on them, then we must not call them stupid. We must rather call ourselves indifferent or afraid.
>
> (Donaldson 1978, pp. 127–8)

Scientific knowledge of the growth of human life can help us appreciate the biology of a child's acting in the world with company. But it is important that the knowledge should not be too narrowly conceived. In the foreword to a book entitled *Early Childhood and Neuroscience* by Mine Conkbayir, published earlier this year, I wrote about barriers to understanding of the playful and affectionate motives for learning in early childhood that result from too narrow, abstract reasoning about the brain as an organ for 'cognition', just active to record information.

> As teachers and parents we need to appreciate how, in every human community, impulses for play inspire rituals of artful creativity and their celebration, and to consider how the source of this imaginative vitality born in our children, and treasured by the musicologist Jon-Roar Bjørkvold and the poet Kornei Chukovsky, may be best supported.... Does the ambitious world of adults searching for profits in knowledge and skills become toxic for the spirit of many children, as the writer and counsellor Johann Christoph Arnold of the Bruderhof Community fears?
>
> (Conkbayir 2017)

I refer to Arnold's book *Their Name Is Today: Reclaiming Childhood in a Hostile World*, published in 2014, and mention two inspiring books on childish artfulness and invention: *The Muse Within* by Bjørkvold (1992), and *From Two to Five by* Chukovsky (1968), a poet who admired the young child's 'genius' for inventing language.

Taking inspiration from how infants share what they know

My work in developmental psychology began with the advice of Jerome Bruner, who, seeking to advance the theory of 'cognition', was inspiring a new study of human cleverness before language (Bruner 1968, 1975). He supported researchers who were taking a fresh look at what a primary teacher in a small rural community in New Zealand, Elwyn Richardson, called life *In the Early World* (Richardson 1964). Richardson's world-famous achievement and the making of a rich philosophy of teaching in a remote rural primary school in New Zealand depended on his belief that children growing up to adolescence are natural artists and scientists who can discover the conventions of cultural practice by free exploration and collaboration in any kind of imaginative task, however artful or technical (MacDonald 2016).

Mentors for the research that I began in Bruner's Center for Cognitive Studies included the paediatrician Berry Brazelton (1979), who showed his medical colleagues how to treat the newborn as a person seeking company; a psychiatrist Daniel Stern (1985), whose observations of infants playing with their mothers led him to believe that a radical reappraisal and transformation of psychoanalytic therapy was needed; and Margaret Donaldson (1978), who led research in Edinburgh on how an imaginative thinking with social awareness inspires the growth of children's minds as they explore the properties and uses of a shared world.

In the past 50 years, research to describe how infants live with those who care for them has revealed remarkable powers of selective awareness in newborn babies, and an eager need to engage with other persons' impulses and imitate them. This research, which flourished in the 1980s, generating deep controversy concerning the development of the human mind, is given a rich review by my colleague Ben Bradley in his *Visions of Infancy* (1989).

> Within a year, before any words are picked up, the infant is an inquisitive and affectionate playmate learning conventional behaviours, including daily rituals and purposeful handling of everyday tools. The child has taught us that we are born with powerful motives that lead to sharing baby songs, action games and use of words with many other tricks and devices for spreading and keeping alive a particular history of meanings. This we describe as the 'nature of culture', in the child, which education has to serve as an assistance for development of self-confident and cooperative practices.
>
> (Delafield-Butt and Trevarthen 2013, 2015;
> Trevarthen, Gratier, and Osborne 2014; Trevarthen and Delafield-Butt 2015, 2017)

Educational practice for early years has a troubled history

> The roots of all sciences and arts in every instance arise as early as in the tender age, and that on these foundations it is neither impossible nor difficult for the whole superstructure to be laid; provided always that we act reasonably as with a reasonable creature.
>
> (John Amos Komensky (1592–1671), known as Comenius,
> in *The School of Infancy*, quoted by Quick 2003, pp. 144–5)

The paradox which wrecks so many promising theories of education is that the training which produces skill is so very apt to stifle imaginative zest. Skill demands repetition, and imaginative zest is tinged with impulse. Up to a certain point each gain in skill opens new paths for imagination. But in each individual, formal training has its limits of usefulness. Beyond that limit there is degeneration: 'The lilies of the field toil not, neither do they spin'. . . . The social history of mankind exhibits great organizations in their alternating functions of conditions for progress, and of contrivances for stunting humanity.

(Alfred North Whitehead 1929, pp. 338–9)

Before obeying instruction in a curriculum for language, literacy, and numeracy—'grammar, logic, and rhetoric', the *trivium* of training for skills of a 'free man' in a rich industrial culture of Hellenistic Greece or the Roman Empire—a child in any human world shares the joy of a curious and clever life with companions, within and outside the family. As Whitehead said, the primary acquisition of knowledge involves freshness, enthusiasm, and enjoyment of learning, in what he called the 'romantic' stage of the educational experience. In class at school, this is transformed. The child's growing curiosity for techniques of doing and thinking leads to the stage of 'precision', which concerns 'exactness of formulation' (Whitehead 1929, p. 18).

Comenius, the Moravian philosopher, pedagogue, and theologian who wrote *The School of the Mother's Breast* (1628), *School by Play* (1630), and *The Gate of Languages Unlocked* (1631), became world famous as a teacher and creator of schools. By appreciating the infant's contribution to human learning he worked to elucidate the best principles for educating children from birth to about the age of six years, when teaching may become more formal.

In the nineteenth century, Robert Herbert Quick developed the study of the history of education at Cambridge University. He described 'a growing science of education' intended to help parents and teachers welcome the initiatives of all children to share interests and feelings about the world in imaginative ways (Quick 1894/2003). The Jesuits of the sixteenth century criticized the restriction of teaching to book learning and advocated that young children must exercise their bodies. Rabelais ridiculed the idea of 'pouring in' formulated knowledge to fill an ignorant mind. Pestalozzi and Froebel worked as teachers to reduce misfortunes of young children obliged to work too soon at prescribed tasks, promoting their freedom to enjoy sociable learning at play in nature with affectionate companions.

At the end of the nineteenth century, James Mark Baldwin (Baldwin 1895) anticipated the discoveries of the pioneering neurophysiologist Charles Sherrington on the importance of proprioception, or 'self-feeling' of the body in movement, for inspiring consciousness (Sherrington 1906). Thus began a science that conceives intentions in movement as the foundation of thoughts and communication. Baldwin named the initiative for action that repeats itself to test stimulation a 'circular reaction', a moving to cause experience. He inspired Piaget's theory of active learning (Piaget 1951) and Vygotsky's explanation of the social development of thought and language with the child as playful agent (Vygotsky 1978).

But Baldwin's enlightened understanding was immediately rejected by the machine psychology of Edward Thorndike's research on conditioning of reflexes, which led to John Watson's behaviourism. Baldwin received appreciation only in the writings of philosophers

Bergson, James, and Dewey, and by Whitehead, who helped his pupil Susan Langer develop a philosophy of art in movement and in community, presented as *Philosophy in a New Key* (Langer 1942).

While greatly advancing appreciation of the child's initiative to solve problems in action with brilliant observations, Jean Piaget failed to notice that attractive expressions by eyes, face, voice, and hands show more than 'pleasure in mastery' of a practical task for that actor alone (see 'Appendix: Piaget's Theory of Intellectual Development' in Donaldson 1978, pp. 129–46). He did not appreciate, as Baldwin and Langer did, that artful 'circular reactions'—movements to feel and explore—are adapted to be shared in affectionate mutual engagements with teachers. They do not only serve technical purposes. They are artful to enable sympathetic awareness and shared intentions.

In short, we are led by more observant science of human nature to recognize that the foundations of education, in every culture, must be inherent in the development from birth of human impulses to test and expand active experience, and to share it joyfully with companions. Education depends on 'storytelling' for fun, with universal emotions of Donaldson's 'human sense'. Loris Malaguzzi of Reggio Emilia in Italy described this gift as the 'hundred languages' of childhood in play with all sorts of media that bring freedom to discover their use in skills of everyday life, and in thinking (Edwards, Gandini, and Forman 1998; see also Chapter 11).

Intuitive motor/affective intelligence of a human being: to move confidently with joy and love—from intentions to do, to intentions to know

Detailed description of the wonderful ease and grace of a healthy newborn baby's movements—their inquisitive and hopeful actions, and their power to communicate interest and feelings with 'rhythms of relating'—has led to discovery of how purposeful meaning-making is shared in play (Delafield-Butt and Trevarthen 2015; Daniel and Trevarthen 2017; Trevarthen 2017; Trevarthen and Delafield-Butt 2017). A baby has learned the mother's voice before birth, and seeks its promise of loving company (DeCasper and Fifer 1980). The newborn commands a complex body as one intelligent self, reaching out, looking, and listening with intuitive measures of time and space, demonstrating an awareness of the body in movement that anticipates a walking, talking life (Figure 2.1).

Eyes, head, hands and arms, and legs dance in harmony, and the mouth sings, inspired by the pulse of a secret melody that attracts and responds to affectionate companionship that supports actions and feelings of the whole body (Malloch and Trevarthen 2010). This is how a young human being is ready to be a personality in a cultural world, moving and thinking with creative conviviality in action, with motives and feelings that guide and reward story-making by a computing cognitive brain (see Chapter 4). As veterinarian Barbara Goodrich, author of the anti-Cartesian principle 'We do, therefore we think' (Goodrich 2010), was pleased to discover there are now brain scientists who accept that the body and mind come alive as one with the consensual rhythms of movement.

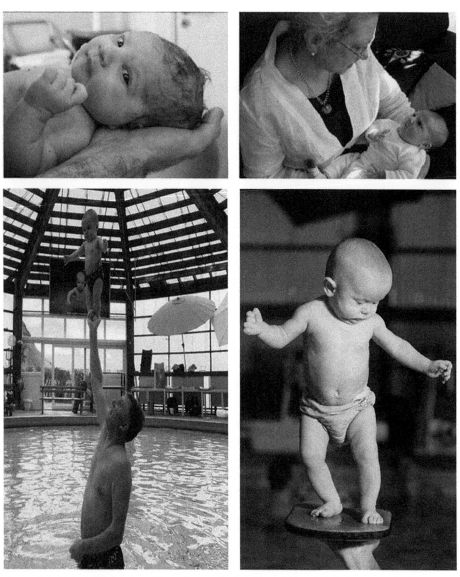

Figure 2.1 *Above left*: A baby girl, one hour after birth, resting on her father's arm, looks with a very intelligent expression, an attentive mouth, and a gesture of her hand towards the photographer, her mother. *Above right*: On day 4, she meets her grandmother and expresses her wish to have a conversation, with a right-hand message and her left hand held towards her body, like Leonardo's drawing of St. John the Baptist. *Below*: Infants three and four months old, assisted to stand by instructor Snorri Magnússon, who is leading his baby swimming class in a large thermal pool in Iceland. *Below left*: A baby girl is held above Snorri's head. *Below right*: A baby boy stands confident on a rubber platform. Normally, infants begin to stand unaided at about nine months of age.

And, as noted by Merlin Donald (2001), we have special human powers of social collaboration in expressive body movements that enable us to share useful objects, and the feelings we have about them. Martin Buber, Jewish philosopher of dialogue and educator, expressed a clear understanding that it is this interpersonal 'I-Thou' awareness that animates the development of an objective 'I-It' awareness.

> On the basis of his relationship with others, the child then comes to a knowledge of the external world, that is, through his social relationships he receives those categories that enable him to see the world as an ordered continuum of knowable and passive objects.
>
> (Buber, quoted in Friedman 2002, pp. 193–4)

The child shows a readiness to be informed by other persons, who can provide support for intentions. This is brilliantly demonstrated by Icelandic swimmer, sport teacher, and baby swimming instructor Snorri Magnússon, in his classes of mothers and babies exercising with him in a thermal pool. He displays how he can aid a baby to stand erect on his hand high above his head, five or six months before any baby is able to stand on its own (Figure 2.1). This exercise in precocious standing, enabled by Snorri's skilled 'understanding', brings benefits in motor development. It is clear that the help Snorri gives depends on innate abilities of the baby that anticipate development of self-confidence with assistance. He is not teaching the babies to stand; rather, he is learning how to support their clever getting ready to stand, and then walk about.

The innate ability of very young infants to coordinate the muscles of their whole body to direct an upright posture depends on practice of moving-with-feeling that begins from the second month of gestation. This forms the foundation of lively consciousness for a mobile self, who will run about full of curiosity to perceive an outside world, learn about its uses, and share experiences of life in expressive movement (Trevarthen 1982).

In the 1920s, a young Russian psychologist, Nikolai Bernstein, used film to examine in minute detail the movements of workmen using tools, athletes racing, and toddlers learning to walk. He revealed the imagination that predicts, with almost no wasted energy, what efficient moving of a purposeful self will feel like and how it should be shaped to make a correct movement, and he called this a 'motor image' (Bernstein 1967). He discovered that a toddler's hopping, twirling, and running about is miraculously regulated to explore the 'degrees of freedom' of movement with such a clever body. Their creative gymnastics is very efficient—it takes brave risks, and rarely makes a mistake.

At first, a newborn, more immature than most other mammals at birth, depends on a mother's protective holding and nourishment from the milk of her breast, but the young person is already looking for communication of well-being with any attentive companion, by movements that communicate inner states of vitality with wonderful ease, grace, and sympathy (Stern 2000, 2010). This hopeful self-making liveliness and its joyful conviviality in play are not learned by conditioning of reflexes, as Pavlov, Thorndike, Watson, and Skinner thought. Bernstein's science of motor intelligence was welcomed by developmental psychologists Vygotsky, Piaget, and Bruner, who, by the mid-twentieth century, agreed that we are born active and imaginative players expecting partners in games of life.

As Dr. T. Berry Brazelton showed his fellow paediatricians over 50 years ago, sensitive parents accept the bright newborn as an alert companion ready for their love and care. He changed a medical practice of acting 'on' the baby as a patient, to one that acted 'with' the baby, as an intimate friend (Brazelton 1979). Teachers, too, at every stage, must teach 'with the child'. Dr. Louis Sander, at the Boston University School of Medicine, studied mother–child communication through the first six years with special attention to the innate sensitivity to precise timing of expressions of communication (Sander 2012). He discovered how they created a world of shared understanding all their own, and more than either could know alone.

Of course the infant person has much to learn—how to move the increasingly powerful body with grace and skill, how to appreciate the art and science of other persons' understanding, and then how to use the symbols of speech and language to tell and preserve stories that may have great beauty as well as important practical information about how to engage with the physical world. Studies of the changes in the first two years show that the innate readiness to enjoy imitating with companions is directed purposefully to learn new conventions of communication (Trevarthen and Bjørkvold 2016). Body and brain undertake a programme of 'age-related changes', which seek confirmation of what is learned from family members, expecting joyful approval (Trevarthen 2001).

Supporting the developing creativity of early childhood, to benefit the community

> We begin our life in unity — the physical unity of the mother and child, to which corresponds the emotional unity of love. We should build on that original unity, extending it first to the family, where the seeds of hatred are so easily and so often sown, and then to the school, and so by stages to the farm, the workshop, the village and the whole community. But the basis of unity at each successive stage, as at the first stage, is creativity. We unite to create, and the pattern of creation is in nature, and we discover and conform to this pattern by all the methods of artistic activity—by music, by dancing and drama, but also by working together and living together, for, in a sane civilization, these too are arts of the same natural pattern.
>
> (Read 1944, p. 32)

The above quote from the art historian, poet, literary critic, and philosopher Herbert Read, the final paragraph from his pamphlet entitled 'The Education of Free Men' sold by Freedom Press for one shilling (5 pence in our present currency), appreciates the artful motives for education that grow in a young human being, and how they depend on affectionate company.

In the 1980s, psychologist Harrie Biemans, in the Netherlands, developed a clinical use of videos recording activities shared by family members in their homes to support the development of attachments, communication, and learning. The method, called SPIN (from the Dutch 'Stichting Promotie Intensieve Thuisbehandeling Nederland' or 'Association for the Promotion of Intensive Home Training in the Netherlands'), has been developed as Video Home Training or Video Interaction Guidance (VIG). It has proved helpful in

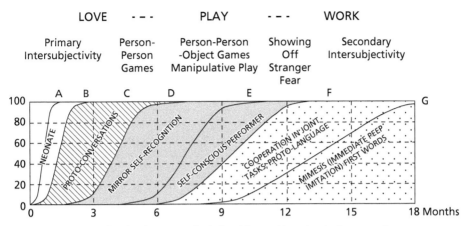

Figure 2.2 Stages in the development of relationships and learning before speech.

improving teachers' communication with pupils in schools, including pupils with developmental disabilities. Figure 2.2 was devised in association with the VIG therapists to summarize age-related developments in the human spirit before that young human being can run about and talk—the first year-and-a-half of the human story (Kennedy, Landor, and Todd 2011).

Below, I summarize what practitioners and researchers in development have learned about the steps that advance motor intelligence and affectionate communication of knowledge in cooperative ways, before speech.

Love

Intimate affection for human company, ready to share imitations in dialogue with the rhythms of intention (Figure 2.2A)

After a healthy full-term birth, an infant, in an active state known as 'birth arousal', may orient two eyes and head to directly gaze at a nearby person, or to track an object moved slowly in a tempting way (Figures 2.1 and 2.3). The baby wants to look at a human face, especially the eyes, has learned the voice of the mother, and can imitate many different expressions.

Emese Nagy, a young doctor and psychologist working in Hungary, pioneered discoveries about the purpose of communication with newborns (Nagy 2011). Her films proved that neonatal imitations are motivated to establish a dialogue. She distinguished 'provocations' where, after the baby imitated and the experimenter had paused and watched the infant expectantly, the baby repeated the imitated act with attention to the experimenter, watching for a reply. The exchange is regulated by the intentions and expectations of the baby as a person with another, as in any conversation (Trevarthen 1979). Giannis Kugiumutzakis and I reviewed evidence that, by imitation, the newborn human mind can read and sympathize with the purposes of another human being (Kugiumutzakis and Trevarthen 2015).

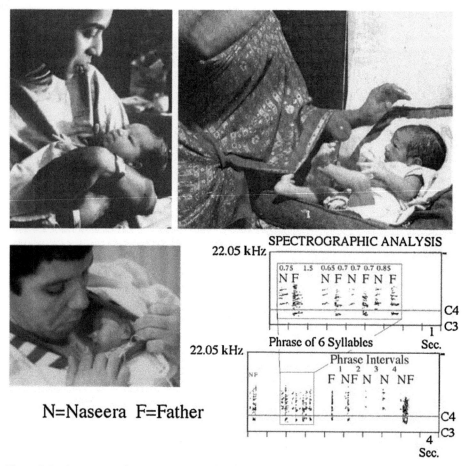

Figure 2.3 *Above*: A newborn, 20 minutes after birth, imitates her mother's tongue protrusion, and a baby tracks a ball with her whole body less than an hour after birth. *Below*: Naseera, two months before term, has a dialogue of 'coo' sounds with her father, who is 'kangarooing' her under his shirt. They alternate syllables at 0.65 or 0.7 seconds, the pulse of *andante*, except for the final interval of 0.85 seconds, which expresses 'final lengthening' to end the phrase. Then, Naseera leads through a set of 4-second phrase intervals. N = Naseera; F = Father; C4 = 'middle C' or 'do'; C3 = one octave below C4; 22.05 kHz = frequency of 22.05 kilohertz, or 1,000 per second; Sec. = seconds.

Saskia van Rees, using films of intimacy in hospital practice, recorded a dialogue of simple 'coo' sounds between a two-month-premature baby girl Naseera and her father, who is supporting her development four weeks after her birth, three months before term, by holding her close to his body in 'kangaroo care' (van Rees and de Leeuw 1993). An acoustic analysis by Stephen Malloch shows that the sounds they share have the timing of movements that form syllables and phrases of mature speech (Figure 2.3). The baby is sensitive to her father's vocal expressions and she knows the score of human dialogue. Paulo Freire (1970), in *Pedagogy of the Oppressed*, recognized the need for an educator to accept this innate skill for synchronizing the expressions of thought in the co-creation of knowledge.

Musical proto-conversations that compose stories of imagination (Figure 2.2B)

In the second month there is a rapid development of focused vision for exploring a greatly expanded world, and the baby's preferential looking at a person's eyes when they offer friendly attention invites an affectionate response. This is the beginning of 'proto-conversations' (Bateson 1979) in 'primary intersubjectivity' (Trevarthen 1979), where the infant enjoys the musical rhythm and intonation of 'infant-directed speech' (Fernald 1989), especially in the familiar voice of the mother (as shown later in Figure 2.6). The infant smiles at an affectionate greeting or touch, often holds a fisted hand up when listening to a companion, and attends with the mouth partly open and the upper lip protruded, signifying attention.

Play

Creative games for fun, teasing curiosity with a companion (Figure 2.2C)

The strength of a baby's body grows in the third month, for extending arms and hands to reach towards a nearby object, with attempts to feel it by touch. The baby's display of curiosity causes a familiar person to offer playful teasing and sharing of discoveries. The baby becomes a self-conscious actor, and a delightful playmate with a sense of humour (Reddy 2008) (Figure 2.4).

More lively and inquisitive person-person–object play, inventing toys (Figure 2.2D)

Months four and five transform these adventures in movement to explore a much larger world. Now the baby often attends to attractive objects out of reach, and likes to manipulate those it can grasp. These new interests direct the baby's attention away from the mother, who, if she is happy and wanting to play, responds by teasing in games that are joyfully shared. The object that the baby was interested in becomes a toy.

Becoming a mobile self finding a new world of adventure (Figure 2.2E)

At six months, the baby attempts to crawl, sitting and pulling up to stand, practising balancing. In Figure 2.1 we saw how a much younger baby, four or five months old, can be assisted to stand on two feet by someone who gives help with balancing. The body is anticipating greater freedom of motor intelligence with the help of a partner in the dance. Objects presented to the baby are grasped and held with delicate movements of the hands, which also make expressive gestures of appreciation. There is a change in articulations of voice sounds leading to babbling which is full of 'proto-language' expression, described by the socio-linguist Michael Halliday (1979), who studied his own son in his first year. Babies of this age become skilled performers of ritual stories of rhythm and melody presented by a parent in traditional baby songs and action games. The six-month

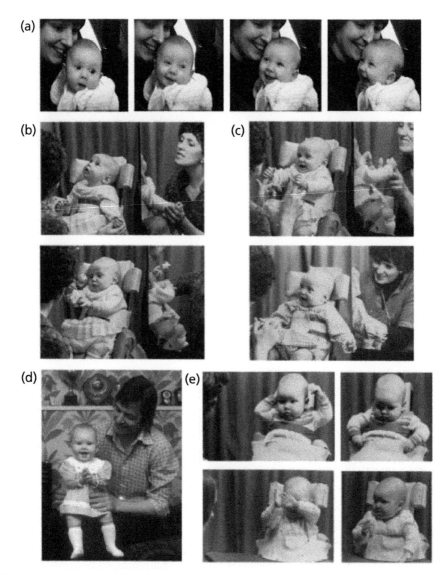

Figure 2.4 A. An 11-week-old shows a 'coy' reaction when her mother holds her up to a mirror (Reddy 2000, p. 188, Figure 1). B. A four-month-old infant is curious about the room, then concentrates her attention on an object presented by her mother. C. When her mother starts a rhythmic body game, the baby is both interested and pleased. At five months she will participate in an action game, 'Round and round the garden', a rhyming four-line stanza with a lively *iambic* pulse. D. A six-month-old sitting on her father's knee smiles with pride as she responds to her mother's request to show 'Clappa-clappa-handies'. E. The same six-month-old shows her uneasiness and withdrawal in front of two strangers, a man and a woman, who attempt to communicate in friendly but unfamiliar ways. The infant appears to experience shame as well as distress.

Reproduced from Vasudevi Reddy, Coyness in Early Infancy, *Developmental Science*, 3 (2), p. 188, Figure 1, DOI: 10.1111/1467-7687.00112 © Blackwell Publishers Ltd. 2000.

old in Figure 2.4 shows proud delight when her performance of 'clappa-clappa-handies' is greeted with admiration.

The baby is also beginning to show a curiosity about what their partner intends to do with objects, and how they want to use them as tools.

Work

Sharing tasks in artificial ways, to co-construct meaning with pride (Figure 2.2F)

After 10 months there is a change: within a few weeks the baby starts to understand another person's request to cooperate in a task (Figure 2.5). Penelope Hubley traced this development of shared actions with a simple task where the mother invited the baby by gesture and speech to pick up small wooden dolls and place them in a toy truck (Hubley and Trevarthen 1979).

Before 40 weeks of age babies did not seem to understand the request, which was not a demonstration but an invitation to complete an intention to do something with the objects—that is, to act like the other person. A month later, babies complied readily. This is the same time as the child is mastering an advance in Halliday's 'proto-language', making 'acts of meaning' and understanding them when they are signalled by combination of vocal sign and hand gesture made by a playmate. An interesting example of the early use of words to recall experience was given by Basilie, one of Hubley's one-year-olds, who is shown in Figure 2.5. Her mother said as she pointed to the toys, 'Put the dolls in the truck.' Basilie said, 'De duck', to which her mother responded, 'Oh yes, it is like the duck in the bath'. An early word recalled a shared experience that had been given an oral label—a name. This is a clear step towards symbolic communication, showing how it can relate experiences given meaning at different times and in different places, mastering what Margaret Donaldson (1992) calls a new 'mode' of human thought.

Toddling into a world of words to describe shared objects of value (Figure 2.2G)

After one year, the adventuring self-aware toddler is beginning to know words, and to use a few for reference to objects of common interest. The world of shared ideas, tasks, and tools begins to expand months before rapid mastery of language begins in the third year.

The two-year-old's sense of responsibility and self-importance grows in challenging ways, but affectionate friendship is greatly valued, and communication with peers is animated joyfully by imitation of acts of meaning using familiar props, such as clothes and toys, in inventive ways. Jaqueline Nadel (2014) made recordings of this in trios of one- to four-year olds and showed how spontaneous imitation 'boosts development'. Mutual imitation in groups of toddlers also enhances leadership and socio-emotional cooperation, developing personalities as well as sharing projects and skills (Corsaro 2003). With affectionate playmates, toddlers are beginning to talk, though the vocabulary is small (Bruner 1983).

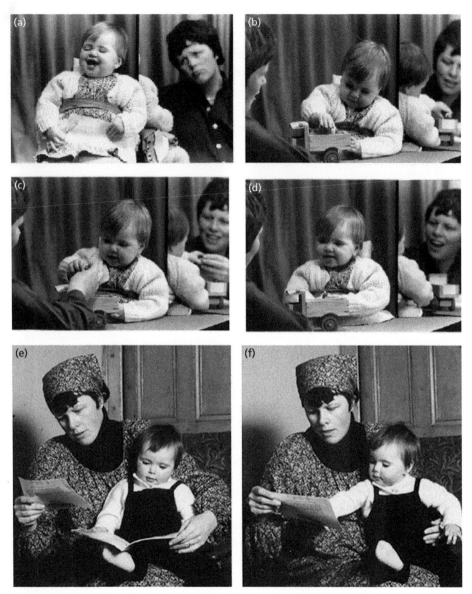

Figure 2.5 A one-year-old shows her talents. A. In the recording room, Basilie enjoys the comedy when her mother pretends to be sad. B, C, D. Mastering a task. She takes the wooden figure offered by her mother, with a request 'Put the doll in the truck'. Basilie carefully puts it in the truck (C), then (D) looks with a self-satisfied expression at her mother, who says, 'What a clever girl!' E. At home, Basilie and her mother read. Basilie is studying her book; the mother is intently occupied with a document, perhaps a telephone bill. F. Basilie drops her book and points to the mother's paper, with a critical vocal comment, without words, but with an intense prosody communicating criticism. This appears to be a response to the concerned expression of her mother.

The musico-poetic foundations of human meaning

After the pleasures which arise from gratification of the bodily appetites, there seems to be none more natural to man than Music and Dancing. In the progress of art and improvement they are, perhaps, the first and earliest pleasures of his own invention; for those which arise from the gratification of the bodily appetites cannot be said to be of his own invention.

(Adam Smith 1777, p. 187)

There are certain aspects of the so-called 'inner life'—physical or mental—which have formal properties similar to those of music—patterns of motion and rest, of tension and release, of agreement and disagreement, preparation, fulfillment, excitation, sudden change, etc.

(Susan Langer 1942, p. 228)

The above quotations by two philosophers who were sensitive to the sensuous experiences of life in movement, not just preoccupied with abstract formulations of thinking, appreciate the 'vitality dynamics' of human life in community, how they are alive from birth, and how they may form the foundation for all kinds of meaning and value in cultural practices (Stern 2010).

Stephen Malloch, a musician and expert in musical acoustics, developed a theory of 'communicative musicality' to explain the engaging narratives of vocal and gestural behaviour I had charted in the early conversations of mothers with their babies. Malloch's analyses of the ways sounds were communicated in delicately timed patterns confirmed that the babies, as well as the mothers, were expecting to share life felt in movement. They were intuitively composing intimate adventures in purposeful synchrony, with all the dimensions noted by Susan Langer.

Stephen described the sounds in a 'proto-conversation' with a six-week-old girl, Laura, and her Scottish mother, Kay, which I had recorded in Edinburgh in 1979. With computer programs designed for acoustic analysis of musical sounds, he made graphs to show the rhythm or *pulse* of the exchange between Laura and Kay, the modulation of subtle features of *quality* such as loudness, pitch, and intonation in their expression, and how the pattern through time created a complete *narrative*. What astonished him was the precision of timing they shared, and Laura's exact cooperation with her mother, who seemed to be led by her tiny daughter. The mother invites the infant to have her turns, just as a good jazz ensemble will invite an instrumental solo from one player (Schögler and Trevarthen 2007). A musical 'holding' is created in which mother and infant express themselves in cooperation.

Figure 2.6 shows the pitch plot Stephen obtained, which shows the melodic story they made together.

The importance of the inner rhythms of life for sharing experience has been proved by accurately measuring how movements of vocalization and gesture are exchanged in dialogues. Stephen and I collaborated with researchers interested in child development and teaching, as well as therapy for disorders of communication, to use this kind of descriptive data to develop and test a theory that motives of 'communicative musicality' are essential

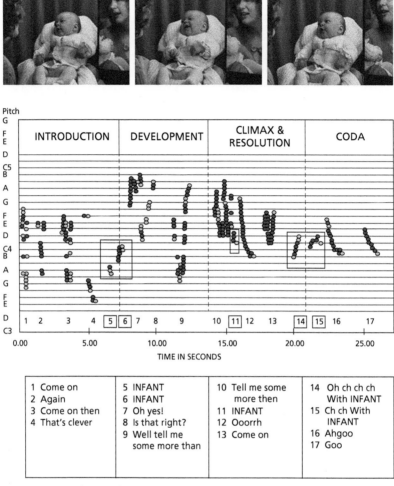

Figure 2.6 Pitch plot of six-week-old Laura and her mother making their melody. The mother leaves space for her infant's vocalizations [5 and 6]. Laura completes a bar with utterance [11], following her mother's three sounds [10] with a vocalization that lasts a quarter of the total length of this bar. The tongue clicks the mother makes with her infant's vocalizations [14 and 15] are spaced 0.2 seconds apart in a group of four, then one of two—at twice the rate of the sub-divisions marked in utterances [9] and [10]. Laura and Kay made a coordinated, playfully negotiated musical 'proto-conversation', as defined by Mary Catherine Bateson (1979).

for human cultural life and learning, and for the well-being and self-confidence of the child (Malloch and Trevarthen 2010; Trevarthen and Malloch 2017).

Why life has to be rhythmic in prospective ways

Musical ways of sharing grow with the same story-making rhythms of proto-conversation in baby songs and action games everywhere, becoming much-loved rituals shared as proof of friendship (Figure 2.7). This is how human meaning is created, in any media of communication. Narrative projects of body movement carry promise of collaborative action with awareness in elaborate forms, as well as offering potential characters for the actors to build and value 'story-telling' negotiation with companions (Bruner 2003; Gratier and Trevarthen 2008).

Evidence that helps us appreciate how the inner self-sensing of time for the body in movement can imagine shared life with a companion is given by a video made by Gunilla Preisler in Stockholm, which records how a totally blind Swedish five-month-old, delicately and with appropriate timing and direction of moving, conducts with her left hand her mother's singing of a famous Swedish baby song (Trevarthen 2012).

The song tells the story of a little boy called Olle who was collecting blueberries in the forest. A bear joined him and they were sharing the berries happily. Then the mother saw them and screamed. The bear ran away and Olle said, 'Why did you chase my friend away. Mother dear, please call him to come back'.

Pairs of lines in the four verses end in rhyming Swedish vowels, all different, two per verse, or eight in all. In the first verse 'gick' rhymes with 'blick', and 'blå' rhymes with 'gå'. A Swedish infant a few months old can hear these as different expressive sounds, and can choose to imitate them. They have been quickly learned as characteristic of the Swedish language. By five months, an English infant, aware of a different language environment, would not perceive the more complex sounds of Swedish, because they are unfamiliar.

Maria is expressing the song as she feels it in her body. She improvises a performance with her fingertip like a player in a jazz duet, sometimes leading her mother's voice by a third of a second, sometimes synchronizing with the beat perfectly. This confirms that the dynamics of language and song are anticipated by her brain and body in a way that bridges the difference between hearing a person singing and an inner feeling of the melody for a dance. This is the IMP, the intrinsic motive pulse mentioned above as the common currency of movements between cooperating individuals of any age.

Cultivating projects for acting in concert

We have studied mothers singing to their infants in many languages, including Japanese, French, Italian, German, and English. They show a common pattern of verses, with four lines and with rhyming vowels (Figure 2.7, Leanne). Lively songs have an *andante* tempo with iambic rhythm. A lullaby to help a baby sleep will be a slow *largo* gently pronounced with a steady, even rhythm. These regularities confirm that adults everywhere have an intuition to match a natural sense for a plan of body movement in the baby. It is the same consensual collaboration as in the proto-conversation with Laura.

The impulsive and persuasive messages of the desire to communicate interests and purposes by speaking with the prosody of the voice combined with gestures of head and hands can be picked up before a vocabulary in language. They form the basis for learning how to comprehend other persons' speech and how to speak like that (Bruner 1983). The sense of timing for separate acts of moving is also essential for the serial ordering of logical thinking.

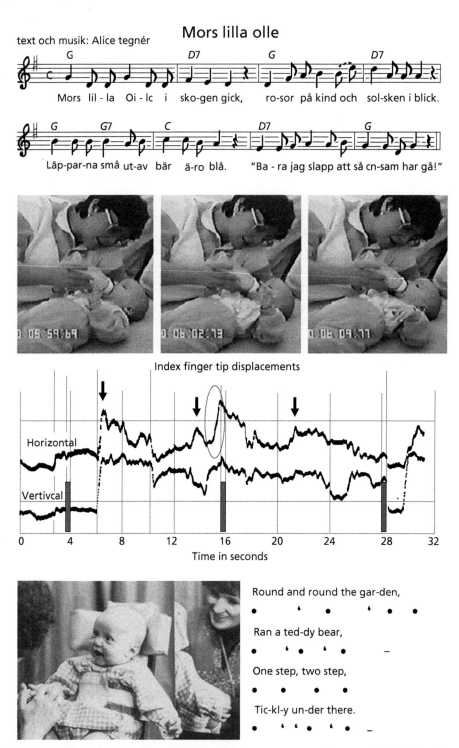

Mors lilla olle

text och musik: Alice tegnér

Mors lil - la Oi - lc i sko-gen gick, ro-sor på kind och sol-sken i blick.

Läp-par-na små ut-av bär ä-ro blå. "Ba - ra jag slapp att så cn-sam har gå!"

Index finger tip displacements

Horizontal

Vertivcal

0   4   8   12   16   20   24   28   32

Time in seconds

Round and round the gar-den,

Ran a ted-dy bear,

One step, two step,

Tic-kl-y un-der there.

Figure 2.7 *Above*: The first verse of the famous baby song composed long ago by Alice Tegnér, Swedish music teacher, poet, and composer. Blind Maria listens to her mother's slow singing of four verses, each line taking 12 seconds. *Below*: Leanne, at five months, enjoys sharing her mother's singing and accompanying movements on her hand, and she imitates the last word 'there', synchronizing with a long matching vowel 'eerh'.

From two to school—discovering common sense and appreciating it with human sense

> It is by natural signs chiefly that we give force and energy to language; and the less language has of them, it is the less expressive and persuasive (pp. 106–7).
>
> Artificial signs signify, but they do not express; they speak to the understanding, as algebraical characters may do, but the passions, the affections, and the will, hear them not: these continue dormant and inactive, till we speak to them in the language of nature, to which they are all attention and obedience (p. 108).

> (Reid 1764, An Inquiry into the Human Mind on the Principles of Common Sense)

As was clear to Thomas Reid 350 years ago, a century before Darwin, our artificial tools of communication, including speech, depend on the sympathy of a 'natural language'. We have to use our natural abilities of expression to learn special symbols for talk and text.

This wisdom was echoed by Margaret Donaldson, who also emphasized the importance of emotions.

> Human sense is understanding how to live in the human and physical worlds that children normally develop in the first few years of life. It is learned spontaneously in direct encounters with these worlds that arise unavoidably everywhere, transcending cultural differences. The learning is always informed and guided by emotion—that is, by feelings of significance, of value, of what matters. And it is highly stable and enduring, once established. It is the foundation on which all that follows must build.

> (Margaret Donaldson, summarizing her account of
> mental development in her book *Children's Minds* 1978)

At every stage in the young child's journey, from an innate 'human sense' of how to move with intentions and communicate them to a cultural 'common sense' of habits of life in a particular community, the tones of emotion in body movement are shared. Young infants are sociable in purposeful ways, seeking a role, and they appraise their identity and knowledge with 'basic complex emotions' of pride and affection, or shame and fear (Panksepp and Biven 2012), feelings that Antonio Damasio finds guide intelligence and growth of awareness (Damasio 2003). The moral feelings of the child regulate actions and roles in the community, and they develop as the scope of activity and self-expression grow, through childhood adolescence and maturity to old age. For the purpose of understanding the child's role in learning after infancy, educators need to look at the developments that occur before attendance to rules of school instruction comes easily—that is, in the first five to seven years.

The debate about the nurture of culture's meaning and how the child's nature is ready for it will continue to exercise psychologists who interpret *The Culture of Education* (Bruner 1996). We have to keep working towards an acceptance of what teachers learn by appreciating the impulses of their pupils—their initiative for getting to know the common sense of the community, and their need for love and joy in sharing with companions what may be pointed out as true and useful. This is particularly important when the societal culture and life of young people is stressed by poverty and violence, as Karsten Hundeide (1991) and Nigel Osborne (2017) show us.

What anthropology discovered in the world of human learning

> From these examples of children's role play, it is clear that such play is not simply an imitation of the adult world. Children are, of course, affected by the adult world, but they collectively appropriate features of that adult world to create innovative play routines in their peer cultures. Role play is especially interesting because it involves children's collective construction and sharing of narratives about their lives in the present and their projections of their lives as adults in the future. Children's constructions of these narratives are creative and fun and are valued aspects of their shared peer culture. In the process of creating and engaging in role play children come to develop predispositions to their futures, and in this way they actively contribute to reproduction and change of the adult world.
>
> (Corsaro 2003, p. 26)

The sociologist William Corsaro, who observed creative play in communities of children, believes 'that the future of childhood is the present'. A science of child invention leads psychology to a richer appreciation for cultural learning, which anthropologist Victor Turner called the 'human seriousness of play' (Turner 1982). Gregory Bateson (1956) also noted the universal importance of dramatic playfulness and intimate live conversation with shared dynamics of expression for sharing cultural meanings and stories. Gregory Bateson's daughter Mary Catherine Bateson, also an anthropologist interested in the social use of language, made a pioneering account of the clever participation of a three-month-old infant in a delicately negotiated 'proto-conversation' of voice sounds and body gestures exchanged with an affectionate mother (Bateson 1979). She was astonished at the subtle sharing of expressions, and concluded that the baby was showing an innate ability to master the rules of prosody and syntax in a language with no need of semantic reference to identify a topic outside their mutual awareness and understanding.

An appetite for a culture is the same everywhere

> In tribal and peasant societies much of the formal and informal education of young people was effected through 'affective culture', and especially by systems of non-verbal communication such as 'dance' and 'music'. During the 1960s and 1970s in the United Kingdom and other industrialised countries, concern for the development of the emotions increased greatly in arguments about educational policy and in the practice of primary and secondary education.... Are then dance, music and other artistic activities peripheral or central to general cognitive development? Are they simply optional extras which can help children to learn in a pleasant way word-based social and technical skills and moral values, and to acquire a sense of group identity? Or are they essential forms of knowledge which are necessary not only for a balanced personality but also for the development of cognitive capacities? ... The most easily accepted argument for the positive influence of affective culture on cognitive development is that which asserts that people learn best in a warm and familiar environment, in which new knowledge can be easily related to the values, symbols and social experience of the home and neighbourhood.
>
> (Blacking 1988, pp. 91–2)

Early in his career, Jerome Bruner, developing a more liberal 'theory of instruction' than that supported by Piaget, proposed three modes of representation through practice by which children develop and demonstrate a sense of their life in company: *enactive* representation, which is action-based in the present; *iconic* representation, which is image-based and remembered; and *symbolic* representation, which is language-based, conventional, and abstracted from immediate essential needs. All three are discovered and transformed in the play of children two to five years of age exploring free body movement and discovering together the fluent use of words.

The Russian poet, and writer of stories for children, Korney Chukovsky, heard the talk of pre-school-aged boys and girls playing on a beach and discovered that they were inventing words fluently in brilliant grammatical displays. In a book published in Russian in 1933, he called them 'linguistic geniuses' (Chukovsky 1968). Barbara Rogoff (2003) found that in very different cultures childish enthusiasm grows to motivate the learning of conventional practices and beliefs no matter how complex and artificial they may intend to become. In New Zealand, the Maoris, who sustain a communitarian oral culture rich in art and song with the proverb, 'let the child lead the way', have inspired a world-famous pre-school curriculum for infants and toddlers, *Te Whāriki*, designed to weave the playful spirit of the young person into the fabric of traditional beliefs and understanding in ways that work in any culture, and in bi-cultural New Zealand (Te Whāriki 1996; Nuttall 2013).

It is clear that planners or administrators of a curriculum for school instruction must accept an obligation to protect grace and kindness of human nature while it is mastering an artificial cosmos of machines that has no life of its own. Allowing the spirit of childhood to lead the way is also how the psychiatrist Russell Meares works to retrieve the 'poetry' of life for a person in need of support for mental health in shared meaning (Meares 2016).

Motives and feelings of a brain for growing cultural cleverness in companionship

From the embryo stage, the nervous system is designed for a purpose. It is mapped out within the dorsal surface of the body as the ground plan of an intrinsic motive formation (IMF) of the person as an agent that will direct the actions and well-being of that person from within (Trevarthen 2016). The first embryonic movements are rhythmic, generating measures of time for action that will be the same in the mature organism. Then, parts of the body surface develop special sensitivities to light, sound, chemicals, temperature, or touch, placed as sense organs to guide beneficial contacts with the environment, or to avoid dangers.

In the human fetus at mid-gestation, a special awareness of the impulses of another human life becomes able to communicate and share vitality, with a twin or with the mother. As the behaviour of Naseera has shown (Figure 2.3), a human being at 32 weeks after conception may cooperate in a dialogue of movements that synchronize and harmonize intentions with smiles, vocalizations, and gestures.

The science of how the brain grows in size and complexity to transform the interests and actions of the person has advanced prodigiously over the past half-century, with new techniques for detecting electrical activities spreading through neuronal circuits, and for locating and tracking anatomical changes. But, as veterinarian and philosopher Barbara

Goodrich (2010) explains, much of the research has been led by a narrow focus on *response* to information from the senses, forgetting the creative *initiative* of 'movement in time', and it neglects the role of feelings in directing cognitive awareness, as described by Antonio Damasio (2003). A new brain science of the affective moral forces in human experience is needed to correct this neglect (Narvaez 2014).

The brain of a newborn is about one-third the size of an adult brain, but it has a unique human anatomy, including cerebral hemispheres with different temperaments and awareness adapted for complementary roles in cultural learning. The two sides of the brain of a child show different periods of growth that relate to changes in social motives for building affectionate *relationships* celebrated in artful ways of self-expression for collective pleasure, and systematic concentration of the individual body and mind to discriminate and identify or represent *tasks* that exploit environmental affordances for profitable 'work', and for their manipulation in technology (Trevarthen 2001).

John Blacking, ethnomusicologist and social anthropologist, identifies two functions of the brain that are essential for cultural learning—compassionate celebration of companionship in performance, and informative definition of facts about practice and the discovery of materials for shared work.

> I find the model of hemispherical differentiation the most useful as a general guide to understanding the languages, uses, and functions of dance and music in different societies. Not only does it correspond with contrasts in communication that are commonly described as 'propositional/discursive' or 'performative/expressive', and with many folk classifications of different kinds of dance and music and of contrasts between 'artistic' and 'non-artistic' systems; it also explains in a more powerful way the intellectual significance of dance and music as systems of non-verbal symbols, and hence the structural relationships between affective culture and cognitive development.
>
> (Blacking 1988, p. 96)

The changing balance of these complementary modes, of the *intellectual* intention and awareness of the individual, contrasted with *value-sensing* of aesthetic and moral feelings in relationships, marks the key stages of a young child's activities and learning. The growth of knowledge is animated by joyful love and responsibilities in a community of values as well as pleasure in mastery of practical ambitions (Richardson 1964; Donaldson 1992; Narvaez et al. 2013). Educational practice must attend to, and work with, these transformations in human ingenuity and compassions, how they may be created in the development of body and mind, and how they are supported in communication and cooperation. It must respect the primacy of interpersonal 'I-Thou' intelligence in dialogue for the cultivation of 'I-It' mastery of objective affordances (Buber, see Friedman 2002).

Acknowledgements

The epigraph at the start of this chapter is reprinted with permission from Crace, John, 'Jerome Bruner: The lesson of the story', *The Guardian*, published 27 March 2007 © Guardian News and Media Limited, 2007.

References

Arnold, J.C. (2014). *Their Name Is Today: Reclaiming Childhood in a Hostile World.* Robertsbridge: Plough Publishing House.

Baldwin, J.M. (1895). *Mental Development in the Child and the Race: Methods and Processes.* New York: Macmillan.

Bateson, G. (1956). The message 'This is play'. In: B. Schaffer (ed.) *Group Processes.* New York: Josiah Macy Foundation, pp. 145–242.

Bateson, M.C. (1979). The epigenesis of conversational interaction: A personal account of research development. In: M. Bullowa (ed.) *Before Speech: The Beginning of Human Communication*, pp. 63–77. London: Cambridge University Press.

Bernstein, N. (1967). *The Coordination and Regulation of Movements.* Oxford: Pergamon.

Bjørkvold, J.-R. (1992). *The Muse Within: Creativity and Communication, Song and Play from Childhood through Maturity.* New York: Harper Collins.

Blacking, J. (1988). Dance and music in Venda children's cognitive development. In: G. Jahoda and I.M. Lewis (eds.) *Acquiring Culture: Cross Cultural Studies in Child Development.* Beckenham, Kent: Croom Helm, pp. 91–112.

Bradley, B.S. (1989). *Visions of Infancy: A Critical Introduction to Child Psychology.* Cambridge: Polity Press.

Brazelton, T.B. (1979). Evidence of communication during neonatal behavioural assessment. In: M. Bullowa (ed.) *Before Speech: The Beginning of Human Communication.* London: Cambridge University Press, pp. 79–88.

Bruner, J.S. (1968). *Processes of Cognitive Growth: Infancy* (Heinz Werner Lectures, 1968). Worcester, MA: Clark University Press with Barri Publishers.

Bruner, J.S. (1975). The ontogenesis of speech acts. *Journal of Child Language*, 2, 1–19.

Bruner, J.S. (1983). *Child's Talk. Learning to Use Language.* New York: Norton.

Bruner, J.S. (1996). *The Culture of Education.* Cambridge, MA: Harvard University Press.

Bruner, J.S. (2003). *Making Stories: Law, Literature, Life.* Cambridge, MA: Harvard University Press.

Chukovsky, K. (1968). *From Two to Five.* Berkley, CA: University of California Press.

Conkbayir, M. (2017). Foreword (by Colwyn Trevarthen): Relating the miracle of young life to mysteries of the growing brain. In: *Early Childhood and Neuroscience: Theory, Research and Implications for Practice.* London: Bloomsbury.

Corsaro, W.A. (2003). *We're Friends, Right? Inside Kids' Culture.* Washington, DC: Joseph Henry Press, https://www.edu.helsinki.fi/lapsetkertovat/lapset/In_English/Corsaro.pdf, accessed 1 Mar 2018.

Damasio, A.R. (2003). *Looking for Spinoza: Joy, Sorrow, and the Feeling Brain.* Orlando, FL: Harcourt.

Daniel, S. and Trevarthen, C. (eds.) (2017). *Rhythms of Relating in Children's Therapies: Connecting Creatively with Vulnerable Children.* London: Jessica Kingsley.

DeCasper, A.J. and Fifer, W.P. (1980). Of human bonding: newborns prefer their mothers' voices. *Science*, 208, 1174–6.

Delafield-Butt, J. and Trevarthen, C. (2013). Theories of the development of human communication. In: P. Cobley and P.J. Schultz. (eds.) *Theories and Models of Communication: Handbook of Communication Science, Volume 1.* Berlin: De Gruyter Mouton, pp. 199–221.

Delafield-Butt, J. and Trevarthen, C. (2015). The ontogenesis of narrative: From movements to meaning. *Frontiers of Psychology*, 6, 1157. doi: 10.3389/fpsyg.2015.01157

Donald, M. (2001). *A Mind So Rare: The Evolution of Human Consciousness.* London/ New York: Norton.

Donaldson, M. (1978). *Children's Minds.* Glasgow: Fontana/Collins.

Donaldson, M. (1992). *Human Minds: An Exploration*. London: Allen Lane/Penguin Books.

Edwards, C., Gandini, L., and Forman, G. (1998). *The Hundred Languages of Children*, 2nd edn. Westport: Ablex.

Fernald, A. (1989). Intonation and communicative interest in mothers' speech to infants: Is the melody the message? *Child Development*, **60**, 1497–1510.

Freire, P. (1970). *Pedagogy of the Oppressed*. Harmondsworth: Penguin.

Friedman, M.S. (2002). *Martin Buber: The Life of Dialogue*, 4th edn. London/New York: Routledge.

Goodrich, B.G. (2010). We do, therefore we think: Time, motility, and consciousness. *Reviews in the Neurosciences*, **21**, 331–61.

Gratier, M. and Trevarthen, C. (2008). Musical narrative and motives for culture in mother-infant vocal interaction. *Journal of Consciousness Studies*, **15**(10–11), 122–58.

Halliday, M.A.K. (1979). One child's protolanguage. In: M. Bullowa (ed.) *Before Speech: The Beginning of Human Communication*. London: Cambridge University Press, pp. 171–90.

Hubley, P. and Trevarthen, C. (1979). Sharing a task in infancy. *New Directions for Child Development*, **1979**(4): 57–80. doi: 10.1002/cd.23219790406

Hundeide, K. (1991). *Helping Disadvantaged Children: Psycho-social Intervention and Aid to Disadvantaged Children in Third World Countries*. London: Jessica Kingsley.

Kennedy, H., Landor, M., and Todd, L. (eds.) (2011). *Video Interaction Guidance: A Relationship-Based Intervention to Promote Attunement, Empathy and Wellbeing*. London: Jessica Kingsley.

Kugiumutzakis, G. and Trevarthen, C. (2015). Neonatal imitation. In: James D. Wright (editor-in-chief) *International Encyclopedia of the Social & Behavioral Sciences*, 2nd edn, vol. **16**. Oxford: Elsevier, pp. 481–88. ISBN: 9780080970868

Langer, S.K. (1942). *Philosophy in a New Key: A Study in the Symbolism of Reason, Rite, and Art*. Cambridge, MA: Harvard University Press.

MacDonald, M. (2016). *Elwyn Richardson and the Early World of Creative Education in New Zealand*. Wellington: NZCER Press, New Zealand Council for Educational Research.

Malloch, S. and Trevarthen, C. (eds.) (2010). *Communicative Musicality: Exploring the Basis of Human Companionship*. Oxford: Oxford University Press.

Meares, R. (2016). *The Poet's Voice in the Making of Mind*. London/New York: Routledge.

Nadel, J. (2014). *How Imitation Boosts Development in Infancy and Autism Spectrum Disorder*. Oxford: Oxford University Press.

Nagy, E. (2011). The newborn infant: A missing stage in developmental psychology. *Infant and Child Development*, **20**, 3–19.

Narvaez, D. (2014). *Neurobiology and the Development of Human Morality: Evolution, Culture and Wisdom*. New York: Norton.

Narvaez, D., Panksepp, J., Schore, A., and Gleason, T. (eds.) (2013). *Evolution, Early Experience and Human Development: From Research to Practice and Policy*. New York: Oxford University Press.

Nuttall, J. (2013). *Weaving Te Whāriki: Aotearoa. New Zealand's Early Childhood Curriculum Document in Theory and Practice*, 2nd edn. Wellington: NZCER Press, New Zealand Council for Educational Research.

Osborne, N. (2017). Love, rhythm and chronobiology. In: S. Daniel and C. Trevarthen (eds.) *Rhythms of Relating in Children's Therapies: Connecting Creatively with Vulnerable Children*. London: Jessica Kingsley, pp. 14–27.

Panksepp, J. and Biven, L. (2012). *Archaeology of Mind: Neuroevolutionary Origins of Human Emotions*. New York: Norton.

Piaget, J. (1951). *The Psychology of Intelligence*. London: Routledge and Kegan Paul.

Quick, R.H. (1894). *Essays on Educational Reformers*. London: Longmans, Green, and Co.

Quick, R.H. (2003). *Essays on Educational Reformers.* Honolulu, Hawai: University Press of the Pacific (paperback reprinted from the 1909 edition).

Read, H. (1944). *The Education of Free Men.* London: Freedom Press.

Reddy, V. (2000). Coyness in early infancy. *Developmental Science,* **3**(2), 186–92.

Reddy, V. (2008). *How Infants Know Minds.* Cambridge MA: Harvard University Press.

Reid, T. (1764). *An Inquiry into the Human Mind on the Principles of Common Sense.* A. Millar, London, and A. Kincaid and J. Bell, Edinburgh.

Richardson, E. (1964). *In the Early World.* Wellington: NZCER Press, New Zealand Council for Educational Research (3rd edn 2012).

Rogoff, B. (2003). *The Cultural Nature of Human Development.* Oxford: Oxford University Press.

Sander, L.W. (2012). *Living Systems, Evolving Consciousness, and the Emerging Person: A Selection of Papers from the Life Work of Louis Sander,* ed. G. Amadei and I. Bianchi. Abingdon: Taylor & Francis.

Schögler, B. and **Trevarthen, C.** (2007). To Sing and Dance Together. In: S. Bråten (ed.) *On Being Moved: From Mirror Neurons to Empathy.* Amsterdam/Philadelphia: John Benjamins, pp. 281–302.

Sherrington, C.S. (1906). *The Integrative Action of the Nervous System.* New Haven: Yale University Press.

Smith, A. (1777/1982). Of the Nature of that Imitation which takes place in what are called the Imitative Arts. In: W.P.D. Wightman and J.C. Bryce (eds.) *The Glasgow Edition of the Works and Correspondence of Adam Smith,* iii: *Essays on Philosophical Subjects.* Indianapolis, IN: Liberty Fund.

Stern, D.N. (1985). *The Interpersonal World of the Infant: A View from Psychoanalysis and Development Psychology.* New York: Basic Books.

Stern, D.N. (2000). *The Interpersonal World of the Infant: A View from Psychoanalysis and Development Psychology,* 2nd edn. New York: Basic Books.

Stern, D.N. (2010). *Forms of Vitality: Exploring Dynamic Experience in Psychology, the Arts, Psychotherapy, and Development.* Oxford: Oxford University Press.

Te Whāriki (1996). *Te Whāriki: He Whāriki Màtauranga mò ngà Mokopuna o Aotearoa. Early Childhood Curriculum.* Wellington: Learning Media. For the New Zealand Ministry of Education.

Trevarthen, C. (1979). Communication and cooperation in early infancy. A description of primary intersubjectivity. In: M. Bullowa (ed.) *Before Speech: The Beginning of Human Communication.* London: Cambridge University Press, pp. 321–47.

Trevarthen, C. (1982). The primary motives for cooperative understanding. In: G. Butterworth and P. Light (eds.) *Social Cognition: Studies of the Development of Understanding.* Brighton: Harvester Press, pp. 77–109.

Trevarthen, C. (2001). The neurobiology of early communication: Intersubjective regulations in human brain development. In: A.F. Kalverboer and A. Gramsbergen (eds.) *Handbook on Brain and Behavior in Human Development.* Dordrecht, The Netherlands: Kluwer, pp. 841–82.

Trevarthen, C. (2012). Communicative musicality: The human impulse to create and share music. In: D.J. Hargreaves, D.E. Miell, and R.A.R. MacDonald (eds.) *Musical Imaginations: Multidisciplinary Perspectives on Creativity, Performance, and Perception.* Oxford: Oxford University Press, pp. 259–84.

Trevarthen, C. (2016). From the intrinsic motive pulse of infant actions, to the life time of cultural meanings. In: B. Mölder, V. Arstila, and P. Øhrstrom (eds.) *Philosophy and Psychology of Time,* Studies in Brain and Mind, vol. **9**. Dordrecht, The Netherlands: Springer International, pp. 225–65. doi: 10.1007/978-3-319-22195-3; ISBN 978-3-319-22195-3.

Trevarthen, C. (2017). Play with infants: The impulse for human story-telling. In: T. Bruce, P. Hakkarainen, and M. Bredikyte (eds.) *The Routledge International Handbook of Play in Early Childhood.* Abingdon: Taylor and Francis/Routledge.

Trevarthen, C. and **Bjørkvold, J.-R.** (2016). Life for learning: How a young child seeks joy with companions in a meaningful world. In: D. Narvaez, J. Braungart-Rieker, L. Miller-Graff, L. Gettler, and P. Hastings (eds.) *Contexts for Young Child Flourishing: Evolution, Family, and Society*. New York: Oxford University Press, pp. 28–60.

Trevarthen, C. and **Delafield-Butt, J.** (2015). The infant's creative vitality, in projects of self-discovery and shared meaning: How they anticipate school, and make it fruitful. In: S. Robson and S.F. Quinn (eds.) *The Routledge International Handbook of Young Children's Thinking and Understanding*. Oxford/New York: Routledge, pp. 3–18.

Trevarthen, C. and **Delafield-Butt, J.** (2017). Intersubjectivity in the imagination and feelings of the infant: Implications for education in the early years. In: J. White and C. Dalli (eds.) *Under-three Year-Olds in Policy and Practice*. Heidelberg: Springer, pp. 17–39.

Trevarthen, C. and **Malloch, S.** (2017). The musical self: Affections for life in a community of sound. In: R. MacDonald, D. Hargreaves, and D. Miell (eds.) *Handbook of Musical Identities*, 2nd edn. Oxford: Oxford University Press, pp. 155–75.

Trevarthen, C., **Gratier, M.** and **Osborne, N.** (2014). The human nature of culture and education. *Wiley Interdisciplinary Reviews: Cognitive Science*, **5**(2) (Mar/Apr), 173–92. doi: 10.1002/wcs.1276

Turner, V. (1982). *From Ritual to Theatre: The Human Seriousness of Play*. New York: Performing Arts Journal Publications.

van Rees, S. and de Leeuw, R. (1993). *Born Too Early: The Kangaroo Method With Premature Babies*. Video by Stichting Lichaamstaal, Scheyvenhofweg 12, 6093 PR, Heythuysen, The Netherlands.

Vygotsky, L.S. (1978). *Mind in Society: The Development of Higher Psychological Processes*, ed. M. Cole, V. Steiner, S. Scribner, and E. Souberman. Cambridge, MA: Harvard University Press.

Whitehead, A.N. (1929). *The Aims of Education and Other Essays*. New York: Macmillan.

Chapter 3

The importance of play

Tina Bruce

What's in a name?

In this chapter there is no attempt to achieve the impossible by defining and pinning
down what play is. Academics writing in the English language such as Catherine Garvey
(1977), Howard Gardner (1982), Corinne and John Hutt (Hutt et al. 1989), and Brian
Sutton-Smith (1997) have pointed out the difficulties of using the term 'play' indiscrim-
inately. Instead, an attempt is made to find some navigational tools which aid the better
understanding of what is needed in both the study of play, and the interconnectivity that
is vital between that study and how early childhood play develops in practice. The way
that adults working with other people's children are trained (Katz 1987; Siraj and Kingston
2015), and more specifically trained to support play—as, for example, in the Scottish
National Practice Guidance document 'Building the Ambition' (Scottish Government
2014, p. 28)—together with an ethos and cultural contexts which value play and open up
opportunities for children and families to play, is of central importance.

One of the challenges to the study and development of play in practice is, as Egan (1997,
p. 8) suggests, that it is difficult for the human mind to escape from the ways of thinking
that have developed in a culture. We might, when we hope to escape from established
grand narratives (Lyotard 1982) of traditional thinking about play, replace them with new
mini-narratives for which we invent new vocabulary. Because these shifting stories (Egan
1997, p. 154) do not link in holistic ways with what went before, they often go off on completely different and much narrower paths of exploration.

An example of this is the way that during the last half of the twentieth century there
has been a steadily increasing use of adjectives which have segmented different aspects of
play. Examples would be manipulative play, water play, pretend play, rough and tumble
play, guided play, and solitary play, with the list becoming longer every year. Recent add-
itions are technology and digital play. Use of the word playfulness (Rogers and Evans
2008; Broadbent, Howard, and Wood 2010) is another example. It is now widely used, but
it has brought an atmosphere in early childhood day care and educational settings which
emphasizes the lighter, enjoyable side of play (Kalliala 2006). The serious side of play is
shaded. This, in turn, separates the therapeutic and educational work of play. The importance of play as a self-healing mechanism is then undermined. So is play's possibility
to help children think, feel, and explore safely major themes of humanity, such as justice,

integrity, anger, jealousy, violence, compassion, difference, cultural variation, and diversity as part of human existence?

Egan (1997, p. 154) helpfully suggests that there are areas of solidarity between those holding different perspectives when examining what play is. Froebelians (Liebschner 1992; Whinnett 2006, 2012; Tovey 2012, 2013; Bruce 2012, 2015) would call this unity. The notion of solidarity or unity is similar to the scientific view that different evidence from diverse research and data often results in overlapping or converging evidence (Polanyi 1958), which in turn leads to convincing messages about the importance of play in early childhood.

Attending to essentials

The focus of this chapter is on features (Bruce 1991) expanded from the work of Rubin, Fein, and Vandenberg (1983), which bring some sense of solidarity and unity within the concept of play but without forcing conformity of view. The emphasis is on the effort to identify navigational tools that support exploration in a range of diverse cultural contexts. This approach aims to keep some degree of continuity with traditional approaches in the search to better understand the essentials of play, but also offers a necessarily wide-ranging framework for illuminating what play can contribute in early childhood education.

There is richness in examining how play is captured as developing ideas, thoughts, feelings, and the physical body (Callois 1961), as well as the part it plays socially, evolutionarily, biologically, and culturally (Smith 1982). Scarlett et al. (2005, p. 13) make the point that animal play is not, in essence, completely different from the play of human children. 'In observing play, we better understand that we humans share a great deal with our nonhuman cousins.' Observation assists the process leading to the identification of conditions which are conducive both to early human childhood play and animal play (Bekoff and Byers 1998; Matthews 2011, p. 351), as well as revealing in useful detail the free-flowing nature of play.

Navigational tools for the study and development in practice of early childhood play

The contribution of philosophy

Play has fascinated thinkers since ancient times, as they observed young children at play. This led philosophers such as Plato (c.428 BCE–c.347 BCE) and Kant (1724–1804) to ponder the subject and take it seriously enough to do so. Before theories about play emerged, which began when disciplines such as psychology, sociology, and anthropology began to be established, support for the importance of play came from philosophers.

Some educators still adhere to the Platonic pursuit of high culture, which makes schools separate places of learning from real life. However, increasingly, research on play suggests that when adults sensitively support and extend play (Bruce 1987, p. 65) children re-create the fundamental aspects of high culture. For example, when they play as characters who are goodies or baddies they investigate the time-honoured themes in Greek and Shakespearean drama of good and evil (Holland 2003; Edmiston 2008). In a lecture on the origins of theatre, the playwright Michael Frayn suggested that children invented Greek theatre and the battles of good versus evil long before the Greeks developed such themes in drama (Frayn 2015).

From his observations of children at play, Friedrich Froebel (1782–1852) pioneered the view that play is important in the education of young children in kindergartens as well as in the home setting. His thinking was influenced by the German philosopher Immanuel Kant (Liebschner 1992, p. 34; Bruce 2015, p. 8). He emphasized the structures of the mind, and the crucial role of direct and real experience in the development of thinking (Robson 2010). Kant saw people as active, rational thinkers when it came to moral issues. This resonates with the constant observations throughout history of children creating goodies and baddies and the struggles between good and evil, which fill childhood play.

There are important links here with other aspects of early childhood play. Young children learn through, and with, the people who love and care for them, and through their senses and active movement. They process what they learn through the structures of the brain, about which there is ever-increasing new knowledge. Play is an integrating mechanism (Bruce 2015, p. 61) which brings together structural form and experiential content during childhood. Stuart Brown (1998, p. 256) describes play as an organizing principle.

> By looking at play as a generator of dynamically integrated affect-laden cortical 'maps' of increasingly complexity, I believe that play can be considered as a *major* organizer and possible sustainer of our human dynamic sense of reality.

Because philosophy deals with areas of knowledge for which there is as yet no clear answer, it is important that early childhood play, about which there is much still to learn, still has a place in it. But the study of play for those working in practice to educate young children demonstrates that descriptions of it need to be tangible enough for governments and policy makers to embrace it as important in early childhood education, and to make available the funds needed to act on this. Those working with other people's children need careful training.

The contribution of psychology

With the emergence of the discipline of psychology at the turn of the twentieth century, theories of play began to develop. However, although they are important navigational tools, neither philosophy nor theories supply evidence about the importance of play. Rather, they provide frameworks through which it becomes possible to make more sense of human behaviour, development, and learning. Philosophical debate helps open up exploration of what is not yet established knowledge. Nevertheless, every theory of play is culture bound and set in a particular time. It is seriously limited and carries the possibility of constraining, rather than opening up, academic study.

The challenge is to integrate with the academic study of play the observation of children at play alone, with other children, with parents, and with practitioners in natural contexts.

When parents, practitioners, and researchers work together, the result has more flexibility to take forward the illumination of what the importance of play is (or is not), and can be useful despite the limitations of human theorizing. Practice and observation need to inform theory as much as theory informs practice, if play is to flourish.

It is helpful to both challenge and see beneficial influences in the traditional thinking and theorizing about play. Theories suggesting that play is recreation, an opportunity to release pent-up energy, a preparation for adult life, or as something producing pleasure, or play placed in opposition to work, emerge, and were followed later by theories which emphasize feelings or thinking, leading to an unhelpful separation of educational play and therapeutic play.

Play as an opportunity to burn off energy, or as recreation

The view that play is an opportunity to 'burn off' excess energy has a great deal to answer for in shaping public and political attitudes to play, undermining the contribution of play to learning by placing it outside the early childhood curriculum and pedagogy. The theory was developed by Herbert Spencer (1820–1903) during the period of the Industrial Revolution in Europe. It proposes that children are like industrial machines and need to release excess energy and let off steam in the playground or out of doors between formally taught lessons. Children were regarded as cogs in the machinery, like those who worked in factories. Rough-and-tumble play and play involving lively chasing were viewed as low-level releases of unwanted energy (Pellis and Pellis 2007). Play was therefore necessary in order to avoid explosions of bottled-up energy.

Play as recreation gave the opposite view, since children were supposed to 'replenish' energy expended during academic work. This is the origin of practice requiring children to finish their work and then rewarding them with play (Spodek 1985, p. 181; Smilansky 1968, p. 48). Goouch (2015) discusses how parents still do not distinguish between recreation and play. In the 1960s most children came to school to work—to 'get down to it and no nonsense' (Dearden 1968, p. 93). At the most, some brief intermissions of 'playtime' could be allowed, as concessions to animal spirits and as a recuperation for the next bout of work.

However, maintained nursery schools—financed by local authorities and led by specialist headteachers to provide education and other services to children aged under five years and their families, the first being established at the end of the twentieth century (many in England now under threat for administrative and financial reasons, Early Education 2015)—and other settings influenced by Froebel, have never subscribed to this view, and so the garden has always been, and still is, regarded as an important area for learning through play (McNair 2012).

Play as rehearsal for adult life

Stanley Hall (1884–1924) developed the theory of recapitulation as central to childhood play. He suggested that children at play work through the history of humanity. They are hunters and gatherers, warriors, builders of settlements, farmers, tool-makers, carers of their young, craft-makers, nomads, law-makers, punishers, justice makers. The child works through the development of the human species. The theory of Karl Groos (1901) also emerged and influenced thinking about play, postulating that children naturally prepare for their adult lives by rehearsing adult events and ways of doing things in their play, both socially and physically. Johan Huizinga (1938) developed this further, suggesting that civilizations are marked by the phenomenon that adults continue their play into adulthood. This was the theory of *homo ludens*. Play keeps the wits sharp and bodies fully functioning, enabling flexibility of thought.

From the 1960s the theory of play as preparation for adult life was again taken forward, this time by the American academic Jerome Bruner. As well as proposing play as preparation for the technical and social aspect of life (Bruner 1966, p. 118) he also saw how play reflects human culture. He suggested that mammals have long childhoods because there is so much for them to learn in preparation for adult life (Bruner, Jolly, and Sylva 1976). Bruner's influence has contributed to the development of what is framed as guided play, adult-led play, structured play, or tutored play (Broadbent, Howard, and Wood 2010; Moyles 2015). Egan (1997, p. 12) points out that when pushed to extremes, this can become totalitarian in its demands for conformity.

Pleasure play

Pleasure play was pioneered by Charlotte Buhler in the 1930s. She saw the joy of active physical movement and the pure motor activity involved in this as the heart of play (Buhler 1945). This theory of play resonates with the health and beauty movement and the outdoor camps for children in woodlands during the summer months in Europe and the USA. It emphasizes the pleasure in movement, which activates unconscious physical and mental learning. Play is seen as a process with no purpose on the part of the child. This is play aiding natural learning. There is a problem here. Lack of purpose is easily conflated with the notion that play lacks function and so has no reason to exist. Lack of purpose is not the same as lack of function. Lack of purpose carries layers of meaning too. Whose purpose is lacking? That of the adult, or that of the child? The child's purposes when engaged in play episodes and scenarios are emphasized and connect with this book's title, *The Child's Curriculum*.

Work versus play

Susan Isaacs (1930, 1933) did not place work and play in opposition, but instead argued that play is transformative. She was deeply influenced by Friedrich Froebel in this. She emphasized that play develops the elements which are needed for a work ethic in ways appropriate to childhood. This located play as a child's work. During play, children concentrate deeply, think of other viewpoints, sustain ideas, and follow them through. They develop manual dexterity. Brehony (2013, p. 62) re-examined the Froebelian perspective of play and suggested that Froebel 'provided a sketch of how play was transformed into work as the child developed'. The features of play (Bruce 2015) do not clash with the traditional Froebelian view of the importance of play in early childhood education, equipping children for lifelong learning. It is not, as Brehony suggests, a matter of work versus play, but rather how play develops the work ethic during early childhood. This raises the status of play as a worthwhile pursuit in educational contexts.

Affective theories of play

The period from the 1930s to the 1960s was probably most significant for the development of what may be termed 'child-centred theories of play'. It was the affective theories which had the most influence during these three decades. However, there was no uniform approach within these theories. The battles between Anna Freud (1895–1982) and Melanie Klein (1882–1960) over their different views about early childhood play were bitter, as noted by Coles (1992, p. 121).

> Anna Freud's preference for respectful observation rather than intrusive assault in clinical exploration as well as selection of candidates is reflected in her well known struggles with Melanie Klein ... who was very much a follower of the early (Sigmund) Freud who explored the unconscious with daring and courageous conjecture. She believed the child analyst can know a lot about the preverbal child, and can work with conviction and dispatch to obtain an analytic intimacy with young children not unlike the kind that develops between analysts and their grown-up patients. Miss Freud was inclined to be wary of what she regarded at best as the surmises and guesses of those who followed Mrs. Klein.

Anna Freud (1969), an outstanding teacher, separated her teaching role from her work as a therapist. In this, she has influenced trained nursery and kindergarten teachers. Like Anna Freud, Vivian Gussin Paley (1986) has been interested in the way that play helps children to control their fears and deal with what frightens them. Anna Freud believed play to have self-healing possibilities and, in her clinic in Hampstead after the Second World War, applied this approach to her work with children who had survived the Holocaust. She tried to give the children as natural a childhood as was possible. As they played, children would, in her view, gain control and experiment with different ways of dealing with situations such that they could escape into play or from it, as was needed by them. As well as the conflicts and sadnesses of life, play also helps children to make sense of experiences and to feel joy and be forward looking, which increases feelings of well-being. Melanie Klein (1932) dismissed Anna Freud's questions to her about how possible it is to psycho-analyze with children scarcely able to speak, or reflect on their relationship with their parents, or whether there are parallels between children's play with toys and the free associations of those analyzed as adults.

Erik Erikson (1902–1994) was a student of Anna Freud. There is an element in his approach which echoes the view that play is a rehearsal for adult life. He was interested in the way that the play scenarios that children invented seemed to serve as metaphors for their future lives and were 'intimately related to the dynamics of the person's life history' (Erikson 1963, p. 95). Visiting them later, as adults, he found that their lifestyles held resonances of their childhood play.

Another major theorist within the tradition of affective theories of play was Donald Winnicott (1896–1971). He developed the notion of transitional objects (Winnicott 1971).

These support the natural and healthy links children have with people they love, but they also encourage the child in early imaginative play. The importance of the transitional object is demonstrated in this example. Jason began primary school in a formal class. After a week he became anxious about going to school each day, and after his mother succeeded in negotiating with the unwilling teacher for him to take his teddy bear each day, returned from school in a less distressed state. He explained to his mother that when he had tears in his eyes he could wipe them with teddy's ears, and teddy would whisper, 'Never mind, you will soon be home'. The transitional object had performed its dual role to perfection. He found comfort when separated from his mother in an environment which challenged him. He engaged in imaginative play with teddy such that his unhappiness was eased and self-managed.

The affective theories of play demonstrate that play is as much about feelings of sadness as they are about happiness. These theories also see pretend and imaginative play as the foundation of future creativity in the arts, sciences, and humanities (Bruce 2011). This chimes with the important place given to the concept of companionship in the development of music, dance, and all forms of art (Trevarthen and Malloch 2002; Malloch and Trevarthen 2009, pp. 4–5). Over the years, Trevarthen and colleagues have developed a body of work embedded in increased understanding of brain development and the child's need for companionship and play.

Cognitive theories of play

Whereas affective theories are often linked to adult life through creativity in literature, drama, dance or music improvisations, artistic happenings or scientific creativity, theorizing or hypothesizing, cognitive theories bring play to an end once childhood is passed. Cognitive theories emphasize the importance of children's ideas and the increasing ability to take part in games with rules during middle childhood.

Jean Piaget (1896–1980) agreed with the affective theories of play that balance (equilibration) is important, although in his view it was not possible to reach a constant state of balance. This connects with the view of Scarlett et al. (2005, p. 3), who argue that 'Play, then, is more aptly defined as *playing*. It is a verb more than it is a noun'. According to Piaget (1962), equilibration has two elements. The first is of accommodation, which involves adaptation to people and situations. The second is of assimilation. This is about adding the familiar to what is known already. Play prioritizes assimilation over accommodation. It is more about applying what has already been learnt than about learning new things. Play through the senses and movements of the child dominate initially, but as walking and talking develop, so does pretend or symbolic and imaginative play. As children move into middle childhood games, rules begin to take over and children begin to participate in sports and rule-bound games such as chess, mathematical equations, notated music or dance sequences, and rules of composition when writing, rather than in play.

Lev Vygotsky (1896–1934) saw play as 'a leading factor in development' (Vygotsky 1978, p. 101). It is 'the highest level of preschool development. The child moves forward essentially through play activity' (Vygotsky 1978, pp. 102–3). By this, he (Vygotsky 1978, p. 95) means imaginative play.

Thus, in establishing criteria for distinguishing a child's play from other forms of activity, we conclude that in play a child creates an imaginary situation.

This means that the emphasis in Vygotsky's theory is on children who are walking, talking, and able to engage in pretend and imaginary play scenarios. Through imaginative play, Vygotsky suggests that young children begin to free themselves from the constraints of reality. Like Piaget, he saw rule-dominated games as central to middle childhood. This contrasts with the affective theories of play which regard symbolic play as the bedrock of later creativity.

Confused practice and muddled use of theories

By the 1950s a steady production of differing theories of play had developed. This often resulted in practice that was confused since many of the theories were mutually exclusive, or differed in important ways. The following extract from Mellor (1950, p. 20) demonstrates this situation. The numbers inserted are to help the reader unravel the confused messages of this statement of the importance of play.

> The irresistible urge in young children to be active, to investigate and discover, to imitate and pretend, to plan and construct, finds its outlet in what we call play. Play means those activities which are not connected with our work and which should perhaps be termed recreation (1). Some of the children's actions are in this category—for example, when he lets off steam (2) and abandons himself to the sheer delight of movement after a period of concentration (3). But if we watch children 'at play' we shall see that much of their activity is of a very serious nature, requiring attention, thought and experiment, and should more truly be termed work, even though it may have no economic value. It is during this so-called play that children learn to work, to concentrate and to persevere until achievement is reached (4), to discover the nature of their surroundings and of the people in their community, to acquire skills of body and mind, and to express their thoughts and feelings in a great variety of ways (5).

The theories drawn upon, some of them at odds with each other, include recreation (1), surplus energy (2), pleasure theory (3), preparation for life (4), and play as an integrating mechanism (5). Statements of the importance of play were (understandably) not convincing to those who continued to dismiss childhood play as having a contribution to make to the education of young children. Those advocating a formal approach to primary school education saw no reason to introduce play into the curriculum or pedagogy of the first years of school. Dearden's accusation (1968, p. 94) appears to have been justified when he wrote that he found practitioners eulogizing play with a continuation of the kind of muddled practice and articulation demonstrated by Miss Mellor.

The contribution of research

From the 1970s early childhood play has been given increased attention by researchers. Bruce (1991, p. 38) suggests the following:

> The unease raised by philosophers of education, typified by Dearden in the 1960s, about the value of play, pervades much of the research of the 1970s and 1980s. It led to a critical examination of the generic concept of play, which sought out those elements which were educationally useful.

Those working practically with children, such as Miss Mellor, intuitively knew its value, but could not easily articulate it or show evidence. The disadvantage lay in the fact that when researchers take control and invade practice, there is a tendency, however unintended, to dictate how pedagogy should develop. An unfortunate power relationship develops in this situation.

Two strands in the research on play are discernible, both of which argue that play is worthwhile educationally. The first proposes that play is educational as it is all about preparing children for their future adult lives. The research undertaken by Jerome Bruner (1980), Barbara Tizard (1984), Corinne and John Hutt (Hutt et al. 1989), and the Department for Education and Skills ('The Effective Provision of Pre-School Education (EPPE) Project' 2004) typify this approach. Play is seen to initiate children into what they will need as adults in ways which are developmentally, and culturally, appropriate. This leads to the role of the adult being to structure and guide the play of young children. As a result of the Oxford studies, play on bikes and trucks in the garden was discouraged, as the research data showed low cognitive challenge. But it did not examine the intellectual aspects of play and social companionship— negotiating skills developing, helping each other, turn taking, collaboration, or joint problem setting and solving—on the part of the children. Nor did it investigate how younger children learn with and through older children as they play together in educational settings. Only practitioners skilled in observation (Isaacs 1967; Katz 1987; Siraj and Kingston 2015) could have picked up on this, and continued to value these elements of outdoor play. Instead, the Oxford research resulted in emphasis on cognitive challenge. Tizard's research emphasized the importance of language for cognitive learning rather than the importance of social gatherings of children, learning through playing together. The Hutts' work on sand and water led to episodic play being valued more than ludic play, and resonating with this the EPPE study emphasized the role of the adult in supporting children's play, with the focus on purposeful play. The purpose was linked to the adult tutoring young children in what they will need to know as adults.

Although the second strand in the research also sees play as education, it is viewed as an integrating mechanism enabling children to sort out their ideas, thoughts, feelings, and relationships; to know themselves physically, mentally, and emotionally; and to come to terms with their knowledge, understanding, and experiences. In this approach, typified by researchers such as Millar (1968), Garvey (1977), Tamburrini (1981), Athey (1990), Bruce (in Gura 1992), Singer and Singer (1990), Fein and Kinney (1994), Goncu, Jain, and Tuermer (2007), and Bredikyte (2011), children are seen to use their play to master, control, innovate, create, imagine, and demonstrate what is important to them as well as to society in their development and learning. Adults, therefore, do not lead and guide, but instead are crucial and sensitive catalysts and supporters in the development of early childhood play. Although she is not a researcher, the observations gathered across the years by Vivian Gussin Paley of children she worked with in schools provide valuable data demonstrating how children understand that play provides them with the possibility to make believe. She writes of the five-year-old Wally (Gussin Paley 1981, p. 81):

> He is not a captive of his illusions and fantasies, but can choose them for support or stimulation without self consciousness. He has become aware of the thinking required by the adult world, but is not committed to its burden of rigid consistency.

The adult role differs in these two strands of research. In the first, adults structure, guide, and lead the play. In the second, adults indirectly structure so that the play free-flows (Bruce 1991, p. 7) and can be supported and extended (Bruce 1987, p. 65), such that sometimes the adult will take a lead, and sometimes the child will do so, as in a conversation. The work of Colwyn Trevarthen (1997, 1998; Trevarthen and Malloch 2002) has been groundbreaking in developing understanding of the importance of this kind of adult role, be it through proto-conversations, musical encounters with babies and young children, or dancing and early childhood play.

Disseminating the importance of play

Because of the intangible nature of childhood play it is difficult, if not impossible, to pin it down. This makes its importance vulnerable to neglect of government funding across the world.

Those who study it or who work with young children, engaging and participating in play with children, tend to be committed to its value. However, the importance of early childhood play in educational contexts has only been accepted at the level of lip service by governments in many countries of the world. Teachers trained to support the learning of younger children to the same level as those educating children from statutory stage (according to the country) are still rarely found. Friedrich Froebel's innovation of the kindergarten for children aged two to seven years, with highly trained teachers, pioneered this approach in the nineteenth century (Bruce 2015). The Froebelian Elinor Goldschmied (1910–2009) further developed Froebelian approaches to play in day care contexts for children from birth to three years during the 1950s (Cousins, Hughes, and Selleck 2013).

A variety of hazards have been identified in establishing the importance of play in early childhood. Philosophizing and theorizing its value does not mean there is evidence for it being beneficial during early childhood. When researchers dictate and dominate how early childhood practice should be, practitioners are undermined rather than supported in their practice. Research needs to empower practitioners and parents (Bruce 1997, Powell, Goouch, and Werth 2013), helping them in understanding so that they are equipped to develop the play of children and families.

If there is no possibility of a tight definition of play, there remains the need to have some kind of shared view, solidarity, and unity of what its importance is. This is so that play can be disseminated and established in practice in homes and early childhood settings of various kinds. As a reaction there have been on the one hand romanticized versions of its importance, and on the other hand great emphasis on the role of the guiding adult, giving play purpose in order to justify its inclusion in the early childhood curriculum. Catherine Garvey (1977, p. 10) summarizes the situation:

In everyday conversation, it is generally unfair and provoking to ask for precise definitions of familiar words. But when a familiar concept like aggression, intelligence, or personality becomes an object of study, then it must be defined or delineated, at least clearly enough so that those who contribute to the study and those who may benefit from it know they are talking about the same thing. Play has been a particularly recalcitrant notion.

Dissemination through government documents

Froebelians have a track record of influencing government documents in the UK in giving play educational status. Susan Isaacs (1885–1948) gave evidence to the committee which led to the Hadow Report (1933). She focused on the way in which play gives children opportunities for understanding their thoughts, feelings, and relationships through their physical selves without being dominated by adult instruction. Dorothy Gardner (1969, p. 75), her student, explains how she believed that:

> Children went further in discovery and learnt more by generous provision of play, with the support of skilled teachers, than they had done by being given instructions in groups or limited occupations on specially selected apparatus.

The emphasis of her approach to play during the 1930s is to see it as the child's work, thereby raising its educational status, and encouraging those adhering to formal direct teaching methods to adopt it. Arnold Campbell (in Gardner 1969, p. 168) writes that 'she was basically a liberal educationalist, but she did not antagonise the formalists'.

Molly Brearley, the Principal of the Froebel Educational Institute in the 1960s, was a member of the Plowden Committee. Working in a later era during the 1960s, she continued to emphasize the need for a broad curriculum with practical direct and real experiences at its heart, taught by highly trained, mature, educated teachers who understood the importance and practice of learning through this kind of informal learning. She took forward the Froebelian thread of argument that play is a serious mechanism for learning. Whereas Susan Isaacs was influenced mainly by Kleinian psycho-analytic theory, a socio-cultural element of learning through play is added to the Plowden Report (Department of Education and Science 1966, p. 194), suggesting that the disciplines of sociology and anthropology, as well as psychology, were beginning to have an impact on primary school education.

From 2000, the legally enshrined documents 'Curriculum Guidance for the Foundation Stage' (Qualifications and Curriculum Authority 2000) and 'Birth to Three Matters' (Department of Education and Skills 2002) were again heavily influenced by Froebelians such as Tina Bruce, Peter Elfer (2015) and Lesley Abbott (Abbott and Langston 2005). In the later combined framework documents 'Early Years Foundation Stage' (Department for Education 2014) this was not the case. There was more focus on adult controlled purposeful play in and less on child initiated play. Despite the efforts of the Tickell Review (2011), a situation has developed such that children could experience a further erosion of their autonomy in learning through their play. However, determined, informed practitioners, who are skilled in their pedagogy can overcome this as the documents do not ban play from the English curriculum framework. The Scottish framework gives greater importance to play, as does the Welsh framework (Department for Children, Education, Lifelong Learning and Skills 2008). The Northern Ireland framework is between the

English and the other countries in the importance it places on educationally worthwhile play (Department of Education Northern Ireland 2013).

Dissemination by those training teachers and other practitioners

Although Susan Isaac's view (1968, p. 133) that 'play has the greatest value for the young child when it is really free and his own' is sprinkled through government documents, these have to be interpreted and implemented by practitioners. This requires training that supports teachers and their colleagues to develop the child's curriculum. The Froebelian tradition of 'freedom with guidance' (Tovey 2012) encourages this. Crucial to this possibility is the training needed in learning how children develop biologically and socio-culturally. Observation of children at play is part of this. Knowing how and when to participate in children's play is a very skilled matter. Some adults have this intuitively in their hearts and actions, but training (Isaacs 1967; Siraj 2017) helps them to be more articulate about how they achieve this, and then to disseminate what they do in supporting and extending the child's own play.

Twelve features of free-flow play (Bruce 1991), identifiable in the vast literature that exists on early childhood play, serve as useful navigational tools for honing observation skills in relation to the absence or presence of play, and subsequent acting in the light of those observations. These navigational tools provide a flexible framework through which to explore play such that the approach is not constrained, ossified, or set in the context of its historic time. Just as the play of the children and adults observed at play needs to flow along, so the thinking of the adults studying play does too. The features of play draw on the areas of agreement that exist between theories and diverse disciplines and the converging evidence available in an effort to provide consistent and coherent help and support to practitioners in developing play in ways which respect the value children place on their own play. But they also provide and open the way for critiquing and challenging current practices, research, theory, and policy making in a very positive and constructive way.

The features of free-flow play as navigational tools

In their play, children draw upon and make use of the first-hand and direct experiences they encounter and are introduced to in life. Early childhood play does not bow to pressures to conform to external rules, outcomes, targets, or adult-led projects. Because of this, children keep control as they play. Play is a process. It has no products. When the play ends, it vanishes as quickly as it arrived. Children choose to play. It is intrinsically motivated. It arises spontaneously when the conditions are conducive, and it is sustained as it flows. Children rehearse their possible futures in their play. Play helps children to learn to function in advance of what they can do in the present. Play has the potential to take children into the world of pretend. They imagine other worlds, creating stories of possible and impossible worlds beyond the here and now, in the past, present, and future. Pretend play transforms children and adults into different characters.

Play can be solitary, and this sort of play is often very deep. Children learn who they are and how to face and deal with their ideas, feelings, relationships, and physical selves. Children and/or adults can play together, in parallel (companionship play), co-operatively in pairs, or in groups. Play might be initiated by a child or by an adult, but adults need to bear in mind that every player has his or her own personal agenda (of which he or she may be unaware). The personal agenda of every participant in the play needs to be respected, and adults need to understand that their agenda should not be privileged above that of the children. Adults who support each child in their personal agenda and interests are likely to develop the children's learning through play.

Children's free-flow play is characterized by deep concentration, and it is difficult to distract them from their learning. Children at play wallow in their learning. And in play, children try out their recent learning, mastery, competences, and skills, and consolidate these. They use their technical prowess and confidently apply their learning. Children at play coordinate their ideas, thoughts, and feelings. They make relationships with family, friends, and culture. Play is an integrating mechanism that allows flexible, adaptive, imaginative, innovative behaviour. Play makes children into whole people, able to keep balancing their lives in a fast-changing world.

The features of free-flow play (Box 3.1) can be put into a shorthand form to aid practice in early childhood settings as a series of memory hooks serving as navigational tools.

The importance of observation—establishing the natural history of play

Observation of children at play has a time-honoured place. Bredikyte (2011, p. 84) suggests, from observations in the play labs at Oulu and Vilnius universities, that when play is given the support required, young children begin to make their own play props. Children use these in conjunction with found props they come across by happenstance, often showing imaginative use of these and giving them greater priority than expensive commercially produced props. It goes without saying that children need time to play. Learning through play is not a possibility in educational settings if children are only allowed to play when their work is finished (Hakkarainen 2006). It takes children time to get into the play so that its pace and rhythms are fine-tuned for the play to deepen into an educationally worthwhile and satisfying experience.

Making rules for discovery and sharing

It is important not to romanticize the freedom of play, and to recognize the sense of agency in making rules which give the player control. Fein and Kinney (1994, p. 193), in a series of observations on a particular young child, noted that Annie did not engage in free-flow play. She chose 'safe, structured materials that required no participation with others or teacher guidance'. These researchers (Fein and Kinney 1994, p. 204) give three reasons why children might be non-players when they arrive at school. They have been led to think that school means no play. Making choices is a threatening process. Impulse control has primacy over making choices of what the child might choose to do.

Box 3.1 Features of free-flow play

First-hand experience is used

Rules are made up

Play materials and props are made and found

Choosing to play or not

Rehearsing and recasting past, present, and future

Pretend play creating possible or alternate worlds

Solitary play

Children play together

Adults and children play together

Deep concentration as children wallow in their play

Using technical prowess as children confidently apply their learning

Play is an integrating mechanism bringing together development and learning

Data from Bruce, Tina, *Time to Play in Early Childhood Education*. London: Hodder and Stoughton, 1991.

> When these children come to a school in which play is a planned part of the curriculum, they must deal with a risky activity that exposes sensitive emotional issues to public scrutiny.

Children like Annie need help in developing their play. Literal play is often a first step to discovery, according to Fein and Kinney. It connects with the safety of knowing the everyday rules of life, such as going shopping, in a way that pretending to become a gibbon seen on a visit to the zoo does not. Annie was able to transfer her writing and paperwork choices to being a shopkeeper and then began to interact with other children at play in this scenario.

Resources for adventure, and a story-making personality

From her observations, the Froebelian Elinor Goldschmied (Goldschmied, Jackson, and Forbes 2015) developed 'treasure baskets' for sitting babies so that they keep a sense of agency as they play. The adult is a companion, sitting near the baby, or two or three babies, sharing the basket, interested and silent, nodding and showing appreciation as a response when the child shows or gives an object, but giving the message that the child is leading. The objects placed in the basket are the result of careful observation of the baby's interests. Observations of babies from experts working with parents such as Cousins, Hughes, and Selleck (2015), Forbes (2004), Elfer and Grenier (2010), Manning-Morton and Thorp (2003), and Manning-Morton (2013) report that babies will often concentrate for nearly an hour. Two things are crucial in this (Tamburrini 1981, p. 138). First, the play environment must be based on careful observation of the children using it, and then materials can be added which might go beyond supporting the play and will extend it. Second, the adult needs to be sensitive to the child feeling in control of their play. Agency is of central importance if the play is to be sustained. The adult might make a suggestion, or might assume a role as a character, but might only do so for a short time in order for the child, or children, to regain control.

Observations by Goncu (1987, p. 118) suggest that real experiences begin to be transformed to less literal play as play scripts with other children develop. Early pretend play is very literal. Bredikyte and Hakkarainen, working in the play labs they have established in Finland and Lithuania, and sharing this approach with colleagues in Moscow, have observed that many children stick at the level of literal play, and that the adults do not see it as a priority to help children extend and deepen the play so that it becomes 'mature' play (Bredikyte 2011, p. 195). Bredikyte (2011, p. 203) expands on 'mature' play:

> Creative, imaginative play is enormously spacious; it can accommodate all possible experiences of the young child and provide the space to explore those experiences and enact them with other children. When we observe children playing we can follow the visible events, the external narrative. Each individual child participating in the same play activity constructs their own version of the narrative. Often children incorporate their own play themes into a bigger play. When we play together for a longer time we realize that there are many different levels of play and many small themes in one big play activity.

Pretend play is about possible alternative worlds which engage children in supposing. This lifts children to their highest levels of functioning. Children develop narratives and characters. From the observations made in their study, Nicolopoulou (in Goncu and Gaskins 2007, p. 249) and the participating teachers in the study found that:

> Young children's pretend play and their storytelling seem to start out as mostly separate and parallel activities, and the potential for fruitful coordination and cross-fertilisation between them is a developmental achievement that children need first to master.

Friedrich Froebel was the first educationalist to give play educational status in the play of young children. Observation was key to the development of his understanding of play. Based on his observations, he made a transition in his views from an earlier more prescriptive approach (Liebschner 1992; Read 1992; Bruce 2015), to a more open-ended way of encouraging the play of young children based on his observations and those of his colleagues.

Froebel (in Lilley 1967, p. 84) famously stated:

> Play is the highest level of child development. It is the spontaneous expression of thought and feeling—an expression which his inner life requires. It promotes enjoyment, satisfaction, serenity, and constitutes the source of all that can benefit the child. At this age play is never trivial; it is serious and deeply significant.

This resonates with the words of Donald Winnicott (1971, p. 54), another pioneer and observer of children at play, working over a century later.

> It is in playing and only in playing that the individual child or adult is able to be creative and to use the whole personality, and it is only in being creative that the individual discovers the self.

So, is play important?

If play is something owned entirely by children, they will be left to get on with it, and it will not be likely to feature in schools, but rather in the home and in places where children play together out of school (Tovey 2012). The question as to whether play benefits children educationally depends to a large degree on how education is perceived. If education is about the transmission of culture, knowledge, and selected values, play will not need to be prominent in educational settings. If education is mainly preparation for adulthood, then adults will need to guide the play. Play tutoring will be a priority with timetabled play that is purposeful, from the perspective of the adult's educational purposes.

This chapter has emphasized navigational tools through which to explore the importance of play in early childhood education. This locates play as a dialogue and shared experience between child and self, children and children, and children and adults (Bruce 1997). Those who spend time with children, observing them, studying, researching, and learning about human development from a variety of disciplines now have the possibility to draw on the increasing wealth of literature which gives support to the importance of early childhood play from this interactionist perspective. There is increasing support for arguing that early childhood education should be full of play. It should be 'play full'.

References

Abbott, L. and Langston, A. (eds.) (2005). *Birth to Three Matters: Supporting the Framework of Effective Practice*. Maidenhead: Open University Press.

Athey, C. (1990). *Extending Thought in Young Children: A Parent-Teacher Partnership*. London: Paul Chapman Publishing.

Bekoff, M. and Byers, J. (eds.) (1998). *Animal Play: Evolutionary, Comparative, and Ecological Perspectives*. Cambridge: Cambridge University Press.

Bredikyte, M. (2011). *The Zones of Proximal Development in Children's Play*. Faculty of Education: University of Oulu.

Brehony, K. (2013). Play, work and education: Situating a Froebelian debate. *Bordón. Revista de Pedagogía*, **65**(1), 59–78.

Broadbent, P., Howard, J., and Wood, E. (2010). *Play and Learning in the Early Years*. London: Sage.

Brown, S. (1998). Play as an organising principle: Clinical evidence and personal observations. In: M. Bekoff and J.A. Byers (eds.) *Animal Play: Evolutionary, Comparative, and Ecological Perspectives*. Cambridge: Cambridge University Press, pp. 243–60.

Bruce, T. (1987). *Early Childhood Education*. London: Hodder and Stoughton.

Bruce, T. (1991). *Time to Play in Early Childhood Education*. London: Hodder and Stoughton.

Bruce, T. (1997). Adults and children developing play together. *European Early Childhood Education Research Journal*, **5**(1), 89–99.

Bruce, T. (2011). *Cultivating Creativity: Babies, Toddlers and Young Children*, 2nd edn. London: Hodder Education.

Bruce, T. (2012). *Early Childhood Practice: Froebel Today*. London: Sage.

Bruce, T. (2015). *Early Childhood Education*, 5th edn. London: Hodder Education.

Bruner, J. (1966). *Toward a Theory of Instruction*. New York: Norton.

Bruner, J. (1980). *Under Five in Britain: The Oxford Pre-School Research Project*. Oxford: Grant McIntyre Blackwell.

Bruner, J., Jolly, A., and Sylva, K. (eds.) (1976). *Play: Its Role in Development and Evolution*. Harmondsworth: Penguin.

Buhler, C. (1945). *From Birth to Maturity: An Outline of the Psychological Development of the Child*. London: Kegan Paul, Trench, and Trubner.

Callois, R. (1961). *Man, Play and Games*. New York: The Free Press.

Coles, M. (1992). *Anna Freud: The Dream of Psychoanalysis*. Wokingham, UK/ Reading, MA: Addison-Wesley.

Cousins, J., Hughes, A., and Selleck, D. (2013). *Discovered Treasure: The Life and Work of Elinor Goldschmied 1910-2009*. London: Froebel Trust.

Dearden, R. (1968). *The Philosophy of Primary Education*. London: Routledge and Kegan Paul.

Department for Children, Education, Lifelong Learning and Skills (2008). 'A Framework for Children's Learning for 3 to 7-year-olds in Wales'. Welsh Assembly Government.

Department for Education (2014). 'Statutory Framework for the Early Years Foundation Stage: Setting the Standards for Learning, Development and Care for Children from Birth to Five'. London: Department for Education.

Department of Education and Science (1966). 'Children and Their Primary Schools: A Report of the Central Advisory Council for Education', vol. 1. London: HMSO.

Department for Education and Skills (2002). 'Birth to Three Matters: A Framework to Support Children in Their Earliest Years'. London: DfES/Sure Start.

Department for Education and Skills (2004). 'The Effective Provision of Pre-School Education Project: Findings from Pre-School to End of Key Stage 1. Final report'. London: DfES/Sure Start.

Department of Education Northern Ireland (DENI) (2013). 'Learning to Learn: A Framework for Early Years Education and Learning'. DENI.

Early Education (2015). 'Maintained Nursery Schools: The State of Play Report'. London: Early Education.

Edmiston, B. (2008). *Forming Ethical Identities in Early Childhood Play*. Abingdon: Routledge.

Egan, K. (1997). *The Educated Mind: How Cognitive Tools Shape Our Understanding*. Chicago, IL/ London: University of Chicago.

Elfer, P. (2015). Babies at play: musicians, artists and scientists. In: J. Moyles (ed.) *The Excellence of Play*. Maidenhead: Open University, McGraw-Hill, pp. 63–74.

Elfer, P. and Grenier, J. (2010). Personal, social and emotional development. In: T. Bruce (ed.) *Early Childhood: A Student Guide*. London: Sage, pp. 141–53.

Erikson, E. (1963). *Childhood and Society*. London: Routledge and Kegan Paul.

Fein, G. and Kinney, P. (1994). He's a nice alligator. Observations on the affective organisation of pretense. In: A. Slade and D. Palmer Wolf (eds.) *Children at Play: Clinical and Developmental Approaches to Meaning and Representation*. New York/ Oxford: University of Oxford, pp. 188–205.

Forbes, R. (2004). *Beginning to Play: Young Children from Birth to Three*. Maidenhead: Open University.

Frayn, M. (2015). 'The Origins and Nature of Theatre'. Lecture to the Richmond Society, 26 February.

Freud, A. (1969). *Normality and Pathology in Childhood*. New York: International Universities.

Gardner, D.E.M. (1969). *Susan Isaacs: The First Biography*. London: Methuen.

Gardner, H. (1982). *Developmental Psychology: An Introduction*, 2nd edn. Boston, MA/ Toronto: Little Brown and Company.

Garvey, C. (1977). *Play*. Cambridge, MA: Harvard University.

Gaskins, S., Haight, W., and Lancy, D. (2007). The cultural construction of play. In: A. Goncu and S. Gaskins (eds.) *Play and Development: Evolutionary, Sociocultural, and Functional Perspectives*. New York/ London: Lawrence Erlbaum. pp. 179–203.

Goldschmied, E., Jackson, S., and Forbes, R. (2015). *People Under Three: Young Children in Daycare*, 3rd edn. London: Routledge.

Goncu, A. (1987). Toward an interactional model of development changes in social pretend play. In: L. Katz (ed.) *Current Topics in Early Childhood Education*, vol. 8. Norwood, NJ: Ablex, pp. 108–26.

Goncu, A. and Gaskins, S. (2007). *Play and Development: Evolutionary, Sociocultural and Functional Perspectives*. New York, London: Lawrence Erlbaum.

Goncu, A., Jain, J., and **Tuermer, U.** (2007). Children's play as cultural interpretation. In: A. Goncu and S. Gaskins (eds.) *Play and Development: Evolutionary, Sociocultural, and Functional Perspectives.* New York/ London: Lawrence Erlbaum, pp. 155–79.

Goouch, K. (2015). Permission to play. In: J. Moyles (ed.) *The Excellence of Play*, 4th edn. Maidenhead: Open University, McGraw-Hill, pp. 138–48.

Groos, K. (1901). *The Play of Man.* New York: Appleton.

Gura, P. (ed.) (1992). *Exploring Learning: Young Children and Blockplay.* London: Paul Chapman.

Gussin Paley, V. (1981). *Wally's Stories.* Cambridge, MA/ London: Harvard University.

Gussin Paley, V. (1986). *Mollie is Three: Growing Up in School.* Chicago, IL: University of Chicago.

Hadow, H. (1933). 'Infant and Nursery Schools Report of the Consultative Committee'. London: HMSO.

Hakkarainen, P. (2006). Learning and development in play. In: J. Einarsdottir and J. Wagner (eds.) *Nordic Childhoods and Early Education.* Greenwich, CT: Information Age, pp. 183–222.

Holland, P. (2003). *We Don't Play with Guns Here: War, Weapon and Superhero Play in the Early Years.* Maidenhead: Open University, McGraw-Hill.

Huizinga, J. (1938). *Homo Ludens: A Study of the Play-Element in Culture.* Boston, MA: Beacon.

Hutt, S., Tyler, S., Hutt, C., and Foy, H. (1989). *Play, Exploration and Learning.* London: Routledge.

Isaacs, N. (1967). 'What is Required of the Nursery-Infant Teacher in this Country Today?' London: National Froebel Foundation.

Isaacs, S. (1930). *Intellectual Growth in Young Children.* London: Routledge and Kegan Paul.

Isaacs, S. (1933). *Social Development in Young Children.* London: Routledge and Kegan Paul.

Kalliala, M. (2006). *Play Culture in a Changing World.* Maidenhead: Open University.

Katz, L. (ed.) (1987). *Current Topics in Early Childhood Education*, vol. **8**. Norwood, NJ: Ablex.

Klein. M. (1932). *The Psychoanalysis of Children.* London: Hogarth.

Liebschner, J. (1992). *A Child's Work: Freedom and Guidance in Froebel's Educational Theory and Practice.* Cambridge, UK: Lutterworth.

Lilley, I. (1967). *Friedrich Froebel: A Selection from His Writings.* Cambridge: Cambridge University Press.

Lyotard, J. (1982). *The Postmodern Condition: A Report on Knowledge.* Minneapolis, MN: University of Minneapolis.

McNair, L. (2012). Offering children first hand experiences through forest school: relating to and learning about nature. In: T. Bruce (ed.) *Early Childhood Practice: Froebel Today.* London: Sage, pp. 57–69.

Malloch, S. and **Trevarthen, C.** (eds.) (2009). *Communicative Musicality: Exploring the Basis of Human Companionship.* Oxford: Oxford University Press.

Manning-Morton, J. (2013). *Exploring Wellbeing in the Early Years.* Maidenhead: Open University.

Manning-Morton, J. and **Thorp, M.** (2003). *Key Times for Play: The First Three Years.* Maidenhead: Open University.

Matthews, J. (2011). *Starting from Scratch: The Origin and Development of Expression, Representation and Symbolism in Human and Non-human Primates.* London/ New York: Psychology Press.

Mellor, E. (1950). *Education Through Experience in the Infant Years.* Oxford: Blackwell.

Millar, S. (1968). *The Psychology of Play.* Harmondsworth: Penguin.

Moyles, J. (ed.) (2015). *The Excellence of Play.* Maidenhead: Open University, McGraw-Hill.

Nicolopoulou, A. (2007). The interplay of play and narrative in children's development: Theoretical reflections and concrete examples. In: A. Goncu and S. Gaskins (eds.) *Play and Development: Evolutionary, Sociocultural, and Functional Perspectives.* New York/ London: Lawrence Erlbaum, pp. 247–73.

Pellis, S. and **Pellis, V.** (2007). Rough and tumble play and the development of the social brain. *Current Directions in Psychological Science*, **16**(2), 95–8.

Piaget, J. (1962). *Play, Dreams and Imitation in Childhood*. London: Routledge and Kegan Paul.

Polanyi, M. (1958). *Personal Knowledge*. London: Routledge and Kegan Paul.

Powell, S., Goouch, K., and **Werth, L.** (2013). 'Mothers' Songs in Daycare for Babies: Report to the Froebel Trust Research Committee'. Canterbury: Canterbury Christchurch University Research Centre for Children, Families and Communities.

Qualifications and Curriculum Authority (2000). 'Curriculum Guidance for the Foundation Stage'. London: QCA.

Read, J. (1992). A short history of children's building blocks. In: P. Gura (ed.) *Exploring Learning: Young Children and Blockplay*. London: Paul Chapman, pp. 1–12.

Robson, S. (2010). *Developing Thinking and Understanding in Young Children: An Introduction for Students*, 2nd edn. Abingdon, UK/ New York: Routledge.

Rogers, S. and **Evans, J.** (2008). *Inside Role-Play in Early Childhood Education*. London: Routledge.

Rubin, K., Fein, G., and **Vandenberg, B.** (1983). Play. In: P. Mussen, L. Carmichael, and E. Hetherington (eds.) *Handbook of Child Psychology*, vol. 4. New York: Wiley, pp. 693–774.

Scarlett, W., Naudau, S., Salonius-Pasternack, D., and **Ponte, I.** (2005). *Children's Play*. London: Sage.

Scottish Government (2014). 'Building the Ambition: National Practice Guidance on Early Learning and Childcare – Children and Young People (Scotland) Act 2014'. Edinburgh: The Scottish Government.

Singer, D. and **Singer, J.** (1990). *The House of Make-Believe: Children's Play and the Developing Imagination*. Cambridge, MA/ London: Harvard University.

Siraj, I. (2017). A review of the current international evidence considering quality in early childhood education and care programmes—in delivery, pedagogy and child outcomes. NSW, Australia: Department of Education.

Siraj, I. and **Kingston, D.** (2015). 'An Independent Review of the Scottish Early Learning and Childcare (ELC) Workforce and Out of School Care (OSC) Workforce'. London: University College London, Institute of Education.

Smilansky, S. (1968). *The Effects of Sociodramatic Play on Disadvantaged Children*. New York: Wiley.

Smith, P. (1982). Does play matter? Functional and evolutionary aspects of animal and human play. *Behavioral and Brain Sciences*, **5**, 139–84.

Spodek, B. (1985). *Teaching in the Early Years*, 3rd edn. Englewood Cliffs, NJ: Prentice-Hall.

Sutton-Smith, B. (1997). *The Ambiguity of Play*. Cambridge, MA/ London: Harvard University.

Tamburrini, J. (1981). Symbolic play. In: R. Roberts and J. Tamburrini (eds.) *Child Development*. Edinburgh: Holmes McDougall, pp. 135–8.

Tickell, C. (2011). 'The Early Years: Foundations for Life Health and Learning. An Independent Report on the Early Years Foundation Stage to Her Majesty's Government'. London: Crown Publishing.

Tizard, B. (1984). *Young Children Learning*. London: Collins.

Tovey, H. (2012). Adventurous and challenging play outdoors. In: T. Bruce (ed.) *Early Childhood Practice: Froebel Today*. London: Sage, pp. 43–57.

Tovey, H. (2013). *Bringing the Froebel Approach to Your Early Years Practice*. London/ New York: Routledge.

Trevarthen, C. (1997). The curriculum conundrum: Prescription versus the Comenius Principle. In: A. Dunlop and A. Hughes (eds.) *Pre-School Curriculum. Policy, Practice and Proposals*. Glasgow: University of Strathclyde, pp. 62–81.

Trevarthen, C. (1998). The child's need to learn a culture. In: M. Woodhead, D. Faulkner, and K. Littleton (eds.) *Cultural Worlds of Early Childhood*. New York: Routledge, pp. 87–100.

Trevarthen, C. and Malloch, S. (2002). Musicality and music before three: Human vitality and invention shared with pride. *Zero to Three*, **23**(1), 10–18.

Vygotsky, L. (1978). *Mind in Society: The Development of Higher Psychological Processes*. London/Cambridge, MA: Harvard University.

Whinnett, J. (2006). Froebelian practice today: The search for unity. *Early Childhood Practice: The Journal for Multi-Professional Partnerships*, **8**(2), 58–80.

Whinnett, J. (2012). Gifts and occupations: Froebel's gifts and occupations today. In: T. Bruce (ed.) *Early Childhood Practice: Froebel Today*. London: Sage, pp. 121–37.

Winnicott, D. (1971). *Playing and Reality*. Harmondsworth: Penguin.

Chapter 4

The emotional and embodied nature of human understanding: Sharing narratives of meaning

Jonathan Delafield-Butt

Introduction: The narrative nature of knowledge

On a hot and humid day in Texas in 1962, John F. Kennedy made an impassioned speech within the grounds of Rice University (Kennedy 1962). His remarks set in motion a space race that would send a man to the moon for the first time in human history. To achieve this technical mastery with rational logic and cognitive foresight, he engaged a fundamental psychological mode of intelligence that has existed in human life from the beginning. He told a *narrative*—a story to be shared—with a grand goal that motivated participation. It was affective—it generated hopes and aspirations in each one of its listeners. And it would set in place America's technical dominance of the world for the next 50 years.

> We choose to go to the moon ... [applause]. We choose to go to the moon ... [applause]. We choose to go to the moon in this decade and do the other things, not because they are easy, but *because they are hard*, because *that goal* will serve to organize and measure the best of our energies and skills, because *that challenge* is one that we are willing to accept, one we are unwilling to postpone, and *one we intend to win.*

> (J. F. Kennedy, Rice University Speech, 12 September 1962; italics mine)

Like an inspiring teacher before his class, Kennedy created a sense of cohesion and belonging that everyone could contribute to. Its biological origin is the power of narrative to motivate, inspire, include, and give direction to individual lives and activity, within the coherence of a community. Kennedy initiated a narrative, a project with a clear collective goal that all individuals could contribute to, no matter their level of knowledge or skill. This is a fundamental source of personal belonging. Served well, it can be a source of inclusion and good health. And it is required by any community of learners in a classroom, too.

Children's agency in the shared generation of meaning

There are two psychological principles that drive human agency. One is, 'I like to move it'—there is deep satisfaction in moving the body, and moving well. The second principle is, 'I like to move it *with you*'—we are fundamentally social creatures with strong emotional ties.

Nobel Laureate Roger Sperry made the profound point that movement is our only means of expression and communication: 'the sole product of brain function is motor coordination' (Sperry 1952, p. 297). All of our psychological experience of feelings, intentions and desires, thoughts, and aspirations can only be made public and evident through movement of the body. And we are naturally compelled to share these experiences with others; it is a simple human need that drives our socialization and personal development. Shaun Gallagher, a phenomenologist or philosopher of direct experience, illustrated this feature of human nature by recalling the pain of solitary confinement (Gallagher 2014). One of the harshest punishments that our penal system can impose is to confine someone *alone*. It is painful not to be social, and goes against our nature.

Moving one's self with another person gives life meaning. An infant moves to generate common understanding in engagement (Delafield-Butt and Trevarthen 2013; Trevarthen and Delafield-Butt 2013a). Movement of self-generated, affect-driven, and intentional acts brings pleasure, and movements made in positive concert with social others create joy, bringing our culture to life (Frank and Trevarthen 2012).

Self-driven, and affective meaning-making is first evident at the very beginning of a human life in how a fetus makes purposeful movements of limbs and careful changes of posture that may be regulated for social contact (Castiello et al. 2010; Delafield-Butt and Gangopadhyay 2013). The first intentions of the baby after birth are adapted to share awareness of life intimately, at first with the mother, in consensuality with her love (Maturana-Romesin and Verden-Zoller 2008).

Successful acts become repeated as schemas of thought, feeling, and action

This wilful, self-generated behaviour first evident in fetal life becomes the basis of learning how the world responds, and what it offers. Learning the echoes or reflections caused by our movements build what Jean Piaget called a 'sensorimotor intelligence', which he claimed is the foundation of later conceptual intelligence. Piaget's predecessor James Mark Baldwin (1895) recognized that these 'circular reactions', which couple self-generated movement with expected sensation, must be the foundation of intelligence that will become more conscious with growing perceptual foresight.

> The self-repeating or circular reaction is seen to be fundamental and to remain the same, as far as structure is concerned, for all motor activity whatever: the only difference between higher and lower functioning being, that in the higher, certain accumulated adaptations have in time so come to overlie the original reaction, that the conscious state which accompanies it seems to differ per se from the crude imitative consciousness in which it had its beginning.
>
> (Baldwin 1895, p. 23)

Acts made consciously that succeed in their purpose bring satisfaction. They are learned and can be repeated to achieve that same sense of satisfaction again and again. They can be adapted to suit new occasions, a schema of intention and action that holds affective value—satisfaction in its success—both intrinsically and shared. Baldwin perceived that circular reactions of human intelligence, even as 'the crude imitative consciousness', are specially adapted to be shared. He perceived that the plans of movement seeking sensory confirmation are ready for communication and the building of a cooperative life.

In the 1980s, Berry Brazelton, Dan Stern, Colwyn Trevarthen, Ed Tronick, Beatrice Beebe, Stein Bråten, and others observed infants closely and proved a contingent, reciprocal nature of infant actions made with another person in dialogue, or 'proto-conversation'. They established evidence for an innate intersubjective, or interpersonal, nature of human minds—a position in agreement with what the philosopher Martin Buber called the primary 'I-Thou' consciousness, from which develops objective 'I-It' consciousness of how we share the use of things in the world (Buber *Ich und Du* 1923, quoted in Friedman 2002, p. 193). We do not need the rational mentalizing of a complex neocortex to begin cooperating with each other's purposes, and acquiring habits of 'common sense'.

Primary intentions are conceived in the embodiment of brainstem, not the rationality of cortex

Contemporary cognitive neuroscience, intending to explain knowledge of facts, reasons, and symbolic language, often forgets that the cerebral cortex sits on top of a more ancient neural structure that nonetheless mediates fundamental psychological functions for thought and intelligence. The brainstem may be anatomically sub-cortical, but is functionally super-cortical in the structuring of thought, experience, and learning. It serves to organize and inform a higher-order, rational intelligence (Merker 2007). In development and through a life of learning, it recruits the activity of the cortex in projects of movement-with-feeling organized through time (Damasio 2003; Goodrich 2010). The brainstem mid-brain system is now recognized as the centre of a primary self-as-agent, and of its emotions and affectivity. It guides rhythms of self-related processing that evaluate the risks and benefits in any action, and responds to the forms and emotions of movements made by other selves (Panksepp 1998).

Observations of the human fetus, with analysis of intentionality in movement recorded by four-dimension ultrasound movies, shows that this basic self-consciousness is developing at 14–16 weeks' gestational age (Delafield-Butt and Gangopadhyay 2013; Reissland and Kisilevsky 2015). This is an age when the cerebral cortex is not yet functional, but there is a brainstem-mediated intelligence, which, studied by Jaak Panksepp, proves to be the seat of the core self (Northoff and Panksepp 2008; Panksepp and Biven 2012), and which is identified by Bjorn Merker as the essential neurological substrate for consciousness of inquisitive vitality in body movement (Merker 2007).

The brainstem integrates and commands three dimensions of activity, which contribute the foundations of intentionality and the affective regulation of the person. It has an *interoceptive* awareness or an awareness of information picked up within the body to sense the 'visceral' functions that sustain life—of heartbeat, blood oxygenation, energy reserves, temperature regulation, digestion of food, and elimination of waste. It has a biomechanical *proprioceptive* sense, which is an awareness of forces of the body in motion, through the system of stretch receptors in the muscles and joints. And it also has an *exteroceptive* awareness of the outside world, which is typically what we think of as our sensory field of consciousness—what we 'know' by vision, smell, touch, and hearing. These senses together give the brainstem a consciousness of the vital needs of the body (interoception), as it is moving (proprioception) through the world (exteroception). This is the intuitive motivator of our person, and it does not require additional cognitive, cortical machinery to integrate purposes in a reasoned awareness of life, or 'theory of mind'. Neuroscientist Philip Winn suggests that 'we need to put the brain back into brainstem' (Winn 2012), the primary site of affective and associative learning often ignored in the neuroscience of intelligence.

Long ago, two pioneering neurosurgeons, Penfield and Jasper (1954), proposed the 'centrencephalic theory' of consciousness at the centre of the encephalon (head), to describe the brainstem complex. Treating brain disorders, they performed a large number of large cortical resections, or inactivated the cortex during operations, and were surprised by the consciousness these patients retained. Children born with loss of most of their cerebral cortices, due to hydranencephaly or anencephaly, may still enjoy affectionate social and emotional lives and control their own actions with conscious purpose, although they are severely cognitively debilitated (Shewmon, Holmse, and Byrne 1999; Merker 2007). We do not need a cerebral cortex to be conscious, to have feelings, to act with intentions, to perceive and appraise the environment, to engage socially and purposefully with others, or to learn. Indeed, experiments with rats demonstrate that, with the cortex removed, these animals are able to navigate over tricky terrain, perform courtship rituals, copulate, and wean litters (Wood 1964).

The cortex is certainly the seat of complex, adult, conceptual intelligence, the constructs of what Thomas Reid (1764) called 'artificial language', a technical language. But we want to understand Reid's other 'natural language', because this is the language of children that remains vital in our adult lives as well—colouring with feeling and emotion everything we do, and giving an embodied and emotional foundation to our advanced technical intelligence.

Child development from simple intentions to ambitious projects

All our activities are composed of elementary units of intention (Figure 4.1). When we reach to grasp something, our intention is carried out in the extension of the arm in a very simple movement, which is followed by movements of the hand that take the object up, then use it. Reaching is organized with anticipation of its goal to use the object; its physical action is organized by its intention. Prospective organization of movement appears to be a biological universal (Delafield-Butt et al. 2012). If the intention differs—for example, to pick up a bottle of wine to pour it or to put it on a shelf—so too does all the preceding structure of the physical acts (Jeannerod 1998).

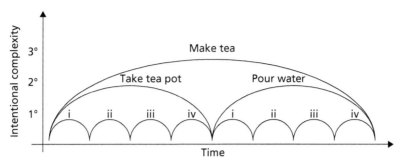

Figure 4.1 Levels of organization of motor intentions built on (1°) individual 'action units' towards immediate goals; (2°) proximal projects that structure and coordinate elementary actions; and (3°) projects of projects that become abstract and conceptually rich. Early skill incorporates intentions from the basic, primary level to the tertiary. For example, the idea to 'make tea' is accomplished by a sequence of secondary levels of intention—to 'take teapot', 'pour water', each composed of a sequence of more proximal sensorimotor actions: (i) reach and (ii) grasp the teapot, (iii) place into position, and (iv) release; (i) reach and (ii) grasp the kettle, and (iii) pour water into the teapot before (iv) returning the kettle to its resting position. This kind of everyday task with imaginative variations may become a favourite 'game' in a children's nursery. Such unitary and embedded organization of practical skill enables learning of a rich repertoire of possible projects.

In the beginning, the fetus can reach with care to touch the umbilical cord, the placenta, or a twin. And it can make grasping movements. The actions of an older child who is playing with a toy, after that initial reach-to-touch, add an accommodating plan to adapt the movement creatively in play, exploring and expanding the child's knowledge of things, and beginning to take many eventualities into account.

These intentional actions are organized in a hierarchy of purpose that expands from its simple beginnings. To have a cup of tea one must reach, grasp, then move the object to one's mouth, then tip the cup and coordinate one's mouth movements to drink from it. Hand and cup are used as tools, in contrast to putting one's head right down to the water to drink, as a dog or horse would do. Manual manipulation of objects requires planning learned within the child's social environment. A one-year-old can drink from a cup using his hands in the proper way, having learned, by 'sharing a task', to use that tool as a parent does (Hubley and Trevarthen 1979). Contrast this with the Wolf-children of Midnapore, who grew up with wolves, rather than with human parents, and who learned the activities of wolf culture and thrived within these (Singh and Zingg, 1942). Learned social intelligence within affective bonds is innate (Packard and Delafield-Butt 2014). This instrumental I-It learning is the beginning of our higher-order cultural intelligence, which needs planning of the serial organization of movement in a conventional way ahead of time. It enables us to achieve more distal goals, further away from us in space and time and in complexity of action—including rituals of art, speech, literature, and manufacturing techniques that may be inherited from ancestors.

To enable this kind of special human 'ritual intelligence' (Merker 2010), the child needs to playfully develop the cognitive machinery of planning—to organize concepts and memory in imagination, and to piece together an understanding of the world that came from understanding the consequences of simple actions (Pezzulo and Castelfranchi 2009). Now the mind of the toddler can extrapolate meaning further into the future, making up stories of make-believe, using creative imagination.

We may plan to drink tea together, performing elaborate, well-organized rituals of sitting together, waiting for the appropriate moment to pour the water, stir the tea, and pour the tea into teacups, all the while sharing a conversation with its grammatical rules and imitative, reciprocal exchange of expression to qualify semantic details. Each act or project has a particular temporal domain. The primary acts always typically last under 1 second, and the small projects 1–3 seconds, while these larger tertiary projects are always over 3 seconds, because now it is going past the immediate present into an abstract, imagined future, as in the 'chronobiology' of a composition of music, a story without words (Osborne 2010).

As adults, we constantly have to organize ourselves in the present moment to achieve goals that are very distant. Students at university stay in and study to achieve a degree years away, so that they can then achieve a good lifestyle, satisfy their parents, or achieve mastery of important facts within a very technical, artificial understanding. They must organize their present moment—to reach for the phone to call their friend to party, or to grasp a pen to take notes on their assignment. Many of them aimed—in the heady days of the 1970s—to go to the moon.

One of the first shared projects of a baby is finding and latching onto the nipple for breastfeeding, or sucking a bottle for feeding. Either way, the task requires skill, focus of attention, and determination to succeed, with shared intentionality. The mother has to align her intentions with that of the infant, to give support and direction, and together they form a shared act that initiates towards a common goal, develops its aim of accomplishment, and finally arrives at its goal. When it is successful, satisfaction is realized that can be vital for sustenance and life (Figure 4.2).

Sometimes it requires professional support to nurture and soothe the mother after the complex experience of childbirth, and to sooth the infant, and to give them both the psychological space needed for joining together in happy and healthy companionship. This becomes the important task of midwifery or grandparenting. Sharing satisfaction or joy in the successful acts of cooperation is fundamental to learning the tasks of our human nature.

Learning to walk is postponed during infancy, and is a very difficult task for a beginner under one year old— putting one foot in front of the other, stepping on something firm, and keeping a heavy body balanced (Figure 4.3). These steps are each organized by their primary goals of putting a foot forward, which are repeated over cycles to form a high-order project that takes the toddler further into the future. They form a project, and on

Figure 4.2 A project shared immediately after birth. A newborn infant is assisted in the task of latching onto the breast for feeding. The project (a) initiates as the infant struggles to latch onto the nipple, (b) develops over repeated small movements of mother's hand and body and baby's head, mouth, and arms, coordinating their interest, arousal, and intention with shared eye gaze before (c) the mother and baby reach completion of their project, delivering both psychological and physiological satisfaction, both of which are required for life to progress in mental and physical health.

their completion, they generate a sense of satisfaction and joy that is both intrinsic to the individual, and can be shared in pride with others (Figure 4.3).

The Russian psychologist Nikolai Bernstein gave us the first scientific proof of 'prospective control' in all kinds of body movement, shown by his very detailed analysis of the forces involved, that an older toddler plays with the agile body, 'testing the degrees of freedom' of elaborate motor activity—running, skipping, hopping, jumping, and twirling—to master its risks safely and with crazy joy, rarely losing balance or making a false step (Bernstein 1967). A bit older, and the child is turning graceful cartwheels through the air like a gymnast. Each of these is a project learned, a project accomplished, and a project to be shared

You see this in toddlers' games of all kinds. The joy at the conclusion of the project, with those motivations and bodily feelings, ensures it will be remembered and repeated, 'Again! Again!' (Featherstone, Beswick, and Louis 2008), echoing the delight of children playing in the playground, and their natural desire to repeat the success of their

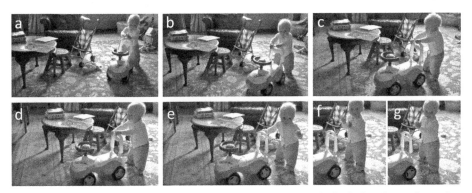

Figure 4.3 A toddler performing a short project, walking with the help of a push-truck. The project (a) initiates with attention to the task and (b–d) develops over repeated steps one in front of the other, maintaining difficult shifts in balance with support from the truck until (e–g) the final conclusion: accomplishment shared with delight and applause with her father filming.

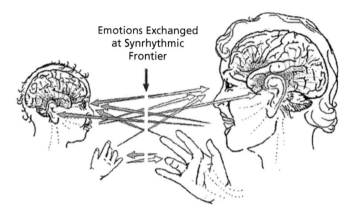

Figure 4.4 Two people with two brains and two bodies connected in intersubjectivity.
Feelings, intentions, and desires expressed with body gesture and posture, facial movements, and movements of the voice are received and reciprocated by the other with sympathy, creating altogether a musicality in the rhythms and shared quality of expression in the exchange.
Reproduced from Kenneth J. Aitken and Colwyn Trevarthen, Self/other organization in human psychological development, *Development and Psychopathology*, 9 (4), pp. 653–77 © 1997 Cambridge University Press.

project—sliding the slide, climbing the wall, spinning the roundabout. This love for challenge and successful accomplishment is embedded into our experience and our learning with its affective, cognitive, and motor dimensions. This is how human consciousness, human intelligence in action, is generated.

It begins with its own agent power, affectivity, and motor intentionality in the late fetus and early infancy, and in early childhood it invites us to enjoy doing and sharing hugely complex projects which mark us as different from the non-human primates. This is the motivation for the 'working theories' of young children and for the support of such theories by understanding teachers, as described in Chapter 16.

How feelings and intentions are shared

We share what we do and what we know through expressive movement of the different parts of the body that together convey feelings and intentions. Dr. Lou Sander found that such movements are coordinated from birth between mother and infant in one time and space with different modalities of sensation (Sander 2008). This is the message Colwyn Trevarthen shares with us in his illustration of the modalities of two brains and two bodies—two embodied consciousnesses alive—two 'subjectivities' in communication, mother and baby becoming a companionship in a single artful and sympathetic 'intersubjectivity' of 'proto-conversation' (Figure 4.4) (Bateson 1979; Trevarthen 1995; Trevarthen et al. 1998).

The hands, the nose, the ears, the face—all interact in harmony to couple the experiences of one person with the experiences of another. The brain functions of one person conveyed in movement are sensed directly by the brain functions of another. This is the collaboration of two persons' 'external synapses' (Bernstein 1967) that connects the experiences of two brains together, that brings two minds together to work as one. We have billions of synapses within our brain that connect one neuron to another, but this is the external synapse of a social engagement, the actions of one particular nervous system interacting with the actions of another nervous system, and importantly those nervous systems are human 'people', not just information-processing organs. This enables an intimate cooperation from birth and shared meaning, sympathy, and understanding to grow in sharing experiences, feelings, and intentions. The mothers' feelings, interest, arousal, and action, and the baby's feelings, interest, arousal, and action work together in sympathy within a reciprocal relationship where the actions of one side are appropriated, felt by the other, and responded to, again with feeling.

Templates of intimate intersubjective engagement are alive between teacher and pupil, caregiver and child. They structure and pattern our intentions and learning, generating trust in the companionship of shared projects. From the start these events are composed in cycles, as when a mother and her newborn are satisfied in breastfeeding. Or when a toddler completes her first steps in walking, or when a child climbs, then slides, down the playground chute, or when an adolescent learns a new mathematical equation in dialogue with her teacher—each of these successful acts completed will be repeated again, again, and again, generating stories of experience and discovery then remembered, and learned from.

This is the active foundation for more complex, cognitive cultural intelligence, using symbols in language and the logic of practice. Karl Lashley summarized the importance of understanding the ordering of movement as a route to understanding the nature of human intelligence and communication.

> There is a series of hierarchies of organization; the order of vocal movements in pronouncing the word, the order of words in the sentence, the order of sentences in the paragraph, the rational order of paragraphs in a discourse. Not only speech, but all skilled acts seem to involve the same problems of serial ordering.... Not only speech, but all skilled acts seem to involve the same problems of serial ordering, even down to the temporal coordination of muscular contractions in such movement as reaching and grasping. Analysis of the nervous mechanisms underlying order in the more primitive acts may contribute ultimately to the solution even of the physiology of logic.
>
> (Lashley 1951, pp. 120–21)

This is the organization of our actions and projects, and what becomes more sophisticated in narratives, or stories, that unfold over time (Delafield-Butt and Trevarthen 2015). Narratives progress with initiative towards a goal, which builds in intensity as the project proceeds, reaching a climactic point with maximal tension and excitement, then releasing that tension to conclude and appreciate the effect of that activity. All the time-based arts share this four-part narrative structure with its rise in excitation and release, through 'introduction', 'development', 'climax', and 'resolution' (Figure 4.5).

This is the psychological and motor organization of an agent acting to achieve something in the future, and our understanding of how actions are organized serially together. It may be an instrumental project to do something practical such as cook a fancy dinner, or to go to the moon, or one made artfully to appreciate the grace and excitement of acting or

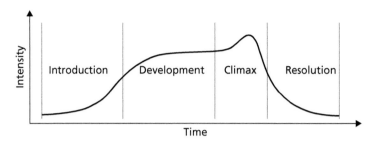

Figure 4.5 The intensity contour of a narrative over its four phases: (i) 'interest' in the narrative begins at a low intensity in the *introduction*, which 'invites' participation in purposefulness; (ii) the coordination of the actions and interests of real and imagined agents intensifies over the *development*, as the 'plan' or 'project' is developed; (iii) a peak of excitation with achievement of a goal in mutual intention is reached at the *climax*; after which (iv) the intensity reduces as the purposes of the participants share a *resolution*, and those who were closely engaged, separate.

Reproduced from Trevarthen, C. and Delafield-Butt, J.T., 'Biology of shared experience and language development: Regulations for the inter-subjective life of narratives', in Maria Legerstee, David Haley, and Marc Bornstein (eds.), *The Infant Mind: Origins of the Social Brain*, Figure 8.5, p. 188, Copyright © 2018, Guilford Press.

performing, or in the sympathy of a caring other to relieve pain, sadness, or loneliness. All our intentions for communication have the same hope and form through a prescribed space and time of moving.

We generate these narratives together in the lived time of intersubjective co-creativity. Narratives are alive in the dynamic and embodied purpose of coming together socially; it is only later that they become written or told in a book or verbal story or a musical composition. The lived experience on which those stories reflect are not pre-scripted, but generated in the natural flow between parent and infant, between friends, and between teacher and pupil. And it's co-created on a basic physiological substrate, which is the substrate of our body, the substrate of our affectivity, and its particular temporal and spatial dimensions. We parse our actions, taking turns to create something woven together, co-created between two or more individuals, to make a story in which each expresses a personality for others' appraisal (see Bruner, 1996, on the importance of narrative for education).

Learning to regulate the arousal of interest, from birth to school

The regulation of arousal and interest, in children and their teachers, is a fundamental capacity to master for school learning. Learning this skill is first evident within the co-regulations between infant and mother (Delafield-Butt and Trevarthen 2015), and in children learning to regulate their attention and interest in school (Delafield-Butt and Adie 2016), both structured by their shared narrative form. I will give three examples to illustrate this and the ways instrumental learning can be combined, first from infancy and then in early childhood education.

Baby B, was born prematurely at 27 weeks, one of a pair of twins. He had intensive care in the hospital neonatal unit, and his mother visited every day for sessions of body-to-body 'kangaroo' care, helpful for the development of a premature baby. A recording was made when the mother and her infant had been in hospital for eight weeks, and B was healthy and due for discharge.

Figure 4.6 shows how lively Baby B was with his mother as she spoke and attended to him affectionately. He made many arm movements, which were recorded (Figure 4.6a), and we plotted these with the pitch plot of the vocalizations they exchanged (Figure 4.6b). The transcript of what the mother said (Figure 4.6c) puts words to their feelings and expressions as they develop a story of their experience together.

Their contour of excitation and arousal in engagement follows that of a drama. It has an 'introduction' that brings the togetherness out of a quiet, quiescent moment, an invitation to a co-created narrative episode initiated through the mother's vocalization and the infant's contributions. These develop over time, with a pulse close to one per second, or *largo* ('slow walk'), creating peaceful musical elements with shared rhythm and timing. The mother's vocalizations start to increase in pitch and intensity and the baby comes to contribute with all of his energy and his creative apparatus (smile, voice, and movement), culminating in a moment of peak excitation, the 'climax'. The mother then regulates this arousal with a long, regular descending pitch glide from the top of the octave above middle C to below middle C (Figure 4.6c: 11). This descending pitch brings the energy and arousal down and concludes the narrative. In this way the mother can be seen to regulate her baby's excitement at a very sensitive early moment in his life, developing small narrative patterns as a template for regulation and in which meaning can be contextualized.

Baby B's mother is trying to regulate him or help him, saying what she is thinking about helping to regulate B's excitement so they share the conclusion where she is calming that activity and bringing quiet again. Then they have a small repeat of the story, a small coda, as in a piece of poetry. The whole piece has a narrative contour—the intensity rises in the introduction, and continues to rise over repeated phrases of this development, until a peak moment of excitation or climax followed by the resolution. They make a shared meaning, now held as memory that can serve to structure the next, future meeting.

Intersubjective resonance of intentions and feelings— how brains link vitalities

This engagement between Baby B and his mother illustrates how affects, feelings, and intentions are conveyed in movement. Advances in brain science confirm our understanding of the shared consciousness required for intersubjectivity, before a more rational 'theory of mind'. There are two systems responsible: the mirror neuron system and the polyvagal system.

The first, the 'mirror neuron system', was discovered by Giacomo Rizzolatti and colleagues in Parma 20 years ago (Rizzolatti and Gallese 2003). It is a very important system

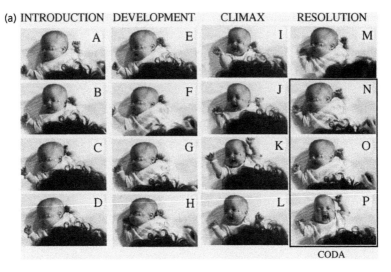

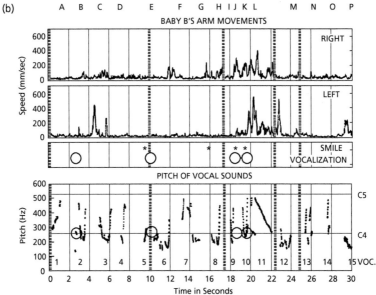

(c) INTRODUCTION [ATTENTIVE]

1 – Are you woken up. mister?
2 – Good afternoon!
3 – Good afternoon, wee B.
4 – How are you doin'?
5 – Eh?

DEVELOPMENT [RESPONSIVE]

6 – Oorh, look at that big smile!
7 – [Oh ... That's all great]
8 – Look at that big smile.

CLIMAX [LIVELY/ENGAGED]

9 – Hi Ya!
10 – Hello there!
11 – Kiss and Glide

RESOLUTION [REFLECTIVE]
[RELAXED]

12 – Oh, you're kicking
your Mum.
13 – Are you kickin me?
14 – Eh?
15 – Have a big wriggle, then.

Figure 4.6 Continued

that appears to be responsible for organizing the actions of the individual, while also serving to recognize those same actions performed by another person. During observation of others' actions, the neurons produce a direct 'resonance' between individuals—the same system is active in both the actor and the observer. In psychological terms, this gives us a basic, implicit understanding of the intentions of the other—so-called 'mind-reading'. This mirror resonance precedes mentalizing, or higher cognitive capacities. It is not necessary to reflect on such sharing or to think about it. No 'theory of mind' is necessary. It is intuitive knowledge of another person's intentions available by correspondence with the motor intelligence of our nervous systems (Sinigaglia and Rizzolatti 2011).

There is another system of the embodied mind important for sharing feelings and intentions directly between individuals, without words. It brings our attention back to the brainstem and originates in the functional regulation of feelings of vitality inside the body. This is the 'polyvagal system' identified by Stephen Porges (2011) of the University of Chicago. He describes this as an evolutionarily advanced system in humans that allows us to share regulatory control of breathing, heart rate, and the energy we need for healthy and expressive body movements (Porges and Daniel 2017).

Porges found that vital autonomic physiology controlled by the ancient vagal nerve, which evolved for visceral motor control of feeding, respiration, and circulation of the blood in primitive vertebrates that had little capacity for imaginative life and social cooperation, has been transformed in the evolution of mammals to afford a rich intersubjective coupling (Porges and Furman 2011). These autonomic organ systems and their adaptation to plans for action are coupled in the brainstem to become an enriched social engagement system that regulates the intonation in our voice and the expressive character

---

Figure 4.6 An early embodied narrative between a young prematurely born infant and his mother demonstrating its embodied, co-created four-part structure. **(a)** Video stills show the expressive actions of the upper limbs, head, and face at different moments in interaction. The columns correspond to the four phases of a narrative of purposes and experiences supported by the vocalizations of his mother. **(b)** Speed of Baby B's arm movements recorded with motion-capture cameras are shown in the top two graphs, with smiles and attempts to vocalize marked below. The mother's speech is shown in the final pitch plot of 30-second dialogue. Baby B's own voice was too hoarse to register a pitch, but the mother's encouraging upward glides can be seen to give rhythmic structure and positive energy to the interaction within the octave above middle C—the area of positive affect. Along the top, the locations of the photographs shown in (a) are indicated by letters A to P. At 11, the mother brings the climactic energy down with a descending pitch glide to settle her baby again, before the whole narrative concludes. **(c)** A transcription of the mother's speech and vocal expression. The utterances are numbered and identified in the pitch plot above. Photographs N, O, and P (utterances 13, 14, and 15) are boxed to indicate that at this phase Baby B is recalling the narrative event in a coda, as his mother's speech gently encourages him.

of our hands, fingers, and facial expressions. Porges discovered that our vital autonomic physiology is directly coupled to expressive gestures and vocalizations, which gives us the powers of what Thomas Reid calls our 'natural language'. Because these expressions announce our vitality, our well-being, and how active, energetic, aroused, and interested we are, as well as what we need as physiological organisms, they are the foundation of the skills and resources we may learn. They enable us to be together in any shared intersubjective space, such as the classroom, to perform tasks together in mutual understanding and enjoyment.

What this allows us to do is directly regulate our autonomic systems, our physiology, one to the other, without thinking about it. It's a feature of shared, pre-reflective primary consciousness (Trevarthen and Delafield-Butt 2017). So, altogether we feel each other's feelings, vital feelings, in their primary intentional acts, which is what Dan Stern described as 'forms of vitality' (Stern 2010). Within the dynamic between subjects, a musicality is formed between feelings expressed with shared timing and reciprocal qualities of voice and gesture (Malloch and Trevarthen 2010). Developments in the cerebral cortex enrich this sympathetic sharing, but the critical evolutionary change occurs in the brainstem, cerebellum, and midbrain, where basic forms of expressive movement and rhythm are generated and regulated in body-related ways.

Co-created narratives become social schemas with significance

Baby B's narrative projects co-created with his mother's sympathy are also recognizable as goal-directed projects. They aim towards something, they build as the act proceeds, they come to a climax of maximal tension and then release into a conclusion. In many cases of human relating, the goal that is planned is one of mutual understanding. When you meet someone in the street and have a chat, you initiate and develop recognition, you shake hands, you chat about this or that, gossip, and make small talk. It may be irrelevant what you're talking about, the goal is manifestly to attune, and then when you're happy, you are satisfied. You say your farewells and off you go to the next project or to continue what you were occupied with before you met.

Such schemas for interpersonal encounters can grow into the habits and recognized rituals of a culture, and their styles will differ. Along with Koichi Negayama, a child psychologist from Waseda University near Tokyo, we have studied the differences between proto-conversations of Japanese and Scottish mothers and babies. Using methods of motion capture to track gestures, expressions, and movements of the body, we found that Japanese mothers follow their babies and wait for the baby to initiate an engagement (Negayama et al. 2015). Even in a task as simple as picking up her baby, a Japanese mother will wait for the baby to take the initiative. A Scottish mother, in contrast, tries to lead or coax her baby, moving on and expecting her baby to follow. If the baby is not following, then she tries many tricks, rattling a toy to attract attention, or making an aeroplane of the spoon to get her baby to join her project. This is a difference in cultural expectations of how to behave, and how a child should respond. In any case it is about expectations and anticipation and what we intend to do, both positive and negative. We become encultured into a particular society with its expected patterns of behaviour that are built on these early rituals of companionship and the value we give to agency within it.

Learning social schemas that enable learning

Frederick Erickson, Professor of Anthropology of Education at the University of California, gives examples of how shared narratives of learning, using prosody of expression to support interest and achievement, help participation and the grasp of conventional ideas of reading, writing, and arithmetic in school (Erickson 2010). He describes musicality in talk and listening as a key element in classroom learning. Narrative patterns active in the school classroom, with their non-verbal musical structure, enable supportive, guided instruction. I give two examples of the use of these principles to help students who find regulation of their arousal and interest difficult, and who therefore struggle with learning in the classroom. By learning the pattern of co-created narrative, they can find the confidence to cooperate with teaching, and enjoy learning.

Nuture-group guidance of affects, interest, and attention to numeracy

In a special school classroom, called nurture groups, children are helped who find the habits of the mainstream class difficult. These children find it difficult to regulate their attention, arousal, and interests to match the intentions of the teacher and wider school system. In a mainstream class they often cannot sit still and find it difficult to integrate socially meaningfully. These children, with so-called social, emotional, and behavioural difficulties, can become a problem for an educational system intended to prepare them for life in a harmonious, intelligent, and sophisticated society. It is assumed their problems arise because of difficulties in early family care. Nurture groups employ techniques of mothering, techniques that work with the emotional and social development of the child to nurture confidence, and to generate more positive attachment relationships.

Together with PhD candidate Jillian Adie, we analyzed the intersubjective patterns of engagement between these teachers and the students. We found the same narrative pattern of embodied, affective engagement evident between caring adults and their younger children, but with a greater degree of cognitive and linguistic skill included (Adie and Delafield-Butt 2016; Delafield-Butt and Adie 2016). In this example, a child in a nurture group was helped to share the walk downstairs (Figure 4.7), a simple task that a teacher may dismiss as irrelevant to the purpose of education, but that served as an important experience of shared learning—affective and cognitive—giving confidence as well as knowledge.

In the recording, he enjoyed the planned participation, and on its conclusion, was delighted with their accomplishment. The teacher held his hand and took him down the stairs. They moved rhythmically, and musically with a basic non-verbal narrative structure, and they

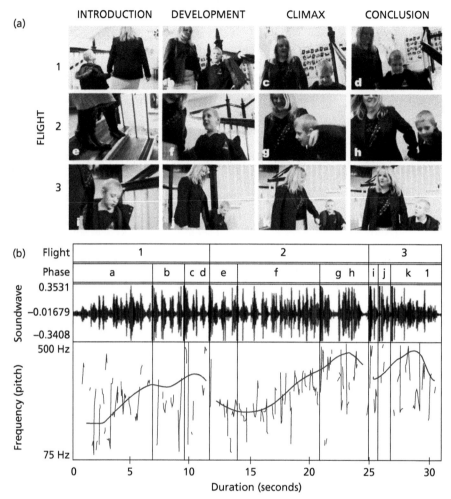

Figure 4.7 A co-created narrative project in school, made while descending the staircase and counting. (a) A picture board illustration (top rows) organized by its three episodes of descending the three flights of stairs. Each episode displays the four phases of introduction, development, climax, and conclusion. The conclusion is tight in between flights with little time to relax, the task demanding immediate preparation for the next flight. Though conclusions are short, the climax of accomplishment in each phase is clearly noted with smiles and increased pitch of the voice signalling delight. Eye contact is made. **(b)** The sound wave shows marked rhythmicity of vocalizations by teacher and student. The sound wave spikes indicate footfalls on the steps. The pitch of each vocalization is calculated (frequency, Hz) and plotted. The full dyadic structure of the child–teacher interaction over the course of the three flights displays a narrative pattern of intensity and progression as the pair move through the phases of **introduction** to the task, **development** of rhythmic shared interaction as they descend the stairs together, a **climax** as they share simultaneous joy on reaching the bottom of the stairs, and a **conclusion** of the activity as they leave this activity behind to commence something new. Narrative contours (black) approximately overlay the rise and fall of vocal pitch to deliver one overarching narrative with three narrative sub-units that correspond to each flight of stairs. The phases are as follows:

added in counting the steps, bringing in maths, something very abstract which requires a conceptual intelligence to understand what it means.

The pitch plot of the video shows how the recitation rises and falls through the different phases in the first flight of stairs, the second flight of stairs, and then the third flight of stairs. The teacher's voice rises and falls as the project unfolds through three sub-narratives or sub-projects that make one whole narrative or project. As the child completes the final flight of stairs he lets out a 'Woo hoo!' before it concludes, a special moment before they go off to do something else. The child has shared something intimately with the teacher, holding hands and sharing their affectivity, and has learned something about what numbers mean, what they can mean with another person, the *value* of those numbers as socially meaningful fun. This catches that child's interest in numbers and in thinking, with the regulation of arousal and attention, and attracts his intentions, which will be required to learn more about those things in a mainstream class.

And after one year of this kind of activity, as little as half a day a week, the children are typically ready to go back into mainstream school. This kind of special education becomes very important, improving the basic psychological skills to succeed in school education, thereby improving the lifelong opportunities for each child and significantly reducing burden to society (Boxall 2002).

Learning expectation and arousal in the narrative of a game

Finally, we draw our discussion of the importance of embodied, non-verbal narratives in education to a close with a second example of guided participation in a nurture group (Figure 4.8). Once again, this is an account of a narrative with a contour, which exhibits the escalation of intensity of expectation until the climax of delight, 'Yeah!', at the end. And then quiet, from which another narrative can unfold. We see the rhythmicity, this

---

(a) introduction as the teacher structures the opening of the interaction, explaining the task ahead as they walk towards the top of the staircase; **(b) development** as they descend the first section of stairs, their footsteps falling into rhythm as they count the stairs together; **(c)** a small **climax** marked by excitement in vocal pitch as they reach the first turning, quickly **(d) concluding** and leading straight into a limited **(e) introduction** to the next task as they negotiate this first turning and make their way to the second flight of stairs; **(f)** a second **development** begins as the child looks to the teacher as she counts the stairs aloud to re-establish their rhythm and **(g)** smiles as they share understanding of their collaborative activity, bringing a second small **climax**, this one larger than the first, as they reach **(h)** the end of the flight of stairs and turn, concluding this episode as they begin to negotiate the second turning, leading to the final sub-narrative. They **(i)** introduce quickly the final episode and **(j) develop** this task by concentrating together on its completion as they descend the final flight of stairs before **(k)** they share a final **climax** of peak satisfaction and joy as they reach the bottom, the teacher smiling as the child lets out a whoop of joy. The piece **(l) concludes** as they leave the staircase behind, now quiet, and head towards a new activity, content with their accomplishment.

Adapted from Jonathan T. Delafield-Butt and Jillian Adie, The Embodied Narrative Nature of Learning: Nurture in School, *Mind, Brain, and Education*, 10 (2), Figure 2, p. 123, DOI: 10.1111/mbe.12120 © 2016 International Mind, Brain, and Education Society and Wiley Periodicals, Inc.

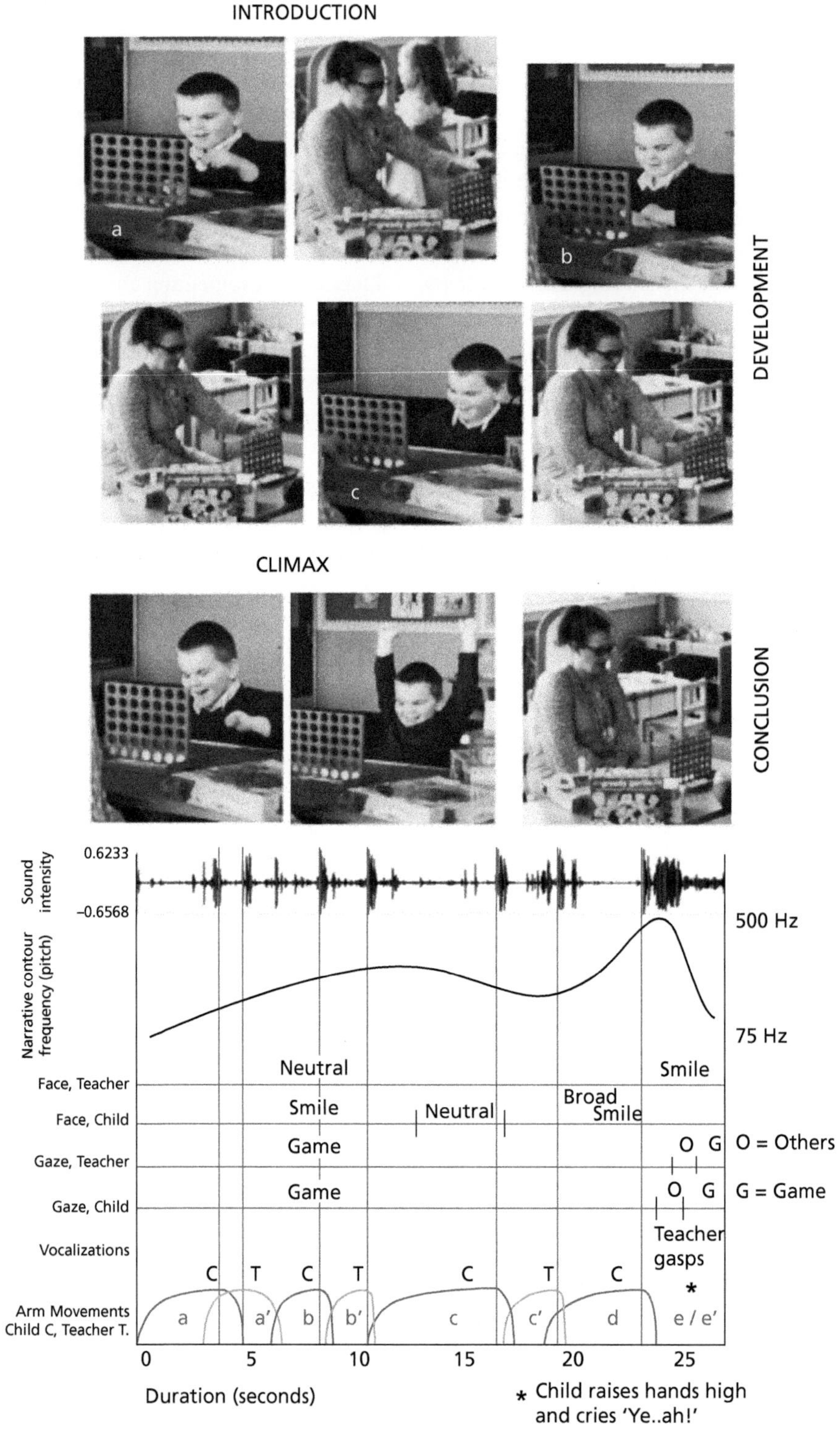

Figure 4.8 Continued

time becoming much more complex with intrusions from the other children and other teachers, but maintaining its coherent form over the act. The same principle, this basic act serving to stimulate confidence and repetition of the project, acts as a bedrock on which higher cognitive intelligence and the stuff of older classroom learning—language, literacy, numeracy, and maths—can be firmly secured.

Narrative intelligence and feelings in the foundation of cognition

I have been describing the development of what Jerome Bruner calls 'narrative intelligence', a form of learning and exploiting the lawful relations between events of people and things and knowing their vital life consequences. This form of intelligence, built on embodied participatory experience of the affective agent, stands in contrast to what Bruner calls a 'logico-scientific intelligence', a conceptual and abstract intelligence that we typically think of as being 'clever', as in 'clever clogs' clever (Bruner 2003). Narrative intelligence is predicated on process—the way things unfold over time in relation to each other. It has also been described as the 'line mode' of the human mind identified by Margaret Donaldson (1992).

A story proceeds through time and space, and therefore is embodied and affective when we create it, in contrast to the logico-scientific or 'construct' mode of concepts that are static and disembodied 'somewhere, some place'. It is built on the structure of experience and it is always coloured with this vital affectivity, which is difficult to get rid of. In fact, we undertake PhDs as a form of scholarship designed to get rid of feelings, to be purely logical and rational, without admitting that affectivity or subjectivity necessarily contributes to form and structure our intelligence.

Logico-scientific intelligence is built on experiences that have to occur within the motivation of a narrative intelligence. And they must be fed back through that narrative

Figure 4.8 The embodied narrative of dyadic child–teacher 'Connect 4' gameplay. The soundwave indicates the fall of the tokens into the game, together with background classroom noise. Acoustic frequency of vocalizations is registered only at the final vocalization of 'Yeah!' by the child—no other vocalizations were made. The narrative contour of intensity approximately follows the combination of vocal pitch, facial expressions of teacher and child, eye gaze, gestures, expressions, and teacher and child vocalizations. The narrative develops through cycles of gameplay turn-taking. The child's turns are identified by the action curves **a,b,c,d**, with the teacher's corresponding turns identified by **a'**, **b'**, and **c'**. Each action curve indicates a reach-grasp-drop—the drop indicated by the red vertical line segmenting the piece—and final return of the hand to the table. The climax to the interaction at **e/e'** is identified by the child's high pitch exclamation, 'Yeah!', at the top of Middle C, with a downward glide as he simultaneously throws his arms in the air and the teacher takes a sharp inhalation of breath. The child and teacher are attentive to the game throughout while recognizing it as part of a greater social interaction as they share their joy with the other teacher ('Other') in the room on completion of the game.

Adapted from Jonathan T. Delafield-Butt and Jillian Adie, The Embodied Narrative Nature of Learning: Nurture in School, *Mind, Brain, and Education*, 10 (2), pp. 117–131, DOI: 10.1111/mbe.12120 © 2016 International Mind, Brain, and Education Society and Wiley Periodicals, Inc.

intellect to be shared with others in communication, whether written or oral, and this then means the affects, with their socio-emotional or poetic value systems, are again placed ahead of 'pure' logico-scientific intelligence. This is why, although we can know facts and figures, we use the intelligence that is lived in the body and in the moment of our actions to explain the truth in the cause of our vitality, to find the natural basis of common sense. 'It is by natural signs chiefly that we give force and energy to language: and the less language has of them, it is the less expressive and persuasive' (Reid 1764/1997, pp. 106–7).

Logico-scientific thought gives us a wonderful abstract world of generalized facts, but they require animation. As Albert Einstein understood, even the laws of physics are stories told about imagined actions in experience. Likewise, a legal trial is, as Jerome Bruner said, just one story versus another and neither is true. That is why he chose to end his career as Professor at New York University School of Law. He wanted to understand how law is about values, what is just and what is unjust, what is criminal and what is not. And his long life had been devoted to understanding how we, and children, are motivated to educate and be educated in shared beliefs and values.

Autism, reduced motor control, and the need for attunement in intentions with affection

Before concluding, I will mention recent ideas about disruption to primary experience in autism spectrum disorder to explain how it affects a child's communication and learning. Autism is a very particular childhood disorder with social, affective, and cognitive aspects (Kanner 1943). All these aspects of the human mind are expressed through movement, as we have seen. It is now clear there is a subtle, but significant, disruption to the physiology of motor control in children with autism that may be a core part of the disorder, evident from birth (Fournier et al. 2010).

Teitelbaum et al. (1998) first recorded movement differences at birth in infants that later developed autism, and since then researchers such as Profs. Nicole Rinehart and Jenny McGinley in Melbourne have worked to characterize and better understand these movement differences in children (Rinehart et al. 2006; Rinehart and McGinley 2010). Using an iPad to record children's movements as they played a game, we recently found we could identify, with 93% accuracy, whether a child had autism simply by analyzing their movements (Anzulewicz, Sobota, and Delafield-Butt 2016), a result that underlines the significance of the disruption in autism, and that is corroborated using similar games (Crippa et al. 2015).

Evidence of the role of agency in movement in child development indicates that disruption to motor timing may lead to a deficit of meaning-making by expressions of the body normally shared in narrative. If the expressive intentions and feelings in movement are confused, this will affect the child's sense of agency and weaken social and affective engagement, leading to secondary consequences of restricted interest, social withdrawal, and cognitive compensations (Trevarthen and Delafield-Butt 2013b).

The expressive 'instruments' needed for communication appear mis-tuned in autism, with subtle timing differences. In consequence, a typical person seeking communication with a child with autism may not readily understand the intentions, interests, and feelings that generate a movement, because the spatio-temporal pattern of a movement is different. They cannot 'read' these intentions and their expressive agency or message as readily, because typical brains are attuned to standard forms of movement with their expected feelings and intentions.

We read the difference as uncertainty or awkwardness in the child's behaviour, and sense a disconnection. Pre-reflective and pre-conceptual awareness of motor intentions is disturbed, part of the direct mind-reading process on which our conscious reflections are based. Therefore, at a primary level of conscious awareness, we find it difficult to read the feelings and intentions of the child with autism as he or she moves. The disjunctions arise between two mis-attuned sensorimotor systems (Cook 2016; Delafield-Butt and Trevarthen 2017).

One way to correct this disjunction is for us—as professional teachers and caregivers—to adjust to the child and attune ourselves differently to the child's actions, so that we can read their feeling and intention, their 'affective vitality', as Dan Stern would describe it (Stern 2010). One way of responding that has proved effective is by imitation, by redirecting our movements to match those of the child (Nadel 2014). This can take place in everyday classroom practice to deliberately attune to the child's embodied feelings, or can be developed into techniques for more regular, focused therapy (Trevarthen et al. 1998; Caldwell 2004; Zeedyk 2008; Athanasiadou and Karkou 2017). Finally, following the child's interests, and bringing these into the curriculum for learning, can offer another route into the child's awareness and interest, helping to generate intersubjectivity and learning in the co-creation of meaning (Gunn and Delafield-Butt 2016).

Conclusion: Reaching for satisfaction in learning, and making sense of the world with others

In this chapter, I have addressed topics of embodiment and feeling with emotion important for learning and education: the importance of *agency* as the power coming to life within the self to engage with the world or with another person; and *embodiment* in how the form of our body in its muscles and skeletal system, with its visceral cycles of arousal and affectivity, can lead to growth of intelligence as these cycles are made meaningful with other people. This is what is required for making contact. To *make contact*, the feelings and intentions must resonate between individuals, and then when they do, each action of the self is contingent on, or cooperative with, the actions of the other. It is this attuned reciprocity that leads to growth in learning to enable the development of more sophisticated projects. Resonance of purposes and feeling in exchange of movements is essential, otherwise the meaning intended, and the complexity we add to it by the use of language, numbers, and other symbolic concepts, is lost.

When we create narrative patterns of meaning-making as a teacher with a child, the stories must come to conclusion in completeness. This, if done well, generates satisfaction and joy. In this positive sensation of success, or pride, confidence is created, and skill is acquired because the child has confidence and inspiration to take on the next cycle with equal or better effect.

All depends on the intuitive foundation of sensorimotor intentionality, first evident in fetal life. Development from primary to secondary to tertiary intentional projects of imaginative action, generating trust in co-action with others, creates shared joy and understanding. It inspires the stories that structure the rituals and games and tasks of our culture. We learn these as children, and we take pleasure and profit by sharing them as the culture of our community. All depends on the embodied narrative intelligence first displayed by a newborn baby.

The urge to share narrative guides experience and knowledge from the beginning of life in projects, such as to touch a twin *in utero*, to share actions with a mother for breast-feeding, or learning to place one foot before the other to walk upright, to more complex projects in social cooperation, such as in learning the rituals of school classroom conversation, or counting. And as these stories become more sophisticated, so they demand an increase in cognitive intelligence. There are many demands to regulate and attend to—to sit upright, wear the right clothes, speak clearly, and attend to your homework with correct academic precision. It is on shared meaning as vital, embodied, and affective creatures developed in narrative on which we build all the cognitive, sophisticated planning capacities that enable us to join in the teacher's imaginative story, and do ambitious, hopeful things—like go to the moon.

References

Adie, J. and Delafield-Butt, J.T. (2016). Social and emotional development in nurture groups: The narrative structure of learning through companionship. *The Psychology of Education Review*, 40(2), 3–9.

Aitken, K.J. and Trevarthen, C. (1997). Self/other organization in human psychological development. *Development and Psychopathology*, 9, 653–77.

Anzulewicz, A., Sobota, K., and Delafield-Butt, J.T. (2016). Toward the autism motor signature: Gesture patterns during smart tablet gameplay identify children with autism. *Scientific Reports*, 6, 31107. doi: 10.1038/srep31107

Athanasiadou, F. and Karkou, V. (2017). Establishing relationships with children with autism spectrum disorders through dance movement psychotherapy: A case study using artistic enquiry. In: S. Daniel and C. Trevarthen (eds.) *Rhythms of Relating: Stories from Children's Therapies*. London: Jessica Kingsley, pp. 272–91.

Baldwin, J.M. (1895). *Mental Development in the Child and the Race: Methods and Processes*. New York: Macmillan.

Bateson, M.C. (1979). The epigenesis of conversational interaction: A personal account of research development. In: M. Bullowa (ed.) *Before Speech: The Beginning of Human Communication*. London: Cambridge University Press, pp. 63–77.

Bernstein, N. (1967). *The Coordination and Regulation of Movements*. Oxford: Pergamon.

Boxall, M. (2002). *Nurture Groups in Schools: Principles and Practice*. London: Paul Chapman.

Bruner, J.S. (1996). *The Culture of Education*. Cambridge, MA: Harvard University Press.

Bruner, J.S. (2003). *Making Stories: Law, Literature, Life*. Cambridge, MA: Harvard University Press.

Caldwell, P. (2004). *Crossing the Minefield: Establishing Safe Passageway Through the Sensory Chaos of Autistic Spectrum Disorder*. Brighton: Pavilion Publishing.

Castiello, U., Becchio, C., Zoia, S., Nelini, C., Sartori, L., Blason, L., D'Ottavio, G., Bulgheroni, M., and Gallese, V. (2010). Wired to be social: The ontogeny of human interaction. *PLoS ONE*, **5**(10), e13199.

Cook, J. (2016). From movement kinematics to social cognition: The case of autism. *Philosophical Transactions of the Royal Society of London B: Biological Sciences*, **371**(1693), 20150372. doi: 10.1098/rstb.2015.0372

Crippa, A., Salvatore, C., Perego, P., Forti, S., Nobile, M., Molteni, M., and Castiglioni, I. (2015). Use of machine learning to identify children with autism and their motor abnormalities. *Journal of Autism and Developmental Disorders*, **45**(7), 2146–56. doi: 10.1007/s10803-015-2379-8

Damasio, A.R. (2003). *Looking for Spinoza: Joy, Sorrow, and the Feeling Brain*. Orlando, FL: Harcourt.

Delafield-Butt, J.T. and Adie, J. (2016). The embodied narrative nature of learning: Nurture in school. *Mind, Brain, and Education*, **10**(2), 117–31. doi: 10.1111/mbe.12120

Delafield-Butt, J.T. and Gangopadhyay, N. (2013). Sensorimotor intentionality: The origins of intentionality in prospective agent action. *Developmental Review*, **33**(4), 399–425.

Delafield-Butt, J.T. and Trevarthen, C. (2013). Theories of the development of human communication. In: P. Cobley and P. Schultz (eds.) *Theories and Models of Communication*. Berlin/Boston: De Gruyter Mouton, pp. 199–222.

Delafield-Butt, J.T. and Trevarthen, C. (2015). The ontogenesis of narrative: From movements to meaning. *Frontiers of Psychology*, **6**, 1157. doi: 10.3389/fpsyg.2015.01157

Delafield-Butt, J.T. and Trevarthen, C. (2017). On the brainstem origin of autism: Disruption to movements of the primary self. In: E. Torres and C. Whyatt (eds.) *Autism: The Movement Sensing Perspective*. Boca Raton, FL: Taylor & Francis CRC Press, pp. 1–41.

Delafield-Butt, J.T., Pepping, G.-J., McCaig, C.D., and Lee, D.N. (2012). Prospective guidance in a free-swimming cell. *Biological Cybernetics*, **106**, 283–93. doi: 10.1007/s00422-012-0495-5

Donaldson, M. (1992). *Human Minds: An Exploration*. London: Allen Lane/Penguin Books.

Erickson, F. (2010). Musicality in talk and listening: A key element in classroom discourse as an environment for learning. In: S. Malloch and C. Trevarthen (eds.) *Communicative Musicality: Exploring the Basis of Human Companionship*. Oxford: Oxford University Press, pp. 449–64.

Featherstone, S., Beswick, C., and Louis, S. (2008). *Again! Again! Understanding Schemas in Young Children*. London: Featherstone Education.

Fournier, K.A., Hass, C.J., Naik, S.K., Lodha, N., and Cauraugh, J.H. (2010). Motor coordination in autism spectrum disorders: A synthesis and meta-analysis. *Journal of Autism and Developmental Disorders*, **40**, 1227–40.

Frank, B. and Trevarthen, C. (2012). Intuitive meaning: Supporting impulses for interpersonal life in the sociosphere of human knowledge, practice, and language. In: A. Foolen, U. Lüdtke, T.P. Racine, and J. Zlatev (eds.) *Moving Ourselves, Moving Others: Motion and Emotion in Intersubjectivity, Consciousness, and Language*. Amsterdam/Philadelphia: John Benjamins, pp. 261–303.

Friedman, M.S. (2002). *Martin Buber: The Life of Dialogue*, 4th edn. London/ New York: Routledge.

Gallagher, S. (2014). The cruel and unusual phenomenology of solitary confinement. *Frontiers in Psychology*, **5**, 585, http://dx.doi.org/10.3389/fpsyg.2014.00585, accessed 7 Mar 2018.

Goodrich, B.G. (2010). We do, therefore we think: Time, motility, and consciousness. *Reviews in the Neurosciences*, **21**, 331–61.

Gunn, K.C.M. and Delafield-Butt, J.T. (2016). Teaching children with autism spectrum disorder with restricted interests: A review of evidence for best practice. *Review of Educational Research*, **86**(2), 408–30. doi: 10.3102/0034654315604027

Hubley, P. and Trevarthen, C. (1979). Sharing a task in infancy. In: I. Uzgiris (ed.) *Social Interaction During Infancy*, New Directions for Child Development, vol. 4. San Francisco: Jossey-Bass, pp. 57–80. doi: 10.1002/cd.23219790406

Jeannerod, M. (1988). *The Neural and Behavioural Organization of Goal-Directed Movements*. Oxford: Oxford University Press.

Kanner, L. (1943). Autistic disturbances of affective contact. *Nervous Child*, 2, 217–50.

Kennedy, J.F. (1962). Video. President John F. Kennedy's address at Rice University, Houston, Texas, 12 September 1962. National Archives and Records Administration. Office of Presidential Libraries. John F. Kennedy Library, https://www.jfklibrary.org/Asset-Viewer/Archives/USG-15-29-2.aspx, accessed 8 Mar 2018.

Lashley, K.S. (1951). The problem of serial order in behavior. In: L.A. Jeffress (ed.), *Cerebral Mechanisms in Behavior*. New York: Wiley, pp. 112–136.

Malloch, S. and Trevarthen, C. (2010). Musicality: Communicating the vitality and interests of life. In: S. Malloch and C. Trevarthen (eds.) *Communicative Musicality: Exploring the Basis of Human Companionship*. Oxford: Oxford University Press, pp. 1–11.

Maturana-Romesin, H. and Verden-Zoller, G. (2008). *The Origin of Humanness in the Biology of Love*, ed. Pille Bunnell. Exeter, UK/Charlottesville, VA: Imprint Academic.

Merker, B. (2007). Consciousness without a cerebral cortex: A challenge for neuroscience and medicine. *The Behavioral and Brain Sciences*, 30, 63–134.

Merker, B. (2010). Ritual foundations of human uniqueness. In: S. Malloch and C. Trevarthen (eds.) *Communicative Musicality: Exploring the Basis of Human Companionship*. Oxford: Oxford University Press, pp. 45–60.

Nadel, J. (2014). *How Imitation Boosts Development in Infancy and Autism Spectrum Disorder*. Oxford: Oxford University Press.

Negayama, K., Delafield-Butt, J.T., Momose, K., Ishijima, K., Kawahara, N., Lux, E.J, Murphy, A., and Kaliarntas, K. (2015). Embodied intersubjective engagement in mother-infant tactile communication: A cross-cultural study of Japanese and Scottish mother-infant behaviors during infant pick-up. *Frontiers in Psychology*, 6, 66. doi: 10.3389/fpsyg.2015.00066

Northoff, G. and Panksepp, J. (2008). The trans-species concept of self and the subcortical–cortical midline system. *Trends in Cognitive Sciences*, 12(7), 259–64.

Osborne, N. (2010). Towards a chronobiology of musical rhythm. In: S. Malloch and C. Trevarthen (eds.) *Communicative Musicality: Exploring the Basis of Human Companionship*. Oxford: Oxford University Press, pp. 545–64.

Packard, A. and Delafield-Butt, J.T. (2014). Feelings as agents of selection. *Biological Journal of the Linnean Society*, 112, 332–53. doi: 10.1111/bij.12225

Panksepp, J. (1998). The periconscious substrates of consciousness: Affective states and the evolutionary origins of the self. *Journal of Consciousness Studies*, 5, 566–82.

Panksepp, J. and Biven, L. (2012). *Archaeology of Mind: Neuroevolutionary Origins of Human Emotions*. New York: Norton.

Penfield, W. and Jasper, H.H. (1954). *Epilepsy and the Functional Anatomy of the Human Brain*. London: Little, Brown and Company.

Pezzulo, G. and Castelfranchi, C. (2009). Thinking as the control of imagination: A conceptual framework for goal-directed systems. *Psychological Research*, 73, 559–77.

Porges, S.W. (2011). *The Polyvagal Theory: Neurophysiological Foundations of Emotions, Attachment, Communication, and Self-Regulation*. New York/London: Norton.

Porges, S.W. and Daniel, S. (2017). Play and dynamics of treating pediatric medical trauma. Insights from polyvagal theory. In: S. Daniel and C. Trevarthen (eds.) *Rhythms of Relating in*

Children's Therapies: Connecting Creatively with Vulnerable Children. London: Jessica Kingsley, pp. 113–25.

Porges, S.W. and Furman, S.A. (2011). The early development of the autonomic nervous system provides a neural platform for social behaviour: A polyvagal perspective. *Infant and Child Development*, **20**, 106–18.

Reid, T. (1764). *An Inquiry into the Human Mind on the Principles of Common Sense.* London: A. Millar; Edinburgh: A. Kincaid and J. Bell (republished 1997, Edinburgh University Press).

Reissland, N. and Kisilevsky, B. (eds.) (2015). *Fetal Development: Research on Brain and Behavior, Environmental Influences, and Emerging Technologies.* London: Springer Verlag.

Rinehart N. and McGinley J. (2010). Is motor dysfunction core to autism spectrum disorder? *Developmental Medicine and Child Neurology*, **52**(8), 697. doi: 10.1111/j.1469-8749.2010.03631.x

Rinehart, N.J., Bellgrove, M.A., Tonge, B.J., Brereton, A.V., Howells-Rankin, D., and Bradshaw, J.L. (2006). An examination of movement kinematics in young people with high-functioning autism and Asperger's disorder: Further evidence for a motor planning deficit. *Journal of Autism and Developmental Disorders*, **36**, 757–67.

Rizzolatti, G. and Gallese, V. (2003). Mirror neurons. In: L. Nadel (ed.) *Encyclopedia of Cognitive Science.* London: Nature Publishing Group, pp. 37–42.

Sander, L.W. (2008). *Living Systems, Evolving Consciousness, and the Emerging Person: A Selection of Papers from the Life Work of Louis Sander*, ed. G. Amadei and I. Bianchi. Abingdon, UK: Taylor & Francis.

Shewmon, D.A., Holmse, D.A., and Byrne, P.A. (1999). Consciousness in congenitally decorticate children: Developmental vegetative state as self-fulfilling prophecy. *Developmental Medicine and Child Neurology*, **41**, 364–74.

Singh, J.A.L. and Zingg, R.M. (1942). The Diary of the Wolf-Children of Midnapore (India): Feral Man and Cases of Extreme Isolation of Individuals. New York: Harper & Row [Facsimile edn, Archon Books 1966].

Sinigaglia, C. and Rizzolatti, G. (2011). Through the looking glass: Self and others. *Consciousness and Cognition*, **20**, 64–74.

Sperry, R.W. (1952). Neurology and the mind-brain problem. *American Scientist*, **40**, 291–312.

Stern, D.N. (2010). *Forms of Vitality: Exploring Dynamic Experience in Psychology, the Arts, Psychotherapy, and Development.* Oxford: Oxford University Press.

Teitelbaum, P., Teitelbaum, O., Nye, J., Fryman, J., and Maurer R.G. (1998). Movement analysis in infancy may be useful for early diagnosis in autism. *Proceedings of the National Academy of Sciences of the USA*, **95**(23), 13982–7.

Trevarthen, C. (1995). Mother and baby—seeing artfully eye to eye. In: R. Gregory, J. Harris, D. Rose, and P. Heard (eds.) *The Artful Eye.* Oxford: Oxford University Press, pp.157–200.

Trevarthen, C. and Delafield-Butt, J.T. (2013a). Biology of shared experience and language development: Regulations for the inter-subjective life of narratives. In: M. Legerstee, D. Haley, and M. Bornstein (eds.) *The Infant Mind: Origins of the Social Brain.* New York: Guilford Press, pp. 167–99.

Trevarthen, C. and Delafield-Butt, J.T. (2013b). Autism as a developmental disorder in intentional movement and affective engagement. *Frontiers in Integrative Neuroscience*, **7**, 49. doi: 10.3389/fnint.2013.00049

Trevarthen, C. and Delafield-Butt, J.T. (2017). Development of consciousness. In: B. Hopkins, E. Geangu, and S. Linkenauger (eds.) *The Cambridge Encyclopedia of Child Development.* Cambridge: Cambridge University Press, pp. 825–39.

Trevarthen, C., Aitken, K.J., Papoudi, C., and Robarts, J.Z. (1998). *Children with Autism: Diagnosis and Interventions to Meet their Needs*, 2nd edn. London: Jessica Kingsley (ISBN 1 85302 555 0).

Winn, P. (2012). Putting the brain into brainstem. *Physiology News*, **88**, 29–32.

Woods, J.W. (1964). Behavior of chronic decerebrate rats. *Journal of Neurophysiology*, **27**, 635–44.

Zeedyk, M.S. (ed.) (2008) *Promoting Social Interaction for Individuals with Communication Impairments*. London/ Philadelphia: Jessica Kingsley.

Chapter 5

Access to enriching environments in early childhood: Paradise lost?

Chris Miles

Paradise lost, and regained

I grew up in a beautiful place. A little mediaeval village with lots of abandoned old buildings to explore, even when, or especially when, they were out of bounds, and woodland
and fields and a sparkly wee burn close to the house, not deep enough to drown in anywhere, but deep and wide enough to increase the level of personal challenge as we grew
bigger, stronger, and more confident. A field that the burn ran through, with a fence
you could climb to get in, and once in, countless play and learning possibilities—from
brambles, thistles, nettles, and barbed wire fences, to the pony we—that is, myself and
occasional playmates—imagined as a wild-eyed rearing stallion, in reality old and un-
threatened by our presence ... but oh how brave we felt, to share his space with him,
watchfully. A paradise for children.

It's been tidied up into a nice play park now, that field, the grass regularly mown, and
with a tasteful dark-stained wooden climbing frame set in sand so that no one is hurt if
they fall, and little bridges in places across the burn. A pale shadow of its former self.

And I grew up in what might now be seen as a reasonably beautiful time, my childhood
spanning the decade of the fifties. Less traffic, more freedom, more room for imagination,
less materialistic. I can remember a lot of time exploring and discovering alone. It left me
with a lifelong liking for my own company, a companion feeling to self- reliance and independence. These are not bad things to have. And I did not know, all the while, that I was
learning, developing, making progress. I was just being.

But my remit is not to give a potted history of my growing up, but perhaps what I have
told you sets me in a context of my childhood reality, and you may feel a need to take
yourself back to my paradise at some point here, as you read, to see what remains, what
can still be achieved, and to ask if paradise is indeed lost. Or to take you back to your own
paradise. Children can make their own paradises out of almost anything or anywhere,
given the freedom to do so. Those of you who cannot recall such a place and time may not
have that problem because the possibility did not exist, but because the permission and
freedom were missing.

Sharing the world with young children

In writing this chapter on 'The Environment', I want to encourage the readers to take their children with them while they read—I mean all the children they once were, who are tucked up inside them like little Russian dolls. We, with our 'adult-ness', can never clearly look through those eyes again, but we must try to remember their feelings, the excitement of discovery, of success, of self-realization, the fear, the facing of challenges, the feeling of emerging with triumph, the moment of understanding—the 'Aaaah, now I see' moment.

Taking these children with us every day, when we are thinking of what we can give children access to, better informs our understanding of what is effective and meaningful, and what is merely an illusion, a current trend, or old habit.

There are things in life that we all need in childhood, building the beginnings of what we all can become. We need freedom. We need challenge. Chances to test ourselves on many levels, physical and intellectual. We need beauty to feed our spirits, and a sense of wonder for all our days. We need independence, a fair measure of autonomy, and opportunities to develop self-reliance. These will carry us through more testing times. We all need support. When we are relatively new to the world, we need to see where the boundaries are, to keep us safe. Most of these are invisible. We need opportunities to solve problems, a skill that will stand by us for life. We need opportunities to acquire knowledge, skills, understanding. So we need permission and freedom to explore, and satisfy our curiosity, with the hope of some glorious serendipity. We need opportunities to be creative, and of a quality that gives us confidence to continue to be creative into adulthood. We need to be able to cooperate, one of the harder lessons of early childhood, along with those of sharing and waiting. And we need other, subtler things, such as peace, silence, visual tranquillity.

The challenge for the teacher, the early years practitioner, the parent, and for all adults who take some responsibility for the development of the young child, is that they need to know how to create, recognize, and allow access to rich environments. And then they need to know when to support, when to set boundaries, and when to leave well alone. Two quotes here may be useful in giving thought to leaving well alone. Ages ago Plutarch said, 'Education is not filling a bucket ... it is lighting a fire', and much later, Antoine de Saint Exupéry, who understood children better than most, said, 'If you want people to build ships, do not send them into the forest to drum up wood, or assign tasks, but teach them to long for the endless immensity of the sea'.

The seductive creativity of a child's play

I remember once, years ago, as a nursery headteacher, doing a home visit on a warm sunny June day. The mother and I ended up finishing our conversation outside on the garden path, which was made up of slabs surrounded by red gravel. Trying to concentrate on finishing the business, I was constantly distracted by watching the three-year-old child, excluded from the business of the grown-ups, quietly playing with the gravel, arranging it in patterns on the slabs, making pictures with it. It was an important learning experience for me in realizing that children, when they are in the mood (and you have to be in the mood to play, not something that you can be ordered to do), will use any re-sources to hand. I might have said there, 'Make a game', but it is something much more important than that. It is creativity, it is experimenting, or whatever else motivates the child at that moment. But the whole drive is to make sense of the world, and 'the world' being that which surrounds us now, our environment. We can only use what we have. And it was a moment when I realized that imagination is not so much what you have, but what you don't have. One of the little Russian dolls reminded me of how I used to play 'houses'. There was no fancy 'home corner' then, but whatever we could use to make a home that existed in our imagination. Ours was a space where we could creep in under some elder-berry bushes. The food was mud or stones, stirred with a twig, in a rusty old can that had found its way under the bushes, and the 'food' was dolloped out onto big leaves, which we children clearly saw as dinner plates.

Structuring and resourcing a quality indoor learning environment

It does seem that not only do we need more people to be consulting one or other of their own Russian dolls, but we also need to more fully realize that you cannot rely on a catalogue of 'resources' to determine what things constitute a rich learning environment. Ultimately, the objective of the 'educational' supplier is to get us to buy what they sell. But our professional training should have led us to understand what we, as qualified pro-fessionals, need to be providing from within ourselves. We should not be looking to the catalogues for 'ideas'; we should be looking for understanding. Time spent discussing our memories might bring very rich plans, and, pleasingly, many of the resources we might seek will cost very little.

Improvisation

Many former little girls will excitedly share memories of collecting flower petals and mixing them with water to make 'perfume'. And perhaps some boys too, budding chem-ists all, or would-be entrepreneurs who also had the innocent thought that someone might want to buy their product, and dreamt up the get-rich-quick schemes that children used to have, and probably still do. Schools do 'Enterprise' now.

Other memories include the various ways in which a den, or a home, or a shelter could be made (Figure 5.1)—old blankets, or curtains, over the clothesline and weighted down made a tent. It didn't matter much that it was a bit makeshift, a bit rough and ready, a bit tacky. As children, we didn't see that; what we did see was that we had improvised and made something for ourselves, and that gave it its own beauty and wonder. It still would. No one is better at improvisation than young children. They can look at one thing and see another, and they can see a creative or an imaginative potential in objects we would be throwing out. An ability to improvise is surely a valuable gift, and in many much-loved children's books (such as *The Famous Five* and *The Secret Seven*, by Enid Blyton (2012a, 2012b)) the central characters—children, or animals with human behaviour—can do this,

Figure 5.1 A den for imagining.
© Gearaidh Matthews

and are, by that means, more self-reliant, more autonomous, more confident—states that all children long for.

How do we provide opportunities in our structured learning environments for children to improvise? Would we do better with less rather than more? And how do we allow them to solve problems? I notice that adults are often uncomfortable with letting problems exist at all, far less standing back and leaving children to make mistakes, muddle through, and get to a place that satisfies them in the end. If we can't bear to watch struggle, we should just go and get on with one of our own!

Among the tasks for us as facilitators of children's learning is surely to see the play potential in many things that might otherwise be discarded—things that will fire up a child's imagination and creativity. For example, we all know about children and big, empty cardboard boxes, but how often do we actually make them available? How much more interesting would things become if we provided several? Many?

Experience has taught me that there is little need for the adult to lead imaginative play, as in, 'Gather round children—here's something interesting we could make with cardboard boxes' (or whatever). Once, I stopped my car to write down a quote I had just heard on the radio, coming from one of the Opies, Iona and Peter, famous for their books for children (Opie and Opie 1969): 'Nothing extinguishes self-directed play more effectively than the attempts to promote it'.

What is more useful is to leave objects with potential you might see if looking through the eyes of one of your little Russians, just 'lying around' in silent invitation. Examples of the kinds of things I leave 'lying around' in my home (for the want of a nursery class) as silent invitations for my grandchildren are: the little bottles that once contained shampoo or shower gel that you get in hotels (after all, the most frustrating thing about marketing your latest home-made scent is a dearth of things to put it into); any little cups for choc-olates or baked goods that are clean (think folks, think, speak to your Russian doll!); clear Perspex packaging (if you want to make a doll's house out of a cardboard box, you might need windows); a bag of smooth wood offcuts to complement wooden building blocks ... and so on. And, like everyone else, I can lay my hands on old blankets or cur-tains or bits of rope or pieces of fabric at a moment's notice. It is about trying to see what children see. And there is no right or wrong aspect to this invitation. You may have had a thought in mind, but children may have a completely different notion, direction, ex-ploration, or enquiry. And sometimes they may not take up your invitation at all, because they are busy doing something else. I could make this list very long, but instead I could just leave my invitation for you to have a chat with your Russian dolls 'lying around'. Your own list will come.

Serendipity ... sometimes contrived!

Henry David Thoreau (1854) went to live a simple life in the woods, by Lake Walden in New England, which he did for two years, two months, and two days. He had a lot of time to ponder on the values people were living by then. He said, 'Every child begins the world again ... and loves to stay outdoors, even in wet and cold. It plays house, as well as horse, having an instinct for it ... at last we know not what it is to live in the open air, and our lives are domestic in more senses than we think.'

When I first visited the nursery school of which I had just been appointed head, I saw, in my mind's eye, in the bright, roof-lit Victorian hallway, which at the time was decorated with cartoon characters, a huge 'conservatory'—lots of tall, impressive greenery reaching up to the roof, a space that would be pleasing and restful to the eye for those of all ages.

When installed, I brought in these plants, and I made a pond among them—basically, a rigid liner with a wall of stones from the seashore, and overhanging plants. It was a dark pool—it had to be—where glittering goldfish lurked. We never told the children that fish were in there.

The story about Harry and the pond

One day, when I was on the phone in the hallway, Harry hurtled by, as was Harry's way, to go to the toilet, planning to have a bit of nonsense with the taps while he was at it, prob-ably. As he drew abreast of the pond, he screeched to a halt (well, his trainers squeaked on the polished floor, but that doesn't add anything to the drama of the moment). Eyes glit-tering, he breathlessly exclaimed, trembling with excitement, 'Ye ken, there's fish in there, come and see!' ... I vaguely implied in my demeanour, without telling a lie, this might be news to me, sharing Harry's excitement. Mercifully, he never spoilt it by asking me where they came from.

Serendipity gives a child the ownership of their findings in a way that 'Children, come see the fish' does not. Harry remained interested and curious about 'his' fish, and retained that feeling of something magical. After all, he found them, didn't he?

There were many 'Harrys' over the years.

Now, voyager, please don't take refuge in anxiety about health and safety . . . no one even tried to fall in. The pond was in an open, public space. It was tiny. And it was a thing of beauty; a thing of great interest; a veritable oasis of peace, tranquillity, and dreaming of faraway and another place; a thing of learning, which gave and gave and gave. Well worth the 'risk' and the wee bit of work keeping an eye on things.

Beauty, visual tranquillity, and a sense of wonder

In creating my little oasis in the hallway, I changed the whole presentation of the main entrance to the school. Hitherto, the walls had been decorated by cartoon characters on the pinboards, saying nothing to or for anyone who came in, bringing about no learning, or any other feeling for that matter. My school catchment area encompassed some areas of deprivation, and I made up my mind that the first steps in the door should bring some peace and tranquillity and convey a message of welcome, and that those who came in were worth this beauty, beauty that did not surround them in the mean streets in which they lived.

I can find no evidence that children's development is impaired in any way by the absence of a kiddy, cartoony, garish environment. When you have spent lots of time painting Mickey Mouse on the window, what have the children gained? But the sky-lit hallway lent itself to huge plants, walls of greenery, nothing on the pinboards but complementary wallpaper, the dark pool with the goldfish sometimes appearing from the greenery. It lent itself to wicker sofas that said come in and make yourself at home. And it saved staff a lot of time in regularly changing faded and torn frieze paper, and cutting frilly bits to go round things that no one looked at. Time that could be better spent, and money saved on these resources.

I realize that beauty is a subjective thing—one person's pride is not another's—and each person who has set up a room or an area may believe it to be beautiful. There has also been a general view, perhaps changing a little now, that children like to be in a highly colourful setting, a blaze of primary colours, with things hanging from the ceiling—a visual cacophony. Although it does seem that the catalogues from which people choose their resources still offer these kinds of resources, with a few admirable exceptions of providers who make well-crafted, durable, beautiful items from natural wood. I found it interesting to note, in going for subdued colours (light greens, magnolia(!), beige, cream—coordinated, restful colour schemes), that some of the headteachers who could not get, or disagreed with, what I was trying to say, did not own up to relaxing at home in the evening on the sofa in a sitting room that was decorated in red, bright blue, vivid yellow, or brilliant green, or that much in their room was plastic. When asked, they owned up to magnolia, beige, cream, white! Why would that be?

In classrooms where staff were supported and persuaded to calm things down visually—and this was often classrooms with high noise levels, with children who did not persevere for long, but flitted from place to place unproductively—those staff members reported an almost immediate change in the children. They were quieter, calmer, persevered longer, were less frenetic. Interestingly, the staff reported that they, too, were less stressed and tired. It seems to me that, often, people working with young children believe it to be a very tiring and demanding job, and it is, but … to tacitly accept this as unchangeable is to stop problem solving.

It costs nothing to introduce children to the beauty of seashells, water-moulded pebbles and cobbles, pinecones, driftwood, and other such found objects. (I have never quite got the learning outcome intended from collecting beautiful autumn leaves and suggesting to the children that they paint them in bright colours. Why not revel in the beauty of them as they are?) And in this way we bring curiosity and wonder about the outside into the room, a connection we can build on.

Likewise, it can cost little or nothing to introduce children to the beauty of objects such as pottery, china, glass, and wood. Charity shops, junk shops, friends, parents, and car boot sales can all yield treasures.

It will cost a little more to buy wooden furniture and play items, but in the end they will still be in use when the cheap plastic ones are in the bin.

Time to have a consultation with the Russians … can you remember a special, intriguing, fascinating, beautiful object from your childhood? Was it a plastic toy, or was it a special ornament on your Granny's mantelpiece? What gave it meaning? In 30 or 40, or 50 years' time, what will be a memory of a lovely thing that brings a smile to the face of today's young children?

Independence, autonomy, self-reliance … and permission

It has to be realized that while a rich learning environment will consist of a well-structured space and resources that are useful to children in their task of making sense of the world, the adults who make this environment possible are absolutely the key element of it. You can provide a high-quality environment and render much of it pointless if it is hard for you to let go. It is only in doing so that the fledglings in the nest will be able to fly. My question when I was a headteacher was, 'Are the children running the school?' Of course the answer to that is no, but the next questions are, 'So how much of it could they be running?' and 'How much autonomy could we allow them to take?' Now that will be very little, if we are stuck with the idea that the baked cake has to be perfect (or even edible); that the Christmas card or the Easter Card, or whatever, has to look like it came from a shop; that our plans are the most important ones; or that the made object must be lovely. That is when we interfere too much. I can remember with new children in my nursery that one of the most exciting things they had to tell their parent about the cake they were taking home, sometimes a less than wonderful piece of work, was that 'I made it ALL BY MYSELF!' And children know when that is the case, and they show less or little interest in the things they know they really had very little hand in.

To be the kind of adult who can let go, who can see their own role as being responsive in providing appropriate resources and 'butting out', is to demonstrate to children that you trust them, that there is space for their creativity to develop in their own individual way ... as leaders, artists, performers, explorers, and discoverers anew; as cooks, decision makers, and thinkers; and as resilient people who can deal with things going wrong, and pick themselves up, dust themselves off, and start all over again. It is my view that this is the most enormous thing we can give children, and the learning space is then the tool whereby we can complement our skills as enablers and facilitators, responsive and re-spectful to children's ideas, struggles, endeavours, and enquiries (Figure 5.2).

It doesn't really take children very long to grasp that they can take initiative, if all the adults are demonstrating trust. Of many of the wonderful memories I cherish from my nursery school days, one is of the child who said, 'I could see that you were busy, so I just mounted my picture myself'. And I have to say that the double-mounted picture, which was how she had seen us do it, was as good a job as the college student whom I had at the time could do.

Another memory I have is of the child, one of five children in a family, under three-and-a-half years old, with baby twins below her in the running order, came to me and

Figure 5.2 Using a tool for my job.
© Gearaidh Matthews

said she would like to create a display (something the staff did a lot of). Responding to her as a peer, I asked her what she thought she would need. She said it was to be about 'two' (guess why?) and that she had two hair ribbons and two hair clasps that matched, and so they would be the basis of the display (not her exact words, but it's all impressive as it is). Having previously noted how it was usually done, she said she would need a table or a box. I knew exactly what she would need, but that wasn't the point. So I suggested she go and have a look for what would suit. A table was found, and then she needed a 'cloth'. She wouldn't have heard us talk about a 'drape'. I had to open that drawer for her as it was too heavy, and she chose something that she liked. I then found a space in the room for this display, and, at her request, I showed her how to write the word TWO and the number 2. Now this display was far from the thing of beauty that was the usual standard in the nursery, but it was very easy to put up a notice by it, one that was simultaneously a celebration and a get-out clause ... 'Lauren made this display ALL BY HERSELF'.

What these children, and many afterwards, knew about the learning environment they were in was that it was *for them*. It was theirs to use as they needed, and the adults would help when asked, or subtly and silently would provide resources from their observations (the unspoken request). The children knew where the resources were kept that were not necessarily in the classroom, and they knew they would be allowed to search for a book, a display item, a drape, and so on, when they needed it. Those children also knew they had permission to take initiative. They were supported by adults who allowed children to take the lead in their learning, and then followed supportively behind. To be able to do this you have to understand, and trust, that young children have very important work of their own to do, serious enquiries of their own to make, big questions to which they must find the answers, and not always factual matters. They will be much bigger and important enquiries than any the adults are likely to set.

Sydney Engelberg, Professor in Social Work, Social Welfare, and Nonprofit Management and Leadership at Hebrew University in Israel, a country where children are welcomed to participate in learning with parents, states that he 'encourages babies to tag along' to his classes with their parents. He says, by way of explaining his rationale, 'The reason is that education for me is not simply conveying content, but teaching values'.

For me, 'teaching' is the intelligence of supporting learning to happen.

Taking charge and running things

In an atmosphere, built up over years, where children know they can take initiative and are trusted, then the business of 'running the school' is much more easily conducted. Thus, able and advanced children could not only take on real tasks, but would then be role models for younger or less advanced children, something attractive to aspire to ... 'Can I do what she's doing?' So it came about, for example, that Larissa, four years old and going on 40, would get the weekly menu from the cook, and copy it out onto a big poster-sized piece of paper so that the parents and children could see what was for lunch each day. Previously, the cook had done this herself. Other children who wanted to could do it too; smaller menus for the day went on each table, and even those whose writing was only emerging could have their efforts respected.

I once went into Larissa's classroom, and I saw little notices all around the room proclaiming what went on in each area … sand, water, home corner, and so on. I asked the staff why they had done this and they told me they had nothing to do with it. Larissa had written them out, cut them up, stuck them on the wall, and told the staff that she had done it 'so that the wee new bairns wid ken whit tae dae'. Of course, her little notices remained on the walls. These are small examples of the ways in which we accepted and respected and supported children's decisions and handed responsibility over to them to sort things out and make things happen, and played to children's strengths. Capable, confident, and mature children are much more likely to motivate their peers than are adults, because the other children want to be like them, or even be them.

I don't have space here to tell you the whole story of how these children ran a sale of work to raise money for our garden, but they served behind the counters and took the money and gave the change and chatted to the adults, and chased a dad who didn't notice he had to pay admission, with great indignation. And made twice as much money as would have been the case if the adults had been helped by the children, rather than the other way round. Our intervention was minimal, after the children were briefed in the morning. They knew this was real stuff, not play; they listened attentively, every one; and they stepped up to the plate. When you were little, didn't you long to work in a shop, behind the counter, selling real things, taking real money?

Of course, when they went to school, there would be a shock for most of them on discovering, in many cases, how little permission they now had, and that taking initiative would not be encouraged, but that's another story for another day.

So what does a rich learning environment look like?

I went to visit my first grandchild on her first day at nursery, and, knowing the likely answer to the question, 'What did you do today?' (for those who have not yet asked this question, the answer is very likely to be 'nothing'), I asked her to tell me three things she had done. After a perfunctory response she then became very animated and said, 'There was SO MUCH STUFF there! Nobody would BELIEVE how much stuff there is! In fact, (arms now akimbo), if you ask ME, there's FAR TOO MUCH stuff!' My heart beat fast with pride at such insight, I can tell you, and it took me back to my days of being a new headteacher, looking at classrooms with trays and trays and trays of plastic construction equipment, which each day ended up in heaps on the floor, with nothing of any note being constructed, no child tidying any of it up, no challenge, no creativity, no problem solving. And remembering the bookcase laden with dozens of books, casually flicked through and left on the floor. Nothing valued, because none of it was precious. Limited resourcing makes each thing precious, and needing to be used and thought about carefully. My analogy would be about buying a new packet of needles, and each disappearing quite quickly (where do all the lost needles go?) until you are on your last needle. You will certainly look after that one, and keep it much longer as a result.

Some staff struggled with my request to provide only one construction activity, but soon saw that the result was more perseverance and better outcomes because there was less distraction and less dabbling and moving on. Eventually we moved towards building, creating, and constructing, which includes with it problem solving, physics, maths, and sometimes cooperation, being provided only through open-ended materials ... clay, woodwork, three-dimensional junk modelling, and wooden blocks—expensive, but ever-lasting, so well worth the money spent on them. And when wondering what to buy, you can never have too many wooden blocks! The quality of everything improved. Quality is not a natural result of quantity, and quantity can often be counterproductive.

Choosing new resources thoughtfully, with a plan

It is rare that we get the opportunity to resource from scratch. We usually inherit what is there, and budgets are a big feature of what is possible. But on those occasions when we have a new budget, or sometimes that end-of-financial-year hurry to get money spent, our purchasing criteria should not be the result of being seduced by sparkly things in the catalogue. For a start, we should be making a shopping list as the year goes on of the resources we realize are missing that we wish we had ... a book about going to the hair-dresser, a microscope, more building blocks, or a picnic bench for outside, for example. So that we already know what we need, and don't waste precious resources on what catches our eye. And when our eye is caught, then the thought process should be, 'When I have bought this with precious financial resources, set it up, and explained its function, etc., to the children, what will they know that they didn't know before?' 'What will they under-stand that they didn't understand before?' 'What skills will they have acquired that they didn't have before?' 'What purpose will it serve?' Think hard. If the answer to these ques-tions is anything from you're not really sure, to a sharp realization that it will be nothing at all, then it really will be alright not to buy it. Even if everyone else has one, and even if there has always been stuff like this around for years!

Consider resources from a child's point of view. As far as sand and water trays are con-cerned, spending extra money on one that is shaped like a fish, for example, does not extend the possibilities for children. Rather, it limits them—less room for water or sand, and less room to explore—and shallow shelves make the real quantity of water difficult for children to reach. Try to think of the length of the arms of small children! Keep it simple ... a rectangular box of water or sand will let the children do the fancy stuff. That's the whole point.

Resourcing ought not to be a matter of habit. So we are used to a facility that has sand, water, home corner, book corner, snack table, art area, and so on, but do we give thought as to why we provide it? A real look at the 'why' would better inform us of the 'what'.

A real-life home corner, of family

The home corner, as probably the most important resource we provide for children, is well worth a detailed examination. This is where children will spend a lot of time rehearsing the dramas and the important issues of life, because that is the connecting thread to their real homes, and whatever they perceive goes on there. A really big issue is the play of preparing and serving food, I believe, because children understand in a deep, deep way that feeding is giving love, caring, parenting, and they are trying that out. So, too, is the caring for baby. A pile of dolls in the cot will not do the trick; one baby in the house is enough (unless you want to provide for the child who has just had newborn siblings). It is in understanding these subtleties that adults can best make provision for children's needs.

Children need to enact the essential Stuff of Life. There must be a place to 'cook', a place to 'eat', a place to 'sleep', and a place to 'sit'. None of these features should be missing. And here daddies will go out to work, or not; there will be fights and arguments; the police will be phoned; and the fire brigade. The doctor will be called, babies will be born, and babies will be cared for. All observed features of their family lives (not necessarily lives like yours) will be acted out, including some things you might find uncomfortable. There is no right or wrong drama here, only the reality of life. Nor is there a place for adults here: observation and eavesdropping need to be so discreet as to be imperceptible to the actors on that stage. When adults enter this space, like Gulliver in Lilliput, they are usually kept out of the way by being given a cup of tea, like unwelcome visitors in any home. A cup of tea ... no more, no less. In the meantime, the important dramas are suspended.

James Reeves (1909–1978) was a poet and writer who began writing poetry for children in 1945. His works, published as *Complete Poems for Children* (Reeves 1994), are said to be 'characterized by lyrical evocations of childhood'. I am reminded of his poem *The Intruder*, which is essentially about the quick disappearance of wildlife when human beings come along

'The Intruder'

Two-boots in the forest walks
Pushing through the bracken stalks.
Vanishing like a puff of smoke,
Nimbletail flies up the oak.
Longears helter skelter shoots
Into his house among the roots.
At work upon the highest bark,
Tapperbill knocks off to hark.
Painted wings through sun or shade
Flounces off along the glade.
Not a creature lingers by
When clumping twoboots comes to pry.
(Reeves 1987, p. 72)

We have to become aware of what our intrusion stops that is rich and important, and from that awareness will come greater respect for the actions of children.

There is a possibility that The Stuff of Life can become endangered by the drive to see every opportunity to interject what adults deem important ... reading, writing, counting.

So it becomes the task of intelligent, informed, and insightful adults to see how they can provide a rich learning environment that cooperates with that drive without damaging the playing out of The Stuff of Life. Where are literacy and numeracy reflected in the least literate of homes? What is the minimum standard?

You know it yourselves, you do it … the telephone directory by the phone, the takeaway menu (that one might need a bit of a rethink!), the writing pad by the phone … What reading materials can be found in a house with few books? Books of road maps? Trashy novels? Can we reflect something in the home corner that is only that which is seen as part of home? I'm not talking of furnishing the home corner with children's storybooks that rightly belong in the book/story corner. I'm talking about harmless, unpretentious adult reading material—that which children may only pick up to role-play, but which creates a subtle awareness. The local newspaper, even if you are only pretending to be granddad looking at the racing results. I have no space here to make up a list for you; that is for a brainstorming session in your staff team.

How often we see that the home corner is temporarily transformed, or 'sacrificed', into another role-play area. Instead we have a shop, a hospital, a school, or such like. This should never happen. It has to be 'as well as' … none of these other role-play areas have any relevance without 'home'. Consider that a hospital role-play area has been set up to meet the emotional needs of a child about to go into hospital—a very necessary thing to do. The learning of the vocabulary of hospital and other such factual information is fine, but it is secondary to the task of allowing an anxious child to act out before, or an upset child to act out after, the drama of the experience. How reassuring is that role playing without a home to return to? A stage play with the entire stage set in the wings rather than on the stage. And when you are pretending to be your own mum, doing the family shopping, and you come out with your bag loaded with groceries, what then? Just take them back to the 'shop'? What really happens is that the child sees, and wants to act out, the weary shopper humping the bags into the house and dumping them on the table and putting the kettle on to boil for a cup of tea while putting the groceries away in the cupboard.

Role playing 'school' surely has leaving 'home' and returning there? There will be those who say that this either/or structure is necessary owing to limited space. Indeed, this will often be a challenge, but part of that challenge is for informed, well-trained staff to be able to see what of the usual run of resources is really important, or an absolute priority, and what is not. How many times I have been told that lack of space is the reason why we take out home or other role-play areas—school, hospital, or shop, for example—or have no woodwork bench, or no solid wooden blocks, when central to the whole space is a big round table with four jigsaws on it that could be housed on a shelf in the book corner, or not bothered with at all, and/or another big table with trays of plastic construction sets.

I have chosen to speak in more detail about the home corner for the reasons I've outlined, and it is for the educator to apply the same depth of thinking to each of the familiar areas of provision we would be offering to children. What is our intention and purpose in providing something? And what do we do to get to where we claim we want to be? And just as importantly, what do we not do to get to where we want to be? How analytical are we about our own role? Do we know when to 'go in' when we are needed, and to know the point at which we get back out again? Do we intervene too quickly, or when we should not intervene at all? Are our resources working for us, to help the children to find the answers to their questions, to hone their skills, to make sense of the world? Have we made useful invitations?

Cutting back distractions—choosing resources with imaginative care

Not only do we need to look at the inherent quality and challenge of the resources we provide. Additionally, the rich learning environment should look inviting and beautiful, and visually peaceful for the best levels of concentration and perseverance. Children should not have to waste mental energy shutting out distractions that the adults have put in their way, with the best of intentions but little thought to their purpose. Plain, simple colours, with different areas visually coordinated so as to be a peaceful backdrop to exploration, will help children to focus on their task in hand.

Resources that are on offer and in constant use should be accessible to children so that they are independent of the adults. And so, too, should the type of resources provided make it possible for the children to clean up after themselves.

Thought should be given with regard to helping children to think carefully about how they use the resources on offer, which can be more precious if their numbers are limited. I have often told the story of the careless 'button sprinkler'. Years ago, I was working in a nursery where a parent brought in a very large cardboard box full of buttons from a factory. This full box was put in the craft area as a resource for the children. For a while then, because these buttons were more than plentiful (thousands of them), the children would take a handful of buttons and drop them from a raised hand onto the glue already spread on their paper, and in a matter of seconds that was put to dry as their 'work of art' for the day. It was hard to tell which child produced which button collage. Better offer children some pretty things in limited numbers and watch how careful and well thought out is the placing of each precious treasure, the time taken to create something individual to be proud of. Do we want painstaking creators or button sprinklers?

During my own specialist nursery training we were taught, having structured a learning environment, to ask ourselves, could 12-year-olds meaningfully occupy themselves in here for a day? It was a good test of the level of challenge and interest that we were providing for children, and it reminded us, too, that while we would not be asked to take in 12-year-olds, from time to time we would be taking in a child of extra-special capabilities whose learning was very advanced. Institutions not understanding and respecting the needs of such children can cause them a lot of dissatisfaction, loneliness, and unhappiness. And of course there is the other question about whether this learning environment is useful for a two-year-old. The answer needs to be yes, because we will also be working with children whose development is not far advanced.

A rich learning environment recognizes that children want to grow up. They want to do real things. They want to grow vegetables in the garden. They want to cook. They want to make things with real wood and real nails and real hammers and saws. They want to learn to write, and read. They want to sweep up, and wipe, and wash things to make them clean. They want to be given responsibility. But they also want to rehearse and enact some Stuff of Life in role play, and need adults to recognize the resources needed from questions that are often not asked aloud.

Much of what we are accustomed to providing for play is an indoor echo of how we used to play as children in my, or your, Paradise Lost. The home corner is a sophisticated substitute for the tent from a blanket or the 'houses' we played in under bushes, the resources being what was there. The sand and water are cleaner versions of the 'guddling' in mud and puddles we did, or if lucky, as I was, in the sparkling burn in the field. The climbing frame is a tidied- up version of the trees that children seldom get the freedom to climb these days, in a world of fearful adults, many from a generation that never had the opportunity to explore out of doors.

Are those sophisticated substitutes better for children's development than what we once had to play with? Or are they much more comfortable for adults who find that giving children freedom is more stressful than they would like it to be?

Recent evidence indicates that many educators are recognizing the need to return to more outdoor experiences. Where there are outdoor spaces for children, opportunities are being provided for the 'guddling', and the gardening, and the physical challenges that children need. I believe that more thought is now being given to the effect the limiting of important life experiences for children by risk-averse adults has had on their development. But many playgrounds are still barren and sterile as places for children to make sense of the world.

Let's go out

Many years ago, when I was doing my nursery qualification with the legendary Margaret Cameron, we learned about 'Big Stuff'. Not that anything undertaken by young children is ever 'Little Stuff'; it's just that some of it is even Bigger.

So what exactly is 'Big Stuff'? It's very hard to describe, but you just kind of get to know. It feels to me that some of it is quite dark, quite primeval. It's about the meaning of life and the core of our existence; it's about 'where I came from'—everything from the womb to the family relationships, to 'from near the sea' or 'from near the forest' or 'from under the sky'; it's about 'where I belong'; it's about, 'Am I brave enough/ skilled enough/ do I matter enough, to do THAT'? It's about poking at the earth, the air, fire, and water, asking big, significant questions out loud or to yourself; it's about deep thinking, searching for meaning, understanding, answers to 'the Big Mysteries'—your own place in the Grand Scheme of Things.

It stands to reason that it is much harder for Big Stuff to be explored in your living room at home, or sitting at a computer, or even in the nursery while singing songs, looking at books, and so on. You have to go out and engage with it all, out into Nature.

Our ancestors knew all that a long, long time ago—longer ago than my nursery training, and as long ago as when much of Europe was forest, and much of the answer to 'Who am

I?' could be found there. As well as being the natural habitat, and a resource for building, heating, and cooking, and a place where food could be hunted, it was also a place of self-discovery. They knew this so well that the challenges of the forest became woven into the folk tales of Europe, where danger lurked and had to be faced, and where skills, energy, wit, endurance, and intelligence were tested.

Over the centuries most of us have moved further and further away from all of this, the forests have receded, and what remains is largely within the folk tales, and we use different skills, and seldom know who we are and of what we are capable.

They haven't left it all behind in Norway, where crisp, bitterly cold days and deep snow are seen as a gift and a thing of beauty, and where the landscape is to be engaged with, and where that begins at a very early age. In so doing, the children develop high self-esteem as they learn to cope with the landscape and be at one with it. Their health is known to be excellent. They know who they are and where they belong. And this knowledge helps with their later learning of industrial and literary skills.

In an ideal world, children would be out in Nature from their earliest months. It would be a way of life, and outdoor experiences would be a golden thread running through childhood, adolescence, and into parenthood, repeating the cycle. As yet, Nature Kindergarten or Forest School is not like this. Children may have Nature or Forest Kindergarten experience during their early years, but this usually dwindles away as they enter formal school. And some children may only experience Forest School much later, or may only access it finally as a result of being troubled and consequently troublesome. This discontinuity of experience impacts on what we do, and the responsibilities we undertake.

Going back to what I said earlier, however, it is most important that adults recognize and respect that children have enquiries of their own, enquiries that demand the freedom to explore and research. These may be factual, scientific enquiries, but they may also be about self-enquiry—for example, in tackling a self-imposed challenge, or in finding out their own levels of courage, resourcefulness, cooperation, compromise, and acceptance. All life is here. Children need to be given open opportunities for self-realization. Adults too ready to direct and control, who make their own role one of devising activities to structure the time, run the risk of heading in the opposite place to the one where they believe they would like to be. Children who have been accustomed to directive adults, and unaccustomed to some autonomy and all that brings, may very well struggle to know what to do with themselves on their early expeditions into a natural environment. Adults providing the solutions to this dilemma will only maintain the status quo and further convince children that they cannot think for themselves.

Being out of doors in nature is a learning experience AS IT IS. I recollect a feeling of despair in finding out about a school with very easy access to local woods not taking the children out until lots of expensive equipment, I know not exactly what, arrived from the company from whose catalogue they had ordered what they deemed necessary, telling me that their parents expected to 'see their children reading, writing, and counting'. In my view they had spent a lot of money to provide a poorer experience rather than a richer one. You really do not need to provide a lot of 'stuff'. It's already there.

How do we learn to live with the silences and contemplation that move us forward in our personal growth? How do we really help people to see themselves as their own most important resource? Nature Kindergarten/Forest School is a journey to self. The young travellers need adults who are rooting for them, respecting them in their struggles, making it all possible, and ultimately letting them get on with it within safe boundaries. In these times of a Curriculum for Excellence (Scottish Executive 2004), these will be the most excellent things a leader can do.

In his book *The Brothers Karamazov*, Dostoyevsky said, 'You must know there is nothing higher or stronger and more wholesome for us in the future than some good memory, especially a memory of childhood, of home. People talk to you a great deal about education. But some good, sacred memory preserved from childhood—that is perhaps the best education. For if a man has only one good memory in his heart, even that may keep him from evil, and if he carries many such memories with him into life, he is safe for the end of his days'.

What do we do outdoors?

While it is always important to recognize and deal with all considerations, if we only focus on the problems, we won't do anything. Firstly, though, I think we need to be clear about what being out there with Nature it *not* about.

It is *not* about:

- trips out to different places in the country
- getting some fresh air
- a picnic on the grass
- doing up the nursery garden and spending more time out there (while that is a perfectly good thing to do as well)
- a good idea now and again
- 'Gather round, children, and I'll show you …'.

It *is* about:

- *at least* once a week visiting the *same* place, having ownership, and a continuity of the experience, a flow to discovery
- trusting that children have serious enquiries, and that you don't have to offer or suggest enquiries for them (You observe their explorations, and prepare yourself to respond, if included.)
- respecting the private, inner world of the child and not intruding upon it
- having things of your own to do, alongside children, in which you are happy to include them, if they wish
- each person being at one with the environment in his or her own way
- challenge … physical, personal, social, emotional … for all ages
- learning to take care of oneself and be responsible
- taking some risks.

Where do we begin?

Find a place

This needs to be as close by as possible. Every minute spent travelling is a minute not spent out in nature. Some people will be more fortunate than others in how far they have to go.

This needs to be cleared with the owners of the land, including what you can and can't do. If there are too many 'can't dos', then the experience for the children may be so much of a lesser thing that you need to look elsewhere. It will, for example, be limiting if you cannot light a fire. This is not a problem in a Norwegian Forest School. That is how the children prepare to make lunch.

Risk-assess the place itself. Try not to create problems that may have arisen from your anxieties.

Keep parents fully in the picture

As this becomes second nature, and a part of what you do in your nursery, parents should know this before their child starts at nursery, so that there are no surprises. If you have a strong relationship with parents, they trust you, and you have high standing in the community, this will go a long way to allaying fears about activities out-of-doors. Be prepared for some parents to be anxious. Be clear that you have planned it all out, and that you are confident. Don't present it to parents as a big deal. This may prove to be the way in which men will engage with their young children (see Chapter 10).

Make sure everyone is well kitted out

The saying in Norway is that there is no such thing as bad weather, only bad clothing. Resource your nursery with a range of sizes of warm, waterproof clothing and suitable footwear. This will, among other things, avoid resistance from parents who are motivated by concern about their child's clothing. (Do remember that for some people this represents hard-earned cash.) It will also mean that no child need be excluded through not being properly equipped. Adults need to be properly kitted out too, so that they can appropriately participate.

Training

Make sure you're familiar with what things are called, and how things are done and made, so that if a child asks, then you have some answers ... not so that you can teach, but so that you can contribute to enquiry and learning.

Getting to fluent literacy and numeracy

Much ado is being made of literacy and numeracy, seen as they are by some as the major ingredient to growing up into a successful adult. Whatever that is. I have no problem in seeing them as useful tools in that process. But I do not see that the journey to engagement with literacy and numeracy begins in a corner of a classroom, with the letter or number of the week to be learned. I see it as a much warmer and richer process of self-discovery, confidence, and the growth of interest in many things, with the desire to know and understand being fuelled and supported by informed adults—the 'building of ships' described by Saint-Exupéry. And it is not only brought about by doing: it is also brought about by witnessing, and wishing to emulate whatever the adult or another child has the responsibility of doing.

The word 'holistic' is bandied about much more often than it is understood or valued as a philosophy. My interest in rich learning environments is in feeding the whole child, in lighting Plutarch's fire. W. B. Yeats made a comment which challenges our thinking: 'Culture does not consist of acquiring opinions, but in getting rid of them'. Perhaps not always, but a useful concept nevertheless?

Summary

I have described paradises, with elements I hope many will recognize, and which those who do not may learn from, in the hope that they lead the educator to think hard about what children really need, to listen to the voice of the child, or hear what the child is trying to tell you through skilled observation and an understanding of emerging and very new humans. I've said something about rooms and furniture and resources, mostly in an attempt to encourage in-depth thinking.

I see a rich learning environment as a woven fabric, each individual element a golden thread intertwined with the other golden threads, but each a vital component part. I'm hoping some people are learning the Russian that their dolls inside speak, or intend to try. For it seems to me that the key is well-informed, well-trained, insightful, compassionate, responsive, and respectful adults, who understand what children need, and do their best to make it happen. You can have all the paradises and all the riches and loveliness as 'that which surrounds you', but when you are wee, you need adults who are clever and brave enough to let you have a go. Without permission to go there, do it, access paradise, then it is only inhabited by sparkling burns and wee ponies, and no excited adventurers bent on exploration and discovery.

References

Blyton, E. (2012a). *The Famous Five: Complete Collection* (22 books). London: Hachette
Children's Books.

Blyton, E. (2012b). *The Secret Seven Collection* (16 books). London: Hachette Children's Books.

Opie, P.M. and Opie, I.A. (1969). *Children's Games in Street and Playground*. Oxford: Clarendon Press.

Reeves, J. (1987). *The Wandering Moon, and Other Poems*. London: Puffin Books.

Reeves, J. (1994). *Complete Poems for Children* (illustrated by Edward Ardizzone). Dubois,
PA: Mammoth.

Scottish Executive (2004). *A Curriculum for Excellence – The Curriculum Review Group,
Edinburgh: Purposes and Principles for the Curriculum 3-18*, Scottish Executive, http://www.gov.scot/
Publications/2004/11/20178/45863, accessed 4 Apr 2018.

Thoreau, H.D. (1854). *Walden; or, Life in the Woods*. Boston, MA: Ticknor & Fields.

Chapter 6

The evolved developmental niche and children's developing morality

Angela M. Kurth and Darcia Narvaez

Introduction

Mammals require nurturing caregiving for optimal postnatal development. It has been some time since Harlow (1958) systematically documented the psychologically devastating effects of long-term isolation of primates from caregivers. Spitz (1947) demonstrated how severely human development and survival were compromised when babies lacked secure human relationships. Bowlby (1951) noted how loss of caregivers at an early age caused extensive separation distress, leading to psychological deterioration. Indeed, decades earlier, Hartmann (1939) identified the 'ordinary expectable environment' to which human morphology, physiology, and behaviour had adapted during biological evolution. Similarly, Bowlby (1980, 1988) conceptualized the profound human need for a natural, evolutionarily adaptive social relatedness that emerged in an 'environment of evolutionary adaptedness' (EEA). More recently, anthropologists have summarized the characteristics of the species-typical niche.

The evolved developmental niche

The human genus spent 99% of its history in small-band hunter-gatherer (SBHG) societies (Ingold 2005; Lee and Daly 2005; Fry 2006; Narvaez 2013). SBHGs are nomadic foragers, living in immediate-return societies (no domestication of animals, cultivation of plants, or resource accumulation). These communities are highly communal, experiencing ongoing deep social embeddedness and enjoyment, positive social support, and relationally purposeful living (Narvaez 2013). Although they have high physical contact with others in cooperative relationships, they also enjoy high personal autonomy with fluid social boundaries, individual freedom, and egalitarian relationships with people of all ages (Ingold 2005; Narvaez 2013). Living close to the earth and to one another, SBHGs are immersed in a world of cooperative give and take, valuing generosity and cooperation with the social and natural world. The natural world forms part of the community and they are relaxed and comfortable within it. They do not tolerate selfish or dominant behaviours, so there is no coercion, even from adult to child. Because meeting basic needs is a part of the flow of life, pent-up frustration or anger is very rare, so their imaginative and abstraction capabilities are kept within a sympathetic cooperative framework.

The evolved developmental niche (EDN), based on the hunter-gatherer childhood model, emerged with social mammals more than 30 million years ago (Konner 2005). The human EDN intensified as humans became bipedal, shrinking the pelvis and requiring offspring to be born highly immature owing to their head size (Trevathan 2011). Because humans are born 9–18 months earlier than other hominids (including apes), much of their growth, and particularly brain development, occurs postnatally (Konner 2010). The characteristics of the human EDN, identified by anthropologists studying present-day SBHGs, include high levels of responsivity, lengthy on-request breastfeeding, extensive positive—and lack of negative—touch (no coercion), multiple adult caregivers, social cohesion and connection to the larger community, self-directed playful interactions, and soothing perinatal experiences (Hewlett and Lamb 2005; Konner 2005, 2010; Kovach and Da Ros-Voseles 2008).

Neurobiological sciences are now demonstrating the importance of each of these caregiving practices for healthy nervous system development (Narvaez et al. 2013b, 2013c). For example, caregiver responsiveness to a child builds his or her prosocial orientation (Kochanska 2002); years of breastfeeding provide the immunogen building blocks fundamental to the construction of a resilient immune system (e.g. Walker 1993; Slusser and Powers 1997); touch facilitates the functioning of the vagus nerve required for autonomic arousal and visceral regulation (Porges 2011); and child-directed social play develops the capacities of emotion regulation (Panksepp 2007) and curtails social aggression (Flanders, Herman, and Paquette 2013).

The mechanisms for the effects of the EDN on social development include the fostering of self-regulation and empathy (Narvaez and Gleason 2013; Gleason and Narvaez 2014). Parents and other caregivers have the greatest impact on moral development in early life during the shaping of what might be called the 'submoral' components of an individual, such as the 'affective core' (Emde et al. 1991). Maternal sensitivity and attentive care foster the development of a 'relational communication system' (Fogel and Branco 1997; Fogel 2000). Within the system, caregiver and child co-modulate behaviour to achieve optimal levels of physiological arousal and coordinated action (Evans and Porter 2009). Successful development of this mutual synchrony is associated with self-control (Feldman, Greenbaum, and Yirmiya 1999) and the development of emotion systems and attachment relationships (Schore 1994). Self-regulation includes physiological, emotional, and social capacities. Constructed on the physiological and emotional aspects of self-regulation, social regulation helps children manage interactions with peers and friends (Narvaez and Gleason 2013). Additionally, in order to behave morally, a person must feel sympathy for others and take responsibility for their welfare.

Narvaez and colleagues have begun to examine how the EDN corresponds with children's outcomes, beyond responsivity. Using an existing dataset in a longitudinal study across the first three years of childhood, they found that EDN-consistent parenting (responsivity, breastfeeding, touch, and social support) was positively related to child prosociality and negatively related to behaviour problems (Narvaez et al. 2013a). After controlling for responsivity, breastfeeding and social support were positively related to prosociality and negatively to behaviour problems, whereas touch was no longer positively related to prosociality, but remained negatively related to behaviour problems. In another study, a questionnaire measuring maternal behaviours and attitudes towards EDN-consistent parenting used with Chinese children showed that EDN-consistent care was a significant predictor of children's development of behaviour regulation, empathy, and conscience (Narvaez et al. 2013d). In summary, in the first years of life, evolved expected care involves a focus on social experience which fosters capacities for social self-regulation and concern for others.

Analysis of group childcare practices in relation to the EDN

One key distinction between the EDN and modern life in large urban and industrial communities is the loss of intimate family life, for example with separation of child from the primary caregiver for much of the day. Although allomothers (caregivers other than the mother) have always been needed throughout human evolution, they typically would have been at the side of mothers who were still present to their children. In contrast, infants and toddlers today are often sent away from mothers and family members to group care settings with non-family members. Lancy (2014) comments that western nations 'helicopter' their children, unlike non-nomadic foraging societies. It is important to distinguish between meeting a baby's needs and coddling or helicoptering. Human babies have built-in needs for the EDN, which helps their brains and bodies grow properly. Denying the EDN sets the child off on a suboptimal trajectory, undermining their confidence and capacities, leading to what looks like a need for helicoptering later. Mother–young child separation causes a great blow to a child's sense of security, which may contribute to the coddling and helicoptering with older children that often occurs in western nations. Perhaps early undercare is why the western child is given additional attention and supports *after* early childhood (rather than during) by parents and other adults.

With the EDN and the societal complexities of non-family childcare in mind, we will examine five approaches to group care which aim for child well-being, and assess their consistency with EDN care: developmentally appropriate practice, the child well-being framework, Resources for Infant Educarers (RIE)®, the Montessori method, and the Reggio Emilia approach. Table 6.1 provides a summary of our basic findings.

Developmentally appropriate practice

Many infant and toddler daycare and pre-school programmes use the framework of 'developmentally appropriate practice' (DAP; National Association for the Education of Young Children (NAEYC) 2009a), which is used by the NAEYC to accredit early childhood programmes. DAP is grounded in research on child development and effective education, and focused on children from birth through to eight years of age. In programmes where DAP is applied, teachers are presumed to have core knowledge in three areas: (1)

Table 6.1 Comparison of five approaches to early life group care

EDN component	Developmentally appropriate practice	McMullen's child well-being framework	RIE®	Montessori method	Reggio Emilia approach
Age focus	0–8 years	Infant and toddler	Infant and toddler	0–3, 3–6, 6–12 years	0–3, 3–6 years
Natural childbirth	×	×	×	×	×
Breastfeeding	×	×	✓	×	×
Responsivity	✓	*	*	*	*
Positive touch	×	✓	*	×	×
Multiple familiar adult caregivers	×	×	*	*	*
Classroom community building	○	○	*	○	*
Embeddedness in larger community	×	○	×	○	*
Free play	✓	✓	*	*	*
Immersion in the natural world	✓	×	*	*	*
Positive climate	✓	*	*	○	*
Social and emotional support	✓	*	*	✓	*
Self-regulation fostered	○	○	*	*	*
Sympathy and compassion fostered	○	*	*	○	*

×, not mentioned; ○, implied; ✓, mentioned; *, substantively mentioned

child development and learning, (2) individually appropriate treatment, and (3) cultural diversity (NAEYC 2009b).

In regard to the first type of core knowledge, the NAEYC (2009a) has laid out 12 principles of child learning and development to be used to inform practice. These are generalizations about children's learning and development—including physical, social and emotional, and cognitive domains—all of which interrelate and are interdependent. Although DAP principles make reference to multiple domains of development, in examining the list of principles the primary emphasis is on cognitive development and learning (https://www.naeyc.org).

The second and third core knowledge components—making decisions for individuals and being attentive to cultural differences—can be combined. Both involve setting challenging and achievable goals for each child by thoughtfully planning activities that build on existing knowledge. For these core knowledge components, teachers must have particular knowledge to enable good decision-making (1) knowledge about child development, including strategies to improve development, and typical developmental trajectories, (2) knowledge about the individual child, from multiple sources, such as observation of the child, conversations with the family, and individual child assessments, and (3) knowledge about the child's social and cultural context outside the classroom. Incorporating these three sets of information allows for effective long-term and short-term decisions about individual children and the classroom as a whole.

Beyond the core components, in their 2009a statement the NAEYC outlined five overarching guidelines for DAP.

1 'Creating a caring community of learners' (NAEYC 2009a, p. 16) encourages teachers to value each member and relationship by providing respect in physically and psychologically safe environments, fostering a positive social and emotional climate.
2 'Teaching to enhance development and learning' (NAEYC 2009a, p. 17) emphasizes the teacher's responsibility for providing an environment and strategic lesson plan to fulfil the programme learning goals for each child.
3 'Planning curriculum to achieve important goals' (NAEYC 2009a, p. 20) states that teachers must have individualized goals for children's learning, to be obtained through application of an effective curriculum.
4 'Assessing children's development and learning' (NAEYC 2009a, p. 21) is attained by implementing a system aimed at assessing children's achievement over time.
5 'Establishing reciprocal relationships with families' (NAEYC 2009a, p. 22) emphasizes the importance of collaboration between teachers and families in encouraging child development.

DAP addresses only some of the characteristics of the EDN. It seems DAP would support responsivity, play (although primarily dramatic play, and more emphasis on academic learning than spontaneous self-satisfying and social play), a positive climate, and social and emotional support, all within the framework of cognitive goals. DAP suggests outdoor play, which can give children chances for immersion in the natural world. However, DAP has little or nothing to say about natural childbirth, breast-feeding, positive touch, multiple responsive caregivers, the nature of classroom community building, or links to the large community. DAP is intended for use from birth to age 8. For the younger end of this range, this framework seems overly focused on academic achievement and learning. While it mentions cooperative adult relationships, it is unclear what particular social-developmental philosophy guides building of the child's relationships. Perhaps the approach would benefit from being split into narrower age ranges to allow more focus on socio-emotional development for the first four to five years, and then more cognitively focused curriculum and assessment for the last few years if developmentally appropriate for the individual child. In all, it is unclear how much *social* self-regulation and sympathy will be built within care centres implementing DAP principles alone.

The child well-being framework

Researchers McMullen and McCormick (2016) provide a framework for group childcare for infant and toddler age groups. They contend that well-being or flourishing should be the primary goal of group childcare. Well-being reaches beyond resiliency and strives towards 'a *general* state of being and feeling well overall, in terms of physical and psychological health and safety, emotional stability and soundness, and overall satisfaction in activities and relationships within the group' (McMullen, Buzzelli, and Yun 2015). Based on a body of research, they outline nine interdependent requirements for achieving well-being in group care settings. When these elements are achieved, individuals should be able to quickly regain equilibrium after distressing experiences, although such circumstances should rarely occur in these environments. McMullen and colleagues place the nine requirements into three overarching categories of well-being: environmental, experiential, and relational well-being.

Environmental well-being

Two aspects encourage environmental wellbeing.

1 *Contentment* gives special attention to the space provided for the children, which should be organized in a thoughtful and pleasant manner, and be visually appealing and comfortable, with natural lighting. The temperature should be appropriate, and the atmosphere within the space should be relaxed.

2 *Security*, the second aspect of environmental well-being, is ensured when all safety and health regulations are followed, and spaces and objects are safe, kept clean, and sanitized. The classroom should have predictable routines and policies.

Experiential well-being

Four aspects provide experiential well-being.

1 *Engagement* is supported with enticing activities and uninterrupted time for exploration and experimentation, alone or with others, including adults who are also available for problem solving. The goal is to foster feelings of fulfilment and satisfaction, rather than boredom or dissatisfaction.

2 *Contribution* results when both children and adults have a sense of belonging through meaningful roles and responsibilities, and use their strengths and talents, which are valued in the same way as their presence in the group.

3 A sense of *efficacy* comes from feeling confident and accomplished, which emerges from caregiver acknowledgement of effort, persistence, or success.

4 *Agency* refers to a sense of empowerment of voice and choice and control as each person—children, teachers, parents—contributes to group planning and decision-making, aiming for the well-being of each child.

Relational well-being

Three components animate relational wellbeing.

1 *Affinity* is promoted when children receive affectionate touch and nurturance within a positive emotional climate with others.

2 *Communication* includes respectful and continuous dialogue between caregivers, children and families to promote mutual understanding.

3 *Self-respect* is fostered when caregivers create and communicate a culture of respect for who the child is, what the child believes, and what the child feels.

In terms of the EDN, the child wellbeing framework for infants and toddlers clearly addresses responsive care and personal autonomy. It mentions the value of positive touch, as well as the need for spaces where children can play freely. It offers no recommendations for natural childbirth or breastfeeding. Although the approach does not require that caregivers remain with children over a long time period, it does emphasize the importance of building a sense of community and a positive social and emotional climate within the caregiving setting. However, it is unclear how this is implemented, leaving it unknown how and whether opportunities for social self-regulation and sympathy are provided. Nor is there mention of connection to the wider community or natural world.

RIE®: Resources for Infant Educarers

The RIE˚ (pronounced 'rye', Resources for Infant Educarers) approach focuses on care for infants and toddlers. It was founded by Magda Gerber while working in Budapest, Hungary, with Dr. Emmi Pikler, who served as medical director of the Lóczy orphanage, a state-run orphanage in Budapest. In 1957, Gerber moved to the United States, and founded the RIE˚ Center in Los Angeles. She coined the term 'educarer', referring to a parent or other caregiver whose role is to care for and educate the child. Whether parent or teacher, Gerber viewed each interaction with a child—even feeding and nappy changing—as an opportunity to show love, trust, and respect. The approach strives to simplify caregiving and focus on being authentic and respectful towards infants as complete and autonomous beings. RIE˚ follows seven basic principles (principles are quoted from Gerber 1998, with additional material cited from Carlisle Solomon 2013 and Lansbury 2014).

1. Basic trust in the child to be an initiator, an explorer, and a self-learner

RIE˚ caregivers trust that infants learn primarily on their own by initiating actions, exploring the world, and signalling needs to the parent or caregiver. In learning to observe the infant, a caregiver must slow down, and spend time in simple, quiet togetherness. The adult learns the subtle signs in which the child initiates interactions or conveys information about her needs and desires. A caregiver receives and follows cues from the children, rather than imposing her own thoughts, lessons, or agenda.

2. An environment for the child that is physically safe, cognitively challenging, and emotionally nurturing

The RIE˚ environment provides the child with a developmentally appropriate space. For young infants, a gated-off area, room, or outdoor space dedicated to safe play with simple household objects or natural elements is appropriate. Toddlers enjoy more challenging climbing areas and sensory materials, like water or sand. Simple, manipulable play objects that allow for creative activity are preferred over complex 'entertaining' toys that elicit passive observation from the child. Examples of appropriate toys for infants include household objects such as a bowl and spoon, some soft scarves, or lightweight stainless steel pots, whereas complex lighted or motorized toys are avoided.

RIE' caregivers provide emotional nurturing by showing authenticity in their interactions. For example, if a child displays a signal, such as a wrinkled nose or a vocalization, the adult does not act abruptly or intrusively to simply quieten the infant, but responds with calm sensitivity and attention in order to understand and appropriately provide what the child needs in that moment.

3. Time for uninterrupted play

RIE' philosophy understands that children do not need to be taught to play, but when given the opportunity, play in the manner for which they are ready. In contrast to some who emphasize exposing babies to targeted stimuli in order to promote development, Gerber (1998) believed that the world itself is naturally a very stimulating place for infants, and no extraordinary stimulation is needed to help them learn. Babies are thought to grow by playing and exploring their new environment, and therefore should not be interrupted when immersed in an activity. Similarly, children explore and self-direct their activities, though with support available from adults—that is, an adult is always on the child's level but might remain near the edge of a play area, available to provide help or comfort.

4. Freedom to explore and interact with other infants

RIE' supporters recognize that children interact with, and learn from, one another in different ways than they do with adults. Children are allowed to play and learn from one another, in multi-aged groups whenever possible.

5. Involvement of the child in all caregiving activities to allow the child to become an active participant rather than a passive recipient

RIE' caregivers collaborate with the child in caregiving activities. For example, during nappy changing, the caregiver describes each step of the process ahead of time, asking the child for participation, building dialogue, and prompting cooperation.

6. Sensitive observation of the child in order to understand her needs

To fully attend to a child's needs, caregivers slow down and become fully engaged with the child. This primarily involves disengaging from the 'hustle and bustle' of life and technology and allowing themself to be emotionally and attentionally present with the child.

7. Consistency and clearly defined limits and expectations to develop discipline

Respectful and compassionate limits and consistency are very important to RIE[*] care-givers in order to encourage a secure developmental environment. Whenever possible, choices are offered to allow the child autonomy in her actions. Similarly, children are given opportunities to solve their own problems within particular limits. For example, if two toddlers are frustrated because they both want the same toy, RIE[*] caregivers closely watch the interaction, but allow the children opportunity to work out their problem. When adults refrain from intervening, children often display the abilities to peacefully resolve conflict on their own. Of course, the time to intervene is if a child is in danger, or if conflict becomes physical, but children learn social competence when they are given opportunities to navigate their own social interactions, rather than when adults rush in to solve such interactions.

RIE[*] emphasizes that eating and sleeping schedules should ideally adhere to the child's cues and needs. For example, a child who is sleepy should never be kept awake for the sake of the parents' or teachers' convenience. In the ancestral social environment (still in existence among small-band hunter-gatherers today), children, and even adults, often fall asleep when sleepy, wherever they are (Gowdy 1998); and as soon as they are old enough community members forage to find snacks when hungry (Hrdy 2009). In many ways the RIE[*] approach fits with the EDN, where the flow of the community varied from day to day.

Outside of the seven principles, Gerber emphasized the necessity of a designated out-door play area for all children. She describes the essential natural stimulation and games provided by the sky, clouds, earth, insects, and animals. 'A sense of nature's presence (sky, trees, flowers) is desirable.... Outdoor play is important because we are the only animals who don't live outside (Gerber 1998, p. 176)'.

RIE[*] does not address some aspects of the EDN for young children, including those outside the purview of early education such as natural childbirth or breastfeeding, leaving these matters to parents and medical professionals. While the EDN emphasizes extensive affectionate touch, RIE[*] believes that fewer, deeply affectionate interactions are more im-portant than constant physical interaction. However, the amount and timing of physical touch should be guided completely by the desires of the child.

Generally, RIE[*] tries to provide the type of responsive allomothering found in the EDN, and emphasizes free, uninterrupted play and deep interpersonal connectedness. In both RIE[*] and our ancestral environment, adults were nearby and non-directive, allowing the child to be immersed in the natural world.

RIE[*] programmes prefer continuity of care, where the caregivers commit to remaining with the same group of children until at least the age of three, and longer if possible (Elam 2005), a practice that seems to help prevent staff turnover, and builds long-term rela-tionships among children and teachers. Overall, RIE[*] practices support EDN principles of community building with familiar caregivers. Social self-regulation and sympathy are likely to be developed within the authentic community of practices.

The Montessori method

The Montessori method is currently used for the age groups 0–3 years, 3–6 years, and 6–12 years. It began with Dr. Montessori, who was the first Italian woman to become a physician. In 1907, she began overseeing a daycare centre for very poor children (Montessori 1966). She had a unique conceptualization of children: 'An adult environment is not a suitable environment for children, but rather an aggregate of obstacles that strengthen their defenses, warp their attitudes, and expose them to adult suggestions' (Montessori 1966, p. 109). 'Children have a deep sense of personal dignity. Adults, as a rule, have no concept of how easily [children] are wounded and oppressed' (Montessori 1966, p. 127). Dr. Montessori believed that a child's outward behaviour is a 'storm' that disguises the child's true spirit, and it is the adult's job to provide an environment which allows the child's spirit to be uncovered. Thus, the goal of the Montessori method is for 'the discovery and freeing of the child' (Montessori 1966, p. 110). Adults should not be an obstacle to child learning by performing activities for a child but instead have a neutral character, a sense of 'intellectual calm', which is not merely a lack of nervousness, but a 'deeper calm, an empty, or better, unencumbered state that is a source of inner clarity. This calm consists of a spiritual humility and intellectual purity necessary for the understanding of a child' (Montessori 1966, p. 137). By maintaining a passive role, adults remove the obstacle of their own activity and authority, allowing the child to become an active agent. Dr. Montessori observed the common developmental stages and preferred activities during each stage. She based her method on the following observations:

1 Children enjoy repetitive exercise or activity. On somewhat rare occasions, children have moments of deep concentration, where they repeat actions over a period of time. She observed that children engage in this repetition after learning a new skill, and that after finishing the repetition, they seem to be filled with joy of accomplishing the task.

2 Children enjoy having free choice of activity, and engage more fully in tasks they choose on their own. Children have little interest in toys chosen for them. 'Since they never freely chose these toys, I realized that in the life of a child play is perhaps something of little importance which he undertakes for lack of something better to do. [...] Since a child is constantly growing, he is fascinated by everything that contributes to his development and becomes indifferent to idle occupations' (Montessori 1966, p. 122).

3 Children are generally indifferent to rewards and punishments but are motivated and fulfilled by learning and choosing their own activities.

Based on these observations, Dr. Montessori provided an environment in which the children learned and grew. She started by helping children develop everyday skills, like preparing meals and cleaning. 'There was no method to be seen; what was seen was the child' (Montessori 1966, p. 136). Rather than describe a particular method, Dr. Montessori focused on providing an environment optimal for learning: one that is pleasant, filled with furniture and objects scaled to the children's size, where a child can be left to her own resources, and feel efficacious to maintain the classroom on her own. Materials and objects are adapted to the children's need, guided by observation. She found that children enjoyed having their own workspaces, defined by a small rug to sit on in an orderly environment. By organizing a child-sized environment where children could take part in everyday activities, the aim was to instil a sense of confidence and independence for the children. A peaceful atmosphere where children are taught basic rules about order and tidiness allows for 'perfect discipline'. By practising silence, children learn to listen carefully, and to move gracefully without bumping objects in their path.

The Montessori approach has become a popular method in the United States for young children (and even for general schooling). Key aspects of the approach, based on Dr. Montessori's observations described above—i.e. (1) child centredness, (2) learning through experiences and a stimulating environment, and (3) child activities—are how the children learn. By allowing children to choose their own projects and activities in a deliberately orderly environment, the approach hopes to instil a sense of intrinsic motivation and love of learning (Seldin 2006).

An additional concept in modern Montessori education is that children are 'stewards of the Earth' and must learn to care for nature, both near and far (Seldin 2006). For example, children are taught to appreciate rich, life-supporting soil rather than thinking of it as 'dirt', which 'implies something nasty to many people'. (Seldin 2006). Children are taught to treat all living things with care. 'Teach your children not to pick leaves and flowers aimlessly and toss them aside, but to gather them only for a good purpose' (Seldin 2006, p. 136).

Some research has examined modern Montessori schools, known for having multi-age classrooms, student-chosen work in long time blocks, and both individual and small-group instruction in academic and social skills (Lillard and Else-Quest 2006). Montessori education has been related to outcomes including positive interactions on the playground, high scores on standardized maths and reading tests, advanced social cognition and executive control, concerns for fairness and justice, and creativity (Lillard and Else-Quest 2006).

Recalling the habits among the SBHGs, it is evident that children who develop within the EDN similarly have high autonomy and freedom in a Montessori setting. With the emphasis on respect and observation, responsiveness is encouraged. Dr. Montessori only discusses touch in regard to newborns: 'The manner in which we touch and move a child, and the delicacy of feeling which should inspire us at the time, makes us think of the gestures that a priest uses at the altar' (Montessori 1966, p. 24). There is, however, no mention of natural childbirth practices or breastfeeding. There is no particular focus on ensuring familiar adult caregivers or community building within a classroom. A positive climate and social emotional support is implied in the idea of respect and a peaceful atmosphere, although not explicitly covered. It is unclear whether social self-regulation or consideration for others will be fostered. The integration into the larger community is implied, but not specified, in the principles.

The Reggio Emilia method

The Reggio Emilia method is designed for use in the age groups 0–3 years and 3–6 years. It is well described in *The Hundred Languages of Children: The Reggio Emilia Experiences in Transformation* (Edwards, Gandini, and Forman 2012b). It is a holistic and constructivist approach to both understanding children and guiding their development (Rinaldi 2012). The pedagogical method is uniquely tailored for each locale and culture but always includes concern for well-being, artistic taste, relationships that enhance belonging and autonomy, continuity of relationships across years, and documentation of children's activities and ideas (Hawkins 2012). The essence of the Reggio approach is captured by its founder, Loris Malaguzzi: 'We think of a school for young children as an integral living organism, as a place of shared lives and relationships among many adults and many children. We think of school as a sort of construction in motion, continuously adjusting itself' (Gandini 2012a, p. 41). 'Adult and child roles are complementary: they ask questions of one another, they listen, and they answer … the system of relationships has in and of itself a virtually autonomous capacity to educate' (Gandini 2012a, p. 46). 'To learn is a satisfying experience … to understand is desire, drama, and conquest … To disappoint them deprives children of possibilities that no exhortation can arouse in later years' (Gandini 2012a, p. 44). The role of teacher is quite flexible: a teacher is a co-constructor of knowledge, creator of the environment as a third teacher, exchanger of understandings, supporter of the competent child, documenter and researcher, partner with parents, listener, provocateur, negotiator of meaning, and 'dispenser of occasions' (Edwards 2012, p. 151).

The Reggio practice is built on notions of multiple intelligences ('a hundred languages') and gives special attention to the design and aesthetics of the physical environment into which children are placed. The building, usually put together by teachers and parents, needs to have an overall softness, provide multiple sensorial experiences (e.g. a flower garden with different colours and aromas), be connected with surrounding environments, and be supportive of social connections. The space should be relational, allowing for a variety of social interactions.

> Exchanges or conversations with children are crucial. It is important to note that the quality of a space (or environment) results from many factors: size and shape, functional organization, and sensory experience, color, light, and materials. The space should represent and allow for flexibility and adaption, community and participation, social constructivism, narration, communication, and documentation. Overall, the setting should provide an intense richness everyday where children can develop and test hypotheses and artistically express what they learn.
>
> (Gandini 2012b, p. 325)

Gandini (2012b) provides an example of typical activities. Teachers value the spaces near the schools, considering them extensions of the classroom space. They take the children to explore neighbourhoods and landmarks. In one example, the group explored how the town was transformed during rainstorms. They first explored the town on days without rain and thought about what to observe, measure, collect, photograph, and record when the rains came. Then, when a thunderstorm came, the children implemented their plans and noticed, 'how people changed their speed and posture in walking, how the shining reflections and the splash from the puddles changed the streets, how the sound of the raindrops differed depending on whether it was falling on the pavement, the hoods of cars, or the leaves of trees. Then after experiencing the rainstorm, and following the customary procedure in Reggio Emilia, the children became engaged in representing their experiences of the rainstorm (e.g. musically and through fine arts). This, in turn, led to more questions and hypotheses, and explorations that the teacher and the atelerista [artistic organizer] thoroughly documented' (Gandini 2012b, p. 322).

In the Reggio approach, each child is viewed as 'an organic unity who needs personal space for action and movement in his or her own personal way' (Gandini 2012b, p. 321). Children are involved in living aspects of the world including multiplicity, circularity, visibility, collectivity, open-endedness, and courage. Children and teachers learn together 'through cooperation, organization, and a strategy of listening and welcoming ... that leads to mutual attention, dialogue and exchange' (Gandini 2012b, p. 324). The setting provides ongoing opportunities for individual and community discovery and creative expression. It emphasizes inclusion and universal access along with involvement of families, citizens, and policy makers.

In regard to the EDN, the Reggio approach appears to be highly supportive of children's full-board development. It is personalized to the individual child, group of children, and community and natural locale, with teachers themselves growing and changing, creating and learning, with the children. It is very much 'spiritual' in promoting the holistic child, beyond cognitive or physical development, suggesting that social self-regulation and sympathy are likely to be fostered. Reggio discussions do not refer to touch or breastfeeding but do emphasize responsivity, play, and multiple layers of positive relational support.

Summary of practices

Each approach to group care concerns itself with the well-being of children. As we have noted, each has a different set of governing practices—some wider than others. One characteristic they all seem to share is the granting of personal autonomy, which may be a way to provide a similar type of autonomy to our evolved setting where adults do not set up environments for children. In fact, SBHG adults do not coerce children in any way, considering them their own agents. Efficacy is built by the child herself, who is granted full autonomy (unless aggressive) and is eager to learn the ways of the group, for example in gathering and preparing food (Morelli et al. 2014).

In evolved conditions, social support is provided to all ages by the 'village' of allomothers. All participate in an ongoing pleasurable social life. Communication occurs through singing, joke telling, and playfulness. No one is coerced, and there are no designated leaders. Individuals have high autonomy but also a sense of communalism. Personal autonomy is always integrated with social concerns. The Reggio method seems the most focused on creating an EDN-consistent learning community that involves parents and the local human and other-than-human communities, but within which children have autonomy to select their own activities and explore their interests in relation to the world around them. The Reggio method seems to provide a highly nourishing, living environment.

One aspect that is found implicitly in EDN settings, but emphasized less in approaches, is interaction with the undomesticated natural world—something vital to mental and physical health (Louv 2016). In our evolved setting, the natural environment would have been enjoyed as a pleasant companion, except perhaps under storm conditions, or when a hungry predator was roaming. DAP says nothing about environmental aesthetics or naturalness. Visual appeal is mentioned by McMullen, but Reggio stresses the aesthetics and connection to natural settings (with plants in urban centres at least). RIE˚ stresses the importance of exploration and play in the natural world, and Montessori emphasizes respect for nature. Play in the wild, natural world should be the emphasis—something that may be required for the development of ecological intelligence.

Moral development in early childhood

Fundamental developments occur during infancy that undergird moral development, including self-regulation, which is reliant on the physical comfort provided by caregivers (Schore 1994)—the sense of self that develops through social-relational intersubjectivity with the mother and the co-construction of rituals of play (Trevarthen 2005). The child prepares for a moral life by practising and learning to value emotional presence and empathy with caregivers (Narvaez 2015).

What happens morally when children live within the EDN? We can see it in the personalities of the children and adults in SBHG societies where the EDN is provided. Members are happy, agreeable, and generous, and moral functioning in these settings is focused on social engagement, or treating others as equals through play and friendship (Ingold 2005). Both companionship in shared adventures of play, and attachment in secure care, are critical in early childhood (Trevarthen 2005).

What is also striking about small-band hunter-gatherers are the high states of mental health and socio-moral well-being among children and adults. Noted by many observers, they appear 'more intelligent, more alert, more expressive, and more interested in things and people around them than the average European or American' (e.g. Diamond 1997). Might these outcomes be related to the EDN? Indeed, initial studies of adult retrospective reports of EDN childhood experiences are also related to adult mental health and morality (Lawrence and Narvaez 2013; Narvaez, Wang, and Cheng 2016; Narvaez et al. 2016c). Thus, the EDN may be important for later outcomes that characterize a society as a whole.

Morality when the EDN is missing

The last 1% of the history of the human genus is very different from the 99% of our past. The 1% exists with the complexities of animal domestication, intensive (some say totalitarian) agriculture, accumulation of possessions, and war (Fry 2006). These concerns have shifted the practices of child-rearing away from the EDN. Cultural narratives and ideologies have also had their effects. For example, messages regarding optimal child-rearing are muddied when people are led to believe that babies are meant to be denied (suffer) 'for their own good' (Miller 1990). Such Calvinist views purvey the child-rearing landscape in the United States. With gene-centric and deterministic views (that children are born a certain way and not much can be done about it), many institutions, policies, and expectations are not structured to help provide the nurturing described by the EDN. Rather, societies seem to be inadvertently experimenting with early care in a way that minimizes the healthy, effective nurturing found in the EDN.

Over the twentieth century, EDN-consistent care diminished in the USA as medicalized birth became the norm, along with infant formula usage, decreased self-directed outdoor play, advocacy of 'scientific' (i.e. detached) parenting (Watson 1928), and the breakdown of extended family networks (Narvaez et al. 2013b, 2013c). Rising rates of psychosocial problems in young children suggest that child development is being undermined in response. The American Academy of Childhood and Adolescent Psychiatry is declaring a 'crisis' in regard to our children's mental health (Campaign for America's Kids 2011). Corroborating data from cohort analyses (Twenge et al. 2009) suggest the decline in well-being is a real phenomenon, particularly for college students.

What happens when a child does not receive evolved expected care? Experiences of suffering depress the child's optimal developmental trajectory, resulting in cascading effects throughout the child's life and social context. Research supports the intergenerational nature of parent–child dynamics. In one study, mothers who maltreated their children were more likely to have experienced physical and emotional abuse, emotional neglect, physical neglect, and sexual abuse in their own childhoods, as well as receive less support from their families as adults (Cicchetti, Rogosch, and Toth 2006). Maltreating mothers were also less likely to be sensitive parents, lacked empathy, used more physical punishment, and had inappropriate expectations of their children. Parenting and child outcomes appear intertwined over generations.

In modern societies, especially in the USA, corporations have a financial interest in advocating *against* EDN practices (e.g. pushing infant formula, and advocating sleep training and baby isolation via all sorts of equipment). Tragically, the USA exports its birthing and child-rearing practices and attitudes around the world (Wagner 2006), contributing to the perpetuation of the misguided practices.

Modern societies foster very different world views and personalities from those found in contemporary 'small-band hunter-gatherer' societies. Mistreatment or neglect of needs in childhood leads to misdevelopment and misperceptions of the world, and to very different personalities and moralities, including a shift to fixedness of habits and ideas, and to materialism (Narvaez 2014). If we isolate mother and child at birth, and separate children from close contact throughout childhood, we are punishing children for their mammalian desire for physical closeness with caregivers, often leading to self-protective moral and social orientations (Narvaez 2008). Undercare impairs multiple physiological functions, including brain systems that control memory and well-being (Meaney 2001), while also undermining social development, which in turn affects moral orientations (Narvaez 2016).

When toxically stressed, the child will necessarily grow in a self-protective manner, one that promotes self-interest, making it more difficult to grow cooperative skills. In contrast, when mutually supportive relationships are emphasized through the structures of the setting and activities, compassion and openness are likely to ensue. In fact, in the Reggio method, cooperative ethics are emphasized, as its founder, Malaguzzi, proclaims:

> When we see young children cooperating, we notice a sort of ethic: they do everything they can to keep the situation stable and ongoing. Some children have more advanced capacities than others. When one such child makes a suggestion or proposal, the others accept it more willingly than if it had come from an adult. Many of them learn the relativity of their own point of view and how to represent their ideas in a delicate way. They say, 'I think,' or 'in my view,' or 'I do not know if my ideas are right for everybody.'

(Gandini 2012a, citing Malaguzzi pp. 68–9)

What kind of morality develops in the group settings we have described for a modern industrial society? Children naturally develop cooperative ethics in a supportive setting, but in the modern environments described here adults may need to be more deliberate about providing a supportive setting. Taking up an intentional approach to ethical education means providing the very sorts of social and physical environments described here (Narvaez 2005; Narvaez and Bock 2014). In a time period when children are exposed to a plethora of vicious and self-centred role models in the media, and with little time spent in a community of familiar, caring adults, educators can be the most consistent presence in a child's life, with special significance for moral development.

Recommendations

For some centuries, civilized nations have been changing standards for early care, bringing us to the point where the bulk of parenting research emphasizes child resiliency and 'good enough' parenting (Narvaez and Gleason 2013), but this aim may be too low. When compared with extreme stress such as war and poverty, low-quality day care seems of little concern. However, we are beginning to understand that low-quality care does in fact compromise development of the sense of good fellowship and shared well-being (e.g. the National Institute of Child Health and Human Development, Early Child Care Research Network 2003). Standards for resilience do not often include evaluation of compassion and a well-formed conscience, but focus typically on the absence of negative outcomes despite risk. In this case, a 'successful' childhood is one that does not result in pathology and incarceration. However, it appears the standard of care is too low, and what defines a successful childhood in the United States is too narrow (Narvaez et al. 2013c, 2016a, b). As we have shown, paying attention to the evolved needs of the young child and the type of human character promoted by EDN-consistent care, child well-being, and socio-moral development can be promoted.

Additionally, as understanding of neurobiology has increased, researchers are less prone to attribute behaviours to genetics, and rather look to epigenetics. For example, babies who die from sudden infant death syndrome are more likely to be deficient in receptors for the neurotransmitter serotonin. Many times, however this problem is discussed using a genetic lens (Talan 2010), failing to consider the epigenetics of serotonin receptor construction that results from breastfeeding and touch.

At a time when motherhood is often overshadowed by the necessity of work outside the home and materialism has dominated goals for life, many children do not receive what they evolved to need within the family. Instead, to accommodate the current way of life, children are often put in the arms of strangers. Although some centres try to approach the kind of care that a child has evolved to need, none that we have identified provide it completely. In light of today's situation, we have several suggestions for changes to foster optimal development in young children.

Public policy recommendations

First, we suggest the following public policy initiatives:

- All nations should provide paid parental leave for at least a year, if not longer, so that parents can focus their full attention on bonding and building responsive care based on the needs of the child. Several European nations are effectively implementing this practice (Cook 2011).

- Workplaces should allow mothers to bring babies to work to facilitate breastfeeding and responsiveness. When well cared for, babies will be quiet (unless traumatized). Grassroots efforts for organizing baby-friendly workplaces are gaining some momentum.

- Child care centres should be available at workplaces so that mothers can breastfeed and be available for other needs.

- Government supplementation of quality childcare would reduce worker turnover. Free market systems do not work properly for this service as most parents cannot afford the cost of a highly educated and trained caregiver who provides quality care. Teachers also struggle within the profession owing to unsustainably low wages.

Recommendations for childcare centres

We have several suggestions for childcare centres so that they better meet the evolved developmental needs of children.

- Support breast milk feeding in the first years.

- Provide extensive positive touch in babyhood for optimizing endocrine systems, and vagus nerve development.

- Support parental involvement, ideally in a manner such as that advocated by Reggio, where parents, mothers, and fathers contribute to the design and ongoing activities of the centre.

◆ Provide multi-aged experiences for children. Placing daycare centres next to elementary schools and nursing homes would provide a chance for cross-age interaction beneficial to all.

◆ Provide more experience in natural world settings with non-human organisms (e.g. trees, animals) and natural features of landscape (e.g. hills).

◆ Focus more on the development of receptive intelligence and creative, playful feelings, not just cognitive, problem-solving development for limited contexts, since this matches up with the brain's early maturational schedule which learns best from self-directed social play. Caregivers need to be aware that optimal development requires intimate social experience with the same responsive adults across time.

◆ Support the continuity of teachers and child groups across time, such that teachers and children build a community that remains together for three or more years. Additionally, when more than one teacher is present, a particular teacher should be designated as primary caregiver for a child (preferably according to natural affinity between the child and the caregiver). This 'primary caregiver' carries out routines with their assigned subgroup of children whenever possible (e.g. nappy changing and feeding).

Conclusion

In economically advanced nations, young children are not being provided with the type of intensive parenting they evolved to need, which undermines their social and moral development. After describing the rich resources of the evolved early nest and discussing several approaches to early group care, we have offered some suggestions to policy makers and to childcare providers on how to adopt policies and practices that better match children's evolved needs and facilitate child flourishing.

References

Bowlby, J. (1951). *Maternal Care and Mental Health*. New York: Schocken.

Bowlby, J. (1980). *Attachment and Loss, vol. 3: Loss: Sadness and Depression*. New York: Basic Books.

Bowlby, J. (1988). *A Secure Base: Parent-Child Attachment and Healthy Human Development*. New York: Basic Books.

Campaign for America's Kids, American Academy of Childhood and Adolescent Psychiatry, Retrieved 18 January 2011, <http://www.campaignforamericaskids.org/11Ajoincampaign.html>.

Carlisle Solomon, D. (2013). *Baby Knows Best: Raising a Confident and Resourceful Child, The RIE Way*. Boston, MA: Little, Brown and Company.

Cicchetti, D., Rogosch, F.A., and Toth, S.L. (2006). Fostering secure attachment in infants in maltreating families through preventative interventions, *Development and Psychopathology*, **18**, 623–49.

Cook, P. (2011). *Mothering Matters*, 2nd edn. Bayswater, VIC, Australia: Freedom Publishing Books.

Diamond, J. (1997). *Guns, Germs and Steel: The Fates of Human Societies*. New York: Norton.

Edwards, C. (2012). Teacher and learner, partner and guide: The role of the teacher. In: C. Edwards, L. Gandini, and G. Forman (eds.) *The Hundred Languages of Children: The Reggio Emilia Experiences in Transformation*, 3rd edn. New York: Praeger, pp. 147–72.

Edwards, C., Gandini, L, and Forman, G. (2012a). Introduction: Background and starting points. In: C. Edwards, L. Gandini, and G. Forman (eds.) *The Hundred Languages of Children: The Reggio Emilia Experiences in Transformation*, 3rd edn. New York: Praeger, pp. 5–26.

Edwards, C., Gandini, L, and Forman, G (eds.) (2012b). *The Hundred Languages of Children: The Reggio Emilia Experiences in Transformation*, 3rd edn. New York: Praeger.

Elam, P. (2005). Creating quality infant group care programs. In: S. Petrie and S. Owen (eds.) *Authentic Relationships in Group Care for Infants and Toddlers—Resources for Infant Educarers (RIE)*. Philadelphia, PA: Jessica Kingsley Publishers, pp. 83–93.

Emde, R.N., Biringen, Z., Clyman, R., and Oppenheim, D. (1991). The moral self of infancy: Affective core and procedural knowledge. *Developmental Review*, 11, 251–70.

Evans, C.A. and Porter, C.L. (2009). The emergence of mother-infant co-regulation during the first year: Links to infants' developmental status and attachment. *Infant Behavior and Development*, 32(2), 147–58.

Feldman, R., Greenbaum, C.W., and Yirmiya, N. (1999). Mother-infant affect synchrony as an antecedent of the emergence of self-control. *Developmental Psychology*, 35, 223–31.

Flanders, J.L., Herman, K.N., and Paquette, D. (2013). Rough-and-tumble play and the cooperation–competition dilemma: Evolutionary and developmental perspectives on the development of social competence. In: D. Narvaez, J. Panksepp, A. Schore, and T. Gleason (eds.) *Evolution, Early Experience and Human Development: From Research to Practice and Policy*. New York: Oxford University Press, pp. 371–87.

Fogel, A. (2000). Developmental pathways in close relationships. *Child Development*, 71(5), 1150–51.

Fogel, A. and Branco, A. (1997). Metacommunication as a source of indeterminism in relationship development. In: A. Fogel, M.P. Lyra, and J. Valsiner (eds.) *Dynamics and Indeterminism in Developmental and Social Processes*. Hillsdale, NJ: Erlbaum, pp. 65–92.

Fry, D.P. (2006). *The Human Potential for Peace: An Anthropological Challenge to Assumptions about War and Violence*. New York: Oxford University Press.

Gandini, L. (2012a). History, ideas, and basic principles: An interview with Loris Malaguzzi. In: C. Edwards, L. Gandini, and G. Forman (eds.) *The Hundred Languages of Children: The Reggio Emilia Experiences in Transformation*, 3rd edn. New York: Praeger, pp. 27–72.

Gandini, L. (2012b). Connecting through caring and learning spaces. In: C. Edwards, L. Gandini, and G. Forman (eds.) *The Hundred Languages of Children: The Reggio Emilia Experiences in Transformation*, 3rd edn. New York: Praeger, pp. 317–42.

Gerber, M. (1998). *Your Self-Confident Baby: How To Encourage Your Child's Natural Abilities—From the Very Start*. New York: John Wiley.

Gleason, T. and Narvaez, D. (2014). Child environments and flourishing. In: D. Narvaez, K. Valentino, A. Fuentes, J. McKenna, and P. Gray (eds.) *Ancestral Landscapes in Human Evolution: Culture, Childrearing and Social Wellbeing*. New York: Oxford University Press, pp. 335–48.

Gowdy, J. (1998). *Limited Wants, Unlimited Means: A Reader on Hunter-Gatherer Economics and the Environment*. Washington, DC: Island Press.

Harlow, H. (1958). The nature of love. *American Psychologist*, 13, 673–85.

Hartmann, H. (1939). *Ego Psychology and the Problem of Adaptation*. New York: International University Press.

Hawkins, D. (2012). Malaguzzi's story, other stories, and respect for children. In: C. Edwards, L. Gandini, and G. Forman (eds.) *The Hundred Languages of Children: The Reggio Emilia Experiences in Transformation*, 3rd edn. New York: Praeger, pp. 73–80.

Hewlett, B.S. and Lamb, M.E. (2005). *Hunter-Gatherer Childhoods: Evolutionary, Developmental and Cultural Perspectives*. New Brunswick, NJ: Aldine.

Hrdy, S. (2009). *Mothers and Others: The Evolutionary Origins of Mutual Understanding*. Cambridge, MA: Belknap Press.

Ingold, T. (2005). On the social relations of the hunter-gatherer band. In: R.B. Lee and R. Daly (eds.) *The Cambridge Encyclopedia of Hunters and Gatherers*. New York: Cambridge University Press, pp. 399–410.

Kochanska, G. (2002). Mutually responsive orientation between mothers and their young children: A context for the early development of conscience. *Current Directions in Psychological Science*, **11**, 191–5.

Konner, M. (2005). Hunter-gatherer infancy and childhood: The !Kung and others. In: B. Hewlett and M. Lamb (eds.) *Hunter-Gatherer Childhoods: Evolutionary, Developmental and Cultural Perspectives*. New Brunswick, NJ: Aldine, pp. 19–64.

Konner, M. (2010). *The Evolution of Childhood*. Cambridge, MA: Belknap Press.

Kovach, B. and Da Ros-Voseles, D. (2008). *Being With Babies: Understanding and Responding to the Infants in Your Care*. Lewisville, NC: Gryphon House.

Lancy, D. (2014). *The Anthropology of Childhood*. New York: Oxford University Press.

Lansbury, J. (2014). *Elevating Child Care: A Guide to Respectful Parenting*. JLML Press, independently published and printed by CreateSpace.

Lawrence, A.V., and Narvaez, D. (2013). 'Psychopathology, ethical identity, and aggression'. Paper presented to the 39th annual international conference of the Association for Moral Education, University of Quebec at Montreal, Montreal, 24–26 November.

Lee, R.B. and Daly, R. (eds.) (2005). *The Cambridge Encyclopedia of Hunters and Gatherers*. New York: Cambridge University Press.

Lillard, A. and Else-Quest, N. (2006). Evaluating Montessori education. *Science*, **313**, 1893–4.

Louv, R. (2016). *Vitamin N: The Essential Guide to a Nature-Rich Life*. Chapel Hill, NC: Algonquin Books.

McMullen, M.B., Buzzelli, C., and Yun, N.R. (2015). Pedagogies of care for wellbeing. In: T. David, S. Powell, and K. Goouch (eds.) *Routledge Handbook of Philosophies and Theories of Early Childhood Education*. London: Taylor & Francis, pp. 259–68.

McMullen, M.B. and McCormick, K. (2016). Flourishing in transactional care systems: Caring with infant toddler caregivers about wellbeing. In: D. Narvaez, J. Braungart-Rieker, L. Miller, L. Gettler, and P. Hastings (eds.) *Contexts for Young Child Flourishing: Evolution, Family and Society*. New York: Oxford University Press.

Meaney, M.J. (2001). Maternal care, gene expression, and the transmission of individual differences in stress reactivity across generations. *Annual Review of Neuroscience*, **24**, 1161–92.

Miller, A. (1983/1990). *For Your Own Good: Hidden Cruelty in Child-Rearing and the Roots of Violence*. New York: Noonday Press.

Montessori, M. (1966). *The Secret of Childhood*. New York: Ballantine Books.

Morelli, G., Ivey Henry, P., and Foerster, S. (2014). Relationships and resource uncertainty: Cooperative development of Efe hunter-gatherer infants and toddlers. In: D. Narvaez, K. Valentino, A. Fuentes, J. McKenna, and P. Gray (eds.) *Ancestral Landscapes in Human Evolution: Culture, Childrearing and Social Wellbeing*. New York: Oxford University Press, pp. 69–103.

Narvaez, D. (2005). The Neo-Kohlbergian tradition and beyond: Schemas, expertise, and character. In: G. Carlo and C. Pope-Edwards (eds.) *Nebraska Symposium on Motivation*, vol. 51: *Moral Motivation Through the Lifespan*. Lincoln, NE: University of Nebraska Press, pp. 119–63.

Narvaez, D. (2008). Human flourishing and moral development: Cognitive science and neurobiological perspectives on virtue development. In: L. Nucci and D. Narvaez (eds.) *Handbook of Moral and Character Education*. Mahwah, NJ: Erlbaum, pp. 310–27.

Narvaez, D. (2013). The 99 percent—development and socialization within an evolutionary context: Growing up to become 'A good and useful human being'. In: D. Fry (ed.) *War, Peace, and Human Nature: The Convergence of Evolutionary and Cultural Views.* New York: Oxford University Press, pp. 643–72.

Narvaez, D. (2014). *Neurobiology and the Development of Human Morality: Evolution, Culture and Wisdom.* New York: Norton.

Narvaez, D. (2015). The co-construction of virtue: Epigenetics, neurobiology and development. In: N.E. Snow (ed.) *Cultivating Virtue.* New York: Oxford University Press, pp. 251–77.

Narvaez, D. (2016). *Embodied Morality: Protectionism, Engagement and Imagination.* New York: Palgrave-Macmillan.

Narvaez, D. and Bock, T. (2014). Developing expertise and moral personalities. In: L. Nucci, D. Narvaez, and T. Krettenauer (eds.) *Handbook of Moral and Character Education*, 2nd edn. New York: Routledge, pp. 140–58.

Narvaez, D., Gettler, L., Braungart-Rieker, J., Miller-Graff, L., and Hastings, P. (2016a). The flourishing of young children: Evolutionary baselines. In: D. Narvaez, J. Braungart-Rieker, L. Miller, L. Gettler, and P. Harris (eds.) *Contexts for Young Child Flourishing: Evolution, Family and Society.* New York: Oxford University Press, pp. 3–27.

Narvaez, D. and Gleason, T. (2013). Developmental optimization. In: D. Narvaez, J. Panksepp, A. Schore, and T. Gleason (eds.) *Evolution, Early Experience and Human Development: From Research to Practice and Policy.* New York: Oxford University Press, pp. 307–25.

Narvaez, D., Gleason, T., Wang, L., Brooks, J., Lefever, J., Cheng, A., and Centers for the Prevention of Child Neglect (2013a). The evolved development niche: Longitudinal effects of caregiving practices on early childhood psychosocial development. *Early Childhood Research Quarterly*, 28(4), 759–73.

Narvaez, D., Hastings, P., Braungart-Rieker, J., Miller-Graff, L., and Gettler, L. (2016b). Young child flourishing as an aim for society. In: D. Narvaez, J. Braungart-Rieker, L. Miller, L. Gettler, and P. Hastings (eds.) *Contexts for Young Child Flourishing: Evolution, Family and Society.* New York: Oxford University Press, pp. 347–59.

Narvaez, D., Panksepp, J., Schore, A., and Gleason, T. (eds.) (2013b). *Evolution, Early Experience and Human Development: From Research to Practice and Policy.* New York: Oxford University Press.

Narvaez, D., Panksepp, J., Schore, A., and Gleason, T. (2013c). The value of using an evolutionary framework for gauging children's well-being. In: D. Narvaez, J. Panksepp, A. Schore, and T. Gleason (eds.) *Evolution, Early Experience and Human Development: From Research to Practice and Policy.* New York: Oxford University Press, pp. 3–30.

Narvaez, D., Thiel, A., Kurth, A., and Renfus, K. (2016c). Past moral action and ethical orientation. In: D. Narvaez (ed.) *Embodied Morality: Protectionism, Engagement and Imagination.* New York: Palgrave-Macmillan, pp. 99–118.

Narvaez, D., Wang, L., and Cheng, A. (2016). Evolved developmental niche history: Relation to adult psychopathology and morality. *Applied Developmental Science*, 4, 294–309, http://dx.doi.org/10.1080/10888691.2015.1128835.

Narvaez, D., Wang, L., Gleason, T., Cheng, A., Lefever, J., and Deng, L. (2013d). The evolved developmental niche and sociomoral outcomes in Chinese three-year-olds. *European Journal of Developmental Psychology*, 10(2), 106–27.

National Association for the Education of Young Children (2009a). 'Developmentally Appropriate Practice in Early Childhood Programs Serving Children From Birth Through Age 8', retrieved 25 February 2015, https://www.naeyc.org/positionstatements/dap, accessed 12 Mar 2018.

National Association for the Education of Young Children (2009b). '3 Core Considerations of DAP', retrieved 25 February 2015, https://www.naeyc.org/dap/3-core-considerations, accessed 12 Mar 2018.

National Institute of Child Health and Human Development, Early Child Care Research Network (2003). Does amount of time spent in child care predict socioemotional adjustment during the transition to kindergarten? *Child Development*, 74(4), 976–1005.

Panksepp, J. (2007). Can PLAY diminish ADHD and facilitate the construction of the social brain. *Journal of the Canadian Academy of Child and Adolescent Psychiatry*, 10(2), 57–66.

Porges, S.W. (2011). *The Polyvagal Theory: Neurophysiological Foundations of Emotions, Attachment, Communication, and Self-Regulation*. New York: Norton.

Rinaldi, C (2012). The pedagogy of listening: The listening perspective from Reggio Emila. In: C. Edwards, L. Gandini, and G. Forman (eds.) *The Hundred Languages of Children: The Reggio Emilia Experiences in Transformation*, 3rd edn. New York: Praeger, pp. 233–46.

Schore, A. (1994). *Affect Regulation*. Hillsdale, NJ: Erlbaum.

Seldin, T. (2006). *How to Raise an Amazing Child the Montessori Way*. New York: DK Publishing.

Slusser, W. and **Powers, N.G.** (1997). Breastfeeding update 1: Immunology, nutrition, and advocacy. *Pediatrics in Review*, 18(4), 111–19.

Spitz, R. (1947). *Grief: A Peril In Infancy* [DVD]. University Park, PA: Pennsylvania State.

Talan, J. (2010). Serotonin abnormalities confirmed in sudden infant death. *Neurology Today*, 10(5), 14–15.

Trevarthen, C. (2005). Stepping away from the mirror: Pride and shame in adventures of companionship—Reflections on the nature and emotional needs of infant intersubjectivity. In: C.S. Carter, L. Ahnert, K.E. Grossmann, S.B. Hrdy, M.E. Lamb, S.W. Porges, and N. Sachser (eds.) *Attachment and Bonding: A New Synthesis*. Cambridge, MA: MIT Press, pp. 55–84.

Trevathan, W.R. (2011). *Human Birth: An Evolutionary Perspective*, 2nd edn. New York: Aldine de Gruyter.

Twenge, J. and **Campbell, R.** (2009). *The Narcissism Epidemic: Living in the Age of Entitlement*. New York: Free Press.

Wagner, M. (2006). *Born in the USA: How a Broken Maternity System Must Be Fixed To Put Women and Children First*. Berkeley, CA: University of California Press.

Walker, M. (1993). A fresh look at the risks of artificial infant feeding. *Journal of Human Lactation*, 9, 97–107.

Watson, J.B. (1928). *Psychological Care of Infant and Child*. New York: Norton.

Chapter 7

Children's aesthetic agency:
The pleasures and power of imagination

Pauline von Bonsdorff

Introduction

In the 1890s a little girl visited her aunts' home in the Finnish inland town of Jyväskylä. She did not know them well, but her parents wished for her to get to know them better, and so did the aunts. They were spinsters and daughters of a priest, and on Sunday they took her to church. The girl had grown up on the monolingual (in Swedish) Åland islands and understood next to nothing of the Finnish sermon. Back at home they asked her, 'Now, Nadine, what did the priest say?' The girl was silent. The question was repeated, and it was evident that silence was not an acceptable answer. 'Now, what did the priest say?' 'He said, he said ... ,' whispered the girl, then raising her voice with hope, 'he said that our Lord is good!' 'You made that up yourself!' was the judgement.

Probably Nadine had lied in order to save her skin, if also to adjust her behaviour towards what was expected of her. As she did not know precisely what she was supposed to say, she invented a likely answer, using her imagination. With the best of intentions, and in a situation of distress, she came up with a white lie and ended up being ashamed.

In this chapter I discuss the relevance of imagination and play for children's well-being from a humanities perspective, where well-being implies cultural agency, human growth, trust, recognition, and participation, in addition to health and development. I am especially interested in how children create and articulate relationships and position themselves socially through play and imagination. The fact that children are subject to rules set by adults and adult power must be taken into account in any discussion of their creative imagination. I discuss imagination in its social contexts on the one hand through the 'mimetic practices' of lying, a form of imagining that is often socially motivated, and on the other hand through the creation of imaginary worlds.

I look at children's play from the perspective of aesthetics and the philosophy of art, and I suggest that these disciplines, which today include only marginal references to childhood and children, can contribute to broadening our understanding of the ontological and existential role of play and imagination in children's lives, and in our own. Childhood, however, demands the renewal and updating of traditional philosophical concepts, and helps us discover the continuity that runs from aesthetic communication in early childhood through imaginative play to art. I introduce 'aesthetic agency' and 'mimetic practices' as conceptual tools that illuminate children's engagement, exploration, and transformation of their life-worlds, and argue that a strict dichotomy between true and false is not helpful in this context. Furthermore, I suggest that engagement and participation are more fruitful than observation as strategies for understanding what goes on in children's play. This also motivates my use of literary narratives.

The existential aesthetics of childhood

That human life in childhood is playful, social, and active is not a new observation, but one that has gained renewed attention in psychology, sociology, and other fields at least since the 1970s. Empirical research with new methods has opened fresh perspectives on what goes on in children's play and communication (Donaldson 1981; Taylor 1999; Corsaro 2003; Reddy 2008; Gopnik 2009; Malloch and Trevarthen 2009). While even the youngest children are now seen as competent social actors, and imagination is valued as a central cognitive resource (Harris 2000; Dutton 2009), one can sometimes detect a bias towards the instrumental value of imagination. Thus, through Alison Gopnik's (2009) account of children's minds, one becomes reassured that the imaginative young child will probably develop into a focused, practical adult. The juxtaposition of the child and the adult is problematic, as is a reduction of imagination to rational capacities, important as they are.

It is necessary to reflect upon what is good for children from the point of view of provisions. But it is my belief that we also need to think about what they find good and interesting to do—about their point of view, situation, and intentions. This is a perspective that childhood studies has advocated for some decades now. Instead of seeing children as 'becomings' in need of protection, the idea is to look at them as 'beings' in their own right, whereby the focus is switched from children's futures to their present lives (e.g. Qvortrop, Corsaro, and Honig 2009). The 'existential aesthetics' of childhood that I propose combines findings from psychological research on young children with impulses from childhood studies. Despite coming from different traditions, these fields share the view that children are intelligent, socially active, and culturally contributing persons. To this, aesthetics and the philosophy of art can contribute with insights about the magnitude of our imagination and its versatile use. In addition, art is meaningful only in human contexts and needs to be understood from within a context. The same goes for children and childhood. To understand children and childhood we need to engage with them (cf. Berleant 1991) rather than just observe.

The aesthetics of childhood and childhood aesthetics

The academic discipline of aesthetics, which for a long time dealt primarily with questions related to the arts, has in the near past broadened its scope. This development is related to a turn towards the roots of aesthetics in eighteenth-century thought. As Terry Eagleton (1990, p. 13) wrote, 'Aesthetics is born as a discourse of the body'. When the term was introduced in the mid-eighteenth century, it was designated 'sensory knowledge'. In his first treatise on the matter, Alexander Baumgarten discussed poetry as a field where this kind of knowledge is at play: it operates with 'sensible imagery', clear but 'confused' images, and has the power to affect its audience emotionally (Guyer 2014). For the purpose of this chapter, it is important to see the full implications of the aesthetic as a synthetic mode of embodied thought, involving senses, emotions, values, imagination, and reflection in activity, and being about particular, individual objects and purposes rather than generalities.

Instead of seeing aesthetic qualities as narrowly defined and specific, or aesthetic appreciation as a connoisseurs' approach that is not available to the uneducated, it is more fruitful to conceive the aesthetic mode as an opening of our minds towards phenomena of our life-world in its various dimensions, whether material or immaterial (such as experiences, memories, and ideas). It includes sensuousness and pleasure (or displeasure), felt qualities, active imagination, and reflection (von Bonsdorff 1998, pp. 58–98). With such an approach we need not draw a line between the arts and their sister phenomena. It lends itself well to an analysis of the 'lantern consciousness' of childhood (Gopnik 2009, p. 129) and is similar to how Iain McGilchrist (2009) describes the work of the right brain hemisphere, which he claims is the locus of values.

If the aesthetics of childhood designates a field of academic aesthetics (von Bonsdorff 2009), then childhood aesthetics refers to its object: the aesthetic dimension of children's life. This dimension may be evident, as childhood is almost, by definition (Bachelard 1999), a period of play and rich imaginings. Infancy research has brought to light the 'communicative musicality' of babies, to use Stephen Malloch's and Colwyn Trevarthen's (2009) telling book title. Rhythm in movement is fundamental to human beings, who, right after birth, turn towards others and communicate in multimodal and highly expressive ways. There is a striking similarity between aesthetic concepts (Sibley 2001) and the dynamic movements common to infants and performing artists (Stern 2010).

Vocal exchanges between infants and their caregivers have been analyzed as musical narratives. This indicates that something that can be remembered is created: infants do not live in the moment only. We might also remember that they are brought up with various practices of play and imagination, such as tickling, peekaboo, and personal greetings, not to speak of songs, narratives, pictures, and objects. These are initially part of shared situations; later, they animate the child's world and afford company even without the presence of other persons (Taylor 1999; Mazokopaki and Kugiumutzakis 2009). Imagination and creativity step in early: it is easier to see continuities than to define a point beyond which they do not exist.

In childhood aesthetics the focus lies on expressive and embodied agency, communication, and performance rather than on objects. Next, I describe its interactive character.

Aesthetic agency

Many authors have noticed children's active and transforming relationship to stories, images, and songs (e.g. Rönnberg 1989; Thompson 2006). This relationship is not very well accommodated by traditional aesthetic theory, where the dominant paradigm is one of non-interference with the work. John Dewey, whose philosophy of art remains one of the most pragmatically oriented, observes that 'artistic' refers to the making of art and 'esthetic' (as he spells it) to enjoyment and reception, and points out that 'the absence of a term designating the two processes taken together is unfortunate' (Dewey 1980, p. 46). Dewey looks at art from the point of view of experience, and emphasizes that aesthetic experience is both active and passive, 'doing and undergoing'. I suggest that the term 'aesthetic agency' can fulfil the function Dewey pointed to.

The aesthetic mode of childhood is typically not one of either contemplative reception or creative production, but rather both at once, in sensuous activity. Aesthetic agency, then, is co-creative, multimodal, and social. First, children engage and interact with works through participation and co-creation, whether in imagination or in play, performing actions and impersonating characters. They often continue on stories and integrate them in their play, as they do with elements from their life-world. Second, in addition to merging the aesthetic and the artistic, children's aesthetic agency is characterized by multimodality. Different expressive media are used simultaneously: children sing while playing, talk while drawing, move while talking, and so forth, probably because they are involved in the creation of imaginary worlds which, as such, are multimodal. Third, childhood aesthetic agency is typically social and intersubjective: it involves the meeting of people rather than of one person and a work.

Aesthetic agency is a way of practising imagination: exploring the world and creating possibilities. It is then important to be precise about what we mean by imagination. While some authors describe it first and foremost as an active exploration and testing of ideas (e.g. Currie and Ravenscroft 2002), others suggest that it is less volitional. Gaston Bachelard's (1999) 'reverie' is of the latter kind, and while aesthetic agency is not confined to lonely daydreaming, the sensuous, emotional, and receptive aspects of imagination are certainly part of it. Imagination is probably best seen as both intuitive and non-volitional and animated by the subject. On both ends it makes visible the reflective, self-aware component of aesthetic agency.

In childhood studies, agency has been a central, if also a debated, concept. As Alison James (2009) writes, the idea that children are social actors rather than merely the subject of various influences was one of its starting points. She maintains that agency represents a 'more developed and rounded conception of what it means to act', for as compared to a social actor, an agent has a wider influence on social and cultural structures (James 2009, p. 41). Yet in the context of play and aesthetic agency, 'agent' is different from 'actor' in other ways too. The analogy of children who play and actors who perform a play on stage is relevant. Agency suggests more goal-directed and focused action, and may fail to do justice to the improvisational and context-sensitive character of play. But depending on context, we need to be aware of children as both actors and agents.

Making sense and making self

I suggest that play, imagination, and aesthetic agency are neither contingent elements of childhood nor preliminary stages of a human mind in the making. Instead they are necessary parts of childhood, which is also the prime reason for characterizing child-hood aesthetics as existential. Play and imagination are ways of making sense and making self: ontologically and existentially relevant practices and modes whereby the child understands the world, creates a life-world, and makes herself visible in that world.

Children are often brought up with narratives and images that are fictive rather than real. Thus it is no wonder that a child places Father Christmas, the Tooth Fairy, and God in the same category: all of them are non-colloquial characters with a connection to specific rituals (cf. Taylor 1999, pp. 90–96). A young child has to trust pretty much what others say, as personal experience is limited and the checking of alternative sources may not be available. Because there are so many aspects in which the world is not given, imagination is a necessity in childhood. Knowledge has to be construed, and this concerns facts and theories as well as words and worlds. When one does not know, one has to imagine, and imagination is stimulated by themes that are important to one's companions. Curiosity and creativity go together: a will to explore and a will to create and contribute.

Play is, among other things, the sharing of imagination. Children's play is typically improvisational even when it has a declared theme. It is also constantly experimental, as contributions are accepted or rejected by playmates. Through play, meaning, structures, and intersubjective relationships are established, often simultaneously in the fictional world of play and in the real world. The participants appear to each other through play, and the self that is made is intersubjective and social, if also embodied.

Finally, an existential perspective on childhood can serve research purposes, where it helps to perceive the child as an individual in a particular situation and stage of life and think about what it would be like to be in that situation. This means that one lays aside normative and generalized ideas about childhood. Such a position can also be taken in engagements with children, where it means that one is 'with' the children, rather than 'above' them (cf. Corsaro 2003).

Mimetic practices: Varieties of social imagination

To demonstrate the manifold functions of aesthetic agency in childhood, I shall now discuss some literary and other examples of imaginative performances in children's lives. I call them 'mimetic practices', borrowing the idea of the 'mimetic dimension' from Jennifer Anna Gosetti-Ferencei (2014), who points out that '[o]ne does not simply 'pretend' a world, but may be subject to its evocation in an imaginative mode' (p. 437). A mimetic practice is the forging of an imaginary dimension, the introduction of elements that may be impossible in this world but possible in another world—a world that both reflects and is distinct from reality (cf. p. 427). The reciprocal influence of the one who imagines and his imaginings is important, but as I pointed out earlier, I consider this primarily as a form of agency where the child does something rather than is only subjected to imagination.

The examples I will shortly discuss can be seen as performative creations or transformations of worlds that, although fictive, are relatively lasting. The examples are meant to deepen our understanding of the complex issues that are involved in mimetic practices and imaginary worlds. I start with lying, a sister phenomenon of imagination, where the claim that something is either a lie or just play involves the use of power. As we shall see, lying is also highly performative and contextual as well as genuinely agentic. Next, I discuss the production of shared and secret imaginary worlds, characters, and idioms, and show that the mimetic dimension fulfils existential and social functions rather than only cognitive ones. I am especially interested in how mimetic practices perform and make visible the relationship between children and adults.

While this book focuses on early childhood, most of my examples are about slightly older children. I do not see this as a major problem, however, as the life of each child is a continuum. A nine-year-old does not emerge from nowhere in that age, but comes from a personal history and a cultural situation. Older children carry the experience of younger children. Additionally, my examples are both from real life and from literature. The advantage of novels is that incidents and behaviours are given a context, which provides the opportunity to reflect on the motivations behind them and their effects. Moreover, in culture for children, protagonists are often older than the audience, and as William Corsaro (2003, pp. 7–35) shows, age and size are not always valid criteria for young children to use in deciding whether someone is a child or an adult.

Lying and imagining

In the first book about Pippi Longstocking, published in 1945, the author, Astrid Lindgren, describes Pippi as a nine-year-old red-haired orphan who moves into a house that her father bought in a small Swedish town, with her monkey and her horse. She soon meets the neighbour's two well-behaved children, Tommy and Annika, and becomes their admired friend. On their first meeting, and in many subsequent scenes, Pippi lies, and admits it. 'It's naughty to lie', said Annika [...]. 'Yes, it's *very* naughty to lie', said Pippi even more sadly, 'but I forget it now and then, you see. And how can you really require that a little child whose mother is an angel and whose father is a Negro king can speak the truth all the time?' (Lindgren 1992, p. 14).

An interesting instance of lying occurs when Pippi is invited to join a coffee party hosted by Tommy's and Annika's mother (Lindgren 1992, pp. 133–41). When the ladies start complaining about their maids, Pippi supports them by providing a story about her grandmother's maid, Malin, who was even more impossible in every respect. Pippi's narrative is an attempt to make contact with the ladies, who close their ears, and a mocking of their bourgeois values. The exaggerated details of her story make clear that she improvises. Pippi's performative intervention has a critical, political function directed at the pettiness and hypocrisy of the adult world. Here, as elsewhere, one can see her imaginings as agency in the strong sense: by a strategy of showing rather than telling, she lures structures and values into the open. A strength shared by such performing and the arts is that they engage the imagination of their audience more fully than a straightforward argument. We have to reflect and decide for ourselves what this is about and how to judge it, and in the process we also reflect upon norms and values.

Lying is not Pippi's only 'vice'. She brags, eats a poisonous mushroom, misbehaves, and excels in non-normative child behaviour, including rescuing two boys from a fire that destroys their home while the fire brigade finds no means to act. She can do this, and carry her horse, and put two nasty boys in a tree, because she is stronger than the strongest man in the world; and she can live independently on account of the bag of gold coins her father gave her. At the same time she is an orphan who does not go to school, lives alone, and wears a dress she made herself. In her mixture of poverty and wealth, vulnerability and strength, lying and straightforwardness Pippi is a complex character living a difficult life.

Pippi is indeed a girl who does and says impossible things. Like some of her own claims, the story about her, taken literally, cannot be true. It is a fiction, a novel for children. Remembering that 'the boundary between truth and falsehood is a key one for assessing the nature of adult–child relations' (Ringrose 2006, p. 231), the impossibilities of the book and its defiance of the logic and mores of adult norms are significant. The author's voice does not take sides with the adult world against the child's. This is also true of the next example.

Like Pippi Longstocking, Pip in Charles Dickens' *Great Expectations* is an orphan, but more vulnerable.[1] Having lost his parents and five siblings he lives under his sister's terror—a state he shares with his sister's husband Joe, who is Pip's friend and the only person to provide safety in his childhood. There are several instances of socially motivated lies in the novel, both direct lies and silences to conceal the truth (cf. Bok 1979; Twain 2008), by children and adults alike.

Chapter nine of *Great Expectations* describes an elaborate scene involving lying, where Pip is interrogated by his sister and her ally, the unsympathetic Uncle Pumblechook, about his visit to the mysterious Miss Havisham, where he was invited to play (Dickens 1992, pp. 53–7). Unwilling to describe his 'perfectly incomprehensible' hostess, he finally takes to imagining the visit. He produces various extraordinary elements, such as 'a black velvet coach', 'cake and wine on gold plates', four 'immense' dogs, and playing with flags. As the novel's grown-up narrator, he describes his childhood self as 'a reckless witness under the torture' and thinks of himself 'with amazement'.

No less amazed is Joe, to whom Pip later that night reveals his lies. Through Joe, Dickens is able to remind the reader of the fear that a lying child might be 'possessed' and evil, and present a naively straightforward, good character who is even more childlike than a child. While Pip feels no 'penitence' about having lied to his sister, who is clearly an unsuitable guardian, he feels the need to tell the truth to Joe. By sharing Pip's perspective the novel suggests that social obligations work towards those whom we trust and love, because they are heartfelt duties, but that those who treat a child 'rudely' can expect no trust in return. Adults' exercise of power is not a given, but it can and should be critically assessed. If we want to communicate with children we must address them with respect and as individuals.

---

[1] Whether Lindgren made a reference to Dickens in naming her character is more than I know, but the homonymy looks like more than a coincidence, and there are other intertextual references in her book.

One reason that Pip lies concerns self-creation. In a couple of scenes he lies in order to appear braver than he actually is, and to boost his self-confidence (Dickens 1992, pp. 47, 67). The reasons for lying about the visit are more complicated. Questioned by Joe, he discloses a feeling of shame about his 'coarse hands', 'thick boots', and general commonness. Thus, while his interrogators' rudeness may have neutralized the duty to tell the truth, the fantasies rather arise from a need to create another world, one where Pip, unlike his sister and her pack, can live a life of pleasure in high society.

My last example of lying is about a childhood fantasy challenged by adults. Two 5-year-old cousins spent a summer as princesses, dressing in pastel cloths and wearing pearls and trinkets. Their uncle, a bearded middle-aged man, at some point felt he had heard enough about princesses and decided to tease his nieces: 'Yes, you are princesses, but not *real* princesses. I am a *real* princess. Real princesses have a beard!' The girls tried to deny this but were not sure about the facts. The debate went on. Then finally, when asked in a video-taped interview by her uncle's friend whether her uncle was a real princess, one of the girls said, 'Well, *maybe* he is a real princess, but he is the ugliest princess of all!'

Here, one adult challenges the children by telling an untruth—whether a fantasy or a lie. Another adult fails a child's trust by making an interview that eventually results in deep regret on her part, possibly because she is lured into making a private reflection public and thereby weakens her own argument. On the positive side, the grown-ups engage with the world of imagination by recognizing the girls as princesses, albeit not genuine ones. They enter the play-world, influence its rules by raising a novel question, and disturb its harmony. They confirm the play-world but also change it in a direction its original creators did not wish. Again, the example shows how complicated it is to judge whether an act is one of playing, lying, or imagining.

Two of the examples of lying I have discussed take place in a work of fiction, while the last one is about the structure of an imaginary world. Next, I shall deepen the discussion of the 'mimetic dimension' by focusing on the functions of imaginary worlds and how they are created.

Imaginary worlds

When children hesitate about accepting a new child in a play, the reason is not necessarily that they are hostile to the newcomer or ungenerous. Often the reason is that they do not want their play to be interrupted but want to 'keep sharing' (Corsaro 2003, pp. 38–47). Playing can indeed be seen as the co-crafting and elaborating of narratives. Like other mimetic practices, it is a serious undertaking, easily disturbed and destroyed. And if play can be shared, it is also a phenomenon that may need to be protected.

A recent novel by Fredrik Backman (2013) tells the story of the 'nearly eight-year-old' Elsa, a child who, like Pip and Pippi, is vulnerable. Elsa's fundamental vulnerability is her 'difference': she is bullied in school and her only friend, as the story begins, is her grandmother. The grandmother is a different person, too: a doctor, now in her 70s, who was exceptionally functional in crisis situations but has problems with people in everyday life, due to her unconventional behaviour. A central ingredient in the novel is the story-world shared by Elsa and her grandmother. It comprises seven kingdoms in the Land of Almost-Awake, with a history and characters, it turns out, that are modelled on the people in the apartment house where they live and who all share part of their history with Elsa's grandmother.

The story really starts unfolding after the grandmother dies. She has left letters in strange places, as a complicated treasure-hunt for Elsa to find, but addressed to the neighbours, whom she asks, one by one, to forgive her. In this process past events, many of them traumatic, surface, and the identities of the neighbours, as well as social relationships, change. The fantasy world and the real world are simultaneous, and the neighbours are both real neighbours and characters in the fantasy. The fantasy is truly a mimetic *world*—and like reality, both in being not fully known, but full of possibility, and in having a future in addition to a past. The reader gradually learns that the fantasy was first created by the grandmother for Elsa's mother and her friend, then developed with another child, then continued with and for Elsa. Finally, when Elsa's brother is born, she promises the baby to tell him all the stories, and an eighth kingdom is about to take shape. The *longue durée* of the fantasy, its generational and societal—vertical and horizontal—broadening, is significant. Throughout the novel the fantasy constitutes a support for Elsa—a space to inhabit and a place to grow.

In Backman's novel imagination and secrets are connected and constitute a dimension that is parallel to what we commonly call reality, and no less real (cf. Van Manen and Levering 1996). Initially, the fantasy world appears to be an elaborate shared secret between the grandmother and Elsa, but as the story unfolds it becomes clear that this world has been shared with others, too. It has been a way to articulate and communicate issues that may be hard to deal with: the grandmother asks forgiveness about events where she has done her best, but not enough. As a secret, the fantasy provides shelter and intimacy for what we may see as affective debts between persons. In a sense, her last deed (asking forgiveness) is a catalyst for new moments where she continues to influence others while her life has actually ended. While the unfolding of the fantasy, in its relationship to reality, mediates intersubjective understanding, this is largely dependent on individual perspectives. Thus, there is a sense in which the neighbours perform for Elsa as persons in a dream who do not know that they are part of it. We also realize that people's identities are not always outwardly visible.

Many of the characters in the novel accept the mimetic dimension. One of them, whom Elsa recognizes as 'Wolf heart' of the fantasy, even knows Elsa's and her grandmother's secret language; it is, in fact, his mother's tongue. Secrets, silence, and concealment are further thematized through Elsa's true friend, the big dog she calls the *wors*, and the 'boy with the syndrome', who is just a little younger than Elsa. She communicates with them through offering food and shelter: both love the kind of cookies that are called 'dreams'.

Imagination in the novel is both reproductive and productive: it enables understanding and communication between the characters, yet also creates something entirely new in several senses. There is the alternative, parallel world of fantasy, but also the new beginnings of shared life in the house that are opened up through novel perspectives. The fantasy provides shelter for Elsa but also the pleasure and power of being a narrator, a creator of a world. Elsa is also an avid reader of fantasy, and so the book about her is a comment on reading and imagination. Pippi Longstocking can be seen in a similar light. The life of her friends is uneventful, but Pippi is adventure: she brings in fun and opens windows to the world outside the little town, telling them that people walk backwards in other places. Pippi might be construed as an imaginary companion of Tommy and Annika. On another level her father, her horse, and her monkey are like the imaginary companions of an orphaned, lonely girl. Finally Pippi, like other fictional characters, is the imaginary companion of generations of readers, remembered in friendship even after they grew up.

Discussion

I would like to add some critical reflections on the relationship between imagining and lying, and the hierarchies that are involved in rejecting or accepting children's imaginations. In his essay, 'On truth and lying in a non-moral sense', Friedrich Nietzsche (1999) radically questions established notions of truth and untruth. From the point of view of experiencing and constructing one's life-world, truth is, suggests Nietzsche, 'dead metaphor'—a perception of the world that once was significant but has become mere convention. Nietzsche instead favours the living metaphors that are born when an individual encounters reality and articulates this meeting in a novel way. This reminds us of how Maurice Merleau-Ponty (1995) describes children's use of language or drawing: the aim is not to depict a world that exists independently of the child, but to convey the meeting of oneself with the object. Furthermore, as our examples indicate, the expression of a child is not innocent or isolated but makes a point in a particular situation and context. If respect for the individual articulation of self and world is one reason to respect imagination, another is the concern for a more equal and creative social community, where people listen to each other regardless of age.

Mark Twain (2008) pointed out that lying is ubiquitous in social life, and while 'courteous lying is a sweet and loving art', injurious lies are not acceptable (pp.7–8). This indicates the relevance of intentions and functions of lying. The intention of telling something that is not true may not simply or primarily be to deceive, to harm, or even to derive an unjust advantage for oneself. Here we enter the field of social imagination, described in the examples above, where a person, by using a mimetic strategy as part of a group, can influence the understanding and values within that group as well as her own position. When looked upon in a non-moral way, lying is a capacity and a performative act that can change contexts and themes, move the discussion to a different level, and, by providing new perspectives, set issues differently. From this perspective imagining, lying, and dreaming can be seen as forms of utopian thought (Bloch 1989; cf. Rönnberg 1989, pp. 12, 188) where the awareness of the possibility that things were different, or oneself someone else, can provide a sense of freedom—as it did for Pip.

Deciding about the status of a communication as true, false, or playful through accepting or rejecting an invitation to imagine involves the exercise of power. It is easy to marginalize others' imaginations, but they can also be taken up and elaborated; in children's play, negotiations about imaginary worlds and narratives go on constantly. In the relationship between adults and children, judging about the status of imaginary constructs is more serious, for it is connected to, or even constitutive of, what Leena Alanen (2009) calls the generational order—the structural relationship between adults (such as teachers or parents) and children in modern society (pp. 161–2; cf. Rönnberg 1989). The strict dichotomy between true and false—that is, the idea that mental constructs belong in one category but not in both—is a pillar of adult hegemony, and often used to dismiss children's communications as unreal, unimportant, or 'nonsense'. Pippi Longstocking violates the generational order by performing childhood in subversive ways. To use Alanen's phrasing, she disregards her '"obligations" … as a dependent being by taking to autonomous living' (Alanen 2009, p. 169). What is more, she does this intentionally, acting like a performer in an improvisational, experimental act of artistic intervention, and her behaviour is 'agentic' in having effects on the community.

In addition to the generational order, several other orders, borders, limits, and rules are involved, made and unmade, in children's play and imagination (cf. Evaldsson 2009, pp. 323–8). Curiosity is a recognized characteristic of children; according to Tyson E. Lewis (2012, pp. 88–114) it closely concerns democracy, the creative unmaking of any given order, and the redistribution of our perceptions—what Jacques Rancière also refers to as 'the poetic labour of translation' (Lewis 2012, p. 103). Children's aesthetic agency and mimetic practices—like the arts of adults—can be seen in terms of appropriations, mediations, and translations between one's own life-world and those of neighbours, in space or time. For Elsa, the fantasy initially created by her grandmother provides points of contact to people around her who turn out to be part of her life story, and access to her family history and new directions for its future. Margareta Rönnberg (1989, pp. 10–11) suggests that we look at culture for children with a view to its 'value and pleasure' *for them*; I suggest that we endorse a similar perspective on children's imaginations.

One interesting issue is finally the distinction between private and public, concealed and shared, which can be used to draw a line between play and imagination on the one hand, and art on the other. As Corsaro observed, play is sometimes protected from outsiders in order to safeguard its character. Personal and aesthetic integrity, as well as authorship, are involved in decisions about with whom to share an imaginary world, and imaginations are often shared secrets rather than either private or public. There is, however, a sense in which a child performs and acts also in playing alone, as indicated by talking or singing. Also, in such cases—as when a scholar mumbles in her study—there is a virtual audience of the performance or production: things are done with a view to how they appear. Even when not shared with others or with everyone, there is, then, a reflective element in play.

To approach truth and lying in a non-moral sense is to waive moral and cognitive judgement. This is extremely relevant for engagements with children, for normative judgements about lying are strong in education, and cognitive and developmental concerns risk narrowing our understanding of imagination to functionality and purpose. If we become too concerned with these aims, I argue, we miss the child's perspective because we step out from the relationship and look at it from outside, often focusing on future adults. In the company of narratives, and more generally in an aesthetic, imaginative mode, we (e.g. adults) can escape from the self-imposed obligation to assess and correct the behaviour of others (e.g. children). Making things up, imagining, including lying, are creative practices, albeit sometimes problematic—but so is always speaking the truth, as Twain emphasized. Furthermore, recognizing the aesthetic, mimetic creativity of children as a personal resource and a resource in communities has a bearing on how we look at human life generally. Perhaps the adult could become more imaginative, which was Nietzsche's point already.

References

Alanen, L. (2009). Generational order. In: J. Qvortrop, W.A. Corsaro, and M.S. Honig (eds.) *The Palgrave Handbook of Childhood Studies*. Basingstoke, UK/ New York: Palgrave Macmillan, pp. 159–74.

Bachelard, G. (1999). *La Poétique de la Rêverie*. Paris: Quadrige/Presses Universitaires de France.

Backman, F. (2013). *Min mormor hälsar och säger förlåt*. Stockholm: Forum.

Berleant, A. (1991). *Art and Engagement*. Philadelphia: Temple University Press.

Bloch, E. (1989). *The Utopian Function of Art and Literature: Selected Essays*, tr. J. Zipes and F. Mecklenberg. Cambridge: MIT Press.

Bok, S. (1979). *Lying: Moral Choice in Public and Private Life*. New York: Vintage Books.

Corsaro, W.A. (2003). *We're Friends, Right? Inside Kids' Culture*. Washington, DC: Joseph Henry Press.

Currie, G. and Ravenscroft, I. (2002). *Recreative Minds: Imagination in Philosophy and Psychology*. Oxford: Clarendon Press.

Dewey, J. (1980). *Art as Experience* (first published 1934). New York: Perigree.

Dickens, C. (1992). *Great Expectations* (first published 1860–61). Ware: Wordsworth Editions.

Donaldson, M. (1981). *Children's Minds*. Glasgow: Fontana/Collins.

Dutton, D. (2009). *The Art Instinct: Beauty, Pleasure, and Human Imagination*. New York: Bloomsbury.

Eagleton, T. (1990). *The Ideology of the Aesthetic*. Oxford/ Cambridge: Basil Blackwell.

Evaldsson, A.-C. (2009). Play and games. In: J. Qvortrop, W.A. Corsaro, and M.S. Honig (eds.) *The Palgrave Handbook of Childhood Studies*. Basingstoke, UK/ New York: Palgrave Macmillan, pp. 316–31.

Gopnik, A. (2009). *The Philosophical Baby. What Children's Minds Tell Us About Truth, Love, and the Meaning of Life*. New York: Farar, Straus, and Giroux.

Gosetti-Ferencei, J.A. (2014). The mimetic dimension: literature between neuroscience and phenomenology. *British Journal of Aesthetics*, **54**, 425–48.

Guyer, P. (2014). 18th Century German Aesthetics. In: E.N. Zalta (ed.) *The Stanford Encyclopedia of Philosophy* (Spring 2014 Edition), http://plato.stanford.edu/archives/spr2014/entries/aesthetics-18th-german/, accessed 14 Mar 2018.

Harris, P.L. (2000). *The Work of the Imagination*. Oxford: Blackwell.

James, A. (2009). Agency. In: J. Qvortrop, W.A. Corsaro, and M.S. Honig (eds.) *The Palgrave Handbook of Childhood Studies*. Basingstoke, UK/ New York: Palgrave Macmillan, pp. 34–45.

Lewis, T.E. (2012). *The Aesthetics of Education: Theatre, Curiosity, and Politics in the Work of Jacques Rancière and Paulo Freire*. New York/ London: Continuum.

Lindgren, A. (1992). *Pippi Långstrump* (facsimile edition of the first printing from 1945). Stockholm, Sweden: Rabén-and Sjögren.

McGilchrist, I. (2009). *The Master and his Emissary: The Divided Brain and the Making of the Western World*. New Haven, CT/ London: Yale University Press.

Malloch, S. and Trevarthen, C. (eds.) (2009). *Communicative Musicality: Exploring the Basis of Human Companionship*. Oxford: Oxford University Press.

Mazokopaki, K. and Kugiumutzakis, G. (2009). Infant rhythms: Expressions of musical companionship. In: S. Malloch and C. Trevarthen (eds.) *Communicative Musicality Exploring the Basis of Human Companionship*. Oxford: Oxford University Press, pp. 185–208.

Merleau-Ponty, M. (1995). *La prose du monde* (first published 1969). Paris: Gallimard.

Nietzsche, F. (1999). On truth and lying in a non-moral sense. In: R. Geuss and R. Speirs (eds.) *The Birth of Tragedy and Other Writings*. Cambridge: Cambridge University Press, pp. 141–53.

Qvortrop, J., Corsaro, W.A., and Honig, M.S. (2009). Why social studies of childhood? An introduction to the handbook. In: J. Qvortrop, W.A. Corsaro, and M.S. Honig (eds.) *The Palgrave Handbook of Childhood Studies*. Basingstoke, UK/ New York: Palgrave Macmillan, pp. 1–18.

Reddy, V. (2008). *How Children Know Minds*. Cambridge/ London: Harvard University Press.

Ringrose, C. (2006). Lying in children's fiction: Morality and the imagination. *Children's Literature in Education*, 37, 229–36.

Rönnberg, M. (1989). *Skitkul! Om sk skräpkultur*. Uppsala, Sweden: Filmförlaget.

Sibley, F. (2001). Aesthetic concepts (first published in 1959). In: J. Benson, B. Redfern, and J. Roxbee Cox (eds.) *Approach to Aesthetics: Collected Papers on Philosophical Aesthetics*. Oxford: Clarendon Press, pp. 1–24.

Stern, D.N. (2010). *Forms of Vitality: Exploring Dynamic Experience in Psychology, the Arts, Psychotherapy, and Development*. Oxford: Oxford University Press.

Taylor, M. (1999). *Imaginary Companions and the Children Who Create Them*. New York: Oxford University Press.

Thompson, C.M. (2006). The 'ket aesthetic': Visual culture in childhood. In: J. Fineberg (ed.) *When We Were Young: New Perspectives on the Art of the Child*. Berkeley, LA/ London: University of California Press, pp. 31–43.

Twain, M. (2008). On *the Decay of the Art of Lying* (first published in 1885). Auckland, New Zealand: The Floating Press

Van Manen, M. and Levering, B. (1996). *Childhood's Secrets: Intimacy, Privacy, and the Self Reconsidered*. New York/ London: Teachers College Press.

von Bonsdorff, P. (1998). *The Human Habitat: Aesthetic and Axiological Perspectives*. Lahti, Finland: International Institute of Applied Aesthetics. Available online: www.helsinki.fi/iiaa/publications/publication%20pdfs/von%20Bonsdorff_The_Human_Habitat.pdf, accessed 14 Mar 2018.

von Bonsdorff, P. (2009). Aesthetics of childhood—Phenomenology and beyond. *Proceedings of the European Society for Aesthetics*, 1, 60–76, http://proceedings.eurosa.org/1/vonbonsdorff2009.pdf, accessed 14 Mar 2018.

Chapter 8

The spiritual strengths of young children

Rebecca Nye

Introduction

Spirituality is a notoriously difficult area for academic study, theory building, and policy development. Yet for many, it refers to an essential area of human experience, representing an intuitive reality that is difficult to speak about, let alone explain, which complements more tangible, explicit forms of experience and knowledge. Spirituality has an elusive and implicit character, further complicated by having a range of claimants (e.g. religious, psychological, existentialist) offering their different explanatory frameworks. Thus, it is a challenging and exciting area of contemporary scholarship, which requires interdisciplinary and open-minded perspectives to glean what *may* pertain to it, rather than prematurely ruling out what *does not*.

Seeking to understand children's spirituality takes these challenges even further. It requires seeing the potential and validity of an ambiguous, perhaps dubious, subject matter in an open and inclusive way—beyond religious constructions, for example. It also depends on particularly generous ways of seeing the child, demanding both sensitivity to their life and setting aside of adult perceptual habits, in order to glimpse the qualities of children's experience. For centuries, this task of noticing the distinctive spiritual features of childhood was carried out by poets, such as Traherne, Wordsworth, Blake, and de la Mare. However, as this chapter describes, in the last two decades a variety of academic traditions have risen to these challenges, creating a more robust compendium of knowledge about children's spiritual strengths and needs, and a firmer basis for re-considering practices that can nurture these.

The first part of this chapter examines the characteristics of childhood spirituality suggested in theory and through research findings—notably, how spirituality in childhood has remarkable strengths and capacities. This resonates with a new determination in developmental psychology to identify children's abilities and differences, rather than their common limitations and deficiencies. Indeed, one of the clearest messages about children's spiritual life is that, quite naturally, it enjoys both quality and quantity, which are rarely sustained into adulthood, where more artificial or more effortful attentions seem required.

The second part of this chapter will explore the implications of these strengths: of children's arising spiritual needs. It will discuss how adults, education, and care environments might provide appropriate nurture and development in ways that value and encourage this potent, but fragile, area of childhood experience.

Spiritual strengths

An unparalleled 'kind of knowing'

The concept of spirituality has been much debated, supporting the conclusion that to define it too precisely endangers recognizing it at all (Sheldrake 2012). With children's spiritual life, it is perhaps an open 'recognition' approach that is most helpful to examining its qualities, rather than trying to apply a definitive identikit or formula. Examples, such as the one below, can often provide a more effective outline of the area intended, by enabling adults to recognize general parameters of childhood spiritual experience which may be both difficult for them to articulate, and distant in time. Conversely, a number of key studies of children's spiritual life have been based on adult recollection (Robinson 1983; Scott 2004), demonstrating the remarkable longevity of this aspect of a child's life in many cases. Thus, while it is difficult to define, a spiritual experience can be a definitive moment, precisely imprinted in memory.

> Despite the passing of five decades it is still vivid. I was four or five years old and staying with my grandmother when it happened. At bedtime I crawled up into my grandfather's bed since he was out of town. My grandmother had arthritis and walked with crutches, so when she got into bed she did so with difficulty and turned out the light. I remember the warm dark and the ticking clock.
>
> The clean sheets sheltered me. The familiar smell of the room made me feel safe. I felt so alive that my skin tingled. Muscles moved for the sheer pleasure of feeling their response. I stretched. Suddenly, as if a huge door opened in front of me, there was nothing there—absolute, lightless, nothing.
>
> 'Grandmother! Why do I have to die?'
>
> My grandmother's words have vanished over time, but her presence in the dark is still with me. She put me in touch with a larger presence that seems to grow to this day. This was my introduction to a kind of knowing that I did not learn at school or in Church. It is an ultimate kind of knowing that puts all other kinds of knowing into perspective.
>
> (Berryman 1990, p. 509)

Key features

Using the example above, it becomes possible to identify many of the fundamental features of child spirituality identified by empirical research, and recognized in theory.

- It can be evident in the *very young* child.
- It can be *a form of awareness*, a kind of knowing (but may also be a 'world view' or set of ideas).
- It is often *relational*: arising through, or drawing attention to, deep-rooted relationships between people or things.

- It can be highly *non-verbal*. It may have very little verbal representation, nor verbal stimulus.
- It can be highly *sensory,* and *within the body.*
- It can arise through *relatively ordinary* life experience (going to bed), not necessarily esoteric practices or events.
- It can be *natural*: not acquired through school or intentional teaching.
- It can be *acutely vivid* and powerful at the time.
- It can have a continuing *effect into adulthood.*
- It can provoke or be manifested in children exploring issues at the difficult *edges of understanding*: engaging with existential and unfathomable questions about death, aloneness, identity, freedom, purpose, and meaning.

Anticipating young children's spiritual strengths: Theoretical models

When applying a cognitive model of development, one might expect little spiritual capacity, let alone spiritual strengths, in early childhood. Lacking powers of complex reasoning, the use of abstraction, and fluency in linguistic and other representational thinking, as well as limitations in social understanding such as an incomplete 'theory of mind', young children would appear to be seriously under-resourced for engaging with spirituality's challenging, conceptual, and often relational kind of knowing and reflection.

However, by drawing on other models of development and reconsidering purposeful qualities of creative thought and awareness, the possibility of children's spiritual strengths becomes more apparent.

Psychodynamic models

Psychodynamic models traditionally highlight the significance and depth of early childhood experience. This period is said to be characterized by a more naked, direct interplay between conscious and unconscious processes than in adult life, when the rationalizing function of the Ego normally establishes dominance. This early freedom may provide children with a greater facility for non-literal conceptions, playful and fanciful excursions of the mind, and the emerging awareness of self through the exploration of significant relationships, especially in search of role models and authority figures (Freud 1923, 1924). Psychodynamic theory therefore implies that early childhood could be rather fertile ground for certain spiritual concepts to flourish (such as the idea of 'God' or transcendent power), as well as a period of heightened sensitivity to other spiritual concerns, such as existing both in relation to others and as an autonomous individual.

While Freud regarded adult religious feeling pathologically as unresolved Oedipal work, he credits its origins to the 'small child's long drawn out helplessness and need of help', and the child's perception of 'how truly forlorn and weak he is when confronted with the great forces of life' (Freud 1957, p. 123). Admittedly, this fails to portray a sense of children's *strength* and *joy*, but it does acknowledge a capacity for profound spiritual encounter in the normal, inevitable course of early child development, particularly in the child's experiences of power and vulnerability.

Freudian theory also provides the concept of 'oceanic feeling', referring to the purported experience of infants before their self has become distinguished from the external world. Without this sense of separation from external contexts, the infant's ego may enjoy a kind of paradisiacal state of oneness or unity. It is certainly possible to see parallels between the phenomenology of this infant state and that of mystical experience reported by adults (James 1916). Supporting this from a neuro-psychological perspective, Johnstone and Glass (2008) argue that spiritual experiences of unity and interconnection achieved by adults in meditation arise when awareness of time and space (governed by the right parietal lobe) is attenuated, which leads Surr (2012) to the view that infants may experience this state without effort. Indeed, Templeton and Eccles (2006) suggest that:

> if the goal of spiritual development is self-transcendence, new-borns are inherently spiritual beings. Many theories in psychology, such as attachment and ego psychology, imply that new-borns do not differentiate self from other and thus exist in a state of 'oneness'.
>
> (Templeton and Eccles 2006, p. 258)

However, these extrapolations from theory (and others below) face a difficult question: to what extent does a child need to be conscious of their spiritual experience for it to 'exist' or make an impact? Clearly, an articulate awareness *can* be a vital asset in spiritual perception and reflection, but is it necessary? Bone (2007), writing from the perspective of New Zealand's *Te Whāriki* early years philosophy, suggests not. She argues that this would unduly limit spirituality to a subjective and individualistic category, overlooking the ways in which this can also be manifest at interpersonal and collective levels of consciousness and unconsciousness. In my view, this aligns well with recent scholarship (such as Malloch and Trevarthen 2010, and Zeedyk 2006) concerning the significance of early relationships and intense emotional interconnection which babies and young children co-create with their carers, in which perhaps the strength the child brings is a propensity to a state unity and connectedness, whilst the adult's contribution can be information-rich intention and awareness.

Object relations theories also provide grounds for looking at the spiritual qualities inherent in early childhood experience. This is particularly clear in Winnicott's discussion of transitional space and the significance of 'transitional objects' (Winnicott 1971). Transitional objects are thought to function as a bridge between inner (subjective) experience and outer (objective) reality, the fusion of which affords an encounter with new meaning that is rich in both a sense of personal significance for the child and a sense of connection with the real world. When transitional objects operate in this way, they open up an intermediate area of experience: the 'transitional space'. That space, Winnicott argues, is the habitat for both play *and* religious experience involving symbols and rituals, since both function by way of the special meanings that capture the fusion, or engagement, of inner significance and outer sign. Thus, a child's natural capacity for symbolic play and use of transitional objects suggests a likely location for spiritually charged activity—a kind of sacred space. This view has been explicitly developed in Berryman's theory and methods pertaining to children's capacity for 'Godly Play' (Berryman 1995, 2013), in which deep engagement in narrative and opportunities for undirected creativity and play with objects are vital conduits for children's capacity for rich spiritual insight.

Psychosocial models

Erikson's psychosocial model of lifespan development offers a different perspective on the spiritual undertones present in early childhood, and has been further developed by Fowler to chart 'stages of faith' (Fowler 1995; Erikson 1998). The youngest child (0–18 months) is said to grapple with the issue of trust, mediated through consistent and caring attention from others, or its absence. When an underlying sense of trust—'it's going to be OK'—becomes established, the child has the resource of *hope*. However, when this fails to become established, the child is beset by hopelessness and mistrust of the world. This resonates with Berger's view that caregivers provide 'signals of transcendence' when comforting the very young by conveying a belief that 'all will be well' and a sense of 'ultimate goodness' in the face of immediate chaos or distress which can become part of the child's internal landscape (Berger 1970).

Slightly older children (18 months to 3 years) are said to wrestle with the conflict between autonomy and doubt as they explore and experience their agency in the world. Successful resolution at this stage is the establishment of a positive sense of *will*. In ordinary senses this stage can be easily recognized in outbursts and defiant tantrums when choices overwhelm them or their decisions are thwarted. But perhaps underlying this, children are implicitly dealing with the vast spiritual issue of free-will versus determinism. For young children this will take place at an emotionally charged, high level of personal significance, but with a paucity of language or concepts to represent and manage this. In contrast, adults can more easily adopt a philosophical distance about freedom/control and draw on formal or informal spiritual world views to manage their personal encounters with such questions. It follows, therefore, that this aspect of children's spiritual experience should be sought in a generous and careful analysis of their emotional highs and lows, and appreciation of the emotional complexity that includes 'pride' and 'shame'—far beyond the simple feelings of 'happy', 'sad', or 'angry'. To recognize that young children are instinctively grappling with matters of shame, pride, and doubt accepts that they are no strangers to some of the persistent categories of adult spiritual turmoil described in many spiritual traditions.

Still older children (aged three to five) face the tension between initiative and guilt, which, when positively resolved, can provide an inner sense of *purpose*—that 'what I do counts, matters, or has meaning'. Again, this psychological work has evident spiritual resonance since it suggests children are involved in a profound weighing up of their worth or worthlessness as they go about their everyday activities. This may be related to the concept of 'chuffedness' used by Tait (2004) as an indicator of well-being in pre-school. Importantly, 'chuffedness' is characterized as a relatively passing moment rather than a sustained state, and perhaps helps clarify that children's spiritual processing and insight, however deep-seated the theme, often occur in brief, easily missed moments.

Fowler's hypothetically religion-free 'faith development' theory (Fowler 1995; Fowler and Dell 2006) builds on Erikson's psychosocial model, and also on Kegan's developmental account of a capacity for meaning-making (Kegan 1982). Fowler expands on the significance and priority of emotional encounter in children aged around two to six years, proposing that this is characterized by an *intuitive-projective* faith style.

> Children attempt to form images that can hold and order the mixture of feelings and impressions evoked by their encounters with the newness of both everyday reality and the penumbra of mystery that surrounds and pervades it. Death becomes a conscious focus as a source of danger and mystery. Experiences of power and powerlessness orient children to a frequently deep existential concern about questions of security, safety, and the power of those on whom they rely for protection.
>
> (Fowler and Dell 2006, p. 38)

In this, imagination plays a central role as children seek out symbol, story, dream, and experience to give order and expression to their heightened emotional-spiritual sensitivity. In particular, they can be drawn to overt representations of good, evil, and supernatural power (monsters, devils, witches, fairies, angels, superheroes, and gods) to help them symbolize and engage with 'urges and impulses that both fascinate and disturb them' (Fowler and Dell 2006, p. 38). Thus children's pretend play and projective investment in particular stories or characters, as well as fears and fantasies, may provide windows through which to see some of their ample spiritual capacity and activity.

A working map of child spirituality

Hay and Nye (1996, 1998) offered another kind of theoretical contribution, which sought to provide a working map of the natural geography of child spirituality, from which their empirical investigation could proceed. Their model largely abstains from making developmental stage delineations, conscious of the fact that evidence points towards spirituality having an erratic or even inverted kind of development (e.g. Nye 1998, and Vianello, Tamminen, and Ratcliff 1992, discussed below). This grew out of Hay's influential studies of adult spiritual experience, which he found frequently occurs outside of social constructs, such as a religious world view.

Hay's position had been to argue that spiritual capacity and experience is a natural, 'innate' human characteristic, at least in potential (Hay 2006). This focused attention on how spiritual awareness could be present in childhood. It also coincided with the Education Act (1996) opting to keep the 'spiritual development of the child' as one of the cornerstones of the education system of England and Wales, which created considerable consternation and questioning about what this could look like in young children in contemporary British society (National Curriculum Council 1993; OFSTED 1994).

Hay and Nye's working map (1996, 1998) proposed three categories and nine subcategories of spiritual sensitivity that seemed plausibly within young children's grasp despite their cognitive limitations, and perhaps even primed by their other psychological characteristics (Table 8.1). It also took into consideration specific features traditionally

Table 8.1 Categories in a working map of children's spirituality

Awareness-sensing	Here and now	Tuning	Flow		Focusing
Mystery-sensing	Awe and wonder	Imagination			
Value-sensing	Delight and despair	Ultimate goodness	Meaning-making and -sensing		

identified in adult categorizations of spirituality and the need to accommodate the many forms spirituality might take, not only discrete experiences (Stark 1965, Watts and Williams 1988).

The category of '*awareness sensing*' and its sub-categories concentrates on the kind of awareness Donaldson (1992) refers to as the 'point mode', a basic mode of the mind's operation, hence available even to young children, and which is also sometimes (not necessarily) a gateway to the spiritual dimension of adult experience.

In everyday terms, this might be recognized in the capacity for a child to become 'transfixed in the moment', fully present to the *here and now*, temporarily impervious to past or future calls on their attention. It might also be evident in the experience of intimate identification between a child and some part of their environment, described by Schutz as *tuning in* (1964). Experiencing 'tuning in' as a childhood sensitivity to the natural world is a frequently mentioned memory in retrospective studies, as well as in poetry and biographies (Robinson 1983; Scott 2004). Csikszentmihalyi's concept of *flow* (Csikszentmihalyi 1990) represents the shift from concentrated attention to a specific task to a sense of liberation of effort, such that the activity appears to manage itself or seem managed by some kind of outside influence. It is experienced often as a kind of pleasure or grace. Children mastering a multitude of new skills, as simple as riding a bike or controlling a paintbrush, have ample opportunities for this potentially spiritual awareness gateway. Finally, young children's predilection for embodied knowing would seem to prime them for Gendlin's idea of 'felt-sense' and the quality of *focusing* that accompanies insight found through attention to how their bodies feel and react, in contrast to adults, for whom this source of information becomes a suppressed awareness in deference to the role of the mind as authority on knowledge of an out-of-body reality (Gendlin 1981).

A quality of transcendence is common in adult conceptualizations of spirituality, but it is not an obvious property of children's experience. The category of *mystery-sensing*, however, represents a way that children might come close to an awareness of transcendence, through encounters which are incomprehensible to them, and for which words cannot suffice. Children are intimately acquainted with ineffability and not knowing, and much less dismissive of its mysterious power than adults. But these moments can jolt against the usual mental processes of perceiving and organizing the patterns of experience, and can prize open the realization in children of their (and our) human limitations and 'tininess' at the same time as bringing into sharper focus the enormity of whatever they perceive to transcend themselves. The memory of the small boy quoted at the start of this chapter is a vivid example of this.

The mystery-sensing sub-category of 'wonder and awe' follows Otto's recognition of two kinds of encounter with 'ultimate mystery' (Otto 1950). *Wonder* is positively tinged fascination, while *awe* may be a negatively charged, fearful reaction. Crucially for children, the parameters of 'ultimate' mystery are likely to be quite different from those of adults. Apparently explicable events (for modern-world adults), such as the twinkling of a star or birth of a sibling or pet, could constitute occasions for wonder or awe, and stimulate further questions and feelings of real significance even if their root material is far from 'really' mysterious. Similarly, children are experts at transcending mundane experience through *imagination*, the second of Hay and Nye's mystery-sensing sub-categories. Experiencing mystery requires some imagination to conceive what is beyond the known and what is 'obvious'. Studies of children's ability to enter into fantasy shows they have a powerful capacity for (and enjoyment of) semi-detaching their inner self-awareness from material reality, and using imagination to discover meanings and depths in response to their life experiences, especially experience for which their current language is inadequate (Cohen and MacKeith 1991; Rosengren et al. 2000).

'Value-sensing' is a term used by Donaldson (1992), pertaining to the progression from self-centred emotion to an experience of deeper value, which transcends purely personal concerns. Clearly, the conscience or moral sense of children is implicated here, but perhaps in a way that is prior to, and more profound than, the kind of cognitive moralizing described in Kolhberg's model of moral development (Kolhberg 1984).

The sub-categories of *delight* and *despair* address the degree to which value-sensing can have an acute and intense impact on an individual, as well as its capacity to progress into something much more than the original stimulus necessarily indicated, such as the startling delight taken from a reflection in a puddle or the crashing despair arising from a broken friendship. Young children's lives seem prepared for moments of delight and despair, where apparently ordinary experiences causing happiness or sadness can escalate, partly thanks to their cognitive immaturity and loose grip on reasoning about their reactions. This can give rise to a progression to some kind of wider, potentially ultimate, vision or concern such as a more wide-reaching sense of '*joie de vivre*' or the sanctity of living things (delight), or an overwhelming sense of nihilism or chaos, not merely in themselves but in the world around them (despair).

To have a sense of *ultimate goodness* may seem beyond the capacity of young children since they lack sufficient comparative data to distinguish 'ordinary' goodness from something beyond that. However, as mentioned previously, Berger (1970) suggests that the instinctively comforting actions and languages which carers transmit to children from the earliest age can convey a sense of ultimate order, pattern, and 'good' in the face of a child's imminent experience of chaos and 'bad'. This means that an emerging awareness of ultimate goodness depends on having some experiences of less intensive protection from carers through which the child can discern the limits of 'ordinary' goodness. Gradual exposure to the limitations of human capacity and experience of good enough, but not *perfectly* good, care, as well as the reality of conditional love inherent in boundary setting, may be crucial in the child's reaching towards an intuitive sense of the existence of unbounded goodness and love which surpasses this, and transcends the 'merely' moral good.

Lastly, the sub-category of '*meaning-making/-sensing*' gives credit to the fact that this is an irrepressible feature of early childhood—a fundamental urge to search for, make, or unexpectedly find underlying connections. This includes meaning-making/-sensing about themselves, such as, 'Who am I?', 'Where do I belong?', 'To whom or what am I connected or responsible?', and 'What is my purpose?'. This experience also encompasses the sense of reward, value, or at least stimulation that arises from trying to do this.

For some researchers, meaning-making is regarded as a principal category (Erricker and Erricker 1996; Hyde 2008). However, in Hay and Nye's model, it is a sub-category because it could represent an unduly cognitive endeavour, limiting attention to the other landmarks in the geography of young children's spirituality. Arguably, these more cognitive signs of potentially spiritual thought are *secondary* products, arising from awareness sensing, mystery sensing, and the other two sub-categories of value-sensing. Children, at least, must regularly enjoy something like what James termed 'noetic' experience (James 1916), a kind of 'penny-dropping' event in which meaning or understanding of something seems to suddenly appear as if from nowhere, like a gift and with a curious sense of authority and truth, but which is also normally beyond articulation.

Research evidence of spiritual strengths: Emerging concepts and debates

Attempts to study children's spirituality empirically are fraught with methodological and epistemological challenges. Initially, most evidence relied on adult retrospection which at least confirmed that childhood was a far from barren spiritual period, with more than 20% of adults choosing a childhood experience as the most salient spiritual moment in their whole lives (Robinson 1983). Since the 1990s, researchers have employed a variety of approaches to studying children's spirituality directly, through interviews, surveys, *in-situ* observations, and mosaic techniques (Ratcliff and Nye 2006). Some common themes have emerged from these studies, which extend the impression of spiritual strengths already suggested in the theoretical contributions above.

Privilege of the young

Using a survey and interview approach, Finnish researcher Kalevi Tamminen explored religious and spiritual issues with more than 1,000 people aged between seven years and adulthood (Tamminen 1991; Vianello, Tamminen, and Ratcliff 1992). In response to a question about whether respondents had ever had what they felt was an experience of 'closeness to God/the divine', 30% of adults affirmed this was the case (a figure closely comparable to adult studies in the UK and Australia). However, 60% of 11-year-olds and 80% of the youngest children (seven-year-olds) were able to identify such an experience. This portrays an inverse relationship between at least this kind of spiritual perception and age. Of course there could be many explanations for the more cautious response of adults, but this clearly attests to the generous sense of spiritual experience children may recognize.

This trend has also been suggested in qualitative studies. Hay and Nye (2006) reported that, when individually interviewing children aged 6–11 years, the older children expressed a need to hide or suppress their spiritual feeling and thoughts from others, and were concerned that these were childish aberrations to 'grow out of', rather than stepping stones to deeper insight, wisdom, or mature contemplation. Similarly, in group discussions with older children (10–11 years), Hyde (2008) uncovered a defensive steering away from conversation about spiritual topics and feelings, as the children either trivialized what they had begun to share or turned their attention to a more materialistic focus.

Together these findings imply that spiritual life is more easily attended to by younger children, but has a tendency to get pushed to the margins, rejected, or reclassified as they get older. Many argue that this may be correlated with formal educational experience that favours the development of rational and logical thinking, usurping the validity of knowing in other ways such as contemplation or wisdom (Donaldson 1992; Hart 2004; Hay and Nye 2006). Thus, while few research studies have studied children in the early years period, the evidence of spiritual strengths in those a little older may be an underestimation of the true capacity and experience of even younger children.

Spiritual signatures

Hay and Nye's empirical studies (1998, 2006) involved 92 individual conversations, mostly child-led, with 40 children aged 6–11 years in English primary schools, of whom the majority had no faith affiliation. A wide range of data was analyzed, including children's recalled experiences and views, but also their on-the-spot spiritual world-view thinking, imaginative detours, and casual chatter. This inclusive approach hoped to make provision for the different ways children's spirituality might be expressed, and circumvent the limitation of relying on their recall of specific memories to order. Using a grounded-theory approach to analysis, initial coding corroborated most areas identified in the working map (1996). However, from further analysis, additional core features emerged.

First, the data yielded a strong impression of individual differences: each child having his or her own *spiritual signature*. This was a unique thread connecting explicit and much more implicit or opaque parts of each child's data. Once recognized, these helped to identify potentially significant passages, even though superficially these might have seemed unpromising. For example, one child's 'signature' centred around nature and beauty, through which she shared a plethora of experiences and thoughts about inspiration, wonder, comfort, and joy. Looking back, often this signature was present even in the earliest parts of the conversations. In another case, Tim's spiritual signature (age 10) seemed to be about engaging in an inner struggle, which came out in his first comments when looking at a picture of a young girl sitting quietly by a fire: he assumed she was lonely and worried, struggling to make sense of some kind of problem she couldn't talk to anyone else about.

This 'struggle signature' also characterized Tim's sense of wonder, awe, meaningfulness, and mystery. Here, he struggles with questions about God and the mystery of infinity:

> Sometimes I think about if there is *one* God and there is ... everybody, well, most people believe in one God and um, there's different people believing in different gods. Which God's real? Um, I just *can't* figure that out. And I sometimes think about after the universe, what's the universe, um ... going on forever? I just don't know ... when I am thinking about the universe that gets me quite annoyed sometimes because I can never thing about ... um ... get the right answer, or even get near it, and, um, then well ... things ... you just wonder ...

> (Nye 1998, p. 199)

And later he contrasted his own pondering approach to spiritual matters, with the style he perceived in other children:

> I think they just look at it and think WOW and then ... forget about it really ... or just ... think about it, but don't *think*, like about how they were made.

> (Nye 1998, p. 201)

The notion that each child has a discernible *unique* spiritual style was also the conclusion of Champagne's delicate phenomenological study of pre-school spirituality in Canada (Champagne 2003). Recording over 100 hours of pre-school daily life, observing words, facial expressions, gestures, and clues to inner dynamics and feelings, she argues that recognizing children's spirituality requires effort to become aware of children's *modes of being*. She explains that '[modes of being] do not reflect attitudes or styles of action. Rather they manifest essential facets of the being of the child' (Champagne, p. 44). In other words these modes are the spiritual component of what Heidegger terms a person's 'Dasein'. What matters here is the sense that the child's spirituality emerges from, and is processed at, the very core of who and how they are. It is not some kind of peripheral or optional appendix. It follows, therefore, that the better a child is, and feels, 'really known', the better the validation of their unique spiritual life.

Relational consciousness

Hay and Nye's (1998/2006) grounded theory analysis eventually yielded a core category. What united the very different kinds of data through which children's spirituality seemed evident was a particular kind of consciousness: *relational consciousness*. They proposed that this is 'the rudimentary core of children's spirituality, out of which can arise meaningful aesthetic experience, religious experience, personal and traditional responses to mystery and being, and mystical and moral insight' (Hay and Nye, p. 109).

The 'consciousness' here refers to distinctive, live mental activity, not limited to the cognitive knowing but also emotional and sensory. It finds that children's spirituality is accompanied by an unusual level of consciousness or perceptiveness relative to the child's 'normal' experience. This alertness to the unexpected was evident sometimes from the observer's point of view, such as in the child's intense concentration, heightened energy, or rich silence and stillness. This special consciousness was also often mentioned by the children themselves—for example, in the use of phrases such as '*waking up (to spring)*', '*switching on (to God)*', '*a tickly feeling in my brain*', or a sense of increased challenge '*like your brains feeling scrambled*'. Some children were clearly fascinated by this 'different kind of knowing', describing it as '*pictures going through my head, like dreams or something... they all seem to fit together like a big puzzle ... like one dream in all, like telling me things*' (boy aged ten, in Nye 1998, p. 242).

However, what defined this further was its 'relational' character. This was far more than children talking about their obvious relationships with people, but was also manifest in the very natural way children turned to relational frameworks and symbols to explore an experience or raise a new spiritual question. For example, a boy (aged six) was trying to wrestle with his own sense of an omnipotent creator, having spotted the fallacy in the claim that 'God makes everything', since his dad was a builder! He turned instinctively to relation-laden language and story (Snow White), honing in on the difficult, severed, and then restored relationship between Grumpy and Snow White to examine how one can '*get into know about life ... and think more better about it*'. After re-telling the story, he added, '*So I think Grumpy and Snow White learned about how clever and good life can be. At the start he doesn't know nothing about life, so he doesn't like life and the planet of God and really later on he finds out all about it ...* [via his relationship with Snow White] *... then* admitting, '*sometimes I get really grumpy at school and then I thought about how life could be, and how happy I could be if I started to try not to be grumpy no more*' (Nye 1998, p. 243). Thus we glimpse how, what starts as wondering about his sense of 'God', also articulates with his emerging and transforming self-consciousness, plagued by his previously disclosed challenging behaviour and unpopularity.

Thus, relational consciousness can be observed in four dimensions: (i) child–people consciousness, (ii) child–world consciousness, (iii) child–self-consciousness, and (iv) child–God/Other consciousness. Examples of each of these dimensions are provided in the box below.

Child–people relational consciousness	*I believe in God's love* [but not God] *... so we can love each other ... If I had three wishes I would make nasty people into good people, rich people gives some money to the poor people, and something for myself, but I'd share it with someone else* (age 6).
Child–world relational consciousness	*Perhaps we've got to ask the* clouds [about the origins and continuation of life]. *The clouds have been there millions and millions of years ... and well there must be somewhere, somehow ... like when flowers are made, where did the wind come from to blow all the petals off to make them fall on the floor and make more? ...* (whisper) *It's puzzling* (age 10).
Child–self relational consciousness	*When I was being rude to my mum and stuff ...* [later] *I felt like I was a new person ... coming out of something ... like ... I don't know what is wrong with me though but I'm a new person from a flower or something. And like I've just grown ... going 'I'm a new person and I'm not going to be rude to my mum'. Makes you feel really, really good actually* (age 10).
Child–God relational consciousness	*Sometimes I feel very lonely when I am alone with God because I can't see God and I can't hear God, I just think about God, I feel really lonely, so I like being with people sometimes too* (girl 10).

Subsequently, 'relational consciousness' has become a much-used heuristic for discussing children's spirituality both in research and practice (e.g. Nye 1999; Scott 2003; Pearmain 2007; Cervantes and Arczynski 2014), in part because it can accommodate both secular and religious perspectives. But more importantly, it provides a clearer indication of the need to look at child spirituality through the lens of relationality—a feature suggesting that in childhood this is especially a process of reaching out rather than the perhaps more individualistic, even narcissistic, spiritual patterns evident in some adults.

Role of language

Brief mention should be made of the huge issue of verbal language and the young child's spirituality. Even when expressing or trying to study adult spirituality, language is as much a barrier as a conduit. It is hard to find the right words for this area of experience—words may even be the wrong place to look. The essentially *non-verbal* qualities of spirituality can be challenging for adults, but for children non-verbal communications, like play and gesture, are their native languages. They have a strong hand in this sense, though adults may fail to see it. However, this makes the acquisition of shared verbal language for spiritual things a sensitive business.

Berryman (2001) explains how it is easy for words to erode and disconnect the child from powerful experiences of awareness-sensing, mystery-sensing, and meaning-making. It is noteworthy that adult retrospective studies of childhood spirituality frequently report that participants 'never told anyone' at the time. Moreover, they feel that their adult ability to articulate their child experience with sophistication in fact adds nothing to the rich and complete quality it had at the time (Robinson 1983).

In Hay and Nye's conversations study (1998), the role played by religious language was interesting, given that most of the children did not practise a faith. Pilot work had made clear that if the researcher first introduced any religious term, the children tended to take this as a request for 'RE' (religious education) knowledge rather than a more personal kind of knowing. So, in their main study, the use of religious language (e.g. God/heaven/Allah/holy) was left for children to make the first move.

Allowing for this spontaneous, 'on their terms' use of religious words produced not only a remarkable amount of religious discussion, but also ensured a different quality, coming from their hearts rather than their heads. However, children used an additional nine kinds of language to give expression to spiritual feeling, thoughts, and experiences, including autobiography, fiction and science fiction, play, science and technology, and nature. Evidently, children are spiritually multi-lingual, and it is perhaps the narrowing down of what their environment deems as 'appropriate' discourse that reduces the aperture of their spiritual perception.

Agency

For some, such as Dawkins (2007), the child's spirituality is regarded as passive—subject to, and at the mercy of, outside influences. However, research studies have repeatedly found that children are capable, active agents in the construction of a spiritual outlook

(Adams et al. 2008). This can be something quite formal as well as heterodox (the few faith-affiliated children in Hay and Nye's research were far from traditionalists). It can also be informal and transient, created and discarded within a few moments—nonetheless demonstrating children's agency.

Studying the manifestations of relational consciousness, Nye (1998) came across children using a wide range of self-taught strategies to help them attend to their spiritual life. These included withdrawing physically or mentally to find space and time for being and thinking, focusing, and a kind of discovered form of mediation with a 'special pencil', seeking dialogue with friends, artistic and physical activity, and deliberate fantasy. For example, one girl spoke of her use of a 'secret garden', a fantasized sanctuary where she hung out in times of need, and mulled over big questions, but where she also sometimes became aware of profound loneliness.

With agency comes an understandable desire and capacity in children for meaningful participation (Kellet 2009). However, older children in many of these research studies report feeling unheard, and quite sure that no one else even has spiritual thoughts and feelings, let alone would regard them as valuable and valid. In areas of school life which seem potential opportunities for this, such as RE (religious education), PHSE (personal health and social education), and collective worship, children are often critical of the tokenistic levels of participation. They have a sense that their viewpoint is suppressed and that their role is to listen to what has already been constructed by adults (Nye 2013). It is significant that 'spiritual listening tools' are now being developed to expand the kind of interventions educational psychologists can offer pupils in difficulty (Gersch et al. 2014).

Spiritual needs

This survey of children's spiritual capacities and characteristics makes clear that teachers, carers, and parents face significant challenges and responsibilities if they are to meet the needs that these strengths and sensitivities create. In this final section, four areas of spiritual need are outlined:

- a need for time to be listened to
- a need for adult presence and respect
- a need for space and silence
- a need for play and creative response.

Listening time

Taking time to 'just listen' has been essential to almost all of the research methods used in the study of children's spirituality, but it is more than an effective method. Researchers have uncovered that for many children this is an unmet need. Many have drawn attention to the importance of listening to children for their well-being and learning (Clark 2011), but the need for this in spiritual life is perhaps especially acute.

In Hay and Nye's study (2006), children were angry and sad when the last interview happened, but were unable to think of anyone else in their lives with whom to have a similar conversation, without fear of ridicule or being told 'there's no time' for that sort of thing. Some adults may be anxious about 'what to say' when children raise 'big questions' or touch on topics such as death, evil, or the sacred, non-verbally signalling their own discomfort or verbally suggesting the child should talk to someone more expert. In fact, adults with less spiritual content knowledge may be better suited to listening, being less inclined to talk, direct, or interrupt a child's seemingly halting articulation or unconventional insights.

Meeting this need requires a child-led listening approach, where a sense of safety, intimacy, and perhaps even privacy is paramount, without judgement or agenda, and which tolerates children's use of humour, evasion, silence, and play to examine and express their thoughts and feelings. This suggests a significant difference from the listening required to develop children's speaking skills, which might typically focus on vocabulary, grammar, articulation, confidence, or fluency. Arguably it may also be different from some 'circle time'-style activities which can be covertly adult-led events, and may be driven by a 'behaviour management or social control of your feelings' agenda, and which not all children recognize as a 'safe' situation (Leach and Lewis 2013). Structured approaches such as Berryman's Godly Play (1995), however, have introduced methods through which adults become more effective spiritual guides by providing an intentionally safe time and space for children's wonder to find its own voice.

Adult presence and respect

If relational consciousness is at the core of children's spirituality, it follows that the adults need to espouse an appropriate way of being in relation to the children. This means adults becoming increasingly aware of what kind of presence they are, and whose presence they are in.

Montessori writes about how the habitual style of teacher–child relations—one of control and knowing better—can actively impede the process of discerning the child's reality, and who and how they really are.

> … the personality of the child is still buried under prejudices that keep adults from seeing the child clearly. Adults must place themselves in the right relationship with the child, in a spirit of humility and respect, in order to learn the child's true nature.
>
> (Montessori 1964, pp. 66–7)

There have been few positive theological perspectives addressing childhood and its spiritual landscape. But, theologian Karl Rahner argues that childhood should be respected as a mysterious and 'abiding quality' of human existence—that childhood is something we might strive to grow into rather than to grow out of (Hinsdale 2001). This invites adults to subvert the traditional developmental maps of progression to human maturity, and encourages a proactive search for the deepest qualities of childhood both in children and adults.

To adopt this kind of view in practice radically alters the mindset of those caring for and educating children. It also invites adults to reconsider their own childlikeness in ways that make clear that the child is not the only 'educational project' in a classroom. Rather, the adult is also engaged in their own developmental project of making sense of themselves, and their spirituality, learning both with and from being amongst children. The challenge for the adult is to aspire to 'a state in which we are open to expect the unexpected, to commit ourselves to the incalculable, a state which endows us with the power still to be able to play, to recognise that the powers presiding over our existence are greater than our own designs' (Rahner 1971, p. 42).

This transforms the relational and power dynamics in the classroom into one that is, potentially, a profoundly democratic community, a spiritually level playing field. Characteristics of this can be found in some educational programmes, such as Reggio Emilia and Montessori, and educational movements such as Palmer's 'Courage to Teach' (Palmer 2007).

Space for the spirit

Space is another basic need arising from children's significant spirituality. This can be 'space' around the child in many senses: physical and visual space, emotional space, and auditory space (Nye 2009)—how the qualities or deficiencies of each of these affect a child's spiritual well-being. Already experts in non-verbal language in even the earliest of interpersonal relations, young children 'read' physical spaces astutely, and will be sensitive to messages of openness, the natural versus the manufactured, care and order, and places of public attention versus areas affording privacy and intimacy.

Children may need to make or find their own spaces for spiritual 'work', such as dens, trees, hiding places, retreats, a swing—'holy ground' (Erricker and Erricker 1996). Adults need to be sensitive, not intrusive or analytical, about visiting such spaces. Depending on home circumstances, the educational setting may be the only viable opportunity for this in the child's life. Hemming's (2013) ethnographic study of children's experience of their school environment demonstrated children's resourcefulness in finding and making the best of spaces, even the privacy of toilets, for spiritual purposes!

Montessori (1964) saw a direct relationship between the child's experience of external, physical space and things in it and their sense of inner space, a place of sanctuary and deep concentration. A chaotic, over-stimulating, restlessly changing, or overcrowded space is unlikely to help a child to cultivate their inner space, or validate the existence of that part of the child.

Walton (2015) examined ways that outdoor natural spaces can be an educative opportunity to meet and develop children's rich spiritual potential. His ten-year study of the benefits of providing opportunity for children to take time, by themselves and in silence, to sit 'in nature' in a spot of their own choosing, provides convincing descriptive data of how spiritually sensitizing this can be, even for children quite unfamiliar with an expanse of nature:

> My magic spot was on a load of wet leaves, with holly in my face and under a conker tree. It was very peaceful because it was so quiet. I could hear the birds and the wind rustling the leaves.... It made me happy, but kind of sad because I was remembering sad things and I felt at peace with myself.
>
> (girl, aged nine, cited in Walton 2015, p. 12)

A large old oak tree caught my eye; I decided to draw it. as I drawed I wondered about that bird and why it made that noise maybe it was angry, sad? Who knows! I'm not sure what came into my thoughts next it was a mixture of anger, sadness and loneliness, I understand the anger, sadness but not the loneliness perhaps it's to do with the amount of space there is around here.

(boy, aged eight, cited in Walton 2015)

Walton also offers an interesting explanation of why this occurs, with the concept of 'metaxic space'—finding and becoming aware of a creative space in-between one and the Other, where relational consciousness is nurtured. He argues that nature, exuding creative spirit by definition, can both 'be' metaxic space, and can be what 'arises from' encounter of awareness between places in nature and the child. Walton suggests that, in the mediation of their experiences of self and nature, the child finds a middle ground in the 'dynamic space between two separate things', which gives rise to 'a sense of deep interconnectedness of the universe as a whole'. Walton is concerned that 'where there is no acknowledgement of this continuing dynamic relational space there is not likely to be space for life. Rather, the more the in-between is closed up, the more spirit is shrivelled and lost' (Walton 2015, pp. 7–8).

The child's spiritual need for *emotional* space can hinge on the potentially intrusive behaviour and attitudes of adults. Spiritual openness thrives when there is no need for self-defence, so intimacy is a key need. This manifests in providing opportunities that are personal, don't have to be shared even with an adult, and which are valid for what they mean to the child alone. This requires careful handling of a 'praise and judgement' culture, in order that children have genuine experiences of the validity of things that are of intrinsic value, of inner life, not merely those that impress others. This helps to honour other kinds of knowing, inner knowing, and also an apophatic kind of 'un-knowing': being at ease with, and in awe of, mystery and wonder, without necessarily attributing that to God.

Time for silence, auditory space, may also be invaluable to meet children's spiritual needs, and positive experiences of silence are clearly in short supply in modern homes and education settings. Walton suggests 'children are more adept, more ready, than adults to discover the secret that is only heard in silence' (Walton 2015, p. 11). Connected to listening and presence, this can be achieved to some extent simply by adults being intentional about speaking less and being more observant. Holding a moment of silence can also be a mark of respect and presence, to mark something the child has said or done that has been extraordinary or that plumbed the depths. Teaching the use of silence in a more formal way can also contribute to acknowledgement of 'being' over doing, and helps children to revel in the richness of non-verbal knowing.

Play and creative response

Doubtless every chapter in this book has highlighted the need for play and the child's own creativity. It is certainly a 'royal road' for child spirituality (Miller-McLemore 2009). Imaginative play endorses and develops children's capacity for possibility and impossibility thinking, beyond what is actually the case, so has a naturally transcendent function.

Berryman (1995) draws analogies between Garvey's (1977) seven marks of play and the spiritual properties of grace and blessing. Free play and non-prescriptive creativity afford children opportunities to make connections, to see and seek relations between things which may be similar to Walton's dynamic 'metaxic' space, or Winnicott's 'transitional space'. In a culture of control, targets, and high-vigilance child protection, free play and creativity, which are about process and not product, can be literally a sanctuary, a place of sacred refuge.

This is not about conventional 'learning through play', which is often used as a catalyst to fast-track intellectual, social, or physical development. Nor is it merely providing for play that is 'fun', which can, in the end, be rather an empty, short-lived experience. Instead this is about meeting the need for child's play that can be a source of deeper pleasure and, potentially, fulfilment. This is play which meets very different, inner needs, and which validates the child's natural propensity to counter-cultural forms of open, flexible, and unpredictable knowing. Through the safety of this play, children can look into the abyss, at infinity, at death, and other looming features of their existential horizon, then pack up and find a safe way back again. Not surprisingly, play is now being recognized as vital for healthy adult spirituality, too (Brown 2010).

Conclusion

It remains to be seen whether scholarly attention to children's spirituality can make a difference to how children are treated, educated, and cared for. Spirituality remains a topic which many find frustratingly non-rational, invisible, and inexplicable, and yet for others it can serve to re-orient them to the vocation which still calls them to be with, and nourish, children's lives, and to advocate for ways of knowing and being beyond being clever or right.

Certainly poets, artists, and authors have expressed this all before. Having become aware of the dimensions and strengths of children's spirituality, their relational consciousness, our challenge is to be sufficiently sensitive to these when they are expressed and to respond creatively. However, it may help to admit that 'the child's spirit is like a child, you can never catch it by running after it; you must stand still, and, for love, it will soon itself come back' (Arthur Miller 1971, *The Crucible*).

References

Adams, K., Hyde, B., and Woolley, R. (2008). *The Spiritual Dimension of Childhood*. London: Jessica Kingsley Publications.

Berger, P. (1970). *A Rumour of Angels*. London: Allen Lane/Penguin Press.

Berryman, J. (1990). Teaching as presence and the existential curriculum. *Religious Education*, 65(4), 509–34.

Berryman. J. (1995). *Godly Play: An Imaginative Approach to Religious Education*. New York: Harper Collins.

Berryman, J. (2001). The non-verbal nature of spirituality and religious language. In: J. Erricker, C. Ota, and C. Erricker (eds.) *Spiritual Education: Cultural, Religious and Social Differences*. Eastbourne: Sussex Academic Press, pp. 9–21.

Berryman, J. (2013). *The Spiritual Guidance of Children: Montessori, Godly Play, and the Future.* Harrisburg, PA: Morehouse Publishing.

Bone, E. (2007). 'Everyday spirituality: Supporting the spiritual experience of young children in three early childhood educational settings', PhD thesis, Massey University.

Brown, S. (2010). *Play: How It Shapes the Brain, Opens the Imagination, and Invigorates the Soul.* New York: J.P. Tarcher/Penguin Putnam.

Cervantes, J. and Arczynski, A. (2014). Children's spirituality: Conceptual understanding of developmental transformation. *Spirituality in Clinical Practice*, 2(4), 245–55.

Champagne, E. (2003). Being a child: A spiritual child. *International Journal of Children's Spirituality*, 8(1), 43–53.

Clark, A. (2011). 'Why and how we listen to young children', National Children's Bureau, https://www.ncb.org.uk/resources-publications/resources/listening-way-life-why-how-we-listen-young-children, accessed 9 Apr 2018.

Cohen, D. and MacKeith, S.A. (1991). *The Development of Imagination: The Private Worlds of Childhood.* London/ New York: Routledge.

Csikszentmihalyi, M. (1990). *Flow: The Psychology of Optimal Experience.* New York: Harper and Row.

Dawkins, R. (2007). *The God Delusion.* London: Black Swan Publications.

Donaldson, M. (1992). *Human Minds: An Exploration.* London: Allen Lane/Penguin Books.

Education Act (1996). 'An Act to consolidate the Education Act 1944 and certain other enactments relating to education, with amendments to give effect to recommendations of the Law Commission, UK Government', , http://www.legislation.gov.uk/ukpga/1996/56, accessed 9 Apr 2018.

Erikson, E. (1998). *The Life Cycle Completed* (extended version). New York: W.W. Norton.

Erricker, C. and Erricker, J. (1996). Where angels fear to tread: Discovering children's spirituality. In: R. Best (ed.) *Education, Spirituality and the Whole Child.* London: Cassell.

Fowler, J. (1995). *Stages of Faith: The Psychology of Human Development and the Quest for Meaning.* New York: Harper Collins.

Fowler, J. and Dell, M. (2006). Stages of faith from infancy through adolescence: reflections on three decades of faith development theory. In: P. King, L. Wagener, and P. Bensen (eds.) *Handbook of Spiritual Development in Childhood and Adolescence.* Thousand Oaks, CA: Sage, pp. 252–65.

Freud, S. (1957). *Eine Kindheitserinnerung des Leonardo da Vinci* (Leonardo da Vinci and a Memory of His Childhood). In: *Standard Edition of the Complete Works of Sigmund Freud*, vol. 11. New York/ London: W.W. Norton, pp. 57–137 (first German edition 1910).

Freud, S. (1923). *Das Ich und das Es* (The Ego and the Id). Internationaler Psychoanalytischer Verlag (Vienna)/ New York/ London: W.W. Norton.

Freud, S. (1924). The dissolution of the Oedipus complex. In: *Standard Edition of the Complete Works of Sigmund Freud*, vol. 19. London: Hogarth Press, pp. 172–9.

Garvey, C. (1977). *Play.* London: Fontana Paperbacks.

Gendlin, E. (1981). *Focusing.* Toronto: Bantum Books.

Gersch, I., Lipscomb, A., Stoyles, G., and Caputi, P. (2014). Using philosophical and spiritual conversations with children and young people: A method for psychological assessment, listening deeply and empowerment. *Educational and Child Psychology*, 31(1), 32–47.

Hart, T. (2004). Opening the contemplative mind in the classroom. *Journal of Transformative Education*, 2(1), 28–46.

Hay, D. (2006). *Something There: The Biology of the Human Spirit.* London: Darton Longman and Todd.

Hay, D. and Nye, R. (1996). Investigating children's spirituality: The need for a fruitful hypothesis. *International Journal of Children's Spirituality*, 1(1), 6–16.

Hay, D., with Nye, R. (1998). *The Spirit of the Child.* London: Harper Collins.

Hay, D., with Nye, R. (2006). *The Spirit of the Child (Revised Edition)*. London: Jessica Kingsley Publications.

Hemming, P. (2013). Spaces of spiritual citizenship: Children's relational and emotional encounters with the everyday school environment. *International Journal of Children's Spirituality*, **18**(1), 74–91.

Hinsdale, M. (2001). Infinite openness to the infinite: Karl Rahner's contribution to modern Catholic thought on the child. In: M. Bunge (ed.) *The Child in Christian Thought*. Grand Rapids, MI: Eerdmans, pp. 406–45.

Hyde, B. (2008). *Children and Spirituality: Searching for Meaning and Connectedness*. London: Jessica Kingsley Publications.

James, W. (1916). *The Varieties of Religious Experience*. New York: Longmans, Green, and Co.

Johnstone, B. and Glass, B. (2008). Support for a neuropsychological model of spirituality in persons with traumatic brain injury. *Zygon*, **43**(4), 861–74.

Kegan, R. (1982). *The Evolving Self: Problem and Process in Human Development*. Cambridge, MA: Harvard University Press.

Kellet, M. (2009). Children and young people's participation. In: M. Kellet and H. Montgomery (eds.) *Children and Young People's Worlds*. Bristol: The Policy Press, pp. 43–60.

Kohlberg, L. (1984*). The Psychology of Moral Development: The Nature and Validity of Moral Stages*, Essays on Moral Development, vol. 2. New York: Joanna Cotler Books.

Leach, T. and Lewis, E. (2013). Children's experiences during circle-time: A call for research-informed debate. *Pastoral Care in Education*, **31**(1), 43–52.

Malloch, S. and Trevarthen, C. (eds.) (2010). *Communicative Musicality: Exploring the Basis of Human*. Oxford: Oxford University Press.

Miller, A. (1971). *The Crucible*. Harmondsworth, UK: The Viking Press.

Miller-McLemore, B. (2009). The Royal Road: Children, play and the religious life. *Pastoral Psychology*, **58**, 505–19.

Montessori, M. (1964). *The Montessori Method*. New York: Schocken Books.

National Curriculum Council (1993). *Spiritual and Moral Development—A Discussion Paper*. London: N.C.C.

Nye, R. (1998). 'Psychological Perspectives on Children's Spirituality', unpublished PhD thesis, University of Nottingham.

Nye, R. (1999). Relational consciousness and the spiritual lives of children: Convergence with theory of mind? In: K. Reich, F. Oser, and W. Scarlett (eds.) *Psychological Studies on Spiritual and Religious Development*, vol. 2. Lengerich, Germany: PABST Science Publishers, pp. 57–82.

Nye, R. (2009). *Children's Spirituality: What It Is and Why It Matters*. London: Church House Press.

Nye, R. (2013), 'Soul Searching: A report for the Church Schools of Cambridge', http://csoc.org.uk/wp-content/uploads/2017/08/Soul-Searching.pdf, accessed 9 Apr 2018.

OFSTED (1994). *Spiritual, Moral, Social and Cultural Development*. London: Office for Standards in Education.

Otto, R. (1950). *The Idea of the Holy*. Oxford: Oxford University Press.

Palmer, P. (2007). *The Courage to Teach: Exploring the Inner Landscape of a Teacher's Life*, 10th edn. San Francisco, CA: Jossey Bass.

Pearmain, R. (2007). Evocative cues and presence: Relational consciousness within qualitative research. *International Journal of Children's Spirituality*, **12**(1), 75–82.

Rahner, K. (1971). Ideas for a theology of childhood. In: *Theological Investigations*, vol. 8: *Further Theology of the Spiritual Life 2*. London: Darton Longman & Todd/Herder and Herder, pp. 11–21.

Ratcliff, D. and Nye, R. (2006). Children's spirituality: Strengthening the research foundation. In: E.C. Roehlkepartain, P.E. King, L. Wagener, and P.L. Benson (eds.) *The Handbook of Spiritual Development in Childhood and Adolescence*. Thousand Oaks, CA: Sage, pp. 473–83.

Robinson, E. (1983). *The Original Vision: A Study of the Religious Experience of Childhood.* New York: Seabury.

Rosengren, K., Johnson, C., and Harris, P. (eds.) (2000). *Imagining the Impossible: Magical, Scientific, and Religious Thinking in Children.* Cambridge: Cambridge University Press.

Schutz, A. (1964). Making music together: A study in social relationship. In: A. Brodersen (ed.) *Collected Papers II: Studies in Social Theory.* The Hague: Martinus Nijhoff, pp. 159–78.

Scott, D. (2003). Spirituality in child and youth care: Considering spiritual development and 'Relational Consciousness'. *Child and Youth Care Forum*, April, **32**(2), 117–31.

Scott, D. (2004). Retrospective spiritual narratives: Exploring recalled childhood and adolescent spiritual experiences. *International Journal of Children's Spirituality*, **9**(1), 67–79.

Sheldrake, P. (2012). *Spirituality: A Very Short Introduction.* Oxford: Oxford University Press.

Stark, R. (1965). A taxonomy of religious experience. *Journal for the Scientific Study of Religion*, **5**(1), 97–116.

Surr, J. (2012). Peering into the clouds of glory: Explorations of a newborn child's spirituality. *International Journal of Children's Spirituality*, **17**(1), 77–87.

Tait, C. (2004), 'Chuffedness', paper presented at the European Early Childhood Education Research Association Annual Conference, 'Quality in Early Education', Malta, September, 2004.

Tamminen, K. (1991). *Religious Development in Childhood and Youth: An Empirical Study.* Helsinki, Finland: Suomalainen Tiedeakatemia.

Templeton, J.L. and Eccles, J.S. (2006). The relation between spiritual development and identity processes. In: E.C. Roehlkepartain, P.E. King, L. Wagener, and P.L. Bensen (eds.) *Handbook of Spiritual Development in Childhood and Adolescence.* Thousand Oaks, CA: Sage, pp. 252–65.

Vianello, R., Tamminen, K., and Ratcliff, D. (1992). The religious concepts of children. In: D. Ratcliff (ed.) *Handbook of Children's Religious Education.* Birmingham, AL: Religious Education Press, pp. 56–81.

Walton, C. (2015). Childhood awaits every person. *International Journal of Children's Spirituality*, **20**(1), 4–14.

Watts, F. and Williams, M. (1988). *The Psychology of Religious Knowing.* Cambridge: Cambridge University Press.

Winnicott, D. (1971). *Playing and Reality.* London: Tavistock.

Zeedyk, M.S. (2006). From intersubjectivity to subjectivity: The transformative roles of emotional intimacy and imitation. *Infant and Child Development*, **15**, 321–44.

Chapter 9

Early human relations set the foundation for adult health and working life

Alan Sinclair and Tam Baillie

Children's rights and the early years

We know that children in different parts of Scotland can lead very different lives, so we have to be careful of sweeping generalizations. That said, it is a reasonable observation that most of our children and young people develop into well-adjusted adults, and as a consequence, are having many of their rights satisfied. For instance, here are some issues that can be directly referenced in the *United Nations Convention on the Rights of the Child* (UNCRC): parents who provide a stable, nurturing, and loving home life for their children (Articles 5 and 18); teachers who provide high standards of education for our children (Articles 28 and 29); health workers who ensure that children and young people experience good health (Articles 23 and 24); and youth workers who enrich young people's lives outside of school settings (Article 31). For all children considered, having a good start in life is a crucial part of their continuing enjoyment of their rights. But there is a flip side to this: we know that too many of our children are living in traumatizing circumstances. For instance, in Scotland, a large number of children live in the same house as alcohol- or substance-misusing parents (Scottish Government 2013), or where there is domestic abuse ('Equally Safe: Scotland's Strategy to prevent and eradicate violence against women and girls.' Scottish Government 2016).

Despite this, the UNCRC reinforces what is, in many instances, already done. It affirms our positive engagement with children and young people; yet parents, professionals, and young people rarely frame our approach to children and young people with reference to the UNCRC. In that sense, many people in Scotland are already contributing to helping children fulfil their rights without realizing it. Human rights are inalienable, fundamental standards that are commonly protected in national and international law. It is instructive to recall the evolution of children's rights.

The UNCRC was in gestation for a long period of time dating back to the 'Geneva Declaration of the Rights of the Child' (1924). Its development predates the synthesis of attachment theory and advances in neurological science providing insights into environmental influences on brain development.

The UNCRC was ratified in 1989 and quickly adopted by most countries in the world, including the UK, which signed up in 1991 (only the USA has failed to ratify). As a signatory, the UK government is subject to periodic review through the UN Committee on the Rights of the Child, which publishes its findings through its Concluding Observations. The most recent report was published in 2016 (UNCRC 2016).

Children are defined by the UNCRC as those under the age of 18 years, and there is no differentiation of children's rights in terms of age or stage of development—if you are a child you have the same rights throughout your childhood, regardless of your age. So, although the UNCRC makes no specific reference to early years, infancy, or anything regarding the importance of early years development, it does contain a number of articles directly relevant to the early years of a child's life, for example: Article 2, a child's right to non-discrimination; Article 3, a child's right for their best interests to be the primary consideration; Article 6, a child's right to life and maximum survival and development; and Article 12, a child's right to have an opinion—even in the earliest years—as we all know that they are active engagers with their environment and development. Of particular importance in the early years are Articles 5 and 18, outlining parental responsibilities and a child's right to receive guidance from their parents in line with their evolving capacities.

It is acknowledged that the UNCRC could be strengthened with respect to concerns around the implementation of children's rights and this has led to the development of a number of General Comments. The General Comment on early years, 'Implementing child rights in early childhood' (UNCRC 2005), is an attempt to update the UNCRC on the importance of early childhood development.

What is interesting is that the UNCRC has had to evolve in line with our increasing knowledge and awareness of the impact of early years experiences—just as most of us have had to assimilate and accommodate the recent mushrooming of evidence demonstrating the powerful link between an infant's early experiences and their future life chances.

Health: the Good Life

A short bit of science explaining the link with what happens in the womb and subsequent health

Vivette Glover is a neuro-chemist and Professor of Perinatal Psychobiology at Imperial College, London. She argues that the most critical time of life is during pregnancy (Glover and Sutton 2012). If interventions could be organized to turn a bad pregnancy into a less bad pregnancy, that would surely be the greatest return on any public spending. Below is a summary of her reasoning.

Environment and genetics are important to a child growing in the womb, but there is firm evidence that prenatal stress increases the risk for later psychopathology (Glover 2011). We often equate stress with a bad day at the office. Glover is concerned about stress during pregnancy caused by violence, alcohol, or drugs. It reduces the blood and nutrition flow for the baby; this could explain why the baby does not grow as well as it might. If the mother has a high level of cortisol, the main stress hormone, so does the fetus.

Sufficient cortisol passes from the mother to the fetus through the placenta to affect the level of it in the fetus. This could affect the development of the brain and the future stress responses of the baby.

In a similar vein, a senior clinician in Scotland ironically told one of the authors that his dream was to have posters across Scotland of a baby drinking a glass of vodka. Why? Well, vodka was the mum's drink, and via the placenta the baby had been plumbed into the mum's habit.

There is strong evidence that one of the occasions when men are most abusive and violent to their partners is during pregnancy (Morewitz 2004).

The growing child of an anxious or stressed mother is more likely to show a range of symptoms, such as attention deficit hyperactivity disorder, conduct disorder, aggression, or anxiety—or to be somewhere on the fetal alcohol spectrum. The child is more likely to have impaired cognitive and language development. Glover's research concurs with the programming hypothesis: conditions and diseases that were once thought to arise near the time of their manifestation in adult life are now known to have roots in the womb or early in life. From here, the prescription follows that we ought to do more to support women likely to become pregnant as well as pregnant mothers, to prevent bigger problems down the line, or if a problem has been identified, to intervene early (Sher 2016).

From Neurons to Neighbourhoods

Vivette Glover was driven by findings in neurochemistry to assert that the most influential period of life is that which occurs in the womb before memory kicks in. It is right to be sceptical of any one study, and it is impossible for most mortals to be sufficiently Stakhanovite (hard working) to have read enough studies, or have a brain big enough to make sense of evidence from different scientific and statistical disciplines. Fortunately for us, over a two-year period the National Research Council of the USA assembled teams of experts for interdisciplinary study.

The National Research Council (NRC; Shonkoff and Phillips 2000) took apart the standard way of framing child growth and adult behaviour as either being about 'nature' or 'nurture'. Science, they conclude, now recognizes that genetic and environmental influences work together in a dynamic way during the unfolding passage of brain development: a central thesis, imprinted in the title of the book, *From Neurons to Neighborhoods*.

Figure 9.1 represents an attempt by the National Research Council to map the pattern and timing of brain development. Growth, it shows, in brain systems for sensing, language, and cognitive functions, is weighted to the last few months in the womb and the first few months of life. Note how the scale of the horizontal axis changes halfway along from months to years, underscoring the significance of the first months of life.

It is worth noting that emerging science demonstrates that brain development continues beyond adolescence into early adulthood (National Institute of Mental Health, 'The Teen Brain'). As before, our increasing knowledge about child development continues to require adjustments in how we think about and perceive the growth of the brain, and how it engages in a human environment with other people and their habits and works.

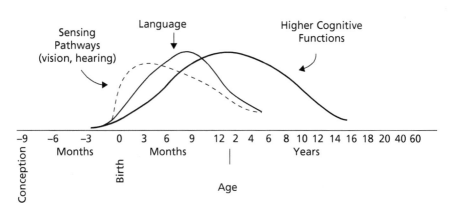

Figure 9.1 Developments after birth in brain systems for learning.

Think of brain development as building a house or baking a birthday cake. First, the foundations are dug, then cement poured, and then the walls go up. With a cake, the ingredients are mixed, then baked, and last of all the decorative piping is added. If we built the walls first and then the foundations, or Mary Berry baked the ingredients before mixing them, both the house and the cake would be a right mess. Brain development is sequential and deliberate—neglect and trauma damages, prohibits, or upsets the order. Scientists cannot say that all children exposed to significant stresses will always develop disorders. But they do say that exposure to toxic stresses will increase the likelihood of physical and mental illness.

If you find this analysis difficult, think of the baby in the womb and in the first months of life as a growing sponge. A healthy pregnancy and a loving warm relationship that helps the child to meet its emotional and physical needs will see the sponge grow. Baby growth, like sponge growth, is a reflection of the world in which it grows, and it is especially responsive to the presence and care of a parent or carer.

Vivette Glover's work, and that of the American Academy of Sciences, demonstrates the critical importance of a good pregnancy and a good first two years of life—a time before our talkative memory recalls any of our own story. The following study shows the profound effect on our physical and mental health of events and patterns in our childhood.

Adverse Childhood Experiences

Why did 50% of the participants in an obesity clinic run by Kaiser Permanente, one of the largest US private health insurance companies, drop out? A physician, Dr. Felitti, was assigned to find out. He interviewed people who had left the programme. A majority of the 286 people he interviewed had experienced childhood sexual abuse (Felitti et al. 1998).

What sense could he make of this finding? In the mid-1990s, in collaboration with the Centre for Disease Control, Kaiser Permanente took the next step. People undergoing a comprehensive physical examination were given the option of providing detailed information about their childhood experiences of abuse, neglect, and family dysfunction. Of 26,000 consecutive patients, 17,000 participants volunteered to do so: 54% were female, 75% were white, 46% were over 60 years old, and 75% had at least some college education—with it being a private health insurance programme, participants were generally financially well off.

In the study, which has become known as 'ACEs' (adverse childhood experiences) ('ACES Too High' News), participants were asked about ten types of childhood trauma. Five were personal: physical abuse, verbal abuse, sexual abuse, physical neglect, and emotional neglect. Five were related to other family members: a parent who abuses alcohol, a mother who is a victim of domestic violence, a family member in jail, a family member diagnosed with a mental illness, and the disappearance of a parent through divorce, death, or abandonment. Each type of trauma is separately counted. So, a person who has been physically abused, and has an alcoholic father and a mother who has been a victim of domestic violence, has a score of three.

Around 66% reported at least one of the adverse experiences. Of the two in three people who reported one adverse childhood experience, 87% reported at least one additional adverse experience. The most prevalent of these additional experiences were: physical abuse; household substance abuse; parental separation or divorce; sexual abuse; household mental illness; emotional neglect; and mother treated violently.

The more adverse childhood experiences an adult reported, the higher the association with high-risk health behaviours such as alcohol and drug abuse, severe obesity, promiscuity, and smoking—correlated with ill-health including depression, heart disease, cancer, chronic lung disease, and shortened lifespan. A score of four adverse experiences was associated with a 7-fold increase in alcoholism, a doubling of the risk of being diagnosed with cancer, and a 4-fold increase in emphysema. An ACE score above six was associated with a 30-fold increase in suicide.

People with high ACE scores are more likely to be violent, and have more broken bones, more marriages, more drug prescriptions, more depression, and more autoimmune diseases, and are more likely to have an early death.

It is comparatively easy to read across from neglect or abuse in early childhood to later behavioural problems such as alcohol abuse, violence, or depression. What is more surprising is the link with adult physical malfunction and premature death. Perhaps we should not be so surprised.

If you feel cramps and recognize that you have eaten something dodgy, you don't think back to the last five or ten minutes but look to the salad bar or the prawn sandwich you ate eight hours ago. Diagnosing a depression at 25 years of age, a heart problem at 50, and cancer at 70 leaves the question open on the origins, the spring, and the foothills of the condition.

Jobs and investment: Return for attention to early life

In 1983, at the time of mass closures of traditional manufacturing, one of the authors of this chapter, Alan Sinclair, started a company called Heatwise Glasgow. Its aim was to draught-proof and insulate houses, and provide temporary paid work to long-term un-employed people and help them get a job in the mainstream market. The company 'grew like Topsy', moved into environmental improvement, created urban forests, set up the first public glass recycling plant in Glasgow, ran a call centre, and expanded into different parts of Scotland and England.

By the time it became the Wise Group, it employed around 300 full-time people and helped, each year, over 2,000 previously long-term unemployed people into work ('The Wise Group'). The Wise Group was acknowledged as a leading UK social enterprise company and frequently called upon by different shades of government to explain its philosophy, operations, and business model: most notably, it played a part in the establishment of the government's New Deal programme.

One of the privileges for those leading the Wise Group for 18 years was to have daily contact with all sorts of people who were long-term unemployed. By getting six out of ten long-term unemployed people into work, it was considered really effective. Perhaps the Wise Group could have been more effective, but despite their best efforts they were unable to get the other four people out of ten into work.

A rule of thumb helped to segment and understand the long-term unemployed people taken on. Easiest to get a job for were the people who, through bad luck, had become long-term unemployed—for example, those who been made redundant twice in quick succession and 'had the wind taken out of their sails', or those who had had an illness or injury that had sidelined them. The middle group of people faced more difficulties. They were reasonably articulate and could, with effort, pick up new skills. Although they were not burning with enthusiasm, they did try. They were in with a shout of getting a job. At the bottom came a group of people who were in need of social or health workers (some with a combination of problems relating to alcohol, drug, violence, or entanglement with the criminal justice system). The Wise Group frontline staff found it hard to engage with this group. They were not interested, did not talk much, stared a lot, were poor at turning up, and got angry or took offence easily. They told staff that they didn't want a job—a view you can understand, because the likelihood of an employer taking them on was so remote, why set yourself up for more failure?

Most of the long-term unemployed people wanted a job, and the biggest problem was the sheer lack of paid work. But that could not disguise a truth: a good many of the people, usually young men aged around 21 years, were not going to get taken on—even if there were lots more jobs. What was doubly depressing was that most of these young men in the hard-to-engage group were already fathers—recycling their despair and hopelessness and almost certainly creating some of the adverse conditions identified in the ACE study ('ACES Too High').

After 18 years of the Wise Group, as well as the stick being applied, the carrot was thrown at the unemployed. Across successive governments the notion of the long-term unemployed being work-shy and scroungers grew, and the support that could be offered shrunk. It was too little, too late.

Whole households are more likely to be either in work or all out of work. As jobs were once passed down the line from father to son, so, too, do we pass unemployment from mothers and fathers to sons and daughters. When Alan Sinclair moved on to a job at the top end of Scottish Enterprise, the economic development and skills organization for Scotland, a number of surprises awaited, one central to this chapter.

One responsibility was establishing 'Futureskills Scotland', to provide labour market intelligence (Scottish Government 2008). Boldly stamped on the Scottish Enterprise tin was, 'Meeting the needs of employers by providing technical or vocational skills and meeting the needs of the emerging workforce'. There was just one problem: the truth got in the way—we did not know what employers wanted. The UK-wide data on employers had a sample size too small for Scotland to represent the geographic diversity and the spread of occupations.

Futureskills Scotland set about correcting these deficiencies by interviewing 22,000 employers in the public and private sector from tiny businesses to large corporations. As the analysts carefully worked their way through the views expressed by employers, a number of stories emerged. The most striking one was this: out of all the employers that had taken someone on in the past year, the biggest problem they had was that the new recruits were poor at talking and listening, working with one another, and working with the public, and poor at elementary planning or problem solving. Employers of people at the bottom end of the labour market, for example in care or retail jobs, had the greatest dissatisfaction. But the same group of complaints applied to the recruitment of graduates, just to a lesser extent.

Policy then, as now, was that society and the economy needed more and more graduates, and then more apprentices. Alan Sinclair felt that he needed to 'road test' the findings with groups of employers before releasing the results. The manager of a fish processing facility that supplied the upper end of the market said, 'We pay more than the minimum wage and although there are lots of unemployed in our area we recruit most of our people from Portugal'. Another said, 'At least the Latvians come in when it snows: I have been telling you for years', and the owner of a conservatory and double-glazing company said, 'that we can't get the right type of young people'.

The labour market results were taken to the Scottish Enterprise Board, eyebrows were raised, and they were perplexed and asked how you acquire these soft, non-cognitive skills?

An exercise to do this was set in motion. The more you think about it, the more you realize that these soft skills are the basic attributes that are needed to manage life, never mind getting a job. It was these soft, or life, skills that were missing in many of the people taken on by the Wise Group. A hotel or coffee bar is more likely to take on a migrant worker who looks you in the eye, and is pleasant and helpful, than a local with poor soft skills.

Around this time, James Heckman came to Scotland to deliver an Allander Lecture (Heckman and Masterov 2005). Originally a mathematician, Heckman gravitated to labour market economics and won the Nobel Prize for the creation of a two-step statistical approach that offered a way to correct non-randomly selected samples. He scrutinized large, long-term, complex data sets to find where the best rates of return came in skill formation. A eureka moment came with the discovery that the best rate of return was from very early investment in parents and children, while the lowest rate of return came from investing in later life. The big gains in human capital formation/ human development came way before school. These were not results that he had expected.

'A major determinant of successful schools is successful families. Schools work with what parents bring them', Heckman told the audience that night. 'They operate more effectively if parents reinforce them by encouraging and motivating children. Job training programs, whether public or private, work with what families and schools supply them and cannot remedy twenty years of neglect. Scottish skill formation policy should be based on this basic principle.'

Heckman's continuing work is summarized in Figure 9.2 (Heckman 2008).

Holding everything else constant, the rate of return to a one pound of investment made while a person is young is higher than the rate of return to the same pound made at a later age. This applies across the economic spectrum. If it is to be successful, remedial work for young people coming out of an impoverished or dysfunctional home becomes progressively more costly the later it is attempted.

In looking at the data that flowed from early interventions, Heckman found no evidence of improved, and sustained, IQ (intelligence quotient) levels. But what he did see was evidence of improved 'character' skills: self-control, openness, ability to get on with people, determination, and empathy. It is these behavioural and life skills, along with intelligence, that determine economic and social failure or success. The problem is that too much education policy focuses on IQ simply because it can be measured.

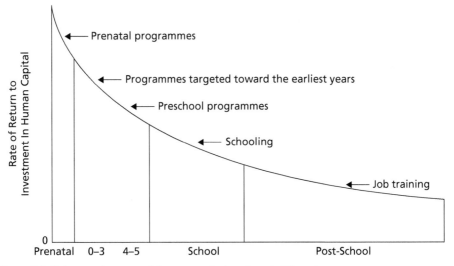

Figure 9.2 Return on investment for care and education at different ages.

Reproduced from James J. Heckman, Schools, Skills, and Synapses, *Economic Inquiry*, 46 (3), pp. 289-324, DOI: 10.1111/j.1465-7295.2008.00163.x, © 2008 Western Economic Association International.

Heckman has arrived at a rate of return in investing in the early years of 7%–10% per year, with the returns continuing to flow throughout life. 'This is not speculation,' Heckman tells us. 'It is a piece of analytic work. Very few government programmes have rates of return close to this.' Where do the returns come from?—improved school attainment, reduction in crime, reduced alcohol and drugs abuse, and in general better mental and physical health, along with increases in productivity and the likelihood of getting a job and not being on welfare. If government wants to decrease inequality and increase productivity, the sense of direction is clear. If you look at Heckman's rate of return analysis and compare it with the American Academy of Sciences' diagram on brain formation, there is a concurrence from two very different starting points.

'There is no trade-off between equity and efficiency, as there is in other social programs', argues Heckman in a recent *New York Times* piece (Heckman, 2013). 'Early investment in the lives of disadvantaged children will help reduce inequality, in both the short and the long run.' Public spending triggered by remedial action is more expensive and less effective than getting it right first time. 'Pre-distribution' to high-quality child and parent support programmes is more effective than cash transfers. In other words, prevention is not only better than the cure—it is cheaper.

Supporting young children and their parents is intrinsically the right thing to do and it is also economically the right thing to do. Current practice flows in the opposite direction. The biggest public investment is made around 20 years of age in degree programmes, then in secondary education, next in primary school, and then, least of all, in the period between pregnancy and school.

Lasting benefits of early care

Across human rights, morality, different types of health evidence, and now from employment and economic rates of return, there is a compelling case for getting the earliest days right, through pregnancy to the first two or three years of life. Of course what happens after age three is important, but if we do not get that first, most malleable and creative bit of life right, it may not be possible to reverse that damage, or as time goes by, there is an escalation in the dosage of the remedial work required. Why, in the face of this evidence and good sense, does the UK treat early years and parenting as a peripheral issue? What can be done? But before we discuss that, it helps to have an assessment of where we are now.

Where are we now?

All statistics can be exercises in selective distortion. Any one anecdote can be as misleading as any one statistic. Across Europe, the World Health Organization study 'Growing up unequal' (Inchley 2016) examines the health, behaviour, and subjective views of school-age children. As far as they can, Innocenti/ UNICEF (United Nations Children's Fund) have used the same categories of data across the OECD (Organisation for Economic Co-operation and Development) countries (Table 9.1). Analysts in compiling Table 9.1

Table 9.1 Twenty-nine developed countries ranked according to the overall well-being of their children. A white background indicates a place in the top third of the table, pale grey denotes the middle third, and white with thick black border the bottom third

	Overall well-being Average rank (all 5 dimensions)	Dimension 1 Mental well-being (rank)	Dimension 2 Health and safety (rank)	Dimension 3 Education (rank)	Dimension 4 Behaviours and risks (rank)	Dimension 5 Housing and environment (rank)
1 Netherlands	2.4	1	5	1	1	4
2 Norway	4.6	3	7	6	4	3
3 Iceland	5	4	1	10	3	7
4 Finland	5.4	2	3	4	12	6
5 Sweden	6.2	5	2	11	5	8
6 Germany	9	11	12	3	6	13
7 Luxembourg	9.2	6	4	22	9	5
8 Switzerland	9.6	9	11	16	11	1
9 Belgium	11.2	13	13	2	14	14
10 Ireland	11.6	17	15	17	7	2
11 Denmark	11.8	12	23	7	2	15
12 Slovenia	12	8	6	5	21	20
13 France	12.6	10	10	15	13	16
14 Czech Republic	15.2	16	8	12	22	18
15 Portugal	15.6	21	14	18	8	17
16 United Kingdom	15.8	14	16	24	15	10
17 Canada	16.6	15	27	14	16	11
18 Austria	17	7	26	23	17	12
19 Spain	17.6	24	9	26	20	9
20 Hungary	18.4	18	20	8	24	22
21 Poland	18.6	22	18	9	19	26
22 Italy	19.2	23	17	25	10	21
23 Estonia	20.8	19	22	13	26	24
24 Slovakia	20.6	25	21	21	18	19
25 Greece	23.4	20	19	28	25	25
26 United States	24.8	26	25	27	23	23
27 Lithuania	25.2	27	24	19	29	27
28 Latvia	26.4	26	28	20	28	28
29 Romania	28.6	29	29	29	27	29

1 to 10   11 to 20   21 to 29

looked at 26 internationally comparable indicators spread across five categories. These include material well-being, health and safety, birth weight, and immunization rates. The 'Education' category includes participation in early childhood education; the number of 15- to 19-year-olds not in employment, training, or education; and the average PISA score (PISA, OECD Programme for International Student Assessment). In the 'Behaviours and risks' category, attention is given to overweight, teenage fertility, rate of use of alcohol and cannabis, and measures on fighting and bullying.

In Table 9.1, each country's overall rank is based on its average ranking for the five dimensions of child well-being considered in this review. Lack of data on a number of indicators means that the following countries, although OECD and/or EU members, could not be included in the league table of child well-being: Australia, Bulgaria, Chile, Cyprus, Israel, Japan, Malta, Mexico, New Zealand, the Republic of Korea, and Turkey.

At the top of Table 9.1 comes the Netherlands, which also manages to be the only country leading for all five categories. At the bottom come three of the poorest countries, all ex-Soviet states—Latvia, Lithuania, and Romania—and one of the richest—the United States.

In sixteenth place is the United Kingdom, a reasonable proxy for Scotland.

Scotland's attention to the needs of children and their parents

To take seriously Scotland's performance in child well-being, we need to take stock. The most repeated words of Scottish cabinet secretaries and ministers are, 'We want Scotland to be the best place in the world to bring up children.'

If this were a football table in 2017, Scotland, we would be comparing Celtic and the top of the Premier League with the sixteenth team in Scotland, Queen of the South. Or in England, Chelsea against Burnley in sixteenth place. If Queen of the South or Sunderland were to top their respective leagues, there would need to be some dramatic financial and managerial changes. It is good to have an aspiration, but if it is a serious intent, actions need to match words. Averages across the UK are presented in the table, but we know that the highs and lows of child-wellbeing do not fall like rain, equally across all children.

For instance, our best estimates suggest Scotland has an estimated 220,000 children living in poor households (Scottish Government 2016)—that is more than one in five of our children—and we know that the gap between the 'haves' and 'have nots' is increasing. Many children will be living with additional negative factors, such as parental alcohol and substance misuse, mental health issue, or domestic abuse problem. We know these are our most vulnerable children, but we struggle to effectively engage with their parents.

The work of Richard Wilkinson and Katie Picket in *The Spirit Level* (Wilkinson and Picket 2009) plots the level of income inequality in society against a number of outcomes in terms of life expectancy, mental health, obesity, educational performance, and levels of violence. Their findings demonstrate the impact of inequality across all sectors of society. For instance, they illustrated that in some countries, life expectancy for the poorest was actually higher than that for the richest in comparator countries. The differences were accounted for in terms of the gap between the 'haves' and the 'have nots', with the smaller the gap, the longer everyone lives. However, this is at a whole-population level, and we know that within populations there are some complex things going on. Being poor doesn't automatically mean you will experience poor outcomes—rather, that your chances of experiencing them will increase. Alcoholism, neglect, and abuse happen in middle-class homes too. Being poor doesn't solely explain the severity of the impact on health within Scotland, and there are, as yet, some unknown additional factors at play.

'Growing Up in Scotland' is a longitudinal study started in 2005 that follows two cohorts of children: a birth cohort (age 0–1 years) and a child cohort (age 2–3 years). They conduct periodic sweeps of data. Light is shed on 'within-population' differences (Growing Up in Scotland 2015). The study identified children who were living in persistently poor households, children who were temporarily poor, and children who avoided living in poverty, and compared the three situations against a range of measures. What they found was that lack of work and lone parenthood were the most influential factors in whether a family would experience persistent poverty. They go on to detail the outcomes for the children living in persistent poverty compared to the other groups of children. Children who lived longer in poor circumstances were more likely to have accidents or injuries and experience social, emotional, and behavioural difficulties. However, once control factors such as other family and area characteristics were taken into account, the direct relationship disappeared. The researchers concluded that the interaction between poverty and measuring outcomes for children was complex, and low income was one of a number of factors contributing to outcomes for children.

This is significant, as the researchers concluded that the impact of poverty could not be simply related to the level of income or the period of exposure to poor circumstances. There were links between persistent poverty and maternal health, low education, and family composition (in terms of lone parenthood), and the researchers suggested that the findings indicated the need for policies that were specific to children who experience persistent poverty, and specific support for families and mothers with risk characteristics.

They noted that at the present time, in Scotland, we have neither policies nor practices that specifically target children living in persistent poverty, nor do we have specific support for families and mothers with risk factors. It is worth noting that the Scottish Government has signalled its intention to maintain child poverty monitoring through the Child Poverty Bill introduced into the Scottish Parliament in February 2017 (Scottish Government 2017), and it remains to be seen what impact the resultant act will achieve.

Parenting and poverty or wealth: Not always related

Despite these findings, most financially poor parents do a wonderful job raising their families. All parents of young children are tested and struggle; it is impossible to survive those sleepless, demanding days as an island of a parent/carer, cut off from other people. Parenting is about what we do personally but also about the population or community effect: what all other parents do and the mindset and behaviour of employers, grandparents, neighbours, and public services. It is a mistake to think that poor parenting is the preserve of income-poor parents who are unemployed or navigating zero-hours contracts. Middle-class children are neglected and abused. Domestic abuse, sexual abuse, self-harm, and alcoholism do not stop and start at a particular salary level. People tend to marry people of similar background and class. There are many two-job households that 'have it all and do it all'; they need to be in early, leave late, work weekends, and travel far and outsource the children. It is hard to hear the cries of help from children who have been outsourced in designer clothes, carrying the latest electronic game. Across the social spectrum in Britain there is abuse of alcohol, domestic abuse, sexual abuse, marriage and family breakdown, drug taking, depression, self-harm, eating disorders, and the use of illicit drugs. Many parents get it more right than wrong, but what is hard to ignore is the entire population effect.

Kaiser Permanente is a private health insurance company in the USA; by definition, the people who pay to be on their books are the 'better off' in America. It was this group of wealthier Americans who reported singular or multiple adverse experiences from their childhood.

Everyone drinks too much is the most plausible public health explanation of high levels of alcohol consumption. Behaviour for good or bad is contagious. Go for a coffee and if the first person ordering has a biscuit or slice of chocolate cake, you are much more likely 3 minutes later to be munching away.

We have already identified the concerns about public services and the impact of unequal income distribution. In Scotland, at a population level, there is another factor at work: we do not care enough about young children. A Dutch woman we know who spent the first half of her life in Holland (top of the child-wellbeing table) and the second half in Scotland expressed the difference: 'In Holland we love children; in Scotland you tolerate them' (Sinclair 2011). It is a serious mistake to frame the problem of early years and poor parenting as synonymous with the poor and feckless. Like alcohol consumption across Scotland, poor parenting runs across the population.

Stretching the public spend

Another dimension of where we are now is how public money is raised and spent. As a result of fiscal devolution, the point is rapidly being reached where 50% of the budget will come from revenues directly raised in Scotland. The pressure is on: in the six-year-period from 2010/11 to 2016/17, public sector capital expenditure has reduced by 12% and revenue expenditure by 5% (Fraser of Allander Institute 2016). Expenditure controlled in Scotland is dominated by the annual Health and Wellbeing spend-forecast to reach £12,767 million by 2020/21.

A bold commitment has been made by the Scottish Government to double the number of hours of free early years education and childcare to 30 hours for vulnerable two-year-olds and all three- and four-year-olds by 2021.

The changing age composition of the population has started to create a care and financial crisis, with the NHS struggling to manage its budget and provide the level of expected care. More is to come. Currently, three people work to support one older person. By around 2035, there will only be two people in work to support each older person.

Older people are living longer, and the older they live, the greater the costs in managing multiple medical conditions and caring for frailty. By 2031, it is estimated that Scotland's population of 85 years-plus will rise by 144%.

Health budgets have largely been protected, and social care and elderly care have been merged across the country. Where we are does not look sustainable. 'In spite of the large financial costs of the (financial) crisis, the major threat to long-term fiscal solvency is still represented, at least in the advanced countries, by unfavourable demographic trends.' So states the International Monetary Fund in its paper, 'The Fiscal Implications of the Global Economic and Financial Crisis'.

Older people already exert a major influence on health expenditure, and that is destined to grow. Somewhere between 25% and 40% of average lifetime health expenditure comes in the last few months of life. Lee, Donehower, and Miller (2011) examined the US National Transfer Accounts between 1960 and 2007. What became clear was the biased and significant growth of welfare-spend towards the over-60s and the over-80s. We have not been able to find a similar piece of work looking at UK trends, but the suspicion is that the picture holds true throughout the UK.

A gravitational pull is compounding existing design failures and making it ever more difficult to find space and money for the very young.

Presented in this way it looks like an unedifying fight between babies and parents on one side of the ring, and frail elderly people in the other corner. This fight could undermine the sustainability of the welfare state. Too few hands in the workplace represent a threat to the older population and undermine the social contract. Scotland needs all young people to be ready and fit for work and paying taxes. Older people need investment in the human capital of the young (Sinclair 2018). What is good for the young is good for the future of society.

Compare the international table on child well-being looked at earlier (Table 9.1) with tables on well-being of older people, and one finds a remarkable fit: the countries doing best in looking after the young do best in looking after the old.

Why does Scotland treat early years and parenting as a peripheral issue?

A car engine is complicated. Traffic-flows in and out of a city are complex, with seemingly unrelated factors such as weather, work start and finishing times, road accidents, public transport failures, and roadworks all conspiring to create the actual conditions on the road. Understanding neurological arguments and time-series data is complicated. There is a similar complexity in fathoming why the first 1,001 days of life are not taken more seriously and what can be done to improve public policy and the culture of what parents do.

A practical illustration of how another complex issue in public policy was resolved can be seen in the ban on smoking in public places in Scotland. Objectively, the message coming from medical science told us that smoking cigarettes, passively or actively, was bad for our health. Increasingly the NHS and the government wanted to act, and it was noted that Ireland had already moved. But before bringing in legislation through the Scottish

Parliament, there was a long-term awareness-raising campaign to get the message across that smoking was a public health issue. There were numerous phases to this awareness and various attempts to shift smoking behaviours. This provided the platform for considering legislative measures on public behaviour. When public opinion was tested and the government found that a big swathe of citizens supported a ban on smoking in public, emboldened government passed the legislation.

Simply blaming government in Holyrood or Westminster is too easy. There is a compelling case for supporting parents from conception through to the first two or three years of life. There was a compelling case for the abolition of slavery and giving women the vote. Change came through a civil war in the USA and much agitation in the UK. Even then, different states maintained their own discriminatory laws, and racists continued to do whatever they could to keep the black person in their place.

In Holland and other countries that do best in child well-being, three features stand out. First, there is the recognition that parenting should be recognized as a high priority in public policy. Second, there is a healthy culture; it is what parents do along with neighbours, grandparents, and friends. Third, there is active public discussion, agitation, and policy to improve on what they are already doing.

What should we do? It helps if we look to the best

Attached parenting is achieved when babies get sensitive care and the watching adult tunes in to their needs. When babies get this care and attention, their capacity increases many times over. Avoidant parenting means that a caring parent is not there, or only inconsistently there. Parents do not pick up on the messages that come from babies. Avoidant parenting is a term most usually applied to individual parents, but in truth it could be applied to Scotland as a country.

Among young children in Scotland there are rising levels of dyslexia, attention deficit hyperactivity disorder (ADHD), autism, obesity, and stresses. For teenagers and young adults, there are high rates of self-harm, suicide, and depression. What is going on, and does our society care enough? A lot of psychopathologizing goes on when the root problem is that 'we', as parents and as a state, do not know how to look after our children.

Compare the inconsistent state support for parenting in Scotland with that in the Netherlands (top of the UNICEF table). During a Scottish pregnancy there will be scans delivered by different practitioners, a very quick in-and-out visit to hospital to deliver the baby, and in most cases contact with the health visitor during the first ten days, and then you are on your own with the reassuring words, 'Come and see us if you have a problem'. Only recently has a health-visitor-led assessment been re-introduced at 27–30 months.

In the Netherlands during pregnancy, usually at week 34, the mother is visited at home by a representative of the Kraamzorg organization to discuss the type of support the mother needs, depending on the mother's choice of a home or hospital birth. A qualified healthcare professional, the *kraamverzorgster*, comes to the home after the birth for eight to ten days to ensure that the mother's recovery is taking place, and that the home and baby are clean, and to support the mother with feeding. The *kraamverzorgster* is also there to ensure that there is good order in the house and that the baby's development is appropriate.

For over a hundred years in the Netherlands, the centrepiece of support from after birth to school age is the local mother and baby well-being clinic (*Consultatiebureau*) (Sinclair 2012). One home visit is made shortly after birth. The parent(s) and child then visit the clinic in weeks 4 and 8, then in months 3, 4, 6, 7, 9, 11, 14, and 18, then at 2 years, 3 years, and 3.9 years, and then at 5 or 6 years as children learn to read and write. Clinics are staffed by doctors who attend to health, social and emotional development, motor skills, language, and general health, and by nurses who concentrate on baby care, parenting, feeding, toileting, and sleeping. Back-up for health and development is provided by walk-in surgeries and a telephone helpline.

Several features are worth stressing. This is a human, very personal service. However, service is not the right word because that suggests an efficient industrial-type process. The basis of the mother and baby well-being clinics is a set of relationships, built up through continuity of contact with a nurse and a doctor. It is truly comprehensive across the country for all babies and their parents and looks at the child from a more holistic perspective: their development, language, and emotional life, and how the parent(s) cope—or do not. Parents who are international management consultants or are unemployed and living on the seventh floor of a tower block appreciate the support and know that if there is a development delay or a sleep or feeding issue, specialist help will rapidly be put to task.

You begin to understand why the Netherlands, with this health and development service and a culture that 'loves' children, is at the top of the child well-being league. And why Scotland, with a threadbare technical health system and parents that largely 'tolerate' children, is an avoidant nation. But it does not stop there. In any field of endeavour you find that people who are really good, at the top of their game, are busy putting in place how to be even better.

Family centres augmenting the mother and baby well-being clinics are being rolled out across the Netherlands. Their genesis comes from the judgement that, for too many children, what was happening in their lives was not as it should be. A group of local authorities authored a report that identified that the 'youth chain' was not working: no one owned the problem; issues affecting children and parents needed to be seen as pivotal; local cooperation between different services was too loose; and help was insufficient. In short, support needed to be timely and tailored.

Central government and its advisors recognized the problem and, as in Scotland, saw a long line of adolescent mental and behavioural challenges: instead of psychopathologizing children, they acted.

Family centres are being rolled out in every neighbourhood, in all 418 municipalities. Their aim was to provide a vehicle for spotting and anticipating problems, giving guidance and counselling, and creating a route for coordinating local care—one family, one plan. Mother and baby well-being clinics and family centres are a formidable preventative and early-intervention bulwark.

Dutch practitioners and policy makers do not see themselves leading the way in bringing up children. There is no triumphalism: they are too aware of the many warts—the human dysfunction in their communities and the intergenerational barriers—to think that it is 'job done'.

Government action

The Scottish Government has come to recognize the wisdom and benefits of services for parenting and early years. Nicola Sturgeon, in her earliest speech as First Minister, signalled a major expansion of day care so that more parents (mothers) can go back to work. In addition, the number of health visitors has been significantly increased and an ambitious early years collaborative across community planning partnerships in each area of Scotland has been beating the drum and setting some firm goals and measures. These originally included ensuring positive pregnancies for mothers and improving the rate of live births—by the end of 2016, 85% of children should reach expected development milestones at the 27- to 30-month health review, and by the end of 2017, 90% of all children should have reached their expected development milestone at the time they start school. However, the date for meeting these ambitious targets has been shunted to 2020 and it is too early to say whether the community planning partnerships, which vary greatly across the country, will be able to deliver.

Day care at two or three years of age does help parents get back to work and manage their money. But day care comes after the first 1,001 days and swerves around the key issue. How do the primary carers, most likely the mother and father, behave during pregnancy and sensitively attend to the first months of life?

Politicians are wary of being painted as a nanny state interfering in parental responsibilities. Political parties and governments, like the banks and the City, jump to the short term, the urgent over the important, a headline and a fashion statement over the long term and the substantial. Public expenditure gets locked into what public expenditure has funded in the past.

Central government creates the climate and works with local authorities and the NHS to deliver public services. Attempting to reorganize public services when the cake of public money is getting smaller presents its own challenge. It is not long before 'producer capture' by the professionals and workers associated with, say, closing a school or hospital or changing a service will vociferously protect their patch. Bigger elbows and the higher you sit in the establishment (as opposed to the wisdom of your case), the better your success.

Older people vote; the middle-aged children of older people have a voice and vote—while babies who have the most number of adverse conditions die young, as we saw earlier. Babies and people who die young have a weak public voice and avoid polling booths. In consequence, as the Institute of Fiscal Studies has shown, families with young children have taken the biggest hit, as the public spending belt gets pulled tighter.

At an executive level, health-board chairs and chief executives have their collars felt if they do not manage budgets and waiting times and reduce hospital-induced infections. Early years, and what parents do, is peripheral—no cause for loss of sleep. Performance measures abound, but the big measures bypass child well-being and child development. If there are no major parent and early years performance measures and no one held accountable, how will the wheel turn?

In arbitrating how public money is spent, finding the best rate of return from that expenditure becomes all the more critical. As was touched on earlier, a very small amount of public money is currently spent on the period from conception through pregnancy until the second year of life. It is the period before school and before day care (Glover 2011; Heckman 2008), when attachment is either made or not made, that has the most profound effect on a child's life. It is what parents do and do not do in this first 1,001 days that matters the most in subsequently reducing the chance of adverse incidents. It would help if Government framed the issue this way and raised it up the political and executive agenda. It would also help if we, the people, as citizens and parents, demonstrated by what we do that we cared more about young children and were a bit louder in our protests.

Conclusion

Evidence on the effectiveness of supporting parents in the first 1,001 days of life is available by the truckload from different fields of knowledge. That children—very young children—have human rights is indisputable. It is the practice that is found wanting: politically and institutionally, favour is granted to older children, adults, and older people. Political and public policy ought to be directed at what it is right to do and what gives the best rate of return. Instead, attention and resources are directed by body weight, age, and the ability to use elbows. The attention being given in policy and political circles to supporting parents and early years is still at a relatively low level and it will most likely continue that way until the public, the citizens, and the chattering classes decide that they, too, need to agitate. There is, of course, a chance that right thinking might win out, aided by the fact that it makes economic sense.

References

'ACES Too High' News, https://acestoohigh.com/, accessed 16 Mar 2018.

'Equally Safe: Scotland's Strategy to prevent and eradicate violence against women and girls', Scottish Government. https://beta.gov.scot/publications/equally-safe/ [Accessed 27/05/18].

Felitti, V.J., Anda, R.F., Nordenberg, D., Williamson, D.F., Spitz, A.M., Edwards, V., Koss, M.P., and Marks, J.S. (1998). Relationship of childhood abuse and household dysfunction to many of the leading causes of death in adults: The Adverse Childhood Experiences (ACE) Study. *American Journal of Preventive Medicine*, **14**, 245–58.

Fraser of Allander Institute (2016). *Scotland's Budget 2016*. Glasgow, UK: Strathclyde University.

'Geneva Declaration of the Rights of the Child' (1924), http://www.un-documents.net/gdrc1924.htm, accessed 16 Mar 2018.

Glover, V. (2011). Annual Research Review: Prenatal stress and the origins of psychopathology: an evolutionary perspective. *Journal of Child Psychology and Psychiatry*, **52**(4), 356–67.

Glover, V. and Sutton, C. (2012). Support from the start: Effective programmes in pregnancy. *Journal of Children's Services*, **7**(1), 8–17.

Growing Up in Scotland (2015). *Tackling inequalities in the early years: Key messages from 10 years of the Growing Up in Scotland study*. Edinburgh, UK: The Scottish Government.

Heckman, J.J. (2008). Schools, skills, and synapses. *Economic Inquiry*, 46(3), 289–324.

Heckman, J.J. (2013). 'Lifelines for poor children', *The New York Times* (from *The New York Times'* opinion pages, The Great Divide series on inequality), 15 September 2013.

Heckman, J.J. and Masterov, D. (2005). Skill policies for Scotland. In: D. Coyle, W. Alexander, and B. Ashcroft (eds.) *New Wealth for Old Nations: Scotland's Economic Prospects*. Princeton, NJ: Princeton University Press, pp. 119–65.

Inchley, J. (2016). *Growing Up Unequal: Gender and Socioeconomic Differences in Young People's Health and Well-Being*, Health behaviour in school-aged children (HBSC) study: international report from the 2013/2014 survey (Health Policy for Children and Adolescents, No. 7), World Health Organization.

Morewitz, S.J. (2004). *Domestic Violence and Maternal and Child Health: New Patterns of Trauma, Treatment, and Criminal Justice Responses*. Dordrecht, The Netherlands: Kluwer Academic/Plenum.

National Institute of Mental Health, 'The Teen Brain: 6 Things to Know', https://www.nimh.nih.gov/health/publications/the-teen-brain-6-things-to-know/index.shtml, accessed 16 Mar 2018.

PISA, 'OECD Programme for International Student Assessment', https://www.oecd.org/pisa/, accessed 16 Mar 2018.

Scottish Government (2008). *Futureskills Scotland: Skills in Scotland 2008*. Edinburgh, UK: The Scottish Government.

Scottish Government (2013). *Getting Our Priorities Right*. Edinburgh, UK: The Scottish Government.

Scottish Government (2016). *Poverty and Income Inequality in Scotland: 2014/15*, Poverty and Income Inequality in Scotland figures, Table A1: Relative Poverty in Scottish Households 1994/5 to 2014/15, http://www.gov.scot/Publications/2016/06/3468/downloads, accessed 16 Mar 2018.

Scottish Government (2017). 'Child Poverty (Scotland) Bill', http://www.parliament.scot/parliamentarybusiness/Bills/103404.aspx, accessed 16 Mar 2016.

Sher, J. (2016). *Missed Periods: Scotland's Opportunities for Better Pregnancies, Healthier Parents and Thriving Babies the First Time … and Every Time*. Glasgow, UK: NHS Greater Glasgow and Clyde.

Shonkoff, J.P. and Phillips, D.A. (eds.) (2000). *From Neurons to Neighborhoods: The Science of Early Childhood Development* (National Research Council, National Institute of Medicine, US; Committee on Integrating the Science of Early Childhood Development). Washington, DC: The National Academies Press.

Sinclair, A. (2011). *Early Years and Transformational Change*. Churchill Travelling Fellowship, Winston Churchill Memorial Trust, http://www.wcmt.org.uk/sites/default/files/migrated-reports/835_1.pdf, accessed 16 Mar 2018.

Sinclair, A. (2012), 'What Chance Scotland?' Parenting across Scotland, http://www.parentingacrossscotland.org/publications/essays-about-parenting/parenting/what-chance-scotland/, accessed 16 Mar 2018.

Sinclair, A. (2018). *Right from the Start: Investing in Parents and Babies*, Postcards from Scotland. Paisley, UK: CCWB Press.

'The Wise Group', https://www.thewisegroup.co.uk/ [Accessed 11/01/17]

UNCRC (2005). General Comment No.7, Implementing child rights in early years, CRCF/C/GC/7/Rev.1.

UNCRC (2016). UK and NI Concluding Observations, CRC/C/GBR/CO/5.

Wilkinson, R. and Pickett, K. (2009). *The Spirit Level: Why More Equal Societies Almost Always Do Better*. London: Allen Lane.

Chapter 10

Gender balance in the childcare workforce: Why having more men in childcare is important

Kenny Spence and Gary Clapton

Histories of unfair segregation and neglect

We are aware that in the past not very many women went to university to study maths or science, and that a concerted effort to address this took place, including the recruitment of more female maths and science teachers, with very successful results. 'Positive female role models are important if we are to transform some of the preconceptions that the public, young girls, their teachers and parents have about who becomes a scientist, technologist, engineer or mathematician' (WISE 2017).

If we accept that this increase in outcomes is due to the fact that women understand how women learn, the converse might apply to boys. Men should understand how boys learn, as they have been boys themselves. Therefore, a greater emphasis might be placed now on the needs of boys—how to ensure better outcomes for them with an understanding of their inherent impulses for activity and gaining experience.

Supporting work with male teachers, including fathers, in their roles relating to child development and parenting in early years, helps all children reach appropriate developmental milestones. Making a positive difference to children they know well, through parenting and productive companionship in teaching, is one of the most important jobs that any adult can have in life. The lack of male staff in early education is recognized as a significant factor in discouraging men from gaining access to childcare services (Cavanagh and Smith 2001, cited by Lamb 2010).

The importance of early paternal care, and its risks

When a baby is born, the brain is developing at a rapid rate. It is at this time that the baby learns about the world, and about relationships. If these pathways for understanding how to act in the world and with others are not animated in the first months and year of a baby's life, that part of the baby's brain will under develop. This is the part of the brain that teaches us how to care for other people and how to have positive relationships with them. The most important teachers the baby has are naturally its main, most intimate, caregivers—its mum and dad.

A baby's best chance in life—is to have a mum and dad who are working together as a team, taking care of them in complementary, mutually supportive ways. However, if this is not the case, if the kindness of parenting is not shared between mother and father, the development of the child suffers.

> Children with involved, loving fathers are significantly more likely to do well in school, have healthy self-esteem, exhibit empathy and pro-social behaviour, and avoid high-risk behaviours such as drug use, truancy, and criminal activity compared to children who have uninvolved fathers.
>
> (National Fatherhood Initiative 2004)

Accepting that the most important teachers every baby seeks are its natural caregivers—their mum and dad—what if there is no dad at home and no male caregiver, and possibly no positive male role model at all? It then becomes vitally important that these children meet and relate to such a role model, a kind and attentive man, while they develop their skills in the early years. Otherwise the role model they may aspire to in later years may be a very different one to the positive one we would want them to emulate.

One of the most exciting things that can happen in a man's life is becoming a father. The emotions a man feels at the time of a child's birth often catch them by surprise. The joy, playfulness, feelings of protectiveness for a child, caring with consideration, and putting someone else first are all things a child needs. A father is in the ideal person to provide this, along with a child's mother.

We know the importance of a mother's love to support a child's development. A father's love is equally important. The caring role of fathers can have a profound impact on both the father and the child, enabling both to feel valued and loved. The positive impact that this can have on a child's life must not be underestimated.

The importance of children having access to both parents is endorsed by the United Nations. The UN Convention on the Rights of the Child affirms that 'States Parties shall use their best efforts to ensure recognition of the principle that both parents have common responsibilities for the upbringing and development of the child' (United Nations 1989, Article 18, paragraph 1). Parents or, as the case may be, legal guardians have the primary responsibility for the upbringing and development of the child. The best interests of the child will be their basic concern.

One of the most important responsibilities that a father can have in life is to make sure that their child can feel supported, valued, and wanted. When we experience someone caring for us, we feel more confident and able to cope with difficulties, challenges, and responsibilities, and we will also do better academically. Fathers talk differently to their children from mothers, and language develops more richly with their contribution. Fathers also play differently with their children, encouraging social and emotional skills to develop more creatively. High-quality (sensitive and supportive) and substantial in-volvement of the father from the first month following birth is connected with a range of positive outcomes in babies and toddlers, including better language development and higher IQs at 12 months and at three years (Yogman et al. 1995).

For many children and fathers, this keeping and building a close and creative relationship has a number of challenges. In the USA and UK, nearly 50% of marriages end in divorce, and within two years of separation two out of three of the children of these divorces no longer see their father (*The Guardian* 2010).

Improving the balance

If the number of qualified male childcare workers increases, fathers and male carers will also become more involved in events at childcare settings and more actively aware of their child's needs and development. By having more qualified men available from the recruitment pool, awareness will be raised that men can look upon childcare as a viable and rewarding career, and more employers will look upon male childcare workers as the 'norm'. Males, either as parents or carers, will feel more at ease interacting within any childcare setting and be more likely to engage in relaxed conversation around insights for improving children's lives in their early years. This will help in building greater parental/community involvement, and more men and women will become aware of the importance of a positive male role model in children's lives, and in the lives of men.

The early months of a child's life are critical in terms of development of the mind, the body, and the spirit. A great deal of a small child's development at this time is social, and that social development would be enhanced with the opportunity to interact with both women and men.

Cooperation between parents enriches the life of both, and their child's world

Men and women are different. They have complementary qualities and talents, and they share different experiences with children. Children themselves are individuals too, who need to share different things with different adult companions. We now know that 80% of a child's brain is developed by the time they are three years old (Ekaban and Sadowsky 1978). If we know that, then we have a responsibility to ensure a rich social and emotional development for young children. Often, this is not available to children because of an absence of gender balance in the childcare workforce.

Imagine for a moment you were a little girl and after you were born you came home from hospital and most of your home environment consisted of your father and his friends. You then went into a nursery and found only male staff, and once you reached primary school you found again almost exclusively male teachers. What opportunities would be provided for you as a little girl to appreciate different role models in life with persons who have different abilities? This kind of lack of gender diversity, and no male role models, is the experience of many boys in early childhood.

Research has consistently shown that positive male role models, both at home and within early years childcare settings, provide significant long-term benefits for children's development and their confidence (Brownhill 2010, p. 12).

The need for qualified male carers was recognized a century ago

The idea of having men in childcare working in an early years environment is not a new one. Robert Owen the industrialist, who created the village of New Lanark so that his mill workers had reasonable accommodation, also thought that young children should not be in the factory. He then set up a nursery, and decided he needed to find a kind man—someone who had unlimited patience with the children of New Lanark. He chose a weaver, called James Buchanan, who was a man with a kind heart. James was joined by a colleague, Molly Young, a girl from the village who was 17 years old.

Thus, the first early years setting in Scotland had a gender balance, and because of its success, when the first nursery in England was set up in London in 1818 to provide a service for children from one to six years old, they recruited James Buchanan to assist the project. James took the ideas that he had developed in New Lanark to the new setting in London.

The situation now

What has changed in our society that brings recognition that the involvement of men is now so important again for our children, for politicians, and for families, to enable us to make progress? There are more single dads. In some areas there are men-only childcare training courses. The media are much more supportive. In most areas the salary for those working in childcare has improved. Government ministers are taking an interest. And because there are more men in related jobs with children, there is more peer support. There have also been more changes in UK legislation, including the implementation of a Gender Equality Duty (Equality Act 2006).

Men in non-traditional occupations may feel they have less to gain and much to lose. Sometimes it is considered that the low level of salary is an inhibitor of male participation, but this is not the primary reason. Early childcare is too often considered an exclusively female task. But this can change.

Steps to gain the benefits of having more men in childcare

A more gender-balanced staff group brings different ways of looking at issues. Fathers benefit because they have someone to relate to and may feel more at ease. Having more men working in childcare provides additional support, and changes the dynamics of childcare settings.

This is a necessary change given that there are very few resources from the past for men, early years settings having been historically feminized. There is still a lack of support for single dads in the community. Men often have difficulty requesting support for parenting. One in four men say they would consider working in the childcare sector, but according to research from the Equal Opportunities Commission (EOC), only 1 in 50 carers in England are male. There is need to change this (Ashcroft 2014).

Early childhood education and care (ECEC) has been on the political agenda of the EU Gender Action Plan for 25 years. In 1992, the EU Council of Ministers produced recommendations to promote and encourage increased participation of men in child-care, with equal pay for men and women for the same work (The Council of Ministers of the European Community 1992, Article 6). The European Social Fund subsequently funded several projects to attract men into ECEC jobs. In 1996, the European Commission Childcare Network recommended an increase in the proportion of men in ECEC to a level of 20% (Peeters 2007). After years of sustained commitment and policy priority, Norway has had the best result in Europe, with a male share of 10%. The other countries with the highest level of male ECEC jobs are Denmark, Germany, and Scotland (Cremers et al. 2010).

The European policy of providing all our children with the best start (Council of the European Union 2011) aims to attract men and boys into jobs and areas of employment such as care work, education, and healthcare, which, until more recently, have largely been regarded as female ones. There is a European-wide acknowledgement that there is a crisis in the care sector and a labour shortage in care jobs. As the Equal Opportunity Commission stated in 2003, male educators could help resolve labour shortages in the area. This becomes especially important when there is a demand to expand early childcare in response to a change in legislation. There is a desire across Europe to increase the amount of early childcare. Institutions involved in ECEC appear to want to employ more men, but often do not succeed in actually recruiting men. Research has identified lack of information and of a peer group working in the area as the main obstacles for young men wishing to enter the area of ECEC. In addition, working with secondary schools and their career advisers might help to correct the shortfall of boys making this a choice of career at an earlier stage.

Gendering of care and education is related to age of the children: the younger the child, the higher the proportion of female employment. Although not as underrepresented as for early years, 'men in primary schools' is also an area that needs to be addressed. There are many more men working in secondary schools.

Children need both

Both male and female behaviours are needed as role models for children (Ruxton 1992; Aina and Cameron 2011). Children need to see both men and women in caring roles in order to challenge the stereotype that caring is women's work. Moreover, MacNaughton and Newman (2001) argue that male childcare workers can induct boys into positive masculinity and may help those who lack positive male role models at home.

Male childcare workers provide children with opportunities to experience different approaches to play and interactions, and are able to model behaviour which would challenge negative male stereotypes. A case study conducted by Sumsion illustrates that male childcare workers are able to identify with, and respond to, boys more effectively than are female childcare workers, because they share an understanding of boys' experiences, perspectives, and masculinity (Sumsion 2005). Robust behaviour might be allowed by male childcare workers to continue a little longer than allowed by female colleagues (Yang 2013). Peeters (2007) argues that unruly play is always viewed as aggressive by female childcare workers, and they often have a negative impression of more masculine behaviours than their male colleagues. Men bring more into play, with active movement, entertainment, and 'rough and tumble' play with their own children, and this vitality is imported into the way they interact with others' children in early years (Lydon 2016).

The benefits of involving males in ECEC do not only apply to boys. A number of studies have shown that more male childcare workers in ECEC could benefit both boys and girls through their observing and interacting with men in a non-traditional role. Male childcare workers help both girls and boys construct new ideas of masculinity (Sumsion 2005). Many researchers agree that if there are more men in early childhood settings, this could help to counter children's sex-stereotyped views of gender roles, reduce sexism, and generally advance gender equality (Milloy 2003; Sumsion 2005; Farquhar et al. 2006; Marsiglio 2009):

> I don't know if it's important what sort of role model you are … I'd like to think that I'm a role model that questions the way men have to be … but I don't consciously go out to do that; maybe I'm rejecting the old sort of stereotypes and role models that I had … by default that means I'm something else … and their role models sometimes … they might want a guy to play football.

> (male childcare worker, in Owen 2003, p .5)

The endorsement of non-traditional gender roles in the early years lays the basis for long-term positive attitudes to gender equality by widening male responsibilities in family life and in children's education (Piburn 2006). For example, a mother interviewed in the blog 'Life Behind The Purple Door' (2016) stressed that her daughter can learn to be comfortable around men who are not family members.

Whether one agrees with the notion that men bring added value, Rolfe observes the following:

> However, while stereotyped notions of male and female qualities might be questioned, it is likely that in practice men will bring different skills to the work, reflecting their own gendered up-bringing and culture. The literature frequently states that such diversity enriches children's experiences.

> (Rolfe 2005, p. 11)

Male childcare workers do not just provide advantages to children; they also provide positive outcomes for their parents. Early childhood services, particularly nurseries and pre-schools, are accustomed to working more with mothers than fathers; in other words, a large number of mothers or females prefer to work and communicate with other women, and therefore fathers may often miss out on information or feeling included in their children's time in early years. Thus, a male figure within the nursey or pre-school can support fathers in their involvement and understanding (Rowell 2007; Baker 2012).

Barriers to men seeking work in early childhood education and care

> As an employer we're not, let's face it, most of us don't employ men as nannies; most of us don't. Now you can call that sexist. I call that cautious and very sensible when you look at the stats. Your odds are stacked against you if you employ a man; we know paedophiles are attracted to working with children. I'm sorry, but they're the facts.

> (Andrea Leadsom, UK Government Environment Secretary, 18 July 2016)

Attitudes and prejudices

Childcare is still largely seen as a job for women. By extension, professional childcare is defined as 'women's work' (The Fatherhood Institute 2014; Lydon 2016):

> In terms of advice for men wanting to go into childcare, I would say it is hard work, and go into it with your eyes open. Things have improved since I started out, but you will still encounter prejudice. Don't be naive and think everyone will love you as they won't, and some staff will find it hard to accept you working in childcare.
>
> (Learner 2013)

Such attitudes are expressed by both sexes: 'They look at me and say, "I couldn't do what you are doing". They are quite blunt with me and say, "It's a girl's job"' (childcare worker about his male friends, Ryan 2009). In a recent study of attitudes of friend and family towards nine male childcare workers, an interesting finding was that whilst family members were generally in favour of such career choice, friends were relatively not:

> Many of their friends feel 'very surprised' when they heard of their current activity. Two informants expressed a little bit of disappointment because their friends feel 'very confused' when they hear of their choices, because they think 'there are a number of choices to choose a job, and men should choose masculine jobs like doing business, science, or academics'. They are quite confused.
>
> (Tong 2016, p. 48)

Financing work with children

In Jones' study of the implementing of policy, salaries of male childcare workers were found to vary, with 32% earning £30,000–£39,000, only 19% earning above £40,000, and 13% currently earning below £10,000. While salaries varied greatly, nearly half of the respondents reported that they were satisfied with their earnings (48%), and only 23% were dissatisfied (Jones 2012). When asked to describe the most rewarding part of their current role, respondents referred to the relationships they were able to create with the individuals surrounding them in ECEC settings, including children, parents, and the community. What is more, responses given can be categorized into concerns regarding administration (such as paperwork), staffing issues (including staff morale and staff tension), and the nature of ECEC—relating to job insecurity and the low status of ECEC (Jones 2012).

Good practice with government support

As we have noted, there are success stories promoting gender equality in some countries, by sustained commitment, policy priority, and high professional status achieved through emphasis on training and qualification, notably in Norway and Denmark and Scotland.

An innovative project in Scotland: Men in Childcare

Before the Men in Childcare (MIC) organization became established in Scotland, there were five men working in early years in Edinburgh and 37 men in childcare training across the whole of Scotland. Now, over 8% of men employed in Edinburgh, and 4% in Scotland, are employed in early years childcare. The success in Scotland has been attributed to the efforts of MIC and their 'men-only' courses, where the advertising for enrolment was directly aimed at men (Men in Childcare Scotland).

Over the last 15 years, MIC has advanced as a project to the extent that countries worldwide have taken on board the fairly simple ideas on which the success of the project is based, especially the idea that men will not look at childcare as a career unless invited to do so. They looked at the training needs of the childcare workforce and provided education, support, and a fully integrated package of training to meet the aspirations of men in becoming fully qualified workers in the field. The project supports new entrants to the childcare workforce and unqualified male childcare workers. There is the provision of mentoring for full-time students, linking them to childcare workers, along with funding for all tuition fees, so training is free. In addition, the courses are advertised in local newspapers, emphasizing the need for a qualified workforce with more men working in it.

MIC use an innovative approach to training consisting of a supportive fast-track access course. The course has enabled those who have not undertaken any formal education for an extended period the opportunity to re-engage in structured learning. This course is followed on with training in the UK Higher National Certificate (HNC) in Childcare and Education. The initial courses are for men only. MIC has found that men accessing training in this way find ways to support and encourage each other. MIC identify and address the barriers to unqualified men taking up and completing training and the needs of the learners undertaking this training. Bringing more men into early childhood education is one of the most important keys to the implementation of gender mainstreaming in the area of education. A better representation of men in fields of professional care is of huge social interest, especially when they are positive and creative role models for children. An increased diversity of gender backgrounds can be seen as a resource for better professional practices in the field.

Having more men working in childcare will help counteract the view that childcare is only 'women's work' (Nursery World 2011). Just as it is important for children to have positive female role models, it is surely equally important to have positive male role models.

The situation in Norway

In Norway, a high priority has been given to getting more men working in kindergarten. There was concern that most children were only meeting women during their first 10–12 years, first in *barnehage* (kindergarten), then in school and school-age childcare. They believe in the long-term benefits of gender equality, and are concerned about the message that the preponderance of female staff gives young girls and boys about gender roles (Haugland 2007).

The numbers of male pre-school teachers has been increasing each year. Norway now has a goal of 20% men; they have already increased the proportion of male pre-school teachers from 3% in 1991 to 10% in 2008. There has been a large increase in services during this time, which means that more men working in early years has not been at the cost of jobs for women.

Several municipalities, which have placed more emphasis on the recruitment of men, have up to 25% male workers, while in open air *barnehager*, men make up a third of the staff. There has also been an increase in male students, with some colleges having more than 20% and one with more than 30%.

The situation in Germany

In Germany, for a number of years, there has been a rise in the proportion of men studying at training colleges for the job of 'educator' (ECEC/youth worker) (Cremers et al. 2010). During the academic years 2009/10 to 2013/14, the proportion of male students increased from 13.8% to 16.3%, which corresponds to a rise of 2.5 percentage points. Since educators trained in Germany can also work with youths and young adults (for example in group homes), this increase does not necessarily correlate with an increase in the number of male ECEC workers.

In Germany, in 2013, a total of 19,055 ECEC male workers, interns, and so on, were employed in ECEC centres. This corresponds to a relative proportion of 4.1%. However, the proportion of male ECEC workers, not including interns, was only 3.4%.

The above are notable success stories, but some countries in Europe have had little success. In 2008, the percentage of male childcare workers in England was only 1%–2% (Bartlett and Davies 2015). During the two years between 2010 and 2011, the proportion of male workers in out-of-school provision was 1%, with the proportion elsewhere tending to be somewhat higher—ranging between 6% in before-school settings to 10% in after-school hours settings in 2014 (Brind et al. 2014). Overall, the proportion of male childcare workers within early childhood education and care services remains significantly unchanged; the UK Government's round-up of 2014's official statistics reported that the proportion of male staff working in the sector remained very low for group-based and school-based settings—circa 2% (Brind et al. 2014). In Scotland, male involvement is slightly higher: 95% of pre-school education and day care staff are female (Naumann et al. 2013).

A strategy for making early childhood education mixed-gender

We need to develop a strategy that considers different models and different ways of recruiting, with the objective of promoting childcare as a professional career that is as attractive for men as it is for women.

The process of changing to a gender-neutral name for an early years worker, has begun. The term 'nursery nurse' is now rarely used and workers are more frequently now referred to as 'early years practitioners'. Government policy documents on provision for early years now make explicit references to the special contribution of fathers and other men to a young child's life.

There is an opportunity now to develop campaigns that will increase the number of men in ECEC, with knowledge gained from the successful campaigns in Denmark, Norway, Germany, and Scotland. We need to make the training more man friendly, and to increase the professional status of males by strengthening and making evident the content of their training and the qualification they obtain. Given the lack of men qualified to work with young children, increased training of men as experts in ECEC promises to transform the early life experience of both boys and girls. Men-only orientation programmes such as MIC in Scotland (Men in Childcare), where over 2,000 men have had various levels of college-based childcare training, can change a world where the care of children is accepted as female work, and childcare is perceived to be based on the care a mother must give her infant. Any effective project will need sustained commitment and policy priority for at least ten years (Moss 2003). Political change is needed to explore a broader range of professions for men, particularly those within the childcare sector and primary school teaching.

The decline of boys' academic performances is often discussed in reviews that focus on the absence of men in early childcare, and at later more formal levels of education. The experiences of creative work and recreation that men bring with them, and the different ways they interact with children as companions, can be seen as a resource to enrich children's education.

Furthermore, the Equal Opportunity Commission stated in 2003 that investment in training of male educators could help resolve labour shortages in education (Equal Opportunity Commission 2003). This is especially relevant given the current need to increase the childcare workforce to meet the aspiration of 1,100 hours a year in Scotland for all three- to five-year-olds and all eligible two-year-olds.

By creating a balance in the workforce between male and female, outcomes for all children will be improved. Men, too, can gain significantly from a policy of greater gender equality, signaling the value to them of more involvement with their own children. More male employees can make childcare centres a more father-friendly space, which could have a positive effect on men's family caring contributions, and women and mothers will be better relieved of the - perceived - sole responsibility of a child's care and development.

References

Aina, O.E. and Cameron, P.A. (2011). Why does gender matter? Counteracting stereotypes with young children. *Dimensions of Early Childhood*, 39(3), 11–20.

Ashcroft, J. (2014). 'Social care employers need to recruit more men', *The Guardian*, 4 March, 2014, https://www.theguardian.com/social-care-network/2014/mar/04/social-care-employers-recruit-more-men, accessed 18 Mar 2018.

Baker, R. (2012). ' "Childcare is not just a woman's job"—why only two per cent of the day nurseries and childcare workforce is male', http://www.daynurseries.co.uk/news/article.cfm/id/1557858/childcare-is-not-just-a-womans-job-why-only-two-per-cent-of-the-day-nurseries-and-childcare-workforce-is-male], accessed 18 Mar 2018.

Bartlett, D. and Davies, J. (2015). *Men in childcare: How can we achieve a more gender-balanced early years and childcare workforce?* The Fatherhood Institute, 10 pp.

Brind, R., McGinigal, S., Lewis, J., Ghezelayagh, S., Ransom, H., Robson, J., Street, C., and **Renton, Z.** (2014). *Childcare and Early Years Providers Survey 2013*, Department for Education, September 2014, 270 pp.

Brownhill, S. (2010). 'The "brave" man in the early years (0–8): The ambiguities of the "role model"', paper presented at the British Educational Research Association Annual Conference, University of Warwick, 1–4 September 2010, pp. 1–18.

Cavanagh, B. and Smith, M. (2001). 'Dad's the word: A study of dads in greater Pilton', unpublished manuscript, Strathclyde University, 25 pp. (cited by Lamb 2010).

Council of the European Union (2011). *Early Childhood Education and Care: Providing all our children with the best start for the world of tomorrow*, Council of the European Union, Brussels, 17 February 2011, http://register.consilium.europa.eu/doc/srv?l=EN&f=ST%206264%202011%20INIT, accessed 18 Mar 2018.

Cremers, M. and Krabel, J. (2010). *Male Educators in Kitas: A Study on the Situation of Men in Early Childhood Education*. Germany: BMFSF.

Ekaban, A.S. and Sadowsky, D. (1978). Changes in brain weights during the span of human life: Relation of brain weights to body heights and body weights. *Annals of Neurology*, 4(3), 345–56.

Equal Opportunities Commission (2003). 'How can suitable, affordable childcare be provided for all parents who need to work?' EOC submission to the Work and Pensions Select Committee Inquiry, http://www.eoc.org.uk, accessed 18 Mar 2018.

Equality Act (2006). The Commission for Equality and Human Rights, Chapter 3, 91 pp.

Farquhar, S., Cablk, L., Buckingham, A., Butler, D., and Ballantyne, R. (2006). Men at Work: Sexism in early childhood education. *Childforum Research Network*, New Zealand, 32 pp.

Haugland, E. (2007). 'Focus on Men in the nursery and kindergarten in Norway', http://www.meninchildcare.co.uk/mencare2/Men_in_early_years.html, accessed 18 Mar 2018.

Jones, C. (2012). 'A policy-to-practice study of male professionals within early childhood education and care in England', paper delivered at the 2012 Conference/AGM of TACTYC - Association for Professional Development in Early Years, http://docplayer.net/38445832-A-policy-to-practice-study-of-male-professionals-within-early-childhood-education-and-care-in-england-charlotte-jones.html, accessed 18 Mar 2018.

Lamb, M.E. (2010). *The Role of the Father in Child Development*, 5th edn. Hoboken, NJ: John Wiley.

Learner, S. (2013). 'Profile: Male nursery worker reveals how he faced sexism and prejudice working in the childcare sector', http://www.daynurseries.co.uk/news/article.cfm/id/1559367/male-nursery-worker-reveals-how-he-faced-sexism-and-prejudice-working-in-the-childcare-sector, accessed 18 Mar 2018.

Life Behind the Purple Door (2016). 'Why I'm OK with a male daycare leader', http://www.lifebehindthepurpledoor.com/2016/04/lessons-male-daycare-leader.html, accessed 18 Mar 2018.

Lydon, D. (2016). 'The influence of male practitioners in childcare settings' (by Kelly): 'How can an increase in male practitioners benefit childcare settings?' Early Years Careers, 10 March 2016, http://www.earlyyearscareers.com/eyc/latest-news/the-influence-of-male-practitioners-in-childcare-settings/, accessed 18 Mar 2018.

MacNaughton, G. and Newman, B. (2001). Masculinities and men in early childhood: Reconceptualising our theory and our practice. In: E. Dau (ed.) *The Anti-Bias Approach in Early Childhood*. Sydney, Australia: Longman, pp. 45–157.

Marsiglio, W. (2009). *Getting Guys Hooked on Teaching Young Children*, Teachers College Record. Teachers College: Columbia University, 4 pp.

'Men in Childcare Scotland', http://www.meninchildcare.com/, accessed 18 Mar 2018.

Milloy, M. (2003). The guy teacher. *NEA Today*, 22(2), 22–31.

Moss, P. (2003). Who is the worker in services for young children? *Children in Europe*, 5, 2–5.

'National Fatherhood Initiative' (2004), http://www.fatherhood.org, accessed 18 Mar 2018.

Naumann, I., McLean, C., Koslowski, A., Tisdall, K., and Lloyd, E. (2013). *Early Childhood Education and Care Provision: International review of policy, delivery and funding: final report, Centre for Research on Families and Relationships*, University of Edinburgh, Scottish Government Social Research, March 2013, 164 pp.

Nursery World (2011). 'Men in childcare: Group to fight "sexist" discrimination', http://www.nurseryworld.co.uk/nursery-world/news/1105549/childcare-fight-sexist-discrimination, accessed 18 Mar 2018.

Owen, C. (2003). *Men's work? Changing the gender mix of the childcare and early years workforce* (Facing the Future: Policy Papers), Daycare Trust, the National Childcare Campaign, http://www.koordination-maennerinkitas.de/uploads/media/Owen-Charlie-Men_s-Work_01.pdf, accessed 18 Mar 2018.

Peeters, J. (2007). Including men in early childhood education: Insights from the European experience. *NZ International Research in Early Childhood Education*, **10**, 15–24.

Piburn, D.E. (2006). 'Gender equality for a new generation: Expect male involvement in ECE', *Child Care Exchange*, Mar/Apr, pp. 18–22.

Rolfe, H. (2005). *Men in Childcare*, National Institute of Economic and Social Research, Occupational Segregation, Working Paper Series No. 35, Equal Opportunities Commission, 68 pp.

Rowell, P. (2007). 'Valuing male child care professionals', *Putting Children First*, The Newsletter of the National Childcare Accreditation Council (NCAC), Issue 24 December 2007, pp. 14–16.

Ruxton, S. (1992). *What's He Doing at the Family Centre? Dilemmas of Men Who Care for Children*. London: National Children's Home.

Ryan, M. (2009). Childcare 'not just for women', http://news.bbc.co.uk/1/hi/education/7838538.stm, accessed 18 Mar 2018.

Scottish Government (2013). *Scottish Government Equality Outcomes: Gender Evidence Review*, Communities Analytical Services, Scottish Government Social Research, http://www.gov.scot/Publications/2013/04/8765, accessed 18 Mar 2018.

Sommers, C. (2000). 'The War Against Boys', *The Atlantic*, pp.1–27.

Sumsion, J. (2005). Male teachers in early childhood education: Issues and case study. *Early Childhood Research Quarterly*, **20**(1), 109–123.

The Council of Ministers of the European Community (1992). 'Treaty on European Union, Article 6', https://europa.eu/european-union/sites/europaeu/files/docs/body/treaty_on_european_union_en.pdf, accessed 18 Mar 2018.

The Fatherhood Institute (2014). 'Careers guidance follow-up: Submission by the Fatherhood Institute (8 July 2014): Boys and girls, men and women, in non-traditional occupations', http://www.fatherhoodinstitute.org/wp-content/uploads/2014/07/Fatherhood-Institute-careers-guidance-followup-submission-08072014.pdf, accessed 18 Mar 2018.

The Guardian (2010). 'Divorce rates data, 1858 to now: how has it changed?' http://www.theguardian.com/news/datablog/2010/jan/28/divorce-rates-marriage-ons, accessed 18 Mar 2018.

Tong, Y. (2016). 'Reasons Men Choose to Work in Early Childhood Education and Care (ECEC) in Scotland and Edinburgh in Particular', MSc in Childhood Studies University of Edinburgh, unpublished.

United Nations (1989). The United Nations Convention on the Rights of the Child, Resolution 44/25, 14 pp.

WISE (2017). 'Inspirational role models', https://www.wisecampaign.org.uk/inspiration/tag/role-models, accessed 18 Mar 2018.

Yang, J.E. (2013). Gender balance in early childhood education: Reasons for the lack of male involvement, encouraging men into early childhood teaching, and the impact on children, families, colleagues and the early childhood sector. *He Kupu (The Word)*, **3**(3), 5–11.

Yogman, M.W., Kindlon, D., and Earls, F. (1995). Father-involvement and cognitive-behavioural outcomes of preterm infants. *Journal of the American Academy of Child and Adolescent Psychiatry*, **34**, 58–66.

Chapter 11

The courage of utopia

Robin Duckett and Catherine Reding

Education: Stuffing in or bringing out?

We are often blinded by the light. In considering concepts of 'education' and 'children' and 'quality', it is, surprisingly enough, politicians with their heads in short-term economic interests and in staying elected who wield the lamps, rather than parents and educators. Our elected representatives set the terms of discussion, and the social arguments and definitions. 'That phrase "improve schools" is the perfect election-friendly catch-all' (Rosen 2016).

Like the citizens of the king wearing his invisible 'new clothes', whole societies are taken in by, or collude with, arrant nonsense. It takes the innocent courage of children to speak the truth. In the UK, and in other countries, children are living through a very difficult time. The adults of the world into which they are born are perpetuating an experience of education for them in which their role is to listen and be instructed. But it does not have to be so, as parents are beginning to articulate. On 3 May 2016, an estimated 40,000 English parents kept their children away from SAT tests, in support of creative learning (Let Our Kids Be Kids 2016).

What if school could be a place of excited, intense exploration, not simply a place where children need to learn their letters? What if education is not primarily an 'essential preparation for adult life' (Gibbs 2015), but a context of learning to live well in the present, to meet and explore the world around us with the best of our intelligence?

We invite you to consider education from a human and 'child-like' point of view. In our work with educators, we frequently invite them to remember their passions and enthusiasms when they themselves were young children—and to then go on to rethink their classrooms, and their practice, holding these memories close. Usually they are impelled to transform their ways of being and working with children: it can be an emotional and complicated awakening.

We invite you to do the same.

The examples which we will show are from work with children of three to six years old. However, the principles with which we are working apply to children, and indeed to adults, of whatever age. The general contextual text was written by Robin Duckett, and the extended example by Catherine Reding.

Curiosity and creativity are in our genes

An awareness that we are born creative is far from new. In 1758, Carl Linnæus, in his tenth edition of *Systems of Nature*, denoted 'humans' as *homo sapiens*: 'humans who seek to know' (Linnæus 1758).

And we have plenty of evidence of this from forebears born 'seeking to know'. Looking back and enquiring into the earliest traces we have left of ourselves, we see humans being curious, expressive scientists and artists, enquiring into the nature of the world, finding ways to express feelings, creating ritual art, living well. Two brief reminders of this are provided in Figure 11.1.

This crucial fact is at once obvious, subjective, and emotive—and yet too often neglected in our society. We can see it plainly in the smiles and games that babies exchange with their parents, and in children's play and exploration. We will remember it of ourselves, thinking back, as Chris Miles reminds us in Chapter 5. However, in spite of what we see and know, regulated society chooses to ignore the evidence: we have become accustomed to the idea of education as instruction, as stuff to be delivered, succinctly and urgently.

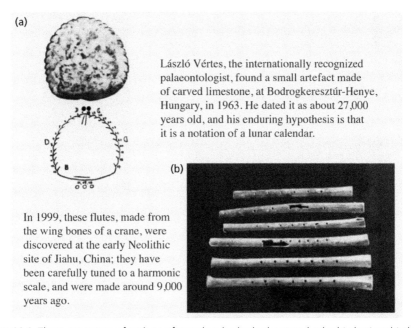

(a) László Vértes, the internationally recognized palaeontologist, found a small artefact made of carved limestone, at Bodrogkeresztúr-Henye, Hungary, in 1963. He dated it as about 27,000 years old, and his enduring hypothesis is that it is a notation of a lunar calendar.

(b) In 1999, these flutes, made from the wing bones of a crane, were discovered at the early Neolithic site of Jiahu, China; they have been carefully tuned to a harmonic scale, and were made around 9,000 years ago.

Figure 11.1 These are traces of actions of people who looked out and asked 'what' and 'why' and 'who'. All people are born to enquire, study, create, celebrate. Being human, this is the essence of what children do—voraciously and expectantly.

(a) From László Vértes, 'Lunar Calendar' from the Hungarian Upper Paleolithic, *Science*, 149 (3686), pp.855–856, DOI: 10.1126/science.149.3686.855 Copyright © 1965, The American Association for the Advancement of Science. Reprinted with permission from AAAS. (b) Reprinted by permission from Macmillan Publishers Ltd: *Nature*, 401 (6751), Juzhong Zhang, Garman Harbottle, Changsui Wang, and Zhaochen Kong, Oldest playable musical instruments found at Jiahu early Neolithic site in China, pp. 366–368, Figure 1, doi:10.1038/43865, Copyright © 1999, Nature Publishing Group.

In England, the education legislation in the Factory Acts 1833–56 set the scene for this very powerfully, with children in rows being instructed, via a monitor system, in 'basic skills', fitting in with their employment in the mills (Wilson 2011). Current politicians, ostensibly talking of education and in their policy-making, frequently instead speak of their overriding concern for growth in the monetary economy: 'the countries that will succeed in this global economy are those that are investing heavily in education and training' [Gordon Brown, 2009, addressing the National College of School Leadership] (Brown 2010). The prime concern is 'education' as a lever for economic advancement, not as a civic quality, or a right of children for their development. Despite all of us being born curious, ready to learn through play and enquiry, other priorities have created an education system that does not satisfy or respect our curious minds.

Loris Malaguzzi's poem 'No way. The hundred is there', first published in 1993 in *The Hundred Languages of Children* (Edwards, Gandini, and Forman 1993), is a passionate observation on the diverse, rich human spirit, the constraining nature of common educational practice, and a call to learn and do differently.

Invece il cento c'è
(*Instead, the hundred is there.*)

The child is made of one hundred.
The child has
a hundred languages
a hundred hands
a hundred thoughts
a hundred ways of thinking
of playing, of speaking.

A hundred.

Always a hundred
ways of listening
of marvelling, of loving
a hundred joys
for singing and understanding
a hundred worlds
to discover
a hundred worlds
to invent
a hundred worlds
to dream.

The child has
a hundred languages
(and a hundred hundred hundred more)
but they steal ninety-nine.
The school and the culture
separate the head from the body.
They tell the child:
to think without hands

to do without head
to listen and not to speak
to understand without joy
to love and to marvel
only at Easter and at Christmas.

They tell the child:
to discover the world already there
and of the hundred
they steal ninety-nine.

They tell the child:
that work and play
reality and fantasy
science and imagination
sky and earth
reason and dream
are things
that do not belong together.

And thus they tell the child
that the hundred is not there.
The child says:
No way. The hundred is there.

Loris Malaguzzi
(Edwards, et al., 1993)

Countless educators are still striving to shape education for curious and creative learners (as have countless past educators), and numbers of adults do remember to value their 'curious child':

> I still see myself as a child—by that I mean I have the curiosity of a child, which I really want to hang on to, because you just want that imagination to fly in every direction; and that's how I need to be. I need to look at something and think 'what do I want to be exploring with this?' and just let that imagination go.
>
> (the percussionist Dame Evelyn Glennie during a 2015 interview, (Glennie 2015)

Easing the window open

So let's begin to look in. Here is a recollection of mine as a young nursery school teacher:

Michael and the leaves, Autumn 1987

Michael, three years old, is by himself, outside at nursery, looking at the leaves in the elder trees. As the teacher outside, I observe from a distance. Some leaves are ready to fall; some have already fallen. Michael touches one and it comes off; and another. He tries to put it back into place, but it doesn't go. Suddenly he runs back into nursery. He swiftly re-emerges with the tape dispenser—I guess he's 'sneaked it'—runs to the trees and starts fixing the leaves back. He was exploring some deep and enduring themes; if we take the trouble to think, it's easy to guess at them. (Pause for a moment: what concepts do *you* think he might be encountering, or considering, in some way?). What did I do? Nothing—well, not quite—I did notice; I didn't shout at him to 'take the tape back where it belongs', and I made sure no other staff did (Duckett 2006).

In 1987, we, in our nursery, did not have the professional structures or expectation to reflect on observations of children's encounters in order to work with them. Our nursery staff were dedicated, for sure, but we understood our role mostly as the presenting of pre-determined educational activities, in parcels of separated skills. But what if we were really set up to attend to Michael and his friends, to really consider his intuitive questioning and seek to work with it?

That is the present and simple challenge: to learn from our observations, and figure out how we can build a pedagogy *with* children, *with* their enquiries.

Discovering principles through practice

As Sightlines Initiative, an independent organization of early childhood educators, we have been endeavouring since 1995 to understand what we could do differently, and to do it differently. We are informed by our own drives of curiosity and understandings, from the observations of past and present colleagues and from our own. Through action-research projects, and reflection, nationally and internationally, we've sought to develop an approach which better connects with all our Michaels.

Some clearly defined grounding principles have evolved.

In this short chapter we will weave principles and examples of practice together: we hope you'll see what we mean, and that these principles can resonate with you also, what-ever your position and endeavours in education or in the world of children.

The first two principles, about children and an education fit for them, are, in a sense, the foundations of all our work:

> Children are rich in curiosity, competence, and potential. They are innately sociable and seek ex-changes. Their desire and predisposition to be curious, to enquire, to hypothesize, to interpret and make sense of their experiences, to be in relationship, are basic human characteristics.

> Education is the creative process of exchange and relationship with the world, ourselves, and others. The task of educators is to support and encourage children's exploration and understanding. The acquisition of skills is not in itself an aim of education. Skills grow in the course of children's en-gagement in their learning, their relationships, and their meaning-making.

To illustrate these two principles, below we will describe an example from abroad, from which we've learnt much (Figure 11.2).

The mountains of the past and of the future

Giorgia, a five-year-old who attends the Sant'Ilario d'Enza municipal pre-school (prov-ince of Reggio Emilia), is participating in an enquiry by her classmates, teachers, and parents into the notion of 'time' and 'the future'. It is part of a 'landscape of thinking', and here she explores her own thinking and expression in graphic, sculptural, and verbal lan-guages: through this revisiting of ideas, she elaborates, refines, and is energized in this expectant place of investigation by the encouragement of friends and the shaping of pos-sibilities through actively attentive educators.

Figure 11.2 Giorgia makes pictures, and a model, to illustrate time and the future.

And now, Giorgia explains her meaning

There's a little door in the mountain of the future that takes you into a place where there are these words that don't mean anything … On top of the mountain of the future there's a path and a little man who can only go uphill; he can't go back down into the past, no way, he can only go on, and on, and on … Instead, on the mountain of the past, where the dinosaurs are, there's a little man that can go backwards, passing through all the years and all times.

But he can't really go—only if he remembers!

In the middle there's a normal mountain—no different. It's a bit small 'cause it was growing: it's the mountain of BEING—of the time of now—and that's where I am, inside it. Thanks to this mountain, the mountains of the past and of the future are separate—they don't get mixed up.

> (five- and six-year-old children of the Fiastri and Rodari pre-schools of
> Sant'Ilario d'Enza, in Reggio Emilia 2001a; see also Smidt 2015)

This is the extra-ordinary ordinary thinking of a five-year-old, —given the time, space, and attention to encounter, enquire, exchange, and express her ideas. We'd say that she is not 'special', or 'gifted and talented'; instead, we see clearly a human sensibility which has been given root-room.

Extending the principles of learning

To go back to the second of our first two principles mentioned above: Giorgia here, and Michael in the earlier example, are engaged in the curiosity of relating to, making sense of, the world. They are driven, not, primarily, to achieve or 'learn new skills', but to wonder, and to give shape to that wondering, and to care. Of course, in giving shape, they will be keen to hone their competences in all sorts of ways, and of course they need the opportunities to grow these skills. But first and foremost, they are inspired by wondering and caring. In the case of Giorgia and her friends, their educators have noticed an important question, 'What *is* 'the future?', have thought deeply about it together, and created the sustained opportunities for the children to delve deeper: they have constructed the opportunity for the children's learning, and given careful pedagogical attention. How do we, also, begin to do this? Firstly, do not fill up our days, and our children's, with mundane, banal 'activities'. Leave space for learning. Second, behave with intelligence and connection.

From these first two grounding principles we derive three further principles:

All human beings are innately sociable, and so effective learning environments must be characterized by opportunities for sociability. Encouraging children engaged in explorations and shared interests to form small learning groups is a key pedagogical strategy.

Listening and exchange are also important activities in our pedagogical practice, and regular analytic reflection by educators in small groups is a necessity. The practice of observation, as a way of trying to see and understand what children are doing and thinking, accompanied by reflection and analysis, enables educators to work with the grain of children's learning.

Our educational work stems from engagement in, and imaginative exploration of, the natural world. Moving indoors, we see the school environment as a studio for the exploration and exchange of ideas, a place where children can bring all of their senses to the business of learning, and use all their expressive languages to make their learning visible.

Our principles owe much to the determined educators in Britain in the 1930s and '40s— (the work of the McMillan sisters, and of Susan Isaacs are notable examples: Giardiello's *Pioneers in Early Childhood Education* (Giardiello 2014) can provide an introduction)— and to our own determination to reflect, learn, and remake, and to encounters with others.

Our articulation of teaching and learning, of children and educators, of schools and education as a whole, owes much to our continuing relationship with the educators of Reggio Emilia, Italy, and their approach. Here, at the close of World War Two, communities came together with educators to reconstruct their worlds, and in particular their children's prospects. Loris Malaguzzi, an inspired and inspirational educator of Reggio Emilia, made it his lifetime's work to develop, with the communities of the city of Reggio Emilia, places of education which are 'hard-working, inventive, liveable, communicable— a place of research, reflection and revisiting, where teachers, children and families feel at home'.

The encouragement of others, within a community of learners, is just as important for us educators as it is for children. As we rub shoulders together, we also better refine, re-consider, and re-articulate our ideas and ways. We aren't simply advocating 'enlightened copying'.

We learn to learn through exchanging ideas with others, through picking up notions, arguing about them, redefining them, learning how to express them, through the experiences of being enchanted by the 'eureka moments' of encounter and revelation, through having good space, opportunity, and encouragement to do this work. And essentially, we are learning about, and how to, live in the natural world into which we are born, which sustains us and of which we are a part. We do not live or learn well in artificial boxes, separated from the world.

Venturing towards an environment of enquiry

Our projects and professional development work with schools and teachers in the course of more than 15 years are contexts in which we've all learnt how to see and understand more closely, and how we might form new possibilities of education. We reflect more fully on this in *Adventuring in Early Childhood Education* (Duckett and Drummond 2007). In relationship with the five principles described, we are teasing out the necessary elements of a holistic pedagogy: an environment of enquiry. In a way lived and developed day by day, it seeks to nourish four 'Es': Encounter, Enquiry, Exchange, Expression.

Encounter: Here, we are describing the full opportunity to meet the new or strange, or the familiar, in new and unexpected ways. The accompanying and motivating desire is to be with the focus of attention, to appreciate it with all our faculties. It is the experience from which we often talk of the feeling of 'awe' and 'wonder'—though there are lots of other possible feelings besides.

Enquiry: By this, we mean with full attention and curiosity to engage in wondering, imagining, and meaning-making; figuring out how we might relate to the subject of enquiry; and the mutual and various significances being met. (Note: certain current educational 'programmes' describe prescribed modules as 'enquiries': we are not intending a reference to anything like that.)

Exchange: We make meaning, not in isolation, but through exchange with others—we bring to others our ideas, puzzles, and inspirations; we present them, hear others' ideas, contest them, modify our own, and reach new understandings.

Expression: Just as we encounter with all the tools of our human perception, so we have the potential to exchange and develop our meanings and our relationships through many faculties of expression. Through working diversely with these faculties, our possibilities of relationship, understanding, and meaning-making also multiply. And with the attitude of real intent to understand, we are motivated to become skilled in the use of all the tools of expression and understanding. Skills are eagerly built as we work 'with the grain' of children's investigations (the converse is also true of course, as we can see in places of education which do not honour children's natural connectivities: teaching and learning can become a drudge—on both sides!).

In the early 1900s, Margaret McMillan wrote, 'Every teacher is a discoverer. Everyone is an inventor, an improver of methods, or he is a mere journey-man, not a master!' (McMillan 1921).

Through the process of learning to listen again to the children in front of them, educators are able to fashion new and qualitatively different—and richer—opportunities for the children. Through making opportunities for enquiry based upon their constant everyday researchful reflections, educators are able to transform the educational environment which they control. The essential shift is from teaching to learning, from delivery of predefined programme to systems and strategies for sociable, meaningful enquiry. Typical classrooms, as Sir Ken Robinson cogently describes in his TED Lecture 'Changing Education Paradigms' (Robinson 2008), are extraordinarily cluttered, literally and metaphorically, with programmes and tools of instruction, on an industrial model, and the 'space for the learner to explore and learn' squeezed out.

Instead, we learnt (and wrote about it in *Adventuring in Early Childhood Education* (Duckett and Drummond 2007)) how educators can create systematic learning environments, built on observation and a reflective cycle approach, which have children's big questions and enquiries at the centre.

Placing children's thinking at the centre

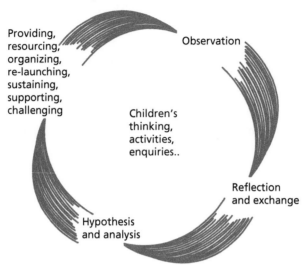

Figure 11.3 The Organizational Cycle.

This organizational and reflective cycle, which we developed as a process tool during our projects (Figure 11.3), is demanding, exciting, and often worrying to teachers: they put down old habits, explore, and learn—sometimes for the first time—to work 'from principle'. For educators more used to 'delivery' than 'enquiry', relearning 'what makes good educational practice', re-creating the ideas and opportunities of the school environment, is involved and challenging.

We are building on our own knowledge and experience, and the close records of many others beforehand—Susan Isaacs, Maria Montessori, Margaret McMillan, twentieth-century educators—and many contemporary others, including the present editors, all of whom saw, insisted upon, children's natural vibrant and sociable learning propensities. In a way, we are simply trying to reclaim their gifts. The practice of the reflective cycle which we elaborate on in *Adventuring in Early Childhood Education* as the foundation for practice is the beginning; it needs persistence, time, and ongoing support. (There isn't room in this short chapter to fully elucidate the processes and characteristics. These will be the subject of a future publication; here, we are opening a window onto the possibilities, and onto some experiences of children and educators.) Worked through thoroughly, it is highly rewarding to all.

There is a fuller reflection on our explorations into background and meaning in the chapter entitled 'Venturing Towards an Environment of Enquiry', in *Adventuring In Early Childhood Education* (Duckett and Drummond 2007); it is from reflections such as those that we've been able to further elaborate on principles *and* practice, and to apply them, as a framework, for reconstructing pedagogy. It is not random or accidental.

> What children learn does not follow as an automatic result from what is taught. Rather, it is in large part due to the children's own doing as a consequence of their activities and our actions.... Value should be placed on contexts, communicative processes, and the construction of reciprocal exchanges among children and between children and adults.... What is most central to success

is to adhere to a clear and open theoretical conception that guarantees coherence in our choices, practical applications, and continuing professional growth.

(Loris Malaguzzi, in Edwards, Gandini, and Forman 1993)

It is very timely that the Independent Review of the Scottish Early Learning and Childcare Workforce and Out of School Care 2015 (Siraj and Kingston 2015) emphasizes just this necessity to work from principle—and the dangers of the current lack of it: 'A lack of such understandings left practitioners unable to defend their own practices, incapable of considering contradictions and alternatives or engaging in critical thinking, and ill-equipped to evaluate policy change and challenge, resulting in naive or inadequately conceptualised amendments to practitioners' methods' (Stephen, Ellis, and Martlew 2010, p. 236). 'Without an underpinning knowledge of the theories, histories, constructions, and beliefs which underlie pre-school practice, practitioners were unlikely to respond appropriately to new ideas or develop them themselves, which is fundamental to a professional workforce' (Stephen and Minty 2012).

Learning to learn

As an example of what is possible, we are going to draw from a recent project of ours: Early Learning in Nature (ELiN). ELiN was a four-year Sightlines Initiative action-research project undertaken between 2009 and 2013, which we published as *Learning to Learn in Nature* (Duckett and Drummond 2014). As part of our long sequence of action-research projects since 1997, we created the opportunity for foundation stage and primary classes of children from north-east England, and their educators, to spend sustained time in local wild areas for the period of the school year. It was intentionally a formation offer to the schools. Can we better learn to 'see' the imaginations, competencies, and explorations of the children if we are away from the classroom and in the wild outdoors? How can educators and children, better use their classroom as a studio for the exploration and exchange of fascinating ideas and questions?

Here is Helen Watson of Holystone Primary School, North Tyneside (Watson 2014), reflecting on two years of work and change, through participation in our ELiN project: 'We changed because we realised we didn't always have to have the answers. When observing children it is always easy to think you know what they are enjoying about an activity. For example, if I observed a child building a rocket I more than likely would have thought the child had an interest in space or construction. I now started to question everything. Are they really interested in the rocket? What is it that really fascinates them? Is it the materials they are using? A fascination with the idea of mysterious and unknown worlds? Different questions pop into my mind now when watching them work'.

It is time now, to introduce you to a sustained example from this project: we hope you will see here our principles in practice. It is an experience which emerged with the reception class of New York Primary School, North Tyneside, during the ELiN project work.

Sarah Hollywood is the main classroom teacher; Catherine Reding and Annette Poulson are from the ELiN team. Catherine here presents and narrates. You can also find her chapter on the subject (Reding 2014) in *Learning to Learn in Nature* (Duckett and Drummond 2014).

Motorbikes and bears

The woods to which we took the children from the reception class at New York Primary School were very large, with steep muddy hills, a stream, and many other exciting features. So that the children could explore these different places and not be constrained to staying near the central camp, we developed a system of dividing the class into groups at the beginning of each session. These groups were negotiated between the children and the adults, depending on the interests of the children and what was organizationally possible. The class would spend the whole morning in these groups, using whichever part of the woods they chose.

A new group begins

One morning in the woods we were deciding on the groupings for the session, and had found that there were a number of boys who weren't decided on what they wanted to do. They were Steven, Kieran, Kie, Adam, Macauley, Christopher, and Ethan. We decided that they could form a group together, and I would be the adult to work with them.

During a recent educators' meeting we had been discussing the learning and dispositions of some of these children. We had noticed that they tended to approach activities with great speed and energy, often moving from one thing to another very quickly, but not becoming absorbed in what they were doing. We felt that it would be beneficial for them to be engaged in some group activities with a sense of shared purpose. We thought that this would encourage social interaction and enable deeper learning to take place.

Working together to develop an idea

That morning in the woods I decided to offer an initial idea and see how the children responded. I suggested that we could collect some large sticks and build something together. All the children seemed excited by this suggestion, and we worked together to find and move large sticks back towards the central camp area. Later, Sarah told us that previously in school these children did not gel together as a group. Once we had a large pile of sticks I asked the children what they would like to do with them. Steven said, 'Build a motorbike', and after some discussion it was agreed amongst the group that they would build a motorbike together.

Figure 11.4A Working to develop an idea. In the woods.

Figure 11.4B Working to develop an idea. Back in the classroom.

During the rest of the morning the boys made three motorbikes from the logs and sticks they had collected, and their play was centred around driving and riding on the bikes (Figure 11.4A). I noticed that their positioning on the bikes was important—the front boy was the 'driver', which was a very sought-after role. At lunchtime I told other staff about the activities of what we started to call the 'motorbike group'. We were very keen for the boys to continue developing this new focus and their sense of being a group, so we decided to offer them the opportunity to continue their work together that afternoon in school.

Back in the classroom

After lunch we encouraged the boys to tell the whole class what they had been doing, and proposed to the group that they could recreate their motorbikes with sticks and clay (Figure 11.4B). We made small stand-up cards so that the children could draw themselves and put themselves on the motorbikes.

All the children were very keen to make the motorbikes. Rather than making them collaboratively, as they had done in the woods, the boys mostly preferred to make their own individual motorbikes. Kie and Ethan were the only two to make a shared motorbike. Even though they worked on separate models, the boys were still acting as a 'group': side by side and with a shared purpose and interest.

Motorbike talk—an emphasis on movement and speed

Watching the group at work I noted down some of their comments about the motorbikes they were building. Kieran told me, 'That's my engine'. Christopher showed me the different sticks he had used: 'That one makes it go faster. That one makes it go flying'. Adam added a stick to his motorbike, and said, 'That's so it goes faster'. He was really proud of his motorbike and took it with him when he went to read with one of the year 6 children.

Steven used a small piece of clay with lots of sticks stuck vertically into it to make his motorbike. The different sticks had different functions. He told me, 'This one makes it go speedy. This one makes it go flying. This one's the backwards flying stick'. Kie asked if they could paint the motorbikes. Once the paint was available, all the children wanted to use it; this added some extra focus and excitement to their work. Ethan and Kie continued to work together on their large motorbike.

KIE: Isn't ours good?

ETHAN: Yeah

I asked the boys where their motorbikes were going to, but this didn't seem to interest them. When I asked them how it felt to be on a motorbike, they had lots of ideas:

CHRISTOPHER: Fast

STEVEN: It feels weird when I'm driving backwards. It feels fun when I'm driving fast.

The speed and feelings of driving a motorbike seemed to be a large part of the attraction for the children. On previous occasions Sarah remembered chasing through the woods at great speed with a group who we called 'the fast group', including many of these children. They wanted to explore the woods with great speed and energy. When reflecting on our documentation during an ELiN project reflection day, our colleague Deb noted, 'What is fascinating is that in settling for longer, far from losing their connection with speed and movement, they were able to go deeper into their explorations—through mechanics (the levers), imagination (driving backwards), and extraordinariness (flying)'.

Apart from Macauley, who left halfway through, the rest of the group stayed with the activity for the whole afternoon. Sarah, the class teacher, was delighted at the way the children had stayed with this group focus for the whole day, as it was usual for these children to flit from activity to activity. During the following week Sarah gave the boys lots of time to play with their model motorbikes together in class, which they did—until they fell to pieces!

Keeping the focus

Maintaining and developing the interest of the motorbike group was our priority for the next woods session. The day before going back to the woods, Sarah talked to the boys about continuing with their motorbike work, so that they had this in mind when they arrived. That morning in the woods Adam was absent, and Alex (not involved previously) was very keen to join in. Together we went back to where the children had built the motorbikes the previous week. When we arrived, the children found that one of the bikes—Christopher's—had been broken into tiny pieces (Figure 11.5).

Figure 11.5 The broken bike.

This prompted a lot of excitement and discussion. I asked the children, 'What do you think has happened?' and wrote down their ideas:

STEVEN: A monster dog came and smashed it.

ALEX: A dog with its really sharp teeth must have come over. It must have bited it really hard. It must have been crying 'cos his teeth must have been hurting off the hard stuff, and his teeth must have fell out.

KIE: A dragon fired it down.

KIERAN: I think I know. I think a dog must have scratched it and then it bited it.

STEVEN: A dog must have stood on it.

KIERAN: A dog must have put his teeth on it.

CHRISTOPHER: Or the monsters might have broken it.

MACAULEY: Someone—a man—must have come and had a knife and chopped it down.

ALEX: He might have chopped it with his axe.

KIERAN: He might have chopped all the bits as well. He has … look!

Welcoming the drama

Although I felt sorry that something so special to the children had been destroyed, I was delighted that it had promoted such an excited and imaginative response. An unexpected event had changed the focus of the group, from building and playing on the motorbikes, to the drama of imagining something unknown, strong, and powerful that destroyed things and put the boys and the woods in danger. The boys' conversations about the bear continued into the morning, and became even more vivid. Christopher, Alex, and Kieran were in a den next to the motorbikes, talking together.

CHRISTOPHER: A bear broken my motorbike then I had to fix it back together.

ALEX: He waited until it was bedtime and then the bear came over and broke Christopher's motorbike. And then in the morning we came into the woods and we said, 'WHY DID THE BEAR BREAK THE MOTORBIKE?'

CATHERINE: Where did the bear go?

KIERAN: Living in a big tree.

ALEX: No, he had a really fast motorbike …

KIERAN: He'll go in a hole. He'll dig a hole, then he'll stay in the big hole, then he'll bury it up. It's under here!

ALEX: Under the tree over there?

KIERAN: It's under here!

ALEX: It's under me?

KIERAN: Yes, under all of us.

STEVEN: I'm getting out now!

ALEX: I'm getting out! I don't like it.

CHRISTOPHER: I like it.

CATHERINE: I wonder what the bear's doing right now …

KIERAN: I know. It's smelling me and it's smelling Christopher.

CHRISTOPHER (TO KIERAN):   And you!

KIERAN: No it's not! 'Cos it's my pet. My pet bear. The bear is on you. The bear is digging under you, and he's going to scratch your bum!

Scary creatures and new stories

The idea of a bear living in the woods was not a new one for these children. Back in January, three months earlier, Annette had worked with a group exploring the woods, who were looking for bears, lions, and monsters. Christopher, Kieran, and Kie had all been part of this group. Maddie had found a tree stump with holes, showing where bears lived underground. Christopher poked a stick into the tunnels, and a lion bit Ella's stick when she put it in a hole. Kieran found a tree with a bear's scratch mark on it, and Faye found a 'monster's hand' coming out of the ground. Back in the classroom Faye used the overhead projector to make her bear huge (Figure 11.6).

Figure 11.6 Faye projects her picture.

There was already an exploration of rich scary stories amongst the class, to which the motorbike boys could add a new, first-hand, dramatic story.

Telling the story through music and drama

The day that we found the broken motorbike happened to be an all-day session in the woods, rather than just a morning. Over lunchtime we played musical instruments and danced with the whole class—something that we often did as a large group. We also gave the children the opportunity to share exciting stories and events from the morning. The motorbike group were very keen to tell the rest of the children what had happened, and the story of the bear destroying the motorbike was retold with great animation. Now these boys were the focus of attention for the whole class, telling of their brave deeds in the face of the bear.

Deepening collaboration

Together, the group acted out the drama of the bears eating the motorbike, with the music expressing the bears' actions.

There was a real sense of engagement and ownership of both the story and its expression in drama and music that was captivating to watch. During the afternoon the children repeated the drama over and over again, with different children becoming the musicians and the bears. Eventually there was just Kie left as the drummer, with me on the violin, and everyone else was being a bear. Particular children were taking on roles suited to their interests and dispositions (for example, Alex and Christopher leading the drama, and Kie drumming). They were organizing themselves and listening to one another, and were totally absorbed in what they were doing (Figure 11.7).

Looking back to the beginning of the year, many of these children had not been focusing for long periods of time on anything, so this was a very significant change. The drama they had authored had real meaning for them, stemming from the motorbikes they had created, played with, and then found destroyed.

There was a real sense of engagement and ownership of both the story and its expression in drama and music.

Bear drawings—the drama of representation

Back in school that afternoon we suggested to Alex and Christopher that they could draw the bear. We wanted to find out more about their ideas, and why the bear character was so important to them.

They worked together all afternoon on their drawing. They carefully drew pointed teeth and 'blood' on his face, and meticulously coloured in the whole picture, then signed their picture—a full witness statement by the people who had seen the bear.

Figure 11.7 Telling the story through music and drama. Deepening collaboration.

We were struck by the level of care and attention that went into the drawing, and the length of time that the boys had spent on it. After he had drawn each spot of blood, Alex took a black pen and carefully outlined every single spot (Figure 11.8).

Figure 11.8 Drawing the bear.

Alex and Christopher loved their bear. The picture showed the bear fierce and bloody, as if he had been in a fight. This fierce creature, which the boys had been initially so angry with for destroying their motorbike, was now being depicted with intense care and respect.

We discovered that these children, some of whom had not previously engaged deeply in classroom activities, could in fact work together on a shared enquiry over many weeks. The nature of what was being explored—speed, power, fierceness, danger—fascinated them, and drove them to continue, along with our acknowledgement and encouragement. The initial offer of clay and sticks to recreate their motorbikes helped to form and build on the idea that they were a group, that they were doing something special together, and that we valued them. We were able to re-present the children's work back to them for discussion, give them opportunities to be together as a group, and offer new forms of expression, such as music. We were active participants and co-explorers, for example when I played my violin for them in the woods.

Through working with this group we learnt some valuable lessons: about the persistence shown by the children, the need for applied thinking by the adults, and the value of using different forms of expressive media.

Researchfulness, and the courage of utopia

In the preceding narrative of the children's encounter with 'motorbikes and bears', we've chosen to keep their experiences to the fore. Vital to their experience, however, are the pedagogical characteristics of adults listening intently to the signs of children's interest, and taking them seriously. The adults equally want to know and understand more: to give time, space, and attention, in the classroom and outside it, enabling the children to become a group exploring together their ideas, through discussion, employing media of drawing, sculpture, talk, drama, music.

In choosing and finding ways to re-construct the classroom and the curriculum, the teachers discovered that these children were full of curiosity, eagerness, vitality, and fun, and eager to exchange ideas. We discovered rich, sociable, competent, creative children. We learned something about how to observe, listen, and discuss together (and the benefits of so doing) as a vital strategy for teachers, and the school learnt how it could re-frame its classrooms to become 'studios of enquiry'. By focusing on the children's sense of fascinated curiosity, the educators discovered that the children 'flowed naturally' into absorption with their subject. Here is Sarah Hollywood, the class teacher: 'By the end of the year, a class which had been big and boisterous became gelled as a unit, and engaged in learning. As educators, we developed our approach to focus on extending children's thinking and ideas. By giving the children the opportunity and freedom to follow their own interests, they developed their 'stickability', and sharing their interests with others also developed the children's personal and social skills. Children who were normally quite reserved and quiet in the class became leaders, boisterous children became listeners, and all became managers of their shared learning and development.

They became a class of sustained thinkers, who adapted their thinking to embrace challenges, persisting when they found things difficult. Whilst in the woods they were free to explore, and develop their awareness and management of their own risks and competences, and back in the classroom they developed their resilience and persistence, something which we had not previously seen'.

Together we worked hard to attend to our statements of principle, and the teachers and the school had the courage to reshape and research their practice. The adults researched as the children researched: both were interwoven. It may be obvious, but it is important to say that this is hard work and requires enormous determination: there is much in the current regimes of education which expects compliance, so moving from compliance to thinking and autonomy, to actually constructing a different paradigm of education, requires courage and persistence. Here is Helen Watson again: 'Our fear of the unknown held us back a lot at first, and it was hard to actually change our habits. However, as our newly keen foundation stage team started to become more confident working in this new way, the unknown became less daunting and actually helped promote reflective discussions between adults about what it is we are seeing. This in turn has shaped the way we adults interact with each other around the classroom, and how we organise our time. ... The last year has been a huge learning curve for me and the children in my class but we achieved so much. We created something meaningful together. The children know I value them and their ideas. They know I listen to them and that their thoughts are important to me. We were partners in each other's journey for the year they were in my class.

I am still learning, to listen, to reflect, to make time in the hectic timetable. It is difficult at times but it is so important to continue this journey we have started' (Watson 2014).

We borrowed the title of this chapter from an article by Professor Carla Rinaldi, President of the Reggio Children—Loris Malaguzzi Centre Foundation. In *Making Learning Visible* (Reggio Emilia 2001b), she writes on research teams of Project Zero and infant–toddler centres and pre-schools of Reggio Emilia.

Rinaldi emphasizes the necessity for constant research, in the re-creation of the life of the educator and the school, re-connecting theory, practice, and culture as renewed tools of educators who are authoring and critiquing principled, mindful pedagogy. 'A new concept of research that is more contemporary and alive might emerge,' she says, 'if we legitimise the use of the term to refer to the capacity to describe the cognitive tension that is experienced whenever real processes of learning and knowledge acquisition occur. Research exists ... within the search for the being, the essence, and the sense of things ... We are talking about the value of research, but also about the search for values.'

In this chapter, we hope you will have seen and heard the innate curiosity of children to research and imagine the possibilities of their world in exploration and play. We hope you have seen educators, with courage and their own researchfulness, beginning to figure out how to frame the educational possibilities which these children deserve. The adults and the children were both researching: their enquiries were interwoven.

> Once children are helped to perceive themselves as authors or inventors, once they are helped to discover the pleasure of enquiry, their motivation and interest explode.... The age of childhood, more than the ages that follow, is characterised by such expectations. To disappoint the children deprives them of possibilities that no exhortation can arouse in later years.
>
> (Loris Malaguzzi *c*.1994, cited in Edwards, Gandini, and Forman 1998, pp. 67–8)

We know that these possibilities are achievable, with moderate persistence, by all educators and educational establishments that recognize the intelligent humans in the children in front of them. It does take determination, and sustained alliances between teachers, parents, communities, and policy makers. Whichever you are, we hope you are encouraged to participate in the making of real environments of enquiry, armed with the courage of utopia—for all our futures.

References

Brown, G. (2010). *The Change We Choose: Speeches 2007–2009*. Edinburgh: Mainstream.

Duckett, R. (2006). Elemental materials. *ReFocus Journal*, **14**, 12–14.

Duckett, R. and Drummond, M. (2007). *Adventuring in Early Childhood Education*. Newcastle: Sightlines Initiative.

Duckett, R. and Drummond, M. (2014). *Learning to Learn in Nature*. Newcastle: Sightlines Initiative.

Edwards, C., Gandini, L., and Forman, G. (1993). *The Hundred Languages of Children*, 1st edn. Westport: Ablex.

Edwards, C., Gandini, L., and Forman, G. (1998). *The Hundred Languages of Children*, 2nd edn. Westport: Ablex.

Giardiello, P. (2014). *Pioneers in Early Childhood Education: The Roots and Legacies of Rachel and Margaret McMillan, Maria Montessori and Susan Isaacs.* London: Routledge.

Gibbs, N. (2015). 'The Purpose of Education' [speech], https://www.gov.uk/government/speeches/the-purpose-of-education, accessed 19 Mar 2018.

Glennie, E. (2015). *BBC Radio 4 'Today'* Interview by C. Paterson: Dame Evelyn Glennie: 'I'd like to collaborate with Eminem' (10 March 2015), http://www.bbc.co.uk/programmes/p02lnjky, accessed 19 Mar 2018.

'Let Our Kids Be Kids' (2016). Kids' Strike 3rd May, https://letthekidsbekids.wordpress.com/what-you-can-do/, accessed 19 Mar 2018.

Linnæus, C. (1758). *Systema naturæ per regna tria naturæ*, 10th edn. Stockholm, Sweden: Laurentii Salvii.

McMillan, M. (1921). *The Nursery School.* New York: Dutton.

Reding, C. (2014). Motorbikes and bears. In: R. Duckett and M. Drummond (eds.) *Learning to Learn in Nature.* Newcastle: Sightlines Initiative, pp. 53–61.

Reggio Emilia (2001a). *The Future is a Lovely Day*, 2nd edn. Reggio Emilia: Reggio Children.

Reggio Emilia (2001b). *Making Learning Visible*, 1st edn. Reggio Emilia: Reggio Children.

Robinson, K. (2008). 'Changing Education Paradigms' [webcast], uploaded by the Royal Society for the Arts, London, https://www.youtube.com/watch?v=zDZFcDGpL4U, accessed 19 Mar.

Rosen, M. (2016). 'Dear Nicky Morgan: schools don't work like the SAS', *Guardian Education* [online], http://www.theguardian.com/education/2016/jan/05/nicky-morgan-schools-sas-improve-teachers, accessed 19 Mar 2018.

Siraj, I. and Kingston, D. (2015). *An Independent Review of the Scottish Early Learning and Childcare (ELC) Workforce and Out of School Care (OSC) Workforce.* Edinburgh: The Scottish Government.

Smidt, S. (2015). *An ABC of Early Childhood Education: A Guide to Some of the Key Issues.* Abingdon, UK/ New York: Routledge.

Stephen, C., Ellis, J., and Martlew, J. (2010). Taking active learning into the primary school: A matter of new practices? *International Journal of Early Years Education*, **18**(4), 315–29.

Stephen, C. and Minty, S. (2012). *Review of SCMA Community Childminding and Working for Families Services.* Falkirk, UK: Scottish Childminding Association.

Vértes, L. (1965). 'Lunar Calendar' from the Hungarian Upper Paleolithic. *Science*, **149**(3686), 855–6.

Watson, H. (2014). A journey into listening. In: R. Duckett and M. Drummond (eds.) *Learning to Learn in Nature.* Newcastle: Sightlines Initiative, pp. 275–85.

Wilson, J.P. (2011). The Routledge Encyclopaedia of UK Education, Training and Employment, 1st edn. New York: Routledge.

Zhang, J., Harbottle, G., Wang, C., and Kong, Z. (1999). Oldest playable musical instruments found at Jiahu early Neolithic site in China. *Nature*, **401**(6751), 366.

Chapter 12

The child's curriculum as a gift: Opening up the early-level curriculum in Scotland

Aline-Wendy Dunlop

Introduction—the nature of education in our community

Accumulated wisdom of past generations provides certain strong threads of thinking about childhood educational practices that transcend time and context. The loss or discarding of this collective history of a pioneering and political early childhood movement risks children's well-being and creativity as learners. These strong pedagogical threads may yet be considered innovative, even best practice, but we need to weigh that up, for one thing is certain: children do not stand still, and nor should adult practices or policy do so. We need, as Giroux (2017) suggests, experience that takes a detour through knowledge and theory, so that the formulation and impact of curriculum and forms of pedagogy are questioned. At the same time the preparation of all early educators should aim for thoughtful, creative, responsive, and imaginative frames of mind. Relationships and interactions with others form the natural core of children's experience and shape their futures. The way in which children step in and out of the world outside the family, forming new relationships with people, places, and in their thinking, is the substance of any child's curriculum. Abiding principles can be re-interpreted for today (Bruce 2015).

At the heart of life lie all the relationships and people with whom our lives have coincided. The primary importance of family must be embraced: as members of a family there is a particular bond, which, when strong and healthy, connects us to others and to the world around us. Working professionally with children also means having relationships at the centre of all we do, but words such as 'love' and 'cherish' are used less professionally, though now we at least talk of nurturing children, but what does 'nurture' mean? Is it the same, or different from, what families offer, and is it enough? We cannot talk only of nurture, growth, and development. We must talk about socio-cultural learning too: children's worlds are defined by the people in them, by their interactions, by the contexts in which they spend their time, and by the political and cultural influences at play.

In this chapter the contribution of early childhood curricula is explored and set against what we know from history and from developmental, socio-cultural, and philosophical understandings of early childhood. Central to this chapter are the ways in which learning and education are fostered through our worlds of relations—companionships, friendship, joint attention on shared projects, being able to take the perspective of others, and being able to regulate our own behaviour for self and in relation to others. Scottish early humanist thinking, which emphasized the value and agency of human beings, and their natural virtues (Hutcheson 1729), has relevance for us today to foster choice, autonomy, and a sense of both individual and collective agency in early childhood, with a focus on a shared sense of well-being and relational pedagogies (Papatheodorou and Moyles 2009).

By using the term 'enlightened' this chapter seeks to explore the extent to which our society is supporting early childhood in ways that are healthy for the being and becoming child: it was Socrates who claimed that a society could be judged by the way it treats its most vulnerable. While not wanting to cast children as 'vulnerable'—terminology that is creeping into the policy field—the state of childhood is open, malleable, new, forming, and therefore affected by what happens around children, and by what others at the daily level, and those at the political level, do. The child is curious, capable, courageous, persevering, contributing, and companionable, but powerless to act upon wider systems and to stop the commodification of childhood, which it may be argued leads to developing children as consumers rather than as contributors (Giroux 2017). People call these essential human attributes 'dispositions'—and young children, more than anyone else, are disposed to relate to others, to their shared world, and to the possibilities this world offers them—or that they manage to find. These are their strengths, which should not be either taken for granted or ignored.

Given such understandings about childhood, this chapter of necessity is about how relationships help us to interpret and to shape curriculum together with children, and why this is so important. Without placing learning within relationships, we cannot have an enlightened early childhood curriculum, policy, or provision. Early childhood is often discussed in terms of children's well-being and happiness: supporting connectedness in childhood means recognizing this is emotion-work for children (Elfer 2012, 2015), and for adults too.

Early childhood in Scotland can be viewed through the lens of the past, present, and future. By taking account of trends in early-years policies and practices over time, we can identify values that withstand time and make for a Scottish approach that always puts children and their families first. Drawing on our history and culture is important, potentially dynamic now, and forward-looking. It is worth considering the following:

Yesterday

◆ *Scottish history and education*
◆ *Enlightened beginnings*
◆ *Scottish early childhood pioneers*

Today

◆ *Current Scottish policy: the Early Level (age 3–6 years)*
◆ *Experience taking a detour through theory: developmental, socio-cultural, and philosophical understandings of early childhood.*
◆ *Curriculum as a gift*

Tomorrow

◆ *A child's curriculum*
◆ *Values and principles*
◆ *Looking forward.*

Yesterday

Scottish history and education

Looking back, the Scottish Enlightenment, Scottish business and philanthropy, and the long cultural tradition of Scottish education have all contributed to the place we have staked out in the world, and how we value ourselves. From very early Scotland reaped the intellectual benefits of a highly developed university system (Herman 2001). For many years this small nation had double the number of universities of its nearest neighbour: only Oxford and Cambridge were older than the four earliest Scottish universities of St. Andrews, 1413; Glasgow, 1451; Aberdeen, 1495, and Edinburgh, 1583.

Hector Boece, appointed in 1500 as the first principal of the newly founded King's College, later Aberdeen University, was influenced by humanist thinking through his studies in Paris, where he met Erasmus and was a committed proponent of humanism (Durkan, 1953) and individual agency: a feature of the early Scottish enlightenment. Here humanism is understood 'a philosophical and ethical stance that emphasizes the value and agency of human beings, individually and collectively' (Wikipedia, accessed 19 August, 2017). The humanist concern with widening education was shared by the protestant re-formers, and as early as 1560 there was a plan for a school in every parish, which was finally ratified by the Parliament of Scotland with the Education Act of 1633. With the advent of the Industrial Revolution came industrial philanthropy: Robert Owen's 1816 in-fant school in New Lanark is often claimed as the first nursery-infant school in Europe. In a modern interpretation, Owen's initiatives in New Lanark included, 'improving social capital and capacity building, social cohesion, healthy living and improved diet and child-birth, raising parental expectations and aspirations for employees and their children, adult training and development, debt counseling, increasing the potential of human resources, establishing patterns for lifelong learning, as well as quality nursery, infant and primary school education and extended care' (Bertram and Pascal 2010, p. 6). This is close to policy ambitions today.

Enlightened beginnings

In Scotland we can, and should be, more aware of the strong roots of our thinking about early childhood education and care. Recently, 'education' has been substituted by the word 'learning' in early childhood policy-speak. While this may be well-intentioned to avoid a top-down view of early childhood, it may also indicate a confusion between 'education' and 'schooling' and a need, as teacher numbers drop in early learning and childcare, to re-establish the ways in which care, learning, and teaching combine in early childhood before and after school entry. The arguments are not simple, and it is important to insist that appropriate pedagogy in early years before school should be sustained in the early years of school: in policy terms this was the ambition of the Early Level 3–6 of Scotland's *Curriculum for Excellence*. The concept of education should not be embargoed for our youngest children, nor in Scottish early childhood policy rhetoric. Education is much more than schooling, and with early childhood firmly in the public sphere pre-school provision becomes, and should be, political.

The pursuit of egalitarian goals 'stems from the Reformation belief in the power of education, reinvigorated by Enlightenment faith in the improvability of humanity, together creating a proffered ideal of the educated person and the enlightened society that is more distinctive and possibly more important to Scotland than its tangible attainments' (Houston 2008, p. 64). Adam Smith's 'Theory of Moral Sentiments' (1789) highlighted the 'greater good' and claimed that human morality depends on sympathy between the individual and other members of society: our moral ideas and actions are a product of our very nature as social creatures.

Against such background it was believed that the provision of the right environment and experiences would overcome an unequal start in life.

Scottish early childhood pioneers

The inspiration of lady pioneers in Scotland for early childhood education was firmly European, based on the teachings of Froebel, Montessori, and Pestalozzi. The first Froebel-inspired kindergarten opened in London in 1851 (Froebel archives, University of Roehampton 2018), and shortly afterwards educated women in Scotland's major cities began to understand the importance of providing encouragement for small children, adopting Froebel's view that 'play at this stage is not trivial; it is highly serious and of deep significance' (Froebel 1826).

A day nursery was established in East North Street in Aberdeen in 1873 (Voluntary Service Aberdeen). The Edinburgh Free Kindergarten opened in 1903. Phoenix Park Kindergarten opened in the densely populated Cowcaddens area in 1913, supported by the Glasgow Froebel Society which had formed in the early 1880s, with Karl Froebel giving an introductory lecture. In 1917, Jessie Porter trained under Margaret McMillan in London (at the Deptford nursery school she had opened in 1914) and returned to open the first nursery school in Dundee in 1921, by which time Edinburgh City was home to five nursery schools. The Edinburgh tradition was to open the early nursery schools in the Old Town, where housing was crowded and there were many young children. It was here that the child gardens were seen to be most needed and were expected to have the most impact.

As a young teacher it was my privilege to work firstly at Moray House Nursery School (which was founded originally in 1908 in Gilmore Place and later moved into a purpose-built nursery school in the grounds of Moray House College), and then at

Milton House, the site to which the Edinburgh Free Kindergarten had moved in 1954. Later, I was to hear much from my mother, also a Froebel-trained nursery and infant teacher, of her experiences at the Edinburgh Free Kindergarten and Grassmarket Nursery School.

This section of my chapter draws on these experiences and places, and finishes with reflections on the practice at Westfield Court Nursery School, where I became head teacher in 1988. Of these places for early formative experiences, only the nursery at Milton House, now Royal Mile Primary, remains open. Their enlightened practice precedes the advent of a national early years curriculum framework for the early years, and was clearly inspired by the work of Froebel.

Edinburgh Free Kindergarten

In each of these early nursery schools the habit was to keep a diary or day-book, to record work undertaken and make a history of developments. Miss Howden, Infant Mistress of Milton House School in 1881, was concerned that babies came to school with their siblings. She left all her savings so that this free kindergarten could be set up. The Edinburgh Free Kindergarten began in Galloway's Entry in 1903, then moved to Reid's Court in 1906, and finally to Milton House School in the Royal Mile in 1954. From her log as a head teacher, Lileen Hardy wrote *The Diary of a Free Kindergarten*, in which she quoted from her own day-book to say:

> It will be a long time before our schools can accord with these theories in practice, but we will supplement the schools. Let us be the pioneers, and, besides benefiting our own children, help on education generally. All this is a dream. Well, the Kindergarten was once a dream and now it is a fact.

> (Lileen Hardy, 11 July 1910, in Hardy 1912, p. 146)

Visiting in 1913, the HMI (Her Majesty's Inspector) of the day observed:

> This school is a bright spot in a rather dark neighbourhood with 2 groups of about 20 children under 5. School lessons are not given: they engage in a variety of kindergarten occupations and they learn to draw and sing. The rest of the time they spend taking care of pets in attempts at gardening and playing at housework. They mostly live in the open air and are obviously happy. Lessons in elementary subjects are given to those children who are aged 5–7.

The Grassmarket Child Garden

The day-book at Grassmarket Child Garden in the Vennel reports that children who had gone to school were welcomed back to what we would now call 'after-school care':

> Two play centres have been carried on for the older children who have left us for the 'big school'. The happy hours spent again in the Vennel do much to maintain the traditions and good habits acquired in the early years with us.

It also describes a warm, dry summer when the children transported water to the sand and the garden using improvised ladders at considerable height and trusted by watchful adults.

My own mother spent her nursery placement at Grassmarket and at Edinburgh Free Kindergarten while undertaking her Froebel course. She wrote:

> The main thing was the actual activity with the children—doing things with the children—with Froebel it wasn't about brushing teeth—although of course that was done— it was about making and doing together with children. It was a whole different approach—watching children—what they did and wanted to do and encouraging them rather than sitting them down to do something—more providing what they need and a much more active child-oriented way—not telling them what to do, but talking with them. I was at the Grassmarket Child Garden and what they called the Free Kindergarten. We learned about the history of Froebel, his principles, their application to children and how the movement started. The Froebel approach was much more what you felt about children—you sat back a bit in a way and watched, then you took part.

> (Looking back: a 93-year-old Froebel teacher recalling her placement in 1937)

An entry in the Grassmarket diary matches her experience:

> Then too there are quiet spells when an adult has an opportunity of playing the important parts of observer and learner

> (1933 report)

Moray House Nursery School

Moray House Nursery School, founded in 1908 in Gilmore Place, was a free kindergarten and a demonstration school set up by the provincial committee for the training of teachers. In 1918 it was moved to basement rooms within Moray House Training College in Holyrood Road, and from there to a nursery school building in the college grounds in 1932, where it remained open until 1988. In 1935, an article in *The Weekly Scotsman* reported that:

> The specially designed interior included glazed panels in sliding timber door frames. These south and west glazed walls could be pushed back so that the indoors merged into an 'open air' environment. A verandah led into the school play area, which included the small playhouse. The two large classrooms were fitted out with child-size furnishings.

This emphasis on the physical surroundings continued to resonate as the demonstration school attached to the college, and flourished into the 1970s following ideas of Isaacs, Froebel and Piaget … with intellectual enquiry from associations with lecturer-headteachers of Moray House: Miss A. F. Mackenzie, Miss Isobel Calder, and Miss Margaret Cameron.

The Colleges of Education in each of the Scottish cities offered specialist programmes in infant and nursery education from ages three to eight, and until the mid-1970s these year-long courses were endorsed and students were visited by an external examiner from the National Froebel Foundation. Those courses shaped early education in Scotland's nursery schools and classes and in the infant departments of primary schools. Essential reading then and now, Susan Isaacs's 1954 pamphlet endorsed Froebel principles when she so boldly stated,

> We have learnt that above every other source of knowledge about children stands the study of their ordinary spontaneous play, whether in the home, the school playground, the street or the parks. The great educators taught us long ago that the child reveals himself in his play.
>
> (Isaacs 1954, p. 6)

She identified space, appropriate play materials, opportunities for self-assertion and independence, skilled help, and companionship as the foundations of professional effort, conceived as an extension of the function of the home and not a substitute for it.

The philosophy of all we did was drawn from a conviction that children's motivations and interests could be trusted, and that responding to them would lead to powerful and deep-level learning in which careful and interested observation was central—for example:

> After the holidays Gordon continued to talk about fishing boats and his holiday in Oban. He said he had a fishing net he'd found that was very big—he was invited to bring it to school—'It's so very big I'd like to measure it'—it stretched the whole length of the classroom and out into the hall. 'It must have come from a huge boat,' the others remarked ... we decided to go to Granton Harbour—imaginative play, drawings, models, stories and book making followed, everything was measured and compared—we talked of fish, bollards, jetties, tugs, trawlers, the sea, the weather and searched for more and more information.
>
> (Moray House Nursery School 1970)

In those early years of my own teaching, understanding of children's and our shared experiences through a dual lens of Froebelian and Piagetian thinking led me to question the concept of the child as a lone scientist, and the stageist or readiness approach. I came to believe that it must be the interactions, timing, relationships, and culture that influenced children's learning and therefore their development. To subsequently find and read the work of Bruner, Donaldson, and Trevarthen confirmed that a child can learn anything at any age provided it makes what Donaldson called 'human sense', building on what he or she already knows and what happens in joyful companionship. I became convinced that the child can create and should be supported to engage with a spiral curriculum of their own recurring and deepening interests (Bruner 1960). Later I was to discover Vygotsky, too, and the importance he gave to learning in conversation (Vygotsky 1981).

The Edinburgh Free Kindergarten—Milton House Nursery Class

Over the three years when I worked at Milton House Nursery Class (1971–1974), our situation on the busy thoroughfare of the Royal Mile meant that the children often heard sirens: sharing their own and family stories of emergency services call-outs, they were particularly interested in the local fire station and the happenings that led to fire engines racing past the nursery gates. Working on an observation model to inform our daily practice, we regularly recorded such interest and the ways in which our responses varied according to the visible interests of the children. One such example follows (illustrated in Table 12.1), in which the children's play was scaffolded by responsive adults ready to note persistent interests and see the potential of extending children's existing experiences and thinking through many conversations.

Table 12.1 Milton House, Fire Engine

Children's interest	Adult response	What next?
In the last few days we've heard a lot of fire engines from the Fire Station at Abbeyhill going up and down the Royal Mile and Holyrood Road near Dumbiedykes, past where the children live. The boys have been rushing about playing with imaginary hoses. The play became very organized with calls of 'There's a fire in the house, get out get out'. The children in the house area had to evacuate—they rushed outside and soon the boys started moving the home area furniture out of the area. Before long, all the furniture had been carried with the help of most of the other children up the stairs and into the garden. Sam and Billy brought in the water play tubes from outside and a pail of water to put the fire out. This went on for some time until one of the mums arrived. She was asked to wait until the fire was out so they could bring the furniture back.	Having watched this interest for a few days, it seems it's now taking off and most of the children are interested. Added stories, and Miss B. to include some firemen songs at singing time or when children go to the music area.	Take interested children out to the school playground for a while to look out for fire engines going up the road.
Thursday: Sam and Billy said there wasn't much point moving the furniture again as the fire was out but they used the big blocks and built a fire engine to play on, going several times to the home area to check the fire was still out. They said to Miss B. that the trouble with the blocks was that they couldn't make a big enough fire engine and they would see what they could find outside to add to it. They came back in with a steering wheel but found it too difficult to bring the tyres in so they asked to take the blocks outside. Later, Billy made a fire engine from two pieces of wood at the woodwork area.	Added more fire engine stories into the book corner from upstairs—lots of requests to read these. Plenty of red paint—children to help make it up—and big brushes—see if we can find a large wooden box (maybe at the beach at the weekend—fish crate?) Make sure to pick up some more wood offcuts. Check dressing up and puppets.	Plan a visit to the Fire Station. Look up more songs and rhymes. Check for photos. Make up a book with the children about their play.

Fire Station visit arranged. This interest continued for three weeks as the children planned and built a fire engine and continued to play on it.

Table 12.2 Observations and planning, Westfield Court Nursery School

Observations/ source of interest	Context	Process	Extension and resources	Content	Evaluation/action
C was carrying the cat around in the basket 'I'm going to the vet—Pepsi's still lost'	From home into room	Imaginative and recall of own experience	'Pets for children'; discussion of animals that can be pets	Reminder of play Information about household pets and care of them	Continue to foster this discussion towards pet shop or vet visit?
M was given a tool set for his birthday: 'It's got everything in it'	Given the birthday card he left on Thursday	Tool using; range of tools; comparison	Crate of tools from cupboard: hammer, saw, drill familiar— what else?	Understanding use of tools	Mastery of skills
Lots of witchy/ monster play Use of long blocks as broomsticks		Discussion — imaginative play	On the way home I met a . . . and *The Jolly Witch*	Understanding and sharing of what frightens	Feeling emotions
Care of dolls	Home area				Not taken up
Talk of snakes		Making fine motor	Snakes and animal shapes at dough	Qualities of snakes—long, thin, supple	B and K enjoyed the press moulds—try at clay?
M and J took over the placing of the goldfish tank in the classroom: added stones previously—a problem—how to get these out? J: 'Climb up'; A: 'Tip it up'	New goldfish tank given		'We got a tank but no fish.' Read 'A Fish out of Water'.		Lively interest including B. Plan for visit to pet shop/ Botanic Gardens. Record pets? (J mentioned 'fish in my toy box')
C and C with small pots at gluing. They talked about planting and planting out their seedlings. Discussed what we'd need. C: 'What's earth? Is it like muck? Where's nature?'	Gluing— nature area	Creative, imaginative; observation of growth and change; learning vocab.	Plant pots, compost, put out a planting instruction book		This interest captured interest of six of the children— talk of seeds and seedlings—extend this
M and J: 'We'll come to story in a minute; we're just moving house.'	Small world	Managing own time; persevering at task	'Moving Molly' into book area or beside small world	Small world toys unloaded; furniture 'next door'	Carried forward to next day

Daily observations of individuals and the group recorded on facing sheet; decisions made in a team chat at end of day about what to 'draw down' for next day.

The Lothian Curriculum for the Early Years 3-8 (1992) brought my thinking together. It encapsulated thoughtful practice and experience and benefited from sound theory. It was open to interpretation, and critique and feedback were requested on taking implementation forward. At the time, three neighbouring nursery schools engaged in dialogue about curriculum planning: Giroux's idea of curriculum as a 'cultural script' whose messages should be subject to critique (Morrison 2001) is important here, as he suggests that such cultural scripts introduce students to 'particular forms of reason that structure specific stories and ways of life' (Giroux 2005, p. 60) and that 'The Enlightenment notion of reason needs to be reformulated within a critical pedagogy' (Giroux 2005, p. 59).

This early version of a curriculum framework brought together the ideologies of nursery and primary education and promoted observational approaches that made human sense of children's learning and development. Observations as sources for curriculum action involved looking at the context and process of learning before engaging with and researching the knowledge content that would serve children's curiosities and interests. Although our project generated a single planner, there was no single script: the template would be populated with children's interests and concerns, and as such, made for a dialogic process (illustrated in Table 12.2): such tools need to be conceived locally, rather than imposed.

Curriculum development and reform as an educational policy tool

At a time when Scotland was developing a national curriculum and assessment framework (for ages 5–14), most of the regional councils of the time were involved in local early years curriculum consultation and discussion; examples are shown in Box 12.1.

Each of these local documents addressed a cycle of observation, identification of interests and needs, resourcing, implementation, recording, reporting, and evaluation. Most developed children's profiles, which would be shared with the next phase of education, and all espoused a child-centred approach that took account of context and of individual contributions. Some documents focused on age 0–5, some on 3–5, and Lothian's on 3–8 years.

Box 12.1 The advent of early childhood curricula in Scotland

- Lothian—A Curriculum for the Early Years 3-8 (1992)
- Fife—Partnership in Early Education: A Continuum 3-8 (1994)
- Strathclyde—Partners in Learning 0-5 (1994)
- Borders—Right from the Start 3-8 (1994)
- Grampian—A Framework for the Curriculum 3-5 (1995)
- Stirling Council—Early Years Curriculum (1996)

The instigators of these local curricula came together to develop the first *Scottish Curriculum Framework for the Pre-School Year*, which was published in draft form in 1996 and in a final form in 1997, to coincide with the entitlement of every child in Scotland to a year of nursery education before starting school. In 1999, this became *The Curriculum Framework 3-5*, and alignment between this early childhood guidance and the 5–14 framework emerged. Each could have been used flexibly as part of an educator repertoire to enhance children's experience, but in fact one remained firmly with early childhood education, and the other with primary education.

As the early stages of 5–14 became increasingly formalized, the Scottish Executive announced curriculum reform through a ministerial statement introducing *A Curriculum for Excellence 3-18* (2004). The then First Minister declared that play-based active learning approaches should move into the early stages of primary school, and thus *Building the Curriculum 3-18—Active Learning in the Early Years 3-6* came about in 2007.

Writing at the time about Scottish early years provision and the Curriculum 3-5, for an international seminar, I identified four distinctive elements. These described: the structure of early childhood provision (which, by then, lay largely with education departments in a coupling with the primary school system); a new approach to curriculum; attention to professional development; and our parental focus. The enthusiasm of this sector for continuing professional development, the importance of teamwork, the desire to collaborate with the next stage of education, and the need to develop the confidence to do so were all evident. There was recognition of the importance of participative approaches with parents, both in the early experience of their children and to promote their engagement with their children's education in the long term.

Within the evolving Scottish early years context of today, what do we hold to now? What have we been led to value, believe in, or understand about children's rights—do they relate to development as the priority that leads to learning, or do they relate to learning that drives development as an alternative discourse of children's rights?

Today

Current Scottish policy: The Early Level 3-6

National frameworks

Scottish Government policy has made a strong case for investing in early childhood. The economic case, the social equity case, and the human rights case are powerfully scripted in Scottish policy (Dunlop 2015). Three 'building blocks' or pillars continue to be influential: *Early Years Framework* (Parts I and II, Sottish Government 2008a); *Achieving Our Potential: A Framework to tackle poverty and income inequality in Scotland* (Sottish Government 2008b); and *Equally Well: Report of the Ministerial Task Force on Health Inequalities* (Sottish Government 2008c). Each of these is reflected in the policy implementation tool *Getting it Right for Every Child*, which is now enshrined in law through the *Children and Young People Scotland Act 2014*, supported by guidance for the youngest children in *Building the Ambition* (2014).

The policy discourse

Our Scottish policy refers to 'the child's world', but for every child there are others in that world who make a difference. Vandenbroeck (2015) warns of the risks of striving for homogeneity: of homogenizing childhood, parenthood, and practice.

Approaching policy as discourse involves seeing knowledge and power as intertwined. For example, Foucault argues that the act of governing has become interdependent with certain sorts of institutionalized analyses, reflections, and knowledge (Foucault 1991). Discourse encompasses the concepts and ideas relevant for policy formulation, and an interactive process of communication serves to generate and disseminate these ideas (Schmidt and Radaelli 2004), and in Scotland such consultation visibly happens. The discursive structures (concepts, metaphors, linguistic codes, rules of logic, etc.), often taken for granted, contain cognitive and normative elements that determine what policy makers can more easily understand and articulate, and hence which policy ideas they are likely to adopt (Campbell 2002).

Our curriculum today, and the debate

We have, on paper, a thoughtful, enabling, and creative curriculum—one that was designed to return professional judgement to educators aiming to develop capacities in our children and young people that would ensure their well-being, confidence, and contribution, so equipping them as lifelong learners. However, the *Curriculum for Excellence* (CfE) has incurred criticism. In 2012, Paterson's critique described it as consensus curriculum with a centralizing plan for secondary education, and later claimed the CfE to be responsible for a drop in Scotland's PISA (Programme for International Student Assessment) ratings (Paterson 2016). Andreas Schleicher, of the OECD (Organisation for Economic Co-operation and Development), stated on *BBC News* on 6 December 2016 that 'Scotland needs to move from an *intended* curriculum to an *implemented* curriculum'.

For early childhood practice this raises two questions—whose intentions, and whose implementation? Subsequently, in June 2017 Schleicher launched *Starting Strong V* (OECD 2017), which reports transitions practices that are much more focused on information-giving than cooperation. In a webinar presentation Schleicher says, 'Challenges still remain for making transitions child-centred, guided by pedagogical continuity, managed by trained staff, and well-informed parental and community engagement'. To achieve any of these, early years practitioners and teachers need the kind of agency referred to by Priestley in the move towards a 'new curriculum' (Priestley and Drew 2016). Scotland's curriculum exemplifies international trends in curriculum change. One of its unique features is the bridging opportunities it provides between early learning and childcare (ELC) and primary school, and between primary and secondary education. Despite the early level of our curriculum emphasizing the years three to six as a whole, there is evidence that the curriculum is enacted in two parts: 'early years' and 'early primary'.

An Early Level Curriculum 3-6

My experience as a transitions researcher, an early childhood teacher, an early years practitioner educator, and a teacher educator has raised deep concerns about curriculum design that falters in the journey from conception to implementation.

Scottish policy discourse for early childhood has aimed to integrate curriculum advice for three- to six-year-olds, up until the age of seven. Valuing the youngest children in their own right is absolutely vital. In *Building the Ambition* (Scottish Government 2014), there a new emphasis on integrating *Pre-birth to Three* advice with the *Early Level Curriculum 3-6*, which eschews 'pre-school' terminology and what it implies for a period of preparation for school. Nevertheless, transitions research shows the importance of continuity into school to avoid the separation of the early learning and childcare sector from early primary education.

There is, in both the *Early Level 3-6* (2007) and the *Building the Ambition* (2014), a certain unity of discourse, embracing a child development model, but each document is distinctive. 'Learning' is foregrounded in both documents, but the route to learning focuses more on teaching in one, and pedagogy in the other. Both speak of the child, of play, of progress, and of the importance of time, literacy and numeracy, intervention, activities, and experiences. The proportion, presence, and absence of these words imply a certain policy-collusion in which the substance of guidance, and its relation to the child, too often remains uncontested.

It is time to move away from a fixed developmental model of the child. All practitioners must have knowledge of development, but we need to embrace how actual learning in socio-cultural engagement and human interaction challenges any fixed view of development. In both documents there is mention of transitions, the changes children go through—more acknowledged and visible in *Building the Ambition*, and less so in the *Early Level 3-6*, a period when children and families face some of the most significant changes.

Is it assumed that if guidance covers the period of the transition to school, it will define the transitions issues? If so, it fails, being in effect split into before and after school start. Ten years on from the publication of the *Early Level*, *Building the Ambition* does not offer guidance on these years as a natural phase of childhood experience, though it addresses a previous disjunction between Pre-birth to Three and the Early Level 3-6 very well. *Building Curriculum 2—The Early Level 3-6* called for mutual cooperation and understanding between what we now call Early Learning and Childcare (ELC) and Early Primary:

> In the early years of primary school there may be some difficulty with the word 'play' itself. Parents often need reassurance that their children will learn effectively through play, because of its association with leisure. What is important is that all staff with responsibility for planning early years

learning recognise that active learning, including purposeful play, has a central role in that process and when necessary can demonstrate this to parents.

(SG 2007, p. 19)

Our Scottish curriculum acknowledges such transitions issues when it makes the following statements:

For nursery schools, partner provider centres and other stand-alone settings, joint planning may present more of a challenge. It will be important for staff in all early education centres and associated primary schools to find ways to work together. Close communication about children's previous experiences and learning is crucial at the time of transition.

(SG 2007, p. 13)

Overall, however, a move like this from a pre-school setting to Primary 1 too often provides an abrupt transition for children which can prove damaging for some children's confidence and progress.

(SG 2007, p. 10)

Why is it so difficult for policy to be holistic even when it acknowledges the rights of the child to the best possible start in life and the nature of lifelong experience? It is unnatural to separate what happens for the four- or five-year-old in ELC from what happens for four- or five-year-olds in Primary 1. This chapter calls not for a 'kindergarten stage', but for a realization that to implement our wise and thoughtful *Early Level 3-6* we need to match resources, staffing ratios, workforce knowledge and experience, and shared common knowledge (Edwards 2011), and promote relational play-based pedagogy all through ELC and Primary 1. There is ample research to support a holistic view of the early years into and through primary school.

Experience taking a detour through theories: Developmental, socio-cultural, and philosophical understandings of early childhood

There is so much theorizing on the early childhood story. Here, I focus on four creative thinkers whose work has been influential in Scotland: Jean Piaget, Margaret Donaldson, Lev Vygotsky, and Jerome Bruner.

Piaget's account of education supplements his study of knowledge—he linked knowledge and development and gave us ideas of the child's autonomy often held and valued in early childhood practice. This explains why we often couple the ideas of autonomy and choice—'teaching is necessary but insufficient' for good learning—which kind of fits with Pasi Sahlberg's paradox of teach less, learn more (Sahlberg 2011). For Piaget too, creativity is important, as is agency in taking charge of one's own learning: he saw the child as an active problem solver.

Donaldson's work has informed my own thinking about the intellectual challenges of the transition to school. She did not think Piaget was entirely right. She redesigned his experiments to discover how the shared purpose of the tasks makes sense for children. Donaldson's idea of a sociable 'human sense' is important for us in education. Piaget called early thinking egocentric, while Donaldson, in her wonderful book *Children's Minds* (1978), writes of thinking which is embedded in contexts that make common sense and thinking which is disembedded and grows 'beyond the bounds of human sense'. This is exactly the transition children are making as they are expected to move from hands-on activity to symbolic activity—a new way of being and knowing that fails to make human sense for our youngest children.

For Vygotsky, too, 'culture is the product of social life and human social activity' (1981, p. 164). The higher mental functions of logical memory, selective attention, decision making, learning, and comprehension of language interested Vygotsky, and in particular the relationship of language and speech to thought. His view was that both development and instruction are socially embedded—and that by recognizing where children are in their understanding, skilled others may help in developing beyond present capacities. Thus, observation and assessment find their importance.

And finally to Bruner, born in 1915 and a regular visitor to Scotland well into his late 90s. He wrote, 'We begin with the philosophy that any subject can be taught effectively in some intellectually honest form to any child at any stage of development' (Bruner 1960, p. 33). Bruner's theory of education has moved over the years, from attention to the limitations of cognitive psychology and what he called 'solo intrapsychic' (inside the head) processes of knowing, to a cultural psychology. He calls on motivation, affect, creativity, perception, personality, thought, language, and intuition. His focus on narratives of learning and interpretive capacities links powerfully with his assertions about human agency, from infancy. He sees agency, collaboration, reflection, and culture as part of play and playful learning (Bruner 1996).

Each of my chosen theorists tells us something about capacities, agency, imagination, creativity, and, by invoking culture, about companionable learning (Trevarthen 2002). The learning challenge of education in early childhood lies in a disjunction of culture, and in human sense making. We need to place the vitality of children at the centre of our thinking, and this may mean shunning 'pre-schooling', 'schooling', and 'schoolification' in favour of 'education' where 'the child leads the way' (Nuttall 2013). Liam, seen on the book's front cover, and in Figure 12.1, was used to his own company: he played imaginatively with his small world animals, reflecting his first-hand experience of zoo visits, the many shared story readings with his parents, and his own lively interest in books.

Already an animal expert, his searching in books is something both self-chosen and offered by family for sharing that interest. Now his concentration on any book follows a mandatory 'look through' first of all to take up what it promises. At the time, he made homes for animals at nursery school, and then explained what was going on to the rest of the group, recalling what he liked to read. More recently as a 4½-year-old, he thought of a game that all the children could play together called 'Super Cheetah': with a little adult support at first, Liam taught everyone the rules of the game—you could be your favourite animal but with a special super-power so that you could rescue any injured or endangered animals. Everyone joined in!

In education, children and adults can jointly create meaning, and groups of children can work together to understand both motivating and self-motivated tasks and their own

Figure 12.1 Journeys of learning take many forms. Here, Liam is absorbed in the enticing world of books.

learning—telling each other about what they have learned links the individual to the collective mind—that children are aware of knowledge and that knowledge can be said in words. It was Bruner who asked, 'Who is curriculum for?' His answer was, of course, 'for adults'.

Curriculum as a 'gift'

What we have called 'the child's curriculum' can be understood as a gift to interpret the Scottish Early Level Curriculum 3-6, to enlighten policy: it is a gift that has not yet been fully unwrapped. In seeking to explore the history, the critical elements of an enlightened Scottish curriculum, and to understand the extent to which the early level is implemented as a 'through' curriculum (Dunlop 2013) embracing continuous experiences embedded in what has gone before, it is proposed that interactions and relationships must work in harmony with understandings of children's creativity, learning, and development if we are to make the most of this gift-giving between children and those who enact curriculum.

Vaughan and Estola (2008) suggest that children and young people in education are required to acquire the kind of knowledge that is sought by the economy, resulting in social inequalities, the fore-fronting of an 'exchange' paradigm (non-nurturing, fostering competition, acquisition, and self-interest), rather than a 'gift' paradigm that respects the views of others, and has empathy or affection for them. In my view, gifts need to be reciprocal: on the one hand children give so much if we are open to receive, while a well-conceived and implemented curriculum can also be just that—a receiving and responsive gift for children.

Transforming the narrative of curriculum to embrace it as a gift, and avoiding metaphors of curriculum as something packaged to be 'delivered' to children, 'the gift paradigm in early childhood will not only allow children to develop values in their individual lives but will help to validate those values in the society at large so that choices and policies can become more consciously life-affirming' (Vaughan and Estola 2008, p. 27).

The idea of early childhood experience as a gift can also be found in the work of Froebel, which focuses on the early years of childhood as a special period of life. Teachers and early educators could populate the spaces between early childhood and primary with a developing discourse of gift-giving, to ensure that curriculum policy in fact works well in practice.

The metaphor of curriculum as a gift arose from thinking about what children contribute and what adults may give in return. If, as Giroux says, curriculum is a cultural script, then this metaphor allows us to embrace the many gifts—the many scripts—that children offer in relation to their creativity, their hope, their dispositions, their working theories, their communicativeness, their imagination, and their possible worlds. The adult world has to be aware of, and open to, those gifts, and if it is, only then can we begin to understand what the child's curriculum is, and what children offer to us and to each other. For me, the concept of curriculum as a gift is a joyful one if we embrace the reciprocity of giving and are able to interpret curriculum as a gift that opens and opens and opens some more. By interpreting curriculum as a gift we can understand it as a relationship between children, between children and the adults in their lives, and between adults within and between the administrative sectors that are together tasked with implementing the Scottish Early Level Curriculum 3-6. The risk, of course, is that gift-giving may not be reciprocal, and so may raise issues of power and control.

The well-connected child

The positioning of parents and families, and parenting

The aspirations of Scottish policy have two dominant discourses when analyzed through the perspective of the workforce and what it should do: an economic discourse that speaks of inclusion, and an aspiration that every child should grow up in a supportive and interested family (Dunlop et al. 2011). However, there is a strong alternative discourse of parenting, of disadvantage, of early years and what it should be—cultural, historical, and political—an unease about the language of 'services', of 'provision', and of 'workforce'.

The relationships with out-of-home adults and with other children are unknown elements for children as they enter early childhood settings. The vast majority of children in our country now go to at least one early years group setting before they start school. An increasing number attend under-threes settings so they are often veterans of change, but what normally sustains them is the connection they make between their already established relationships to the new. The central role of supportive and interested families, coupled with the continuity they provide, is visible in the examples of transitions described below, told with the parent's voice.

Timing when to let go

Liam has a loving home experience, and I know he feels, and is, respected in his decisions, and has been to many different places with both of us and to a variety of early childhood arts, music, and play opportunities in my company. The choice of nursery centre was important to all the family. I had consistently said, 'I don't want him going anywhere until he has the language to tell me about it': at 3½, that time has arrived and a place has been offered at a nearby nursery school. After a number of different visits we found somewhere that understood we would like consecutive days, a steady peer group, a named teacher who would look out for our boy, an interesting environment indoors and out, and a staff team that could articulate their early childhood philosophy. Isn't that what all families should expect of the places where they entrust their children? In turn, as Liam's family we were keen to make a contribution, and after visiting a couple of times we asked if we could give the nursery a hen—so 'Cloudy' arrived to join the chickens already in the hen coop. Before his starting date, Liam and I agreed he would tell me when he was ok about my leaving. On Liam's first day he tried out various things to do; then, after a while, he went over to the outside sandpit where some bigger children were playing—a boy looked up at him and said, 'This is how you do it'. Liam joined the other children and said to me, you can go now', and so I did (feeling both proud and devastated). On the second day Cloudy had laid an egg and Liam was able to bring this home—we made breakfast pancakes with banana in them—a two-way connection between home and nursery had begun.

I've been speaking with Liam about nursery school on his days away. He speaks of Hilary frequently, relays stories of things she's said and has quite the giggle. He said, she's very funny and also that he loves her. This morning upon arrival, he ran to Hilary to say good morning. She outstretched her arms and asked him for a cuddle, and he didn't hesitate. Hilary has reported back that Liam is quietly observing and taking his time to explore and play with the different areas around the room. He is exploring each area section by section and enjoying the detail. As a result, he's been quite immersed and hasn't really embarked on the social aspect of nursery school yet. That will come (and now has: see 'Super Cheetah' on page 226.

Moving on from childminder to nursery

Amber is excited that she's going to the 'big girl's nursery'. She's told her granny that she would see the babies there—she is very much into baby dolls—feeding, dressing, bathing, and telling them stories. At 2¾, she is about to start at the private nursery where her older brothers spent their pre-school years. With working parents, Amber is already well-established at her childminder's, where she has been going since she was ten months. Margie was a known adult as Amber's brother Will had also spent a couple of years in Margie's care. Amber is used to change and takes the new in her stride.

Her home, childminder, new nursery, and brothers' school are all in the same area, and Margie takes her out and about to playgroup, the wildlife garden, and the park often. She is in a small group of other children as her childminder works in partnership with another childminder. This network of relationships is fluent and easy and will sustain beyond a change of setting. Amber speaks often about the fact she is soon to start nursery and regularly seeks confirmation that she is now a 'big girl'. She is very pleased when we agree she is, and a little cross with her brothers when they tease her for still being a baby. She tells Will and Eddie that the nursery had a garden 'with a squirrel in it' which she spotted on the tree when she visited with her mother. She knows that it is 'next to the boys' school' and that she can 'hang up my coat' on a peg like Maisie Mouse in her storybook. On her one visit to the nursery so far, she opened drawers and cupboards to see what was inside them.

Most mornings Amber asks where she will be going that day, nodding sagely when they tell her that she has some more days left at Margie's house. 'I'm going to play with my friends', she announces, before telling them what plans she has in store.

The manager of her new nursery, her room leader, and her named carer are all coming to visit before she starts, and she will have a short settling-in period. Amber firmly declares that Margie can come to visit her home too and is pleased when this is confirmed. I feel emotional about her leaving such a loving childminder, but am confident that Amber will take it all in her stride and will flourish. She is very interested in the world around her, and we think this will help her get through the initial change.

Deciding to wait a year before starting school

When our February baby was born I knew that four years later I would be given the choice to send her to school at either 4½ years old or 5½ years old. We spoke to many of our friends and family about the decision and had a mixed response. Many suggested that our child would do well either way (she had excellent verbal skills and was a good team player). However, one comment stuck in my memory most of all: 'Some people regret sending their children to school early, but you will never find someone who regrets sending their kid later'. I also found it interesting to talk to a secondary school teacher who commented that parents almost always focused their decision on their child's ability to settle into primary 1, but she had noticed teenagers struggling to be the youngest (in a variety of ways) in the upper years of their secondary schooling.

As the enrolment date drew nearer I found my decision all the more easy as I could see Sacha lagging behind her friends in confidence and in toilet training (my daughter had several minor medical reasons to delay continence). As a mother who was affected by bullying at school, I grew concerned that my child was trying so desperately to fit into the girl group at nursery; worrying about how she looked and acted, and not showing confidence to ever take the lead, she was striving—at the tender age of 4—to be what everyone else wanted her to be!

So the decision was made and my daughter was prepared for not joining her friends in going to school. She began another fully funded year at nursery with the additional activities of a weekly dance class and one full day a week at the local outdoor woodland nursery to supplement her routine.

Now, with only five months to go before she finally starts primary 1, we have absolutely no doubts that we made the right decision. She remains a strong team player but has increased exponentially in confidence and has recently even approached the headmistress with an idea for a charity campaign, which has been implemented across the whole nursery! I have also loved seeing her compassion and care for the new younger children at nursery whilst she engages in a lovely new group of friends, all the while maintaining her previous relationships.

What she has achieved in this extra year she has passed on to her siblings and to us. For that, I am greatly thankful!

Island life

Living on a remote Scottish island allows my children to experience a freedom that not many mainland locations can offer. The beach and fields are the playgrounds, and family hikes and bonfires with neighbours and friends are the norm. With a small population most people know each other either intimately or at least the family gossip. For the most part houses and cars are left unlocked, and with such a tight-knit community the 'old values' of looking out for every child, whoever they belong to, plays a part in island community living. Children know each other from when they were babies, through nursery, and into school, as well as socializing outwith. Relationships, therefore, with nursery and school staff are close; they have been developed not only on site but at social occasions and day-to-day living. Continuity of relationships is most definitely advantageous in knowing the child, their family, and their circumstances. Most of the teachers are of a similar age and part of my social life, some being close friends. Professional and personal boundaries can become blurry and relationships tested. With others, I have seen trust destroyed and a sour taste left, parents almost scared to bring up any problems for fear of community and social retribution. But on the whole it is a wonderful thing being part of something close. This year the community came together to fundraise for school trips and the target was smashed, leaving a small amount to be raised by families. As a family we are also involved in developing a community garden where people of all ages and skills are coming together; such a richness of relationships is becoming part of each of my children's lives and sense of belonging to the island.

In conclusion: Tomorrow

The child's curriculum

Human babies have a far more prolonged growing-up period and arrive in the world much more vulnerable than other species, but the baby should not be underestimated for what he or she brings to making sense of the world. In this book we have been looking at what we have called the 'child's curriculum'—at how children respond to the world, how the child makes meaning, and how the child shows us not only what they need, but also what they are capable of, and how they can instigate new learning and take their development forward: not alone, but in the company of, and in relationship with, others in their world.

It can be seen that for more than 200 years there has been a strong commitment to appropriate and relevant experience for the youngest of children here in Scotland. The focus was on their day-to-day experiences, and yes, too, upon how these early experiences would open up a world of later opportunities for them. The focus was firmly on what the 'here and now' looked like, with a recognition of what small children needed from adults in their world, but also a respect for the meaning-making of children.

This built on the principles of the Scottish Enlightenment, the early recognition of the importance of a 'school in every parish' in Scotland, and fed into the primary school system of the day, where 'infant' classrooms were very often also staffed by Froebel-trained teachers.

Values and principles

These traditions, which can so inform current practice, have been swallowed up in the banking model of early childhood, in curriculum definition which, by its very nature, risks being curriculum stricture with increasingly narrow aims, and with a pressing need to revisit first principles, to embrace the complete necessity of an enlightened approach to children's early experiences, valuing the bedrock of the past but at the same time questioning tradition.

In early childhood people talk about their principles of practice: my early experiences in the Edinburgh child gardens and Nursery and Infant classes laid the values for a career. They taught me about the importance of relationships; the innate capacity of children; the importance not just of educational culture but primarily of home culture; the tools to do a good job that theory provides us with; the importance of evidence to inform teaching; the curiosity, motivation, and drive of nearly all children to find out, experience, and learn, so driving their development; the central importance of children's interests and curiosities and how to capture the interest of children who are less able to focus and delve deep into exciting and interesting discoveries; and the very important skill of 'following ahead' of children as we pay attention to transitions, so that they, too, may be a tool.

Looking forward

In this chapter I have tried to weave in the values I hold and share with others in the early childhood enterprise into a kind of colourful tartan or celebratory narrative of childhood, informed by experience, taking a detour through theory and real family experience to bringing a critical eye when looking at policy and practice. To conclude with what this means for practice, this is not about 'improving children's readiness for learning'—the title of a talk I was recently asked to give—but about children being learners from the very start of life and about considering how we might ensure that capacity is fostered rather than inhibited. We need to ask not whether children have agency, but what happens when that is denied.

Returning to what makes an enlightened early childhood educational policy at the beginning of the twenty-first century, we need not go much further than Froebel's words:

> But I will protect childhood, that it may not, as in earlier generations, be pinioned, as in a strait-jacket, in garments of custom and ancient prescription that have become too narrow for the new time. I shall show the way and shape the means, that every human soul may grow of itself out of its own individuality.

> (Weston 2000, p. 23)

In drawing from our rich heritage and questioning its relevance today, we can use it as a contemporary springboard to ensure a full implementation of the Scottish Early Level Curriculum 3-6 in both Early Learning and Childcare and in school. For children, this is a glorious time in their lives when they have so many gifts to bring and we have a curriculum that is a complete gift to the profession.

It is a time of real opportunity.

References

Bertram, T. and Pascal, C. (2010). Robert Owen 1771–1858: mill owner and educationalist. *Nursery World*, Spring 2010.

Bruce, T. (2015). *Early Childhood Education*, 5th edn. London: Hodder Education.

Bruner, J.S. (1960). *The Process of Education*. Cambridge, MA: Harvard University Press.

Bruner, J.S. (1996). *The Culture of Education*. Cambridge, MA: Harvard University Press.

Campbell, J.L. (2002). Ideas, politics and public policy. *Annual Review of Sociology*, **28**, 21–38.

Donaldson, M. (1978). *Children's Minds*. London: Harper Collins.

Dunlop, A-W., Seagraves, L., Henderson, S., Henry, J., Martlew, J., and Fee, J. (2011). *A Policy-Based Functional Analysis of the Children's Workforce*. Edinburgh, UK: Scottish Government, Children and Young People Social Care Directorate, Workforce and Capacity Issues Division.

Dunlop, A-W. (2013). Curriculum as a tool for change in transitions/practices/transitions practices as a tool for changing curriculum. In: K. Margetts and A. Kienig (eds.) *International Perspectives on Transition to School: Reconceptualising Beliefs, Policy and Practice*, Chapter 12. London: Routledge, pp. 135–45.

Dunlop, A-W. (2015). Aspirations and actions: Early childhood from policy to practice in Scotland. *International Journal of Early Years Education*, **23**(3), 258–73.

Durkan, J. (1953) The beginnings of humanism in Scotland, *The Innes Review*, **4**(1), 5–24.

Edwards, A. (2011). Building common knowledge at the boundaries between professional practices: Relational agency and relational expertise in systems of distributed expertise. *International Journal of Educational Research*, **50**, 33–9.

Elfer, P. (2012). Emotion in nursery work: Work Discussion as a model of critical professional reflection, *Early Years*, **32**(2), 129–41.

Elfer, P. (2015). Emotional aspects of nursery policy and practice—progress and prospect. *European Early Childhood Education Research Journal*, **23**(4), 497–511.

Foucault, M. (1991). *Discipline and Punish: The Birth of the Prison*. London: Penguin.

Froebel, F. (1826). *Edinburgh Froebel Network*, http://edinburghfroebelnetwork.org.uk, accessed 22 Mar 2018.

Giroux, H.A. (2005). *Border Crossings: Cultural Workers and the Politics of Education*, 2nd edn. Abingdon, UK: Routledge.

Giroux, H.A. (2017). *In Conversation with Henry Giroux: Rethinking Education in the Age of Emergent Authoritarianism*, Seminar 5 July, School of Education, University of West of Scotland, Paisley.

Hardy, L. (1912). *The Diary of a Free Kindergarten*. Boston/ New York: Houghton Mifflin and Co., https://archive.org/details/diaryoffreekinde00hardrich, accessed 22 Mar 2018.

Herman, A. (2001). *How the Scots Invented the Modern World*. London: Crown Publishing Group.

Houston, R.A. (2008). *Scotland: A Very Short Introduction*. Oxford: Oxford University Press.

Hutcheson, F. (1729). *An Inquiry into the Original of Our Ideas of Beauty and Virtue; In Two Treatises: I. Concerning Beauty, Order, Harmony, Design; II. Concerning Moral Good and Evil*, 3rd edn corrected. London: J. and J. Knapton.

Isaacs, S. (1954). *The Educational Value of the Nursery School*. London: The British Association for Early Childhood Education (now available in a 2013 reprint from Early Education).

Morrison, K. (2001). Henry Giroux. In: J.A. Palmer (ed.) *Fifty Modern Thinkers on Education, from Piaget to the Present*. London: Routledge, pp. 280–5.

Nuttall, J. (2013). *Weaving Te Whāriki: Aotearoa. New Zealand's Early Childhood Curriculum Document in Theory and Practice*, 2nd edn. Wellington, New Zealand: NZCER Press (New Zealand Council for Educational Research).

OECD (2017). *Starting Strong V: Transitions from Early Childhood Education and Care to Primary Education*. Paris: OECD Publishing, http://dx.doi.org/10.1787/9789264276253-en, accessed 22 Mar 2018.

Papatheodorou, T. and Moyles, J. (eds.) (2009). *Learning Together in the Early Years: Exploring Relational Pedagogy.* Abingdon, UK: Routledge.

Paterson, L (2012). 'Do we have an excellent curriculum or not?' *The Scotsman* [online], http://www.scotsman.com/news/opinion/lindsay-paterson-have-we-excellent-curriculum-or-not-1-2191644, accessed 22 Mar 2018.

Priestley, M. and Drew, V. (2016). 'Teachers as agents of curriculum change: Closing the gap between purpose and practice', European Conference for Educational Research, Dublin, 23–26 September 2016, http://www.eera-ecer.de/ecer-programmes/conference/21/contribution/39307/ and http://hdl.handle.net/1893/24179, accessed 22 Mar 2018.

Sahlberg, P. (2011). Paradoxes of educational improvement: The Finnish experience. *Scottish Educational Review,* **43**(1), 3–23.

Schmidt, V. and Radaelli, C. (2004). Policy change and discourse in Europe: Conceptual and methodological issues. *West European Politics,* **27**(2), 183–210.

Trevarthen, C. (2002). Learning in companionship. *Education in the North: The Journal of Scottish Education,* New Series, **10**, 16–25.

University of Roehampton (2018). 'Froebel History page', https://www.roehampton.ac.uk/colleges/froebel-college/froebel-history/, accessed 22 Mar 2018.

Vandenbroeck, M. (2015). '*La socialisation des jeunes enfants: approches démocratiques des diversités*' (Early childhood: Socialisations and transitions) conference, Paris, 13 November 2015.

Vaughan, G. and Estola, E. (2008). The gift paradigm in early childhood education. In: S. Farquhar and P. Fitzsimons (eds.) *Philosophy of Early Childhood Education: Transforming Narratives.* Oxford: Blackwell Publishing, pp. 24–41.

Voluntary Services Aberdeen website, https://www.vsa.org.uk/about-vsa/history-and-origin/, accessed 22 Mar 2018.

Vygotsky, L.S. (1981). The Genesis of Higher Mental Functions. In: J.V. Wertsch (ed.) *The Concept of Activity in Soviet Psychology.* Armonk, NY: Sharpe.

Weston, P. (2000). *Friedrich Froebel: His Life, Times and Significance,* 2nd edn. London: University of Surrey Roehampton, https://www.froebel.org.uk/app/download/2478564/pwbookmedium.pdf, accessed 22 Mar 2018.

Policy documents

'Children and Young People (Scotland) Act 2014', http://www.legislation.gov.uk/asp/2014/8/contents, accessed 22 Mar 2018.

Scottish Executive (2004). *A Curriculum for Excellence – Ministerial Response.* Edinburgh: Scottish Executive.

Scottish Government (2007). 'Building the Curriculum 2: Active Learning in the Early Years', https://www.education.gov.scot/Documents/btc2.pdf, accessed 22 Mar 2018.

Scottish Government (2008a). 'The Early Years Framework', http://www.gov.scot/Publications/2009/01/13095148/0, accessed 22 Mar 2018.

Scottish Government (2008b). *Achieving Our Potential: A Framework to tackle poverty and income inequality in Scotland.* Edinburgh: Scottish Government, http://www.gov.scot/Publications/2008/11/20103815/6, accessed 22 Mar 2018.

Scottish Government (2008c). *Equally Well: Report of the ministerial task force on health inequalities.* Scottish Government, http://www.gov.scot/Resource/Doc/229649/0062206.pdf, accessed 22 Mar 2018.

Scottish Government (2014). *Building the Ambition: National Practice Guidance on Early Learning and Childcare (Children and Young People Scotland Act),* http://www.gov.scot/Resource/0045/00458455.pdf, accessed 22 Mar 2018.

Chapter 13

Early childhood education and care policy: Beyond quantity and quality, for human development

Ingela K. Naumann

Introduction—a new century of the child?

Children are in the spotlight today, more so than ever before in modern times. Their development and education are receiving enormous attention from parents, early childhood experts, policy makers, and even economists. In the rich countries of the Organisation for Economic Co-operation and Development (OECD), public debate is buzzing: about the right nutrition, the right cots, the right toys, and in particular, the right education and care for young children. There are myriads of conferences and workshops, bookshelves full of new publications on childhood, child development, and early years education, and new academic degrees and professional training programmes for young people who wish to 'work with children'. Notably, governments are spending more money than ever on 'early interventions', and in particular, early childhood education and care (ECEC). Large international organizations such as the European Union (EU), the OECD, or UNICEF (United Nations International Children's Emergency Fund, now named the United Nations Children's Fund) have made recommendations and formulated targets for early childhood policy. The World Bank has made early child development through ECEC one of its core topics and areas of support also for lower-income countries (OECD 2006, 2012; UNICEF 2008; Jenson 2009; European Commission 2013; Mahon 2013).

At the beginning of the twenty-first century, we see an extraordinary, broad, and international consensus gathering force about the importance of a good early childhood experience for the well-being and later success of individuals and for society as a whole. There is a real chance for change towards more child-friendly politics and practices, and with this, for more general transformative social change in today's societies. For it is children who tend to suffer most from the great ills of society: war, poverty, exploitation of human and natural resources, repression, social exclusion. There are examples across different countries and cultures of new policy initiatives and programmes focused on children, giving hope that the twenty-first century may become the true 'century of the child' (OECD 2011, 2012; European Commission 2013).[1] In particular, ECEC services

---

[1] In 1900, in her influential book *The Century of the Child* (translated into English in 1909), the Swedish educationalist Ellen Key argued for a transformational change in children's education and set out her vision for the twentieth century, where education would centre on the child and help him/her develop into a free and independent, yet considerate, individual (Key 1909; Lengborn 1993).

Figure 13.1 Children jumping on a big bouncy mat.

have been developed extensively in many countries as a means of combating child poverty (by supporting parental employment), compensating for social disadvantage, and creating more equal opportunities. For the first time in history there exists universal, or near-universal, access to ECEC for pre-school children in most OECD countries (Esping-Andersen 2002; Morel, Palier, and Palme 2012; Van Lancker 2013).

However, the importance given to ECEC today also carries risks: it can mean increased pressure and expectations on children to reach developmental milestones at certain intervals, tightened control over children's behaviour and that of their families, or decreased appreciation of children's intrinsic value in favour of human capital generation and a narrow focus on cognitive development. The amalgamation of neuroscientific findings about brain development in young children and economic cost–benefit calculations in current policy debates has led to an oversimplification of the positive link between ECEC and child outcomes (Cantillon 2011; Wastell and White 2013). It matters not only *that* children have come into the focus of politics and policy-making, but *what* policies, practices, and discourses are developed for children. Not all early childhood policies are also 'child-friendly' or suited to genuinely improving children's well-being and life chances. There is a strong trend today towards the commodification of children. This chapter argues for a renewed moral debate about the forms and content of state intervention into children's lives, and in particular, a critical discussion about the role of ECEC in supporting the development and flourishing of the 'whole child', alongside the child's integration and participation in their cultural community (Figure 13.1).

The following section will first give a broad overview of the international development of ECEC since the end of the nineteenth century, with particular focus on the accompanying moral debates and conflicts. It will then take a critical look at current debates around children's development and new ECEC policy trends, thereby discussing a series of policy-mismatches and policy-myths that may obstruct some of the positive developments under way. The final section reflects on what ECEC could mean, both for children and society.

The rise of the early childhood education and care policy

When Friedrich Froebel opened his first kindergarten in 1840, the concept of a 'children's garden' was revolutionary, and a rarity: according to Froebel, small children should be given the space and opportunity to develop their sense of self, their wonder of the world, and their skills in a creative and playful manner under the auspice of caring and mindful pedagogues (Hebenstreit 2003). This vision was quite contrary to the 'children's crèches' or 'infant schools' that had begun to crop up at various places across Europe in the early nineteenth century, and were reactions to the 'Social Question'—the fact that small children of industrial workers, who were still too young for the factories themselves, had nowhere to go and no one to look after them during their parents' and siblings' long working days. These 'childcare' initiatives of the Churches or philanthropic individuals were often inspired by concerns to get working-class children off the street, maybe giving them a meal, some safety, and to 'save their souls' by educating them to become disciplined, obedient citizens (Reyer 1987; Scheiwe and Willekens 2009). These two drivers have shaped the development of early childhood education and care across the last two centuries: the needs created by modern economic production that separates work place and home, parents and children, during the day, thereby creating a 'care deficit'; and the recognition of the intrinsic value of childhood and of children's zest for learning, exploring, and participating in the world they live in, as portrayed and promoted by philosophers, educationalists, and children's activists of many colours (see, for example, Palmer 2001).

The unwieldy term 'early childhood education and care' (ECEC) only came into fashion in recent years, and was introduced by large international organizations such as the EU and the OECD as a technical umbrella term that would somehow manage to denote and encompass the many different types and organizational forms of services for young children that exist within and between countries. By pulling 'early childhood education' and 'childcare' linguistically together, the term 'ECEC' also carries normative connotations, or even a sense of policy objective: it implies an understanding that small children have a right to consistent quality of care *and* education. In practice, however, the general use of the term 'ECEC' has come to mask great variations in the purposes and quality of different services for children—not all types of ECEC are equally 'caring' about children or provide equally rich learning experiences for children. The term 'ECEC' also glosses over the fact that in most countries a split system developed historically out of the above two drivers, with institutions of 'early childhood education' on the one hand, and 'childcare' on the other.

Kindergarten before school, and children's rights

Building on the practical understanding of visionary educators such as Pestalozzi, Froebel, Montessori, and Malaguzzi, a rich kindergarten or pre-school culture developed in Europe in the nineteenth and early twentieth century, and was taken up in various forms across the countries of the OECD. Educational settings specially designed for young children first originated as private initiatives, but in time the State took responsibility in some countries—for example in France, where *écoles maternelles* were set up in the second half of the nineteenth century, to further the 'natural development' of children aged 2–5 years and support the making of French citizens (Scheiwe and Willekens 2009).

By the mid-twentieth century most governments of wealthier nations were devising programmes of education intending to support young children's growth and learning, a policy that was stimulated in 1957 across the western world by the fear that the Soviet Union might be ahead of the game in educating for technological innovation after launching Sputnik (Slobodin 1977; Kirp 2009). Development of early childhood education policy was also promoted at the same time by the International Children's Rights movement, which urged recognition of children as full persons with inalienable rights based on their emotional needs and virtues, and prevention of the exploitation, discrimination, and marginalization of children in industrial society, thus raising awareness of the need to create spaces for children to grow, develop, and learn, in safe and healthy environments. This movement culminated in the signing of the UN Convention on the Rights of the Child in 1989, which confirmed the moral right to education for all children, of both sexes and from all backgrounds (United Nations 1989; Therborn 1993).

In most OECD countries, however, early childhood policy remained, for the duration of the twentieth century, an add-on to education policy for older children. The raising of very young children as healthy social beings was generally understood as the private responsibility of parents, with the state only intervening in the case of manifest need, and kindergarten and pre-school services were not part of the formal education system (Scheiwe and Willekens 2009). 'Childcare' services remained in most countries very scarce and directed at 'children in need'—children whose mothers could not take care of them, either because they had to work, or for other reasons.

Public childcare and maternal employment

From the 1960s onwards, new understandings and interpretations of 'childcare' entered public and political debate, triggered by the demands of the new women's movements for public childcare. Questioning the dominant norms about the gendered division of labour that presumed mothers' 'natural caring role' while leaving women and children dependent and exposed to patriarchal family structures, feminist activists demanded women's right to gainful employment—supported by state-provided childcare (Ruggie 1984; Marchbank 2000). However, this gender equality-inspired childcare movement remained marginal in most OECD countries, leading more often to private parent cooperatives and playgroup initiatives than public childcare services (Randall 1996; Naumann 2005). Furthermore, the 'childcare' and 'early education' movements often stood in tension to each other, with educationalists and children's rights activists questioning whether women's demands for equal rights and full access to employment might be harmful to children by disregarding their need for closeness and loving care, a concern often fuelled by positions of radical feminists who wanted to free themselves altogether from family ties and care obligations (Naumann 2005).

Interestingly, due to a series of economic, cultural, and political circumstances in the post-war period, in some European nations public opinion came to understand women's and children's rights not as contradictory but as mutually inclusive of each other. In these countries, mainly the Nordic nations, comprehensive and integrated public early childhood education and care systems developed from the 1970s onwards with the dual aim of providing high-quality childcare for working parents as well as supporting the development and learning of small children. In these countries, a culture and policy framework became established that recognized high maternal employment and high participation rates of children in (full-day) ECEC as beneficial for children, families, gender relations, the economy, and society as a whole (Hinnfors 1992; Leira 1992; Sipilä 1996). As a result, in the Nordic countries both participation of children in ECEC and women's employment rates have been consistently higher than in most other OECD countries, and with participation rates of mothers with children similar to those of women without children (Thévenon 2016).

It is important to note that this dual-policy approach, which embraces both women's and children's rights, does not include a 'the sooner the better' perspective: alongside the extension of ECEC services, extensive parental leave policies were developed so that, today, children in Nordic countries stay at home with their parents at least until their first birthday (often longer)—due to generous leave entitlements and financial state support— before they start to attend ECEC facilities (O'Brian 2012). Neither is ECEC conceptualized simply as a preparation phase for school, but as an important space for children to develop and thrive, and with no hurry to send them on to school: in Sweden and Finland the compulsory school age is 7 years, while it is 6 years in most OECD countries, and even five years in some English-speaking nations.

Similar attitudes to maternal employment and ECEC could also be found in the Eastern Bloc countries during the cold war era, resulting in extensive childcare provision for example in East Germany, and contrasting starkly with the policy approach in most continental countries of Western Europe.

Contrasting policies and practice

The two parts of Germany arguably stood most starkly for the two different approaches to early childhood services in the second half of the twentieth century: on the one hand the economically driven expansion of childcare in the German Democratic Republic that also supported a certain independence of women and gender equality, and on the other hand a pronounced traditional and conservative stance in West Germany where, in a Froebelian tradition, there existed mainly part-time kindergartens for pre-school children from age 3 with the understanding that the family, and in particular the mother, was responsible

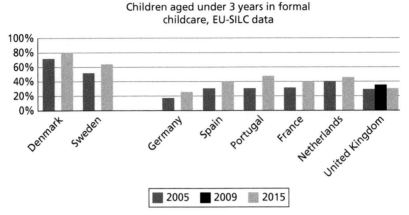

Figure 13.2 Percentage of under-3s in formal childcare (selected European countries).

for childcare (Moeller 1993; Von Oertzen and Rietzschel 1998). Strong ideological attacks were levered at both ECEC systems: East Germany was criticized for 'forcing' mothers to work and subjecting children to uniform and standardized daycare practices and indoctrination, while West Germany was, more recently, criticized for 'forcing' mothers into a housewife existence, with the effect of very low fertility rates amongst well-educated and professional women, as well as failing to provide educational support to young children from disadvantaged backgrounds (Budde 1999; Kolbe 1999; Riedel 2008).

In recent years there has been a veritable U-turn in early childhood policy in (unified) Germany: since the 1990s, consecutive governments have made great investments in the expansion of daycare services, which also accommodate children aged under 3 years. A legal entitlement for all children to an ECEC place was introduced, first for 3–5 year-olds in the 1990s, then for children aged 1 and over in 2013, increasingly emulating the Nordic, integrated approach to ECEC (Riedel 2008; Naumann 2014). At the beginning of the 1990s childcare places existed only for around 2% of the under-3s in West Germany. By 2007 this had increased to 15.5% in unified Germany, and to 24% in 2011. However, large regional variations reflecting the different cultural and institutional trajectories of East and West Germany still persist: in 2008, 43% of 1 and 2 year-olds in the East German *Bundesländer* were in childcare settings, versus 7% in the West German *Länder* (Oberhuemer, Schreyer, and Neuman 2010, p. 174; Naumann et al. 2013).

Similar developments have taken place in other countries that, until recently, saw childcare to be primarily a private family responsibility, and where there had been modest public investment in early education, such as in Spain, Portugal, the Netherlands, or the UK (European Commission et al. 2014) (Figure 13.2).[2]

---

[2] In the UK, participation of under-3s in formal childcare rose steadily to 35% in 2009, but then decreased again to 30.4% in 2015. Most children under 3 who attend childcare services in the UK do so on a part-time basis; this is also the case for the Netherlands. In the Nordic countries such as Sweden and Denmark, the majority of children attend formal ECEC for thirty hours or more per week, which is more conducive to supporting maternal employment (European Commission et al. 2014).

So what caused this massive expansion of ECEC provision?—what made ECEC become a central policy focus causing such pronounced investments in this policy field, and this in a period when governments generally have scaled back on public service funding?

The social investment turn and the political economy of the infant brain

The popularization of neuroscientific knowledge in the 1990s, the 'decade of the brain', coupled with evidence of massive brain development in infants and young children, led to a general acknowledgement of the importance of the first years of life for developing cognitive and behavioural skills, which have life-time consequences on educational attainment, health outcomes, and well-being (National Research Council and Institute of Medicine 2000; Sylva et al. 2004, 2010). The mainstreaming of neuroscientific findings about early child development happened at about the same time as OECD countries started to define themselves as 'knowledge-based economies'—that is, countries that were competing in the globalized market not so much through availability of natural resources or cheap labour, but through the high skill levels and expertise of their citizens, and their potential for technical progress and innovation (OECD 1996). If brain development in young children was central to later educational attainment and success, then taking care of young children's brains was key to a country's economic competitiveness. Early childhood education is now promoted by governments and international organizations as the first phase of lifelong learning, and worthy of investment (Esping-Andersen 2002; Morel, Palier, and Palme 2012; European Commission 2013; World Bank 2016; OECD 2017). It is seen as a means of compensating for potential disadvantages some children may experience in their emotional and cognitive growth, due to the poverty and lack of community support of their families, early neglect, or intrinsic disorders of development and disabilities. Good early education institutions, and special education for disabilities, are conceived to create more equal life opportunities for all children because they favour attainment of normal brain growth, intelligence, and social abilities.

By this logic, and focusing on the 'product', the emphasis on ECEC is given an economic justification in current policy discourses, as a means to supporting future employability and the generation of wealth. Economists offer evidence that investing in human capital formation at the earliest stage will yield higher returns and be more cost-effective than programmes that aim at later life stages, such as training to improve the lives of low-skilled unemployed adults (Heckman 2008; OECD 2012).

The World Bank states this plainly on its website 'Early Childhood Development (ECD)':

> In fact, investing in young children through ECD programs—ensuring they have the right stimulation, nurturing and nutrition—is one of the smartest investments a country can make to address inequality, break the cycle of poverty, and improve outcomes later in life. Evidence from both developed and developing countries suggests that an additional dollar invested in high quality preschool programs will yield a return of anywhere between US$6 and US$17.

But there is a second appeal behind the push for more ECEC provision: in the harsh economic climate of the last few decades and with expanding public costs of their maturing
welfare states, countries have sought to find ways for making social expenditures sustainable. One approach has been an emphasis on 'activation'—that is, bringing as many
people into gainful employment as possible, as a means of increasing tax revenue and cutting welfare bills—in other words, devising programmes that help people support themselves. Early childhood services thus not only help to make children more 'employable'
in the future, but support the employment of their parents, particularly mothers, thus
also helping to reduce the risk of poverty for families and related welfare costs (Esping-
Andersen 2002; Jenson and Saint-Martin 2006; Jenson 2009; Morel, Palier, and Palme
2012). ECEC has thus become a core element of the 'social investment turn' in affluent
countries with mature welfare systems: a turn towards an understanding where passive
'hand-outs' of the welfare state have lost acceptance and are being replaced with measures
that enable individuals to support themselves economically.

The new ECEC hegemony: Throwing out the child with the bath water?

Undoubtedly, this new social investment approach, supported by governments across the
OECD and by international organizations such as the World Bank, the IMF (International
Monetary Fund), and the EU, has led to an extraordinary investment in ECEC policy over
the last few decades, with more children than ever having access to ECEC settings. Many
countries have moved the governance of their ECEC provision from social or family min-
istries into education departments to highlight the new emphasis on early education, and
innovative early years curricula have been developed (see, for example, Te Whāriki 1996).
This has also led to a strengthening of children's rights (Naumann 2011): in many OECD
countries, children now have a legal entitlement to pre-school education, at least for some
period before they start school, and there is increasing evidence that children from disadvantaged backgrounds in particular are benefiting from participating in good-quality
ECEC (Mathers et al. 2014). The increase in ECEC places has also benefited women in
their ability to participate in the labour market: across the OECD, female employment
rates amongst women aged 25–54 years rose steadily from an average of 54% in 1980 to
71% in 2010 (Thévenon 2016). There is thus much to be positive about when looking at
recent policy trends in ECEC.

And yet, have we truly entered the 'century of the child'? Or should this unprecedented
international consensus on ECEC policy also make us wary? There have always been,
and still are, great variations between countries, and even within countries, in the types,
forms, and extent of ECEC. These differences reflect national and regional educational
traditions, different welfare state designs, and differently composed ideological battles
and political compromises. ECEC is located at the interface of various societal spheres: the
family, public education, the labour market, the welfare sector, and so on (Mahon 2002).
Specific formations of ECEC give insight into dominant understandings and norms about

the relation between the public and the private realms in society, acceptable levels of state intervention, the appropriate place and form of care for young children, intergenerational and gender relations, and differing constructions of 'the child'.

Early campaigners for early childhood education and/or childcare were well aware of the way ECEC reflected dominant norms and hierarchies in society, and of its transformational potential. Froebel believed his kindergartens would not only help children to flourish, but also saw them as a basis for developing a religiously grounded national citizenry (Hebenstreit 2003; Sauerbrey 2013). Second-wave feminists saw childcare facilities not only as a means to their liberation, but also as a place where new collective and solidaristic forms of community life could be developed and practised (see, for example, Bernd 1995). Thus, over the last 150 years public debates and politics around childcare and early education have always involved normative conflict between competing visions of society. These older disputes around ECEC have gone ominously silent today, giving way to the just-described dominant policy discourse that reduces ECEC, ultimately, to its economic function. In this process, the role of ECEC becomes rather narrow and focused on the techniques that support human capital development, rather than, for example, the development of moral sensitivity or cultural understanding. There is, then, also the risk that in this process, the child—as an imaginative and affective participant of a cultural community—is thrown out with the bath water of moral debate. We shall return to this issue later.

There are, however, more immediate tensions inherent in the currently dominant ECEC policy paradigm: a primary issue is that existing ECEC systems, and the directions within which they currently develop, are in fact ill-equipped to deliver on the great expectations of the social investment agenda. There exists a pronounced mismatch between policy discourses and objectives and the actual organizational forms ECEC has taken in most countries. In particular, a core problem lies in the inequality of access to high-quality ECEC, with respect to both age and socioeconomic background.

There is no space here to go into detail about the effectiveness of different ECEC systems and cultures in supporting children and their families; instead, I shall discuss a series of general international trends in ECEC policy and dominant discourses below, and the pitfalls that come with them.

Failure to appreciate and provide for the under-3s and their families

Neuroscience identifies the first period in life, ages 0–3, as the crucial phase for development and learning as this is the fastest period of brain growth with special adaptation for care and communication (Davis and Dobbing 1981; Schore 2001; Narvaez 2014) (Figure 13.3).

In contrast, international ECEC policy has focused predominantly on the 3–5 year age group, arguably demonstrating a truncated transmission of research discourse into policy. In around two-thirds of OECD countries, participation rates in early years settings of children aged between 3 and school age is over 70%, and in most European

Figure 13.3 Baby with blocks.

countries, New Zealand, and Japan, enrolment rates are even over 90%. For the under-3s age group, large differences exist, with enrolment rates of below 10% in some countries such as the Slovak Republic, Czech Republic, or Mexico, and over 50% in others such as Denmark, Iceland, Norway, Belgium, or the Netherlands (OECD 2017).

Reflecting the 'split' tradition of ECEC, early *education* services are usually set up for 3–5 year-olds, mostly on a part-time basis, although there are exceptions, such as France or Italy, where state pre-schools run a full-day provision. Under-3s are more likely to attend *childcare* settings, which often have to cater for the need of employed parents who require full-time provision. Early education institutions tend to be public and are often free of charge, while 'childcare' in many countries, such as the UK, USA, Australia, or the Netherlands, is provided via privatized 'childcare markets' that can mean considerable costs for families (see, for example, OECD 2006, 2017; Lloyd and Penn 2012; Naumann et al. 2013). The professionalization of staff tends to be higher in early education than in childcare settings, and, in an increasing number of countries, the early years teaching curricula are planned to lead to primary school learning, and the 'childcare' settings do not receive the same degree of guidance and regulation (UNICEF 2008; Oberhuemer, Schreyer, and Neuman 2010). There is thus strong focus in early education settings on guidance and practices aimed at supporting pre-school children in reaching specific cognitive 'milestones' understood as necessary for successful transition into school learning, while there is often little pedagogical input in childcare settings for the youngest children. In fact, owing to often very low pay levels and low qualification requirements in childcare settings, there is a tendency for the care of the youngest children—arguably the most crucial developmental phase—to be left to very young, poorly trained, and poorly paid women working in these settings. Turnover rates can be very high on account of poor work conditions and lack of career prospects, particularly in marketized childcare—adding to unfavourable conditions with respect to the consistency and sensitivity of responses to the affective and social needs of children under the age of 3.

There is thus a gap in understanding between the neuroscientific and child development research—which has established the importance of a supportive and responsive environment from birth and through the first 5 years of a child's life, with creative experiences that become richer as the child develops greater agility, mastery of language and artful skills—and the emphasis on ECEC policy in educating the 3–5 year age group to prepare for learning at school.

The lesser attention to services for the under-3s may also reveal the inadequacy of the social investment formula with its strong focus on ECEC services, with respect to the well-being of infants and toddlers and their families. In most societies there is a cultural unease about extra-familial care of very small children based on an understanding of the importance of the parent–child relationship in the earliest phase of life, a view that is supported by psychological knowledge on early child development (Belsky et al. 2007; Music 2011). Other policy measures, such as financial family support and leave entitlements that enable parents to care for their babies themselves, may be more beneficial and wholesome for the child than the new activation policies favoured by governments today. As mentioned earlier, it is primarily in the Nordic countries that we find a more comprehensive approach to supporting children and families, while other rich countries such as the UK or the USA lag behind in developing adequate parental leave and other family support measures (Esping-Andersen 2002; O'Brian 2012).

There is now a strong expectation on parents to fight poverty and its negative consequences on children on an individual basis by actively engaging in gainful employment, when in fact few ECEC systems and their wider policy contexts respond particularly well to the requirements of labour markets or the needs of families. There are thus mounting pressures—stress and 'time poverty'—for families with young children today—pressures that are particularly felt by families with lower financial and social resources. The psychological consequences of this policy-mismatch for children and their families are rarely acknowledged in policy discourse.

Inequality of access widens the gap

Equal access of all children to high-quality ECEC services has, to date, remained more a vision than a reality in practically all OECD countries: despite the strong emphasis on policy discourse around 'disadvantaged' children, or children from low-income family background, it has been shown that it is precisely the children most in need that have least access to ECEC services—a trend that has been found across OECD countries (Riedel 2008; Greenberg 2010; Speight et al. 2010; Van Lancker and Ghysels 2012; Zachrisson et al. 2013). This is the case in particular for children aged under 3 years. The lower participation rates of under-3s from lower socioeconomic groups are partly due to the fact that low-skilled mothers are less likely to be in gainful employment than well-educated women—and then prefer to care for their children themselves. Even when only looking at children with gainfully employed mothers, it has been found that children from poorer households are less likely to participate in ECEC than their more affluent peers (Van Lancker 2013). There are, however, large differences between countries in the extent to which children from low-income households have access to ECEC services. In the Nordic countries, for example, access to ECEC is almost the same for all children, while in the UK children from households in the lowest 20% income bracket are 2.5 times less likely to attend any form of ECEC than the children from the most affluent 20% of households (Van Lancker 2013).

The institutional set-up of ECEC seems to have a strong influence on access. Unitary or integrated systems offering care and learning together are better able to reach all children than systems that have different forms of provision in place for 'childcare' and 'early education' (Naumann et al. 2013). Of course, the level of state subsidies influences access as well. Only where the state covers the majority of the service costs can it be ensured that all children receive access. Where, however—as is the case in the UK—parents have to cover the majority of the costs for early care, low-income families tend to become priced out of the market. Thus, in countries where investment in ECEC more readily reaches children from middle- and upper-class backgrounds, rather than children from low-income backgrounds, there is the risk that the expansion of ECEC provision will actually increase educational inequalities linked to family resources rather than mitigating these, and further widen the 'school readiness' gap between children from different backgrounds (Cantillon 2011; Naumann 2014).

Risks of misunderstanding science, and forgetting the Whole Child

A further issue arises from the popularization and circulation of distorted understandings and mis-readings of the neuroscientific findings about the link between brain development and learning in young children. One such 'neuro-myth' has been the idea that evidence on brain growth, and its 'plasticity' or response to stimulation, supports the starting of 'teaching' as early as possible, leading to initiatives—as in the UK—of expanding free nursery education for 3 and 4 year olds down to 2 year olds, especially those from disadvantaged backgrounds (House 2011), without much consideration of how the nursery education system would have to be transformed to meet the special affective needs at the developmental stage of 2 year olds.

The 'human capital investment' approach that has come to dominate early childhood policy debate also continues to focus on the development of cognitive skills, and neglects other aspects such as motor skills, emotional and social well-being, and especially the importance for children of rich and secure relationships with their human and natural environment. Important evidence from 'affective neuroscience' is not attended to (Panksepp 1998, 2005). The emphasis on 'education' of young children may carry the risk of a 'schoolification' of ECEC, constraining the development of institutional practices that open space for children's affective and creative activities, and learning in free play, identified as essential by developmental psychology and neuroscience for laying down the foundations for long-term development of human talents and social qualities (Bruner, Jolly, and Sylva 1976; Donaldson, Grieve, and Pratt 1983; Göncü and Klein 2001; Reddy 2008).

A fundamental critique of current developments in ECEC policy has been put forward by children's rights advocates: that the 'investment' focus conceptualizes children as 'becomings' or 'citizen-workers of the future' rather than as 'beings' in the here and now (Lister 2003). If children are not valued as persons in their own right and for their genuine contribution to society, but rather for their potential to achieve performance and productivity as adults in a world planned for them, their self-confidence and resilience will suffer.

There is one compensatory change. The push for early education as a form of 'human capital investment' has led to an extension of children's rights: in most OECD countries children aged between 3 years and school age now have a statutory right to early years education, and in some countries this is extended to 1 year olds. A rights approach that places the child as a person and citizen in the centre can set boundaries against an economic instrumentalization of children and their future, and encourage the creation of genuine child-friendly spaces (Moss and Petrie 2002; Naumann 2011). That said, both the children's rights perspective and the social investment perspective conceptualize the child as an autonomous individual. We should not forget that all children are fundamentally relational beings, dependent on secure attachments with other human beings. Intellectual abilities and technical skills cannot be separated from impulses for affectionate relations and shared meaning in creative projects.

What is the purpose of early childhood education and care?

The idea that education is for children, both for exploration and criticism of accepted wisdom and values, and for understanding the entire range of knowledge and struggles that has characterized the human condition is rapidly disappearing.

(Apple 1988, p. ix)

A striking feature of ECEC, both within countries as well as internationally, is the absence of any significant conflict about its *content*. This is extraordinary considering that, for centuries, the education of children has been a prime battlefield between different forces in society—prominently between the State and the Church—about shaping the values and principles of society. The emotive and moral debates about 'children's needs' or 'maternal deprivation' of the twentieth century and the accompanying ideological clashes have disappeared from public debate and politics.

There is a trend for governments to favour the creation of 'ECEC markets', providing a bazaar of educational styles, where parents can choose from a range of institutions with different pedagogical orientations and practices according to preference. Many recently developed early years curricula avoid normative statements and focus instead on laying

Figure 13.4 Girl on a tractor.

out 'quality' criteria and providing standardized and rationalized measurements of 'desirable outcomes', 'school readiness', and 'efficiency', thereby rendering any discussion about the content and purpose of education into one about technical and managerial process and optimization rather than an ethical question (Dahlberg and Moss 2005; Dahlberg, Moss, and Pence 2007). The avoidance of normative expressions in ECEC policy may be politically safer in today's culturally diverse societies, but it impedes children's engagement with, and appreciation of, the culturally and socially complex contexts within which they grow up.

The dominant discourses and orientations on ECEC have thus become strangely detached from the fundamental experiences of young children, who, in their playful everyday learning practices, creatively seek and explore their integration into the culture, beliefs, and life duties of their societies (Rogoff 2003, 2008) (Figure 13.4). The strong focus on ECEC as social investment—as an economic strategy for human capital development and national and international competition—risks 'robbing children of any organic sense of the relationship between curricula and their own cultural pasts and presents' (Apple 1988, p. x; see also Chapter 12).

There do exist, however, examples of self-reflection and cultural re-centring of ECEC policy. The early child curriculum in New Zealand draws its internationally recognized strengths from the communitarian culture of the Maori, explicitly setting out to weave each child into the fabric of a society of relations linking family with the community and its traditions (Te Whāriki 1996). The original 1996 version of Te Whariki from the New Zealand Ministry of Education opens with this quotation from a group of educational psychologists from Scotland, Australia, and England:

> [Early childhood is] … a period of momentous significance for all people growing up in [our] culture … By the time this period is over, children will have formed conceptions of themselves as social beings, as thinkers, and as language users, and they will have reached certain important decisions about their own abilities and their own worth.
>
> (Donaldson, Grieve, and Pratt 1983, p. 1)

Conclusion: The humanitarian and moral purpose of early childhood education and care

For over 150 years social institutions, philanthropists, educationalists, and activists of various camps campaigned for the development of ECEC—for the sake of 'saving children's souls', for helping them thrive and develop, for generating a responsible citizenry, and for achieving gender equality, amongst other motives—and yet, ECEC policy remained a rather marginal policy field during the building and expansion of modern welfare states. Then, at the end of the twentieth century, changes in ideological orientations, along with new economic predicaments (the challenges of global competition and the sustainability of mature welfare states) and the popularization of neuroscientific findings about the importance of the first phase of childhood for a successful life course, fused into a new, powerful social investment agenda, with ECEC becoming its flagship policy. The expectations are high: ECEC services for young children are supposed to level social inequality and create more equal opportunities, reduce child poverty, compensate for social disadvantage and disabilities, and produce competitive, highly skilled, responsible, and productive citizen-workers.

It is of course debatable whether one policy alone can ever achieve such extensive objectives, and in this chapter and on other occasions we have pointed to the importance of a more holistic policy approach to supporting the development and well-being of children and their families (see, for example, Naumann 2014). At the same time there is a trend for ECEC to be reduced to rather narrow objectives of cognitive development in pre-school children, with a focus on 'school readiness' and ultimately 'human capital development'. Ironically, ECEC is supposed to achieve far more than it would ever be able to do, but with a far more restricted content and function than would be beneficial for children and society.

This chapter has pointed to a puzzling misperception of neuroscientific knowledge in policy-making that may lie at the heart of this mismatch between policy objectives and policy orientation. The neuro-scientific research of the last thirty years amounts to nothing less than a celebration of the brain and human development: the human brain is magnificent in its 'plasticity' and its ability to grow, adapt, and learn. Children, from the moment they are born, are magnificent in their ability to engage and communicate with their environment, in their yearning for learning and creative exploration, and in their innate drive to connect emotionally, physically, and cognitively with other human beings and their material and natural environment. Neuroscientific and psychological research could thus inspire us to be confident in the human condition: children will grow and develop—in a far more complex fashion than narrow 'school readiness' benchmarks might predict—and integrate as active and moral participants into a cultural community, as long as provided with a 'good' environment. And yet, policy orientations today are driven by concerns about 'developmental deficiencies' in children, resulting in controlled and tightly monitored state interventions from the very beginning of their lives.

A precondition for any successful economic investment is trust: trust that the institutional arrangements are stable, that ethical standards are adhered to, and that agreements are honoured. Social investment, in turn, will only succeed if policy makers can develop trust in the basic components of human development: that children will thrive and develop into responsible citizens that contribute to society, as long as there is a stable and secure environment they can grow up in; that there are ethical standards that are adhered to; and promises that are not broken.

What we need is a new moral debate about what a 'good' environment constitutes for children and their families. In the twenty-first century such a moral debate should not need to pitch children's and women's rights against each other, or reduce individuals to

Figure 13.5 Boy, barefoot, embarking on outdoor adventures behind the house.

specific functions of 'workers' or 'carers'. Instead, it could acknowledge the rights of all human beings as full persons with ambitions for creative expression, development, and self-fulfilment, and take on the challenge of envisioning what a society might look like that reconciles productive and caring aspects of humanity. Such a moral debate would further address how to integrate and balance in society the two innate human drivers—of autonomous action and individual expression on the one hand, and affective relational interdependence with other persons on the other—of which both are crucial for healthy development in childhood, as much as throughout later life, for men and women alike. With other words, the debate would shift the focus from 'fixing the child' to fixing the broader conditions within which children live and grow up. Such a perspective could draw inspiration both from educationalists, of the past and in the present, who have reflected on the ethical value of ECEC, and from neuroscientists who inform us about the organic building blocks of human development.

So let us end this chapter by opening up for exploration how our modern-day psychological and neuroscientific knowledge about children's development may weave into Friedrich Froebel's vision of the kindergarten: what does a seed need to grow? Good soil (a diverse cultural and natural environment), sunshine (stable affective relationships, i.e. love), and water (material and cultural resources that allow a child to explore and learn about its environment, and about himself/herself, other human beings, and the cultural community he or she is born into), and with this, the seed will germinate into a seedling, set roots, and reach for the sky. And the gardener knows: she does not need to pull at the plant to make it grow—it knows how to do that all by itself (Figure 13.5).

References

Apple, M.W. (1988). Series editor's introduction. In: K. Egan (ed.) *Primary Understanding: Education in Early Childhood*. New York/ London: Routledge, pp. ix–xiii.

Belsky, J., Vandell, D.L., Burchinal, M., Clarke-Stewart, K.A., McCartney, K., Owen, M.T., and the NICHD Early Child Care Research Network (2007). Are there long-term effects of early child care? *Child Development*, **78**(2), 681–701.

Berndt, H. (1995). Zu den politischen Motiven bei der Gründung erster antiautoritärer Kinderläden. *Jahrbuch für Pädagogik*, Sonderdruck, 231–50.

Bruner, J.S., Jolly, A., and Sylva K. (eds.) (1976). *Play: Its Role in Development and Evolution*. New York: Basic Books.

Budde, G. (1999). Women's policies in the GDR in the 1960s and 1970s: Between state control and societal reaction. In: R. Torstendahl (ed.) *State Policy and Gender System in the Two German States and Sweden 1945–1989*. Uppsala, Sweden: Opuscula Historica Upsaliensia, pp. 199–218.

Cantillon, B. (2011). The paradox of the social investment state: Growth, employment and poverty in the Lisbon era. *Journal of European Social Policy*, **21**(5), 432–49.

Dahlberg, G. and Moss, P. (2005). *Ethics and Politics in Early Childhood Education*. London: Routledge/ Falmer.

Dahlberg, G., Moss, P., and Pence, A. (2007). *Beyond Quality In Early Childhood Education and Care: Languages of Evaluation*, 2nd edn. London: Routledge/Falmer.

Davis, J.A. and Dobbing, J. (eds.) (1981). *Scientific Foundations of Paediatrics*. London: William Heinemann.

Donaldson, M., Grieve, R., and Pratt, C. (1983). *Early Childhood Development and Education: Readings in Psychology*. Oxford: Basil Blackwell.

Esping-Andersen, G. (2002). A child-centred social investment strategy. In: G. Esping-Andersen with D. Gallie, A. Hemerijck, and J. Miles (eds.) *Why We Need a New Welfare State*. Oxford: Oxford University Press, pp. 26–67.

European Commission (2013). *Barcelona Objectives: The Development of Childcare Facilities for Young Children in Europe with a View to Sustainable and Inclusive Growth*. Luxembourg: Publications Office of the European Union.

European Commission/EACEA/Eurydice/Eurostat (2014) *Key Data on Early Childhood Education and Care in Europe, 2014 Edition*, Eurydice and Eurostat Report. Luxembourg: Publications Office of the European Union.

Göncü, A. and Klein, E.L. (eds.) (2001). *Children in Play, Story, and School*. New York: Guildford Press.

Greenberg, J.P. (2010). Assessing policy effects on enrollment in early childhood education and care. *Social Service Review*, **84**(3), 461–90.

Hebenstreit, S. (2003). *Friedrich Fröbel—Menschenbild, Kindergartenpädagogik, Spielförderung*. Jena: IKS Garamond.

Heckman, J.J. (2008). Schools, skills, and synapses. *Economic Inquiry*, **46**(3), 289–324.

Hinnfors, J. (1992). *Familjepolitik. Samhällsförändringar och partistrategier, 1960-1990*, Göteborg Studies in Politics 26. Stockholm, Sweden: Almqvist & Wiksell International.

House, R. (ed.) (2011). *Too Much, Too Soon? Early Learning and the Erosion of Childhood*. Stroud: Hawthorn Press.

Jenson, J. (2009). Diffusing ideas for after Neoliberalism: The social investment perspective in Europe and Latin America. *Global Social Policy*, **10**(1), 59–77.

Jenson, J. and Saint-Martin, D. (2006). Building blocks for a new social architecture: The LEGO paradigm of an active society. *Policy and Politics*, **34**(3), 429–51.

Key, E. (1909). *The Century of the Child*. New York/ London: G. P. Putnam's Sons.

Kirp, D.L. (2009). *The Sandbox Investment: The Preschool Movement and Kids-First Politics*. Cambridge, MA/ London: Harvard University Press.

Kolbe, W. (1999). Gender and parenthood in West German family politics from the 1960s to the 1980s. In: R. Torstendahl (ed.) *State Policy and Gender System in the Two German States and Sweden 1945–1989*. Uppsala, Sweden: Opuscula Historica Upsaliensia, pp. 133–68.

Leira, A. (1992). *Welfare States and Working Mothers: The Scandinavian Experience*. Cambridge: Cambridge University Press.

Lengborn, T. (1993). Ellen Key. *Prospects: the quarterly review of comparative education*, **XXIII** (3/4), 825–37.

Lister, R. (2003). Investing in the citizen-workers of the future: Transformations in citizenship and the state under New Labour. *Social Policy and Administration*, **37**(5), 427–43.

Lloyd, E. and Penn, H. (eds.) (2012). *Childcare Markets: Can They Deliver an Equitable Service?* Bristol, UK/ Chicago, IL: Policy Press.

Mahon, R. (2002). Gender and welfare state restructuring through the lens of child care. In: S. Michel and R. Mahon (eds.) *Child Care Policy at the Crossroads: Gender and Welfare State Restructuring*. New York/ London: Routledge, pp. 1–30.

Mahon, R. (2013). Social investment according to the OECD/DELSA: A discourse in the making. *Global Policy* **4**(2), 150–59.

Marchbank, J. (2000). *Women, Power and Policy: Comparative Studies of Childcare*. London: Routledge.

Mathers, S., Eisenstadt, N., Sylva, K., Soukakou, E., and Ereky-Stevens, K (2014). *Sound Foundations: A Review of the Research Evidence on Quality of Early Childhood Education and Care for Children Under Three: Implications for Policy and Practice*, Oxford University and The Sutton Trust, https://www.suttontrust.com/wp-content/uploads/2014/01/1sound-foundations-jan2014-3.pdf, accessed 25 Mar 2018.

Moeller, R.G. (1993). *Protecting Motherhood: Women and the Family in the Politics of Post-War West Germany*. Berkeley, LA/ Oxford: University of California Press.

Morel, N., Palier, B., and Palme, J. (eds.) (2012). *Towards a Social Investment Welfare State? Ideas, Policies and Challenges*. Bristol, UK: The Policy Press.

Moss, P. and Petrie, P. (2002). *From Children's Services to Children's Spaces: Public Policy, Children and Childhood*. London: Routledge Falmer.

Music, G. (2011). *Nurturing Natures: Attachment and Children's Emotional, Sociocultural and Brain Development*. Hove, UK/ New York: Psychology Press, Taylor & Francis Group.

Narvaez, D. (2014). *Neurobiology and the Development of Human Morality: Evolution, Culture, and Wisdom*. New York/ London: W.W. Norton.

National Research Council and Institute of Medicine (2000). *From Neurons to Neighborhoods: The Science of Early Childhood Development*, ed. J.P Shonkoff and D.A. Phillips. Washington, DC: National Academies Press.

Naumann, I. (2005). Child care and feminism in West Germany and Sweden in the 1960s and 1970s. *Journal of European Social Policy*, **15**(1), 47–63.

Naumann, I. (2011). Towards the marketization of early childhood education and care? Recent developments in Sweden and the United Kingdom. *Nordic Journal of Social Research*, **2**(1), 39–54.

Naumann, I. (2014). Access for all? Sozialinvestitionen in der frühkindlichen Bildung und Betreuung im europäischen Vergleich. In H.H. Krüger, W. Helsper, and U. Deppe (eds.) *Elite und Exzellenz im Bildungssystem. Nationale und internationale Perspektiven*, Sonderheft 19. *Zeitschrift für Erziehungswissenschaft*, **17**, Supplement 3, 113–28.

Naumann, I., McLean, C., Koslowski, A., Tisdall, K., and Lloyd, E. (2013). *Early Childhood Education and Care Provision: International Review of Policy, Delivery and Funding*. Edinburgh: The Scottish Government, Research Report Series.

Oberhuemer, P., Schreyer, I., and Neuman, M.J. (2010). *Professionals in Early Childhood Education and Care Systems: European Profiles and Perspectives*. Opladen, Germany/ Farmington Hills, MI: Barbara Budrich.

O'Brian, M. (2012). *Work-Family Balance: Report for the 20th Anniversary of the International Year of the Family 2014*. New York: United Nations.

OECD (1996). *The Knowledge-based Economy*. Paris: OECD Publishing.

OECD (2006). *Starting Strong II: Early Childhood Education and Care*. Paris: OECD Publishing.

OECD (2011). *Doing Better for Families*. Paris: OECD Publishing.

OECD (2012). *Investing in High-quality Early Childhood Education and Care (ECEC)*, OECD Education and Training Policy, https://www.oecd.org/education/school/48980282.pdf, accessed 25 Mar 2018.

OECD (2017). *Starting Strong 2017: Key OECD Indicators on Early Childhood Education and Care*. Paris: OECD Publishing.

Palmer, J.A. (2001). *Fifty Modern Thinkers on Education: From Piaget to the Present*. London/ New York: Routledge.

Panksepp, J. (1998). The periconscious substrates of consciousness: Affective states and the evolutionary origins of the SELF. *Journal of Consciousness Studies*, **5**(5–6), 566–82.

Panksepp, J. (2005). Affective consciousness: Core emotional feelings in animals and humans. *Consciousness and Cognition*, **14**(1), 30–80.

Randall, V. (1996). Feminism and Child Day Care. *Journal of Social Policy*, **25**(4), 485–505.

Reddy, V. (2008). *How Infants Know Minds*. Cambridge, MA/ London: Harvard University Press.

Reyer, J. (1987). Geschichte der öffentlichen Kleinkindererziehung im Deutschen Kaiserreich, in der Weimarer Republik und in der Zeit des Nationalsozialismus. In G. Erning, K. Neumann, and J. Reyer (eds.) *Geschichte des Kindergartens. Vol.1: Entstehung und Entwicklung der öffentlichen Kleinkindererziehung in Deutschland von den Anfängen bis zur Gegenwart.* Freiburg i. B., Germany: Lambertus, pp. 43–82.

Riedel, B. (2008). Kinder bis zum Schuleintritt in Tageseinrichtungen und Tagespflege. *Forschungsverbund Deutsches Jugendinstitut/Universität Dortmund,* 41 pp.

Rogoff, B. (2003). *The Cultural Nature of Human Development.* Oxford: Oxford University Press.

Rogoff, B. (2008). Observing sociocultural activity on three planes: Participatory appropriation, guided participation, and apprenticeship. In: K. Hall, P. Murphy, and J. Soler (eds.) *Pedagogy and Practice: Culture and Identities.* Los Angeles, CA/ London/ New Delhi/ Singapore: Sage/The Open University, pp. 58–74.

Ruggie, M. (1984). *The State and Working Women: A Comparative Study of Britain and Sweden.* Princeton, NJ: Princeton University Press.

Sauerbrey, U. (ed.) (2013). *Friedrich Fröbel. Die Entstehung des Kindergartens und der Spielpädagogik im Spiegel von Briefen,* edited and commented by U. Sauerbrey. Leipzig, Germany: Evangelische Verlagsanstalt.

Scheiwe, K. and **Willekens, H.** (eds.) (2009). *Childcare and Preschool Development in Europe: Institutional Perspectives.* Basingstoke, UK/ New York: Palgrave Macmillan.

Schore, A.N. (2001). Effects of a secure attachment relationship on right brain development, affect regulation, and infant mental health. *Infant Mental Health Journal,* **22**(1-2), 7–66.

Sipilä, J. (1996). *Social Care Services: The Key to the Scandinavian Welfare Model.* Aldershot, UK: Ashgate.

Slobodin, C.S. (1977). Sputnik and its aftermath: A critical look at the form and the substance of American educational thought and practice since 1957. *The Elementary School Journal* 77(4), 259–64.

Speight, S., Smith, R., Coshall, C., and **Lloyd, E.** (2010). *Towards universal early years provision: Analysis of take-up by disadvantaged families from recent annual surveys,* Research Report DFE-RR066. London: Department for Education.

Sylva, K., Melhuish, E., Sammons, P., Siraj-Blatchford, I., and **Taggart, B.** (2004). *The Effective Provision Of Preschool Education (EPPE) Project: Findings From Preschool To End of Key Stage 1.* London: University of London, Institute of Education.

Sylva, K., Melhuish, E., Sammons, P., Siraj-Blatchford, I., and **Taggart, B.** (2010). *Early Childhood Matters: Evidence from the Effective Pre-school and Primary Education Project.* Oxford: Routledge.

Te Whàriki/He Whàriki Màtauranga mò ngà Mokopuna o Aotearoa. Early Childhood Curriculum (1996). For Ministry of Education, New Zealand Government. Wellington, New Zealand: Learning Media.

Therborn, G. (1993). The politics of childhood: The rights of children in modern times. In: F.G. Castles (ed.) *Families of Nations: Patterns of Public Policy in Western Democracies.* Aldershot, UK/ Brookfield, WI/ Hong Kong/ Singapore/ Sydney: Dartmouth Publishing, pp. 241–91.

Thévenon, O. (2016). Do 'institutional complementarities' foster female labour force participation? *Journal of Institutional Economics,* **12**(2), 471–97.

UNICEF Innocenti Research Centre (2008). *The Child Care Transition: A League Table of Early Childhood Education and Care in Economically Advanced Countries.* Florence: UNICEF.

United Nations (1989). 'Convention on the Rights of the Child', https://downloads.unicef.org.uk/wp-content/uploads/2010/05/UNCRC_united_nations_convention_on_the_rights_of_the_child.pdf, accessed 25 Mar 2018.

Van Lancker, W. (2013). Putting the child-centred investment strategy to the test: Evidence for the EU27, *Working Papers* 1301, Centre for Social Policy, University of Antwerp.

Van Lancker, W. and Ghysels, J. (2012). Who benefits? The social distribution of subsidized childcare in Sweden and Flanders. *Acta Sociologica*, 55(2), 125–42.

Von Oertzen, C. and Rietzschel, A. (1998). Comparing the post-war Germanies: Breadwinner ideology and women's employment in the divided nation, 1948–1970. In: A. Janssens (ed.) *The Rise and Decline of the Male Breadwinner Family?*—International Review of Social History Supplements, vol. 5. Cambridge: Cambridge University Press, pp. 175–96.

Wastell, D. and White, S. (2012). Blinded by neuroscience: Social policy, the family and the infant brain. *Families, Relationships and Societies*, 1(3), 397–414.

World Bank (2016). 'Early Childhood Development Overview', World Bank Group, http://web.worldbank.org/WBSITE/EXTERNAL/TOPICS/EXTCY/EXTECD/0,,contentMDK:20207747~menuPK:527098~pagePK:148956~piPK:216618~theSitePK:344939,00.html, accessed 25 Mar 2018.

Zachrisson, H.D., Janson, H., and Naerde, A. (2013). Predicting early center care utilization in a context of universal access. *Early Childhood Research Quarterly*, 28, 74–82.

Chapter 14

Communities raising children together: Collaborative consultation with a place-based initiative in Harlem

Joshua Sparrow

Acknowledgements

The author would like to thank Geoffrey Canada, Anne Williams-Isom, Marilyn Joseph, the late Caressa Singleton, and other colleagues at the Harlem Children's Zone; Halle LeBlanc, Lisa Desrochers, and the late T. Berry Brazelton at the Brazelton Touchpoints Center, Division of Developmental Medicine, Boston Children's Hospital; and David Saltzmann, Carron Sherry, and the Robin Hood Foundation for their support, guidance, and wisdom over the course of this collaboration. Additional thanks go to Marty Lipp and others at the Harlem Children's Zone for their careful review of this chapter and for permission to use the stories that follow and photographs from its Baby College and Harlem Gems programmes.

Introduction: The human curriculum

Like other human beings, children dance, sing, and tell stories. They arrange sounds, movement, and meaning into patterns, rhythm, and melody. They explore, inquire, and make discoveries about their world, and they invent and create, using their minds, bodies, and objects close at hand (Figure 14.1).

They do these things alone, alone with others in mind, and with others—real or imagined—whom they invite, or who have invited them, to enter into each other's stories, creations, and discoveries. These activities, solitary and social, are constructed of the histories and environments of the time and space in which they unfold—disassembled and reassembled with infinite variation. A young child who has voyaged to the moon on a daydream will find desolate prairies and aliens constructed from her own front stoop and the strangers passing by. Stories also come from other stories, songs from other songs.

Contexts for development

The immediate world that children inhabit is the source of the energy and matter from which their stories and creations will be made, of the companions with whom they will

Figure 14.1 Harlem Gems. Sharing discoveries and tools.
Courtesy of Harlem Children's Zone.

sing and dance, and sets the tone for their relationships that will emerge. This is probably also true for mothers, fathers, and other adults who care for children. But the songs,
stories, movements, and moods in which they immerse their children also emerge from
expanses of time and space beyond the child's experience.

Under what conditions can humans explore, discover, and create a range of possibilities
with and for their young, and for each other? Parents and other adult caregivers both open
up and set boundaries for the time and space in which children learn. Among the conditions for parental mediation of children's experience are:

◆ the quality of being together of child and parent—in the story or in discovery; this
may include the quality of the adult's affordances (protecting, respecting, honouring,
acknowledging, ignoring, leaving a private space) for the child's solitary expressions
and inventions-to-be

◆ the quality of the adult caregiver's being, both in the child's immediate world, and in
the world beyond, which the adult carries into the child's space and time.

Both of these conditions are influenced by forces within the child and within the adult
caregiver, and by external ones as well—some still within their control, some that they
can influence, and others that are beyond their control or influence. An adult caregiver's
sense of community (Sonn and Fisher 1998), and experiences of social connectedness and
engagement in a community, are among the forces that may change both of these ways
of being, and mediate the experiences from which children derive the elements of their
stories, creations, and discoveries.

Child-rearing social capital

People construct their environments with each other. Constructs such as 'social capital'
(Coleman 1988) and 'cultural capital' (Lee and Bowen 2006) are theorized as potential

benefits of human interaction that make the things people do together more than the sum of their parts. The nature and qualities of these human interactions, and their products, vary in correspondence with environmental affordances and constraints, and with cultural variations including those that pertain to individualistic vs. collectivist beliefs, values, and practices. Often, social capital constructs refer to concrete, material things that emerge from human interaction, or to the aggregation of individual political will into a collective one. The possibility that there are characteristics—structures, processes, or functions—of social capital that are specific to child-rearing has been explored to some extent in the literature (Putnam, Feldstein, and Cohen 2004). Yet in their child-rearing roles, parents and other adult caregivers may create social phenomena that result specifically from their child-rearing interactions (Sampson et al. 1999). Within the theory of social capital, there may be some value to conceptualizing a construct for 'child-rearing social capital'.

Child-rearing social capital has not been a major focus of research on the effects of neighbourhood poverty on infants, toddlers, and young children, perhaps because the literature suggests that parents can buffer their children from negative influences of the communities they live in (Brooks-Gunn, Duncan, and Aber 2000). When parents don't provide this protection, their individual shortcomings or challenges are often invoked as the explanation. But if we look beyond the individual level to the community and societal level, we might ask who or what buffers the parents?

One source of protection for parental functioning can be positive social supports and networks beyond the family. The benefits of shared beliefs and aspirations among parents in communities have been more clearly established in research on school-aged children and adolescents, demonstrating advantages in 'social control' in the behaviour of their children (Sampson et al. 1999; Vieno et al. 2010). However, for the parents of young children as well, social isolation has certainly been established as a threat to parental protective functions (Burchinal, Follmer, and Bryant 1996; DePanfilis 1996; Gracia and Musitu 2003; Lee 2009; Leininger, Ryan, and Kalil 2009).

One distinctive feature of 'child-rearing social capital' that may set it apart from the wider social capital phenomena (Coleman 1988) is that parents bring to the construction of this intimate kind of social capital a unique experience and knowledge of their individual children. Who their individual children are, what they do and say, give and take, along with their individual strengths and vulnerabilities, constitute some of the unique and overlapping knowledge that each parent brings to other parents as they construct child-rearing social capital together. Together, parents in a community can create a kind of aggregate of both their shared and distinctly individual knowledge and experience, bringing together what each of their children teaches them. To the extent that each individual child's unique characteristics represent but one facet of the larger environment in which the child was conceived, gestated, and is being raised, such aggregated knowledge also helps parents put together the pieces of a far more complete picture of where they are, what they are contending with, and what their environmental opportunities and constraints may consist of.

Figure 14.2 Harlem Children's Zone Annual Children's March for Peace, 9 August, 2017, Lenox Avenue, Harlem (Marty Lipp).

The story of the collaboration between the Brazelton Touchpoints Center and the Harlem Children's Zone is the story of a community coming together to reclaim and reconstruct environments for raising children, and connect adult caregivers so that they can support each other in that process (Figure 14.2).

Harlem Children's Zone

Starting early

When Berry Brazelton and I, and our colleagues at the Brazelton Touchpoints Center (BTC), were first invited by the Robin Hood Foundation to collaborate with the Harlem Children's Zone (HCZ) to assist with the development of its early childhood programming in 1999, we were told that this organization had come to recognize that their services for youth and adults could have been more effective if they were preceded by health, education, and a wide range of other services for these same children far earlier in their lives, beginning before birth. HCZ and the Robin Hood Foundation had been listening to the call that Brazelton had been delivering to health and education providers around the world: 'We must start earlier'.

Place-based

Alongside this new effort to begin early and connect services over time, the Harlem Children's Zone intended, as a place-based initiative, to connect services across space in this historic African American community, now also home to recent West African, indigenous Mexican, and other immigrants. By improving and linking existing services and creating new ones to fill gaps across all of the sectors affecting families with infants and young children (education, health, mental health, social services, employment support and training, and housing, among others), place-based approaches strive to weave together a community's resources to create a stronger social fabric, a shield against adversity. In contrast, singly focused projects are more like patches that may cover over one gap, but if surrounded by fraying material, are unlikely to hold (Schorr and Schorr 1989).

In some earlier versions of place-based initiatives, the innovation thought to drive change was the improved collaboration and coordination of agencies and their services within a community. The assumption often was that the professionals and their institutions would, in this way, better 'meet the needs' of the local residents, and of course this often proved to be true. Yet the resources of communities and their members to generate their own contributions to overcoming many of their challenges were often overlooked. The Harlem Children's Zone model sought to combine both improved coordination and collaboration of professional service agencies with the activation of intrinsic community problem-solving capacities.

The work of the Brazelton Touchpoints Center

In the early days of its partnership with the Harlem Children's Zone, the Brazelton Touchpoints Center had been focusing on providing a developmental, relational, and strengths-based approach to infant, child, and family development for paediatric healthcare and early education professionals, often embedded in community-based organizations around the country. From the start, the thrust of the work had been to elevate the meaningful and purposeful behaviour of the child, beginning in the newborn period, along with parents' corollary expertise about their own children, and the collective wisdom of local communities and cultures about child-rearing in their contexts. Over the course of the next few years, the Brazelton Touchpoints Center would embark on adaptations of the Touchpoints approach in Harlem and other communities, including tribal communities with American Indian/Alaskan Native 'Early Head Start' programmes. We developed a process of adaptation called "collaborative consultation" (Sparrow 2010), creating open spaces to welcome and honour the wisdom of families and communities. Through these experiences our center came to see that its potential as a change agent depended not only on paediatric healthcare and early educational professionals and their institutions, but on their capacity to build community-wide partnerships, to listen and respond to family and community members' voices, and to share power with them.

The Brazelton Touchpoints Center and Harlem Children's Zone in collaboration

The Brazelton Touchpoints Center—Harlem Children's Zone collaboration began with efforts by both organizations to help each other understand the experience and expertise each would bring. On the surface this was a reach across vastly different worlds. On the one hand, the Harlem Children's Zone is a community-based organization in a materially impoverished community with a history of generations of discrimination, persecution, disinvestment, and cultural and spiritual vibrancy, which had produced or harboured many of the United States' great political and civic leaders, thinkers, writers, artists, and other luminaries. On the other, the Brazelton Touchpoints Center is based in an academic teaching hospital in a university with a long tradition of privilege and entitlement, through whose halls many great leaders and thinkers had passed. A closer look, though, revealed similarities that, in retrospect, may have contributed to the success of this long and multi-faceted partnership. There are commonalities in the approaches of both organizations that the story of our partnership illuminates. Both share a developmental, relational, strengths-based, culturally responsive approach rooted in systems theory, and a commitment to social justice and racial and economic equity.

In addition, both were led by extraordinarily effective leaders building new organizations within older ones, striving towards convergent missions to which they were single-mindedly dedicated. For both, their missions, and the strategies for achieving them, hinged on amplifying human potential within an individual that is often overlooked or dismissed—for example, in a newborn baby or an adolescent father. Several years into our collaboration, when we travelled regularly from Boston to Harlem to work with parents and HCZ staff, Geoffrey Canada, the founder of the Harlem Children's Zone, and a forceful voice for the rights of all children, asked me,

'How does Dr. Brazelton keep up this grueling pace? He's 86 years old and he's got more energy than I have—and you know I have a lot!'

'Geoff,' I answered, 'he's the same as you. He's got an urgent mission, and he's not done yet.'

'Oh, I do get that.' (Figure 14.3)

The Harlem Children's Zone vision

Canada (2010) grew up in a not dissimilar neighbourhood in the South Bronx, and was keenly aware of the still not fully realized potential of the people of Harlem—their cultures, their communities, and the burden of discrimination and injustice that impeded their full expression. We were privileged to witness, through our participation in the work of 'The Zone', elements of his approach to activating the community's strengths, which included:

◆ a crystal clear vision: 'The children of Harlem deserve the same opportunities for high quality education and health care as the children in upper middle class communities on Long Island.'

◆ a relentless sense of urgency: 'There are children dying in the streets here every day. We don't have time to waste.'

◆ a laser-like focus on achieving results that the community could rally around—starting with the survival and flourishing of the community's young: 'We are not just saving children from the cradle to prison pipeline. We are sending them to college and beyond. They will be doctors, lawyers, scientists, teachers and the leaders of the next generation.'

Figure 14.3 Geoffrey Canada and T. Berry Brazelton.
Courtesy of Harlem Children's Zone.

◆ high expectations for everyone—babies, children, adolescents, parents, and other family members, staff, community members, funders, and collaborators like us: children come to school in uniforms, begin learning a second language at age 4; parents and community members are recruited to serve each other; and staff—many from Harlem, a few from elsewhere—are expected to learn, grow, and push forward their careers. They are held accountable for clear performance measures, such as numbers of parents recruited to family support programmes, or students' academic achievement. Demanding expectations are consistent with a culture of respect and a commitment to realizing the promise of the community and its hopes for its future.

◆ careful, skilful facilitation of the organization of time and space through which community members would come together, consider, and commit to action: to date, the Harlem Children's Zone has built Early Head Start, Head Start, and pre-kindergarten programmes in neighbourhoods where they are easily accessed and have become beacons of strength and hope, along with two sparkling kindergarten to 12th-grade charter schools that are also hubs for the community—one on the corner of one of Harlem's most animated thoroughfares, and the other in the midst of one of the most materially deprived public housing projects, where its staff are actively building bridges to the residents, and bringing hope.

First lessons from the Harlem Children's Zone

Social determinants of health

Nearly a decade before the World Health Organization (WHO) began to draw the international healthcare community's attention to the social determinants of health (Braveman, Egerter, and Williams 2011) with the founding of its Commission on the

Social Determinants of Health in 2005 and that commission's report in 2008 (WHO 2008), and several years before publication of the economic equations 'justifying' investments in early education based on return on investment (Rolnick and Grunewald 2003; Heckman and Masterov 2007), and of the widely cited synthesis of early childhood development research (National Research Council and Institute of Medicine 2000), HCZ leaders had mapped out 24 square blocks in Harlem. The map identified where schools, housing, police protection, and health and mental health services were either unavailable or of vastly inferior quality to those just 10 or 20 blocks south. It also showed where families with infants, toddlers, and young children lived whom the early childhood programmes that they were preparing to develop would serve. Although we had been invited to collaborate in the development of these early childhood and parenting supports and to improve access to, and quality of, paediatric healthcare, our colleagues at HCZ lost no time showing us how health and mental health are also constructed—or undermined—in the streets, on the stoops, and in the hallways and stairways of housing projects.

Concentrated poverty, concentrated capital, and environments for raising children

The city housing authority's ownership and management of the housing projects left many residents with little reason to believe that this was where they could truly put down roots and invest their energy in maintaining and improving the quality of their environment. The lack of sense of ownership by residents, the experience of living within the dehumanizing design and layout of the public housing projects, and the lack of basic maintenance by the housing authority—all were social determinants working against the mobilization of social capital, of individual and collective motivation to contribute to the physical betterment of neighbourhoods.

A history of overcoming, and the capacity to imagine what might be

Among the community's leaders—an informal source of social cohesion and control—were sometimes physically frail but reliably authoritative grandmothers and grandfathers. Many of them could be counted on as upholders of shared expectations, a strong moral code, hope for a better future no matter how unjust and destructive the past had been, and with the capacity to 'imagine what might be' (Obama 2015). The elders were among the first to be engaged by HCZ to bring about the neighbourhood renaissance that residents became committed to in the many focus groups and community convenings that HCZ conducted. When Geoffrey Canada, the founder and first visionary leader of HCZ, asked us to join one of the convenings of community elders and informal leaders to learn about the community's strengths and challenges pertinent to raising their children, and to receive their guidance and their blessings, he told us, 'These folks are busy people. Their time is valuable. Don't waste it.'

One other early lesson came from the history of academic researchers entering into Harlem and other 'otherized' communities to extract data without recognizing the costs to the community—including the loss of precious time, and often the contamination of precious meanings (Metraux 2013). Often, the damage that was inflicted was neither acknowledged, nor repaired. It ranged from blatant examples such as the Tuskegee syphilis experiment (Poussaint and Alexander 2001) or more subtle ones that perpetuated internalized oppression and disenfranchisement, or that deflected time and other resources from local demands for sustainable capacity building (Tuhiwai Smith 2012). Many researchers had also created a reputation for themselves, and those that would follow, of failing to leave anything of value behind them once the research grant had been spent. Often, they interpreted the data they took without consultation with those they took it from, sometimes in ways that caused further damage, reinforcing hopelessness and stereotypes. HCZ, however, was committed to conducting its own research, collecting its own data on child, family, staff, and programme progress for continuous quality improvement. We have learned similar lessons in the Native American communities where we have entered into collaborative consultations (Sparrow 2010).

There was another early lesson we were offered, although it would only be through experience that we could fully understand it. This work, we were told, is carried out through, and depends on, the quality of the relationships that we make: 'When you enter into this community, you never leave. When you do this work with us, we become family.' And that is what happened here, and also in several of the Native American communities where we began working at roughly the same time (Sparrow et al. 2011).

Baby College

HCZ's first programme for expectant parents, parents, and other adult caregivers of infants and young children was Baby College. Its name was intended to create new expectations and convey a sense of possibility and hope for the future of the community's youngest children. Its logo—a baby wearing a graduation cap and brandishing a college diploma—encouraged parents and other adult caregivers to be ambitious in their dreams for their children, and to talk about them with each other. These aspirations helped motivate parents to commit to participating in nine consecutive Saturday morning sessions held in a Harlem public school's classrooms. Outreach workers from the community, who usually had entrée into the neighbourhood's apartment buildings, recruited parents by knocking on every door.

Brazelton thought that to connect with reticent parents they might try commenting on something positive about their child's behaviour. To build this engagement skill, we observed children's behaviours together, thought together about their possible meanings for parents, and—in role plays—practised commenting on children's positive behaviours and parents' positive interactions with them. In subsequent Baby College sessions, the outreach workers would point out to us the parents that they'd recruited, and the ones with whom they'd 'used the child's behaviour' (Sparrow and Brazelton 2011) to make their initial connection (Figure 14.4).

Parents were grouped according to the ages of their children, and there were also separate classes for expectant parents and for adolescent expectant parents. Infants and

Figure 14.4 Mother and baby at Baby College.
Courtesy of Harlem Children's Zone.

toddlers stayed with their parents in the classes, which is not true of all parenting inter-ventions, but which allows parents to learn about their own children, rather than the ones in textbooks. We would go from one classroom to the next, and listen to the parents' questions—often the same ones as those we'd been hearing during these same years every-where else in the United States—about sleep, toilet training, and tantrums, and less about sibling rivalry. We saw our role as helping them find the answers from their observations of their children, from within themselves, and through dialogue with their peers.

Like most parents, they were hungry to understand their children, and urgently sought to ensure their children's health, well-being, and development, openly sharing their con-cerns, most often about delayed language development, and the inaccessibility of quality healthcare and early intervention services, and sometimes about the effects of whatever hardships the family had had to endure. Yet most parents also tend to be uncomfort-able with advice that they haven't asked for. When parents at Baby College seemed to be looking for advice, Dr. Brazelton would always ask, simply and straightforwardly, for per-mission before offering it: 'Would you like some advice?'

The older children were cared for in separate classrooms. After the first few years, the director of the programme, Marilyn Joseph (later promoted to plan and oversee all of HCZ's early childhood programming), realized that there was one missed opportunity that she quickly seized: the childcare staff began to offer activities to the children that were designed to reinforce each week's particular topic for the parents. Yet parents were not only learning about their children's development. They were learning about them-selves, and each other. The official programme evaluation tested parents before and after Baby College on what they knew about typical child behaviour and related knowledge. But after a few weeks into each nine-week session, we noticed that parents would start to turn to each other, compare observations about their children, share their challenges, exchange phone numbers, and then offer to help out by trading play dates and helping each other out with errands. We began to realize that Baby College was not only transmitting parenting information, and connecting families to professional services, but also creating a parent-to-parent peer network and catalysing the development of their social capital.

Once the age-based instructional time had ended, the parents would collect their children and congregate in the windowless school cafeteria for announcements, songs, celebrations, and lunch. This was a chance for parents to connect happily with each other, and for us to get to know them as well. One mother, from West Africa, told me over a plate of rice and beans that she'd been a pharmacist there but could not use her degree here to work. Another mother, as she took in with eyes as big as saucers the sliced turkey roll on her plate, said, 'This looks SOOO good!', as if she couldn't remember the last time she'd had a helping of protein. Each interaction opened up new ways of understanding the next.

In addition to childcare, breakfast, and lunch, outreach workers helped connect Baby College families to whatever services they might need—from assistance with filling out their tax forms, to food pantries and homeless shelters, to mental health or early intervention services. We would routinely encourage parents to speak to their Baby College outreach worker and the director when they were in need of services, or dissatisfied with the ones they had, and let them know that we would do the same.

'Sorry, not my department'

One of the reasons why it was possible to surface parents' most pressing and sometimes overwhelming concerns at Baby College was that it was designed to connect parents to the other services and programmes at the Harlem Children's Zone and beyond. The 'Zone' had created a well-coordinated safety net for families and for workers. The staff—outreach workers, parent instructors, and childcare providers—all seemed to have the sense that they could take on whatever challenge came their way because someone else always 'had their back'. One Saturday morning, for example, a mother of three young children, in great distress, confided in her outreach worker that she had HIV AIDS and was seriously contemplating suicide. The worker took her hand, and together they went to the director to make plans for an emergency psychiatric evaluation (to which the worker accompanied her), and arrangements for the temporary care of the children.

One of the advantages of well-designed and well-run place-based initiatives is that the services they offer are more effective because they are woven together, and more readily accessible. The usual barriers between divisions, departments, and services are lowered or removed, and workers in every service in a place-based initiative know that it is their responsibility to make connections across departments and agencies, and that it is never acceptable to say, 'Sorry, I can't help you with that' without also saying, 'but I know who can, and I'll make sure you get in to see them' (Schorr and Schorr 1989).

At the end of the ninth Saturday morning, a graduation ceremony was held—with performances by the children, videos documenting the families' experiences over the past nine weeks, and a Baby College diploma for each parent. With each diploma, there was a hug or a handshake from the director of the programme, Dr. Brazelton, and me. As each parent walked up to the elementary school auditorium stage to receive his or her diploma, it was easy to see how deeply meaningful this was to almost every one of them. They had committed themselves to their children, and to each other. And for some, their eyes and faces and the bounce in their step seemed to be saying that this was the first diploma of any kind that they had ever received—an affirmation of their efforts, and a new vision of their own possibilities.

Families with perfect attendance at the nine weeks of classes were entered into a raffle draw on graduation day: first prize was one month's rent; second, an air conditioner; and third, $150 worth of groceries. Funders of programmes serving those living in material poverty sometimes balk at incentives like these, believing that these buy parent participation and render it less meaningful. Yet the designers of Baby College knew what it cost parents to take nine Saturday mornings out of their busy lives. They offered such incentives out of respect for the value of parents' time, particularly when there wasn't enough money to purchase the help that families with more material resources may have taken for granted.

Everyone wants a Baby College

Several years after Baby College's inception, people across the United States began clamouring for their own Baby College. Around the country, non-profit agencies and foundations asked us how they could build their own Baby College, and sometimes had already come up with names like 'Parent University'. Of course we referred them to HCZ's Practitioner Institute, which had been designed to respond to the growing demand to learn about and apply the entire HCZ model. Eventually, under the Obama administration, HCZ became the model for federally funded comprehensive place-based initiatives called 'Promise Neighborhoods', which were seeded across the United States (Komro, Flay, and Biglan 2011).

Some of the well-intended requests for assistance in starting a local Baby College that came to our attention in the years before the Promise Neighborhood Initiative began seemed to envisage Baby College as a short term, stand-alone programme, leaving out the four-pronged paradigm shift necessary, in our view, for its effectiveness:

1 community leadership and control of the initiative
2 family and community co-construction of child development and child-rearing knowledge, and a balance of parenting knowledge with contextual social supports and networks for parents and other adult caregivers
3 comprehensive, coordinated services, linked by shared organizational mission, culture, and practices
4 longitudinal commitment to, and funding for, comprehensive services over time.

Community leadership and control

First, many of these requests came from agencies and funders in which leadership and upper management levels were staffed predominantly by individuals who came from, and lived in, very different communities from those that they hoped to build a Baby College in. Often, they were not fully aware of the knowledge and experience of local families and communities that would be critical to their success (Sparrow 2011). There was a step to take beyond community 'buy-in': a transformative re-equilibration of power dynamics—a transformation that would also fundamentally change them, and their organizations as well (Kania, Kramer, and Russell 2014).

Family and community co-construction of knowledge and social supports

Second, Baby College was misunderstood by some to be based on a theory of change that assumed that parents' child-rearing behaviours were inadequate or problematic, that this was due to lack of information, and that these behaviours could be improved by supplying information that largely derived from the halls of academe. For example, many parenting interventions, designed for the most part by Caucasian upper-middle-class academics, promote warm, sensitive, contingently responsive caregiving, and attempt to reduce what they characterize as 'harsh' parenting. When these are brought to communities that are socioeconomically and culturally distinct from those of Euro-American academics, it can lead to a range of reactions.

In one parent group for parents of four-year-olds in the HCZ pre-kindergarten pro-gramme, one parent stood up at the back of the auditorium and said to a teacher who was leading the group, 'You can say what you're going to say, but when I get home, I'm going to do what I'm going to do'. Many parents told us that outsiders just didn't understand the world they were raising their children in: 'Look, you white people raise your children to become lawyers, so you teach them to negotiate and argue back at you as soon as they can talk. But when I tell my child, '"Duck!"—she just needs to do exactly what I say and as soon as I say it. There's no time for negotiating—there's bullets in the air'.

When the topic of corporal punishment came up, parents often would say, 'My mother whipped me, and I turned out just fine'. A very wise social worker and HCZ leader, the late Caressa Singleton, born and raised in the community, would pointedly ask, 'Now, tell me, did you turn out alright because she whipped you, or in spite of it?' One day, over fried chicken and collard greens at Amy Ruth's on 116th Street, she talked about how desper-ately she wanted to stop using corporal punishment:

> Why do you think we have this tradition of whipping our own children? Now if you look back at our history in this country, you know where that comes from.... It is complicated for us. People are not going to be able to let go of this just like that. So instead of telling our people, 'Listen to the white lady who knows what's best for your children', we tell them straight up that if they hit their kids, A.C.S. (Administration for Children's Services—New York City's child protective services agency) will take them away. We do not want that to happen to our children. We need to hold onto them and raise them ourselves.

She went on to say,

> You know why discipline is so important in Harlem? Because one-quarter of our boys end up in jail. If you're a black boy in Harlem, you need to not only stay out of trouble, you need to stay as far away from it as you possibly can.

(For drug-related offences, African Americans are incarcerated at 10 times the rate of Caucasians who are found guilty of the same crime (NAACP 2015).)

Over time, in relationships, we were offered knowledge like this that carried with it a responsibility to build understanding and bring change more broadly. This is one reason why attempts at Baby College 'replications' that are not co-constructed with community representatives who bear their community's wisdom seem more likely to fail, and one reason why child-rearing knowledge is more likely to be relevant if generated in co-construction with those who live the history and contexts in which their children's development is shaped.

Parents need, and almost always want, information to help them raise their children, and indeed some important and in some instances life-saving knowledge is—of course—generated through academic research. Yet much of the research on child development and parent–child interaction was performed on middle-class Euro-American graduate students' children and was often then presumed to be universal (Henrich, Heine, and Norenzayan 2010). It is often held out as 'the science', leaving little room for what families and communities already know and are learning as they raise their children—the contextually informed approaches to child-rearing. As a result, approaches to sharing information derived from Euro-American research that do not also elicit and uplift local family and community knowledge may undermine parental self-efficacy and confidence, both of which are essential to effective parenting. In addition, some of the academic knowledge content may simply not be appropriate or relevant for culturally specific contexts. The Baby College curriculum, however, was home-grown—a contextualized adaptation of highly relevant academic research, professional clinical practice, and local wisdom and best practices. Its theory of change extends beyond the one-way transmission of information—from instructors to parents and other adult caregivers, to include the creation of social capital by:

- 'connecting' parents and other community members to each other
- 'facilitating' the exchange of social support, material resources, and child-rearing wisdom and best practices derived through lived experience
- 'co-constructing' shared social norms, expectations, aspirations, and mutual commitments to each other's children.

(These processes will be described in more detail later in this chapter.)

Comprehensive, coordinated services linked by a shared organizational culture

Third, before the Promise Neighborhood national initiative, some agencies, in search of a silver bullet, mistook Baby College for a relatively quick and inexpensive bandage for a set of broken systems—education, healthcare, and housing, among others. It is an understandable wish, but not realistic, to imagine that nine Saturday mornings can help families overcome generations of societal neglect and exploitation. Baby College is not a stand-alone programme. The place-based strategy upon which HCZ is built requires that Baby College, this short-term parenting support programme, be embedded in a neighbourhood where major investments are being made in comprehensive services that are synchronized through a shared set of values and goals. The services for children and parents include high-quality early education and K-12 charter schools, healthcare, mental healthcare, social services, and adult educational and vocational advancement services, among others (Schorr and Schorr 1989).

Longitudinal commitment and funding

Fourth, short-term parenting support programmes such as Baby College, embedded in an array of carefully coordinated and often spatially co-located resources in communities like Harlem, also must be articulated over time if they are to generate long-term results. Human development occurs in complex systems through adaptive processes rather than technical ones, and adaptation occurs over time (Heifetz and Linsky 2009; Kania and Kramer 2011). Just as there is no single-focus programme that can ensure the healthy unfolding of human development, there is no single chronological period to be invested in that would obviate the need for resources during other periods of human development. Human development can't be advanced far into the future by a short and temporary infusion of resources, especially if children's subsequent developmental steps must be taken in poor-quality schools, in food and healthcare 'deserts', and in communities where jobs for their parents are scarce and mostly pay poverty-level wages. Complementing the unique return on investment of the early years (Rolnick and Grunewald 2003; Heckman and Masterov 2007), subsequent years obviously require investment as well.

Even the best early education, health, nutrition, and family environments do not prepare five-year-olds to rescue themselves from overwhelming adversity on their own. Because resiliency may be constructed during the first years of life, it too has been erroneously nominated as another silver bullet. Geoffrey Canada once poked holes in this notion with a story about graduate students investigating resilience in rats. They dutifully submerged a pack of rats in vats of boiling water, and sure enough a few would clamber to the surface and up over the edge of the vats. The students then sliced up their brains to search for the secret to their resilience. 'But,' Mr. Canada asked, 'why are we putting our children in vats of boiling water?'

Of course the primary motivation for identifying a single focus for a programme, or a single chronological period for intervention, is to use scarce resources as efficiently as possible. But in some instances the benefits of starting early may have been oversold, as if once a child's brain has optimally developed over the first six years, it is ready for 'whatever', including sub-standard schooling, dangerous neighbourhoods, and other deprivations associated with poverty and social injustice. But 'whatever' is not the follow-up to Baby College. Instead, in the words of Geoffrey Canada, it is 'whatever it takes' (Tough 2009). In this instance, what it takes is for Baby College to be embedded not only in a community-wide configuration of development-promoting services and activities, but also in a 'cradle to college and career pipeline' that extends from before birth all the way through college and beyond.

The cradle to college pipeline

To this end, the Harlem Children's Zone developed several higher 'dosage' programmes for young children and their families, for which Baby College became an entry point into a 'conveyor belt' of high-quality education buttressed by comprehensive services for two generations—the child and the parent. 'Head Start' may be the first two-generation model (Zigler and Styfco 1995), which has more recently been promoted by initiatives such as Ascend at the Aspen Institute (Lombardi et al. 2014). The 'Zone' applied to start its own Head Start programme (for three- and four-year-olds), but because this was delayed by one logistical hurdle after another, a pre-kindergarten programme, Harlem Gems, was created first. This 'we'll build it ourselves' response was typical of Mr. Canada's sense of urgency, and of his 'whatever it takes' (Tough 2009) approach to obstacles of this sort. Eventually, the HCZ Head Start did come to pass, and with the significantly increased funding provided for Head Start by the Obama Administration in later years, an Early Head Start programme (for expectant parents, infants, and toddlers) was later created as well. By that time, the Zone, convinced that the public schools in Harlem were unlikely to significantly improve any time soon, had already built its first kindergarten to 12th-grade charter school, and had begun planning the second one.

Before the Early Head Start programme began, Mr. Canada and the HCZ early childhood leadership were concerned that their Head Start and pre-Kindergarten programmes were missing the opportunity to start even earlier children. At that time there were no resources to create programmes for infants and toddlers, but Mr. Canada decided that he would build a programme for the parents of the Harlem Gems children that would begin during the year before the children's classes did—that is, when the children were still only three years old. The idea was that these children would benefit from their parents' engagement with Harlem Gems during the year before they began. Harlem Gems was a highly sought after programme, not only because of its rigour and high expectations, but because once accepted (by lottery, which seemed the fairest way) children were guaranteed a slot in Promise Academy, HCZ's kindergarten to 12th-grade charter school. For parents raising children in Harlem, an alternative to the poor-quality public schools was a rare opportunity to advance their dreams for their children.

Because parents were so highly motivated to keep their child's coveted place in the Harlem Gems programme, HCZ could require that they participate in a parenting programme that came to be called 'The Three Year Old Journey', consisting of 14 consecutive Saturday morning sessions. This was a lot to ask of busy parents of young children, sometimes raising them alone. But Mr. Canada, who asked us to help develop the curriculum for this programme, persevered: 'If we can't get to the kids before they're four, at least we'll get to their parents while they are still three'.

The Harlem Gems

In the years before the Three Year Old Journey was created to prepare parents for the Harlem Gems pre-kindergarten programme for their future four-year-olds, we had been asked to create various sessions for the Harlem Gems parents. These were based on our understanding that children, from the newborn period on, shape their caregivers' behaviour at least as much as their caregivers' shape theirs. Babies bring with them into the world from their *in utero* experience specific behaviours shaped by that experience, that reflect the specificities of the caregiving context and broader environment in which the baby will be raised (Lester et al. 2012). When parents are ready to observe carefully, and listen, their baby's behaviour will teach them who their own baby is, how to become that baby's parents, and how to respond to the early effects of local context on growing up (Brazelton and Sparrow 2006).

A corollary of this assumption is that parents are the experts on their children (Brazelton and Sparrow 2006), with expertise derived from their observations and interactions with their children, and from their cultures, communities, and contexts. As a result, our approach to developing these sessions was to elicit from parents what they already knew, to catalyse the circulation among them of this knowledge in ways that might create something larger and more powerful than the individual bits of information themselves, and to uplift their experience of mastery and reinforce their sense of self and collective efficacy (Sampson, Raudenbush, and Earls 1997). Although it may seem paradoxical, such growing convictions about one's own strength as a parent make it easier to face one's questions, doubts, and vulnerabilities openly, and without the defensiveness that can interfere with learning and growth.

Learning through play

Rather than enter into a Harlem Gems parent night with a canned curriculum of questionable relevance, we listened, modelling, in a way, the listening that parents might engage in with each other and with their children, and opened up a moment for self-reflection. On one evening, we asked the parents to seat themselves in the children's classroom, on the small chairs, meant for four-year-olds. These were grouped around the children's worktables upon which we had distributed an assortment of materials, bristle blocks, Lego bricks, and rubber farm and zoo animals. We had been hearing from the parents that their children did not have time for play. They needed to learn the alphabet, and their colours, shapes, and numbers, if they were going to be ready for school. Play, they thought, was a luxury reserved for middle-class children, and a waste of time for theirs, who needed to devote their time to 'learning'.

We asked the parents simply to play with the materials on their tables. Most of them were hesitant at first, but soon all of the parents at every table began handling the materials, and talking with each other about them. Then they began narrating stories with the toys; sharing ideas; venturing possibilities; disagreeing; negotiating; taking turns; embarking on exotic journeys; constructing ambitious playgrounds, zoos, and parks; handling their own and each other's enthusiasm and frustration; and occasionally tossing a bristle block at each other, or threatening to do so.

None of them wanted to stop when the time had come. When they finally did, we first asked, 'Tell us about what you did, and what it was like'. Each table then took turns to eagerly explain their exploration of the materials, the ideas that they sparked, and the process of co-constructing their play agenda—of inviting each other into their stories. Most of them agreed that at first they felt inhibited and awkward, but that once they got going, they had fun. One parent said that she had never had the chance as a child to play, and didn't really know how. This felt foreign to her, and out of reach, at first. Others nodded their heads in agreement.

We then asked one more question: 'What did you learn about as you played together?' Almost every parent spontaneously had something to say: 'We learned about animals'—'Colours'—'Numbers'—'Geography'—'Putting things together'—'Making the blocks balance'—'Listening to each other'—'Taking turns'—'Compromising'—'Putting our ideas together'—'About each other'. Through their own experience, their interactions, and their shared reflection, they all seemed to be exploring their theories about what and how young children learn.

Hopes and dreams

On another evening, we asked an entirely different question: 'What are your hopes and dreams for your children?' And then we listened, and wrote down each parent's answers on large sheets of paper, so that all could see. There were two related premises for this question:

◆ First, there seemed to be an expectation among many parents in this community that outsiders and clinicians would focus on problems, not strengths. Yet when there are multiple problems, in order to solve them it is necessary to know what strengths are available to be brought to bear on them. Our question was designed to begin with the positives.

◆ Second, it may be difficult for people with material resources, social supports, and experiences of positively influencing the course of their own lives to understand the effects of the lack of these on raising a child. When much in a parent's life has seemed to happen to the parent, rather than as a result of the parent's actions, and when most of this has led to more hardship, the capacity to positively envision one's child in the future may be curtailed. With the loss of hope for one's child's future may come the loss of expectations and direction, along with the loss of energy for emotional investment. Our question was intended to stimulate reflection about possibilities, to articulate known hopes and dreams, and to set off the search for them, if none were readily apparent.

Although many spoke of their hope for their children's success in school, and later, in work, the theme that emerged most resoundingly was: 'I want my child to be a good person, to care about other people, and to take care of them'. The group's discovery of the collective strength emerging from their shared values and vision for their children was palpable, and unspoken until one parent said, 'It seems like we all want the same thing for our children. And what we want for our own child will be good for all of them'. They would be helping each other as they taught their children to help each other.

Conclusion: The Three Year Old Journey

So when the HCZ leadership asked us to come 'teach' the parents in the Three Year Old Journey about the development of three-year-olds, they were not surprised when we told them that we would be honoured to work with them. By this time they were also not surprised to hear us say that we did not think that parents learn to be parents by being taught. Parents learn to be parents from their children, and from their own experiences—for better or worse—of being reared by their parents, from their culture and their community, and through a process of trial and error. On the Saturday morning when we were to address three-year-old development, instead of teaching, we simply said to the 20 or so mothers and fathers assembled in a circle in the over-heated public school classroom:

'So, you all know a lot about three-year-old development.'

'We do?' they asked, surprised, doubtful that they did, and even more doubtful that we would think so.

'Well you all have three-year-olds at home, don't you?' we persisted.

'Well yes, we do.'

'Well don't your three-year-olds know a lot about you?' we teased.

'Oh yes,' they laughed. 'They sure do know a lot about us.'

'Well then, tell us, what do they know about you, and what do you know about them?'

Then we were quiet, markers poised in our fingers, ready to record their every word on our flip charts. There was silence. We waited, hoping that someone would rescue us. And of course, eventually, all the parents did. The brave ones spoke first, and the shy ones spoke later. After about 45 minutes, together they had written the best textbook chapter on three-year-old development one would ever hope to read. When they had finished, and it was time to talk over what we'd just done together, that's what we told them. Of course no one parent knew it all, but together, they did. Yet it was not until this moment that they realized how much each one of them already knew, how much each had to contribute to all the others, and how much more powerful their individual observations and reflections became when shared with each other.

As they reflected on their children, and surfaced their knowledge about them, they invited each other into their stories, and began to envisage writing future chapters of their stories together:

One father leaned back in his chair and said, 'You know, when I heard I had to come to 14 Saturday morning classes in a row, I figured you people had to be out of your minds. You don't know what it's like to raise a child alone in Harlem. This is my only time off work, and I've got to do the laundry and get the grocery shopping done. But you know what? This is like my therapy! Everybody should have this!'

And then, a mother, again entirely unsolicited, slowly looked into each parent's eyes, one by one, and said, 'This is really old school. This is like back in the day. The way things used to be'. She paused, to gather herself, and said, 'And to think that we're going to be raising each other's children until the day they graduate from high school!'

References

Braveman, P., Egerter, S., and Williams, D.R. (2011). The social determinants of health: Coming of age. *Annual Review of Public Health*, **32**, 381–98.

Brazelton, T.B. and Sparrow, J.D. (2006). *Touchpoints 0-3: Your Child's Emotional and Behavioral Development*, 2nd edn. Cambridge, MA: Da Capo Press.

Brooks-Gunn, J., Duncan, G., and Aber, J.L. (eds.) (2000). *Neighborhood Poverty: Contexts and Consequences for Children*, vol. 1. New York: Russell Sage Foundation.

Burchinal, M.R., Follmer, A., and Bryant, D.M. (1996). The relations of maternal social support and family structure with maternal responsiveness and child outcomes among African American families. *Developmental Psychology*, **32**(6), 1073–83.

Canada, G. (2010). *Fist, Stick, Knife, Gun: A Personal History of Violence*. New York: Beacon Press.

Coleman, J.S. (1988). Social capital creation in the creation of human capital. *American Journal of Sociology*, **94**, S95–S120.

DePanfilis, D. (1996). Social isolation of neglectful families: A review of social support assessment and intervention models. *Child Maltreatment*, **1**(1), 37–52.

Gracia, E. and Musitu, G. (2003). Social isolation from communities and child maltreatment: A cross-cultural comparison. *Child Abuse and Neglect*, **27**, 153–68.

Heckman, J.J. and Masterov, D.V. (2007). The productivity argument for investing in young children. *Review of Agricultural Economics* **29**(3), 446–93.

Heifetz, R. and Linsky, M. (2009). *The Practice of Adaptive Leadership: Tools and Tactics for Changing Your Organization and the World*. Cambridge, MA: Harvard University Press.

Henrich, J., Heine, S.J., and Norenzayan, A. (2010). The weirdest people in the world? *Behavioral and Brain Sciences*, **33**, 61–83.

Kania, J. and Kramer, M. (2011). Collective impact. *Stanford Social Innovation Review*, Winter 2011, http://ssir.org/articles/entry/collective_impact, accessed 27 Mar 2018.

Kania, J., Kramer, M., and Russell, P. (2014). Strategic philanthropy for a complex world. *Stanford Social Innovation Review*, Summer 2014, http://ssir.org/up_for_debate/article/strategic_philanthropy, accessed 27 Mar 2018.

Komro, K.A., Flay, B.R., and Biglan, A. (Promise Neighborhoods Research Consortium) (2011). Creating nurturing environments: A science-based framework for promoting child health and development within high-poverty neighborhoods. *Clinical Child and Family Psychological Review*, **14**, 111–34.

Lee, Y. (2009). Early motherhood and harsh parenting: The role of human, social, and cultural capital. *Child Abuse and Neglect*, **33**(9), 625–37.

Lee, J. and Bowen, N.K. (2006). Parent involvement, cultural capital, and the achievement gap among elementary school children. *American Educational Research Journal*, **43**(2), 193–218.

Leininger, L.J., Ryan, R.M., and Kalil. A. (2009). Low-income mothers' social support and children's injuries. *Social Science and Medicine*, **68**, 2113–21.

Lester, B.M., Marsit, C.J., Conradt, E., Bromer, C., and Padbury, J.F. (2012). Behavioral epigenetics and the developmental origins of child mental health disorders. *Journal of Developmental Origins of Health and Disease*, **3**, 395–408.

Lombardi, J., Mosle, A., Patel, N., Schumacher, R., and Stedron, J. (2014). *Gateways to Two Generations: The Potential for Early Childhood Programs and Partnerships to Support Children and Parents Together* (part of the *Ascend at the Aspen Institute Presents: Two-Generation Solutions* series), http://ascend.aspeninstitute.org/pages/gateways-to-two-generations, accessed 27 Mar 2018.

Metraux, J.C. (2013). *La Migration Comme Métaphore*. Paris: La Dispute.

NAACP (2015). 'National Association for the Advancement of Colored People, Criminal Justice Fact Sheet', http://www.naacp.org/pages/criminal-justice-fact-sheet, accessed 27 Mar 2018.

National Research Council and Institute of Medicine (2000). *Neurons to Neighborhoods: The Science of Early Childhood Development*, ed. J.P Shonkoff and D.A. Phillips. Washington, DC: National Academies Press.

Obama, B. (2015). Remarks by the President in eulogy for the Honorable Reverend Clementa Pinckney, College of Charleston, Charleston, South Carolina.

Poussaint, A.F. and **Alexander A.** (2001). *Lay My Burden Down: Suicide and the Mental Health Crisis among African-Americans*. New York: Beacon Press.

Putnam, R.D., Feldstein, L., and **Cohen, D.J.** (2004). *Better Together: Restoring the American Community*. New York: Simon & Schuster.

Rolnik, A. and **Grunewald, R.** (2003). *Early Childhood Development: Economic Development with a High Public Return*, Federal Reserve Bank of Minnesota, https://www.minneapolisfed.org/publications_papers/studies/earlychild/abc-part2.pdf, accessed 27 Mar 2018.

Sampson, R.J., Morenoff, J.D., and **Earls, F.** (1999). Beyond social capital: Spatial dynamics of collective efficacy for children. *American Sociological Review*, **64**, 633–60.

Sampson, R., Raudenbush, S.W., and **Earls, F.** (1997). Neighborhoods and violent crime: A multilevel study of collective efficacy. *Science*, **277**, 918–24.

Schorr, L. and **Schorr, D.** (1989) *Within Our Reach: Breaking the Cycle of Disadvantage*. New York: Anchor Press.

Sonn, C.C. and **Fisher, A.T.** (1998). Sense of community: Community resilient responses to oppression and change. *Journal of Community Psychology*, **26**(5), 457–72.

Sparrow, J.D. (2010). Aligning systems of care with the relational imperative of development: Building community through collaborative consultation. In: B. Lester and J.D. Sparrow (eds.) *Nurturing Young Children and Their Families: Building on the Legacy of T. Berry Brazelton*. Oxford: Wiley-Blackwell Scientific. doi: 10.1002/9781444324617.ch2

Sparrow, J.D. (2011). Child justice, caregiver empowerment and community self-determination. In: B.S. Fennimore and A.L. Goodwin (eds.) *Promoting Social Justice for Young Children*. New York: Springer, pp. 35–46.

Sparrow, J.D. and **Brazelton, T.B.** (2011). Touchpoints for anticipatory guidance in well childcare visits in the first three years. In: B. Zuckerman, S. Parker, and M. Augustyn (eds.) *Zuckerman and Parker's Handbook of Developmental and Behavioral Pediatrics*, 3rd edn. Philadelpia, PA: Lippincott Williams & Wilkins.

Sparrow, J.D., Ironpipe Armstrong, M., Bird, C., Tatsey Butterfly, R., Grant, E., Hilleboe, S., Olson-Bird, B., Wagner, S., Yellow Kidney, M.A., and **Beardslee, W.** (2011). Community-based interventions for depression in parents and other caregivers on a northern plains native American reservation. In: P. Spicer, H.E. Fitzgerald, and S.A. Denham (eds.) *Child Psychology and Mental Health: Cultural and Ethno-Racial Perspectives*. Santa Barbara, CA: ABC-CLIO/Greenwood.

Tough, P. (2009). *Whatever It Takes: Geoffrey Canada's Quest to Change Harlem and America*. New York: Mariner Books.

Tuhiwai Smith, L. (2012). *Decolonizing Methodologies: Research and Indigenous Peoples*. London: Zed Books.

Vieno, A., Nation, M., Perkins, D.D., Pastore, M., and **Santinello, M.** (2010). Social capital, safety concerns, parenting, and early adolescents' antisocial behavior. *Journal of Community Psychology*, **38**(3), 314–28.

World Health Organization, Commission on Social Determinants of Health (2008). *Closing the gap in a generation: Health equity through action on the social determinants of health*, http://whqlibdoc.who.int/hq/2008/WHO_IER_CSDH_08.1_eng.pdf?ua=1, accessed 27 Mar 2018.

Zigler, E. and **Styfco, S.J.** (1995). *Head Start and Beyond: A National Plan for Extended Childhood Intervention*. New Haven: Yale University Press.

Chapter 15

Involving parents in their children's learning

Cath Arnold and Tracy Gallagher

The history

In 1950, Corby, Northants, which is situated in the middle of England, was designated a New Town. The main industry was steel production at the huge and dominating Stewarts & Lloyds steelworks in the town (Figure 15.1). At this time of rapid growth, Corby earned the title 'Little Scotland' owing to the many Scots who migrated to Corby for work during those early years. Workers came from all over the UK as well as from Eastern Europe for work and for a better life for their families, but Scotland was the main source of labour.

The area of Corby near to the steelworks where houses were built specifically for steelworkers is known as East and West Lloyds. In this area, there was also a girls' and boys' secondary modern school building, again to accommodate and educate the children of the steelworkers. Following nationalization in 1967 and other changes, what, by then, was British Steel closed down much of its production in 1980. This meant huge social change and deprivation in the very area of the town that had been prospering for many years. On top of this major change, the secondary schools in the area closed down.

So, in 1982, when a local councillor had the idea of opening a Centre for Under Fives and their Families to serve the people of this area by using the empty building that had been a school, there was an active 'Action Group Against the Centre' formed by local parents. The parents were worried about a centre located in their area that might become '... another problem family centre in Corby. What they really wanted was an institution that would be flexible and responsive and driven by local need' (Whalley et al. 2017, p. 4).

Margy Whalley, with experiences in community projects in Brazil and Papua New Guinea, was appointed Head of Centre. Margy's experience and vision, coupled with the energy of the parents, meant that the area, over time, became rejuvenated, with small factories being located in Corby, more jobs for women, and a 'sense of community' around a centre for children and families located within pram-pushing distance of family homes. Margy actively listened to the parents' concerns and trusted parents to appoint the first staff team. Margy was also prepared to learn from history—'from Margaret McMillan's work with families in Deptford and Bradford'—and from Europe—'where fully integrated services, such as those in Scandinavia or Italy, have a long history' (Whalley et al. 2017, p.4).

Figure 15.1 Houses with steelworks in the background, Corby.

In this way, the Pen Green Centre for Under Fives and their Families opened in 1983 as a centre that integrated education with care. The vision from the beginning included long daytime opening hours (currently 8 till 6 with some evening and weekend activities) and year-round opening (48 weeks a year), working with children aged two to five years in the nursery *and* their families, and making regular home visits to all families. From the beginning, a 'strengths-based view' of parents was promoted. In her book about the setting up of the Pen Green Centre, Margy Whalley says:

> From the beginning, parents made decisions about how rooms should be used, which services got priority, how services were delivered and by whom.

> (Whalley 1994, p. 15)

The centre is called Pen Green because it is situated on Pen Green Lane. The centre has been shaped over the years by the families and staff who use the centre. By 1986, staff and parents had written a Curriculum Document that has stood the test of time, in which we state our philosophy about children:

> Children should feel strong Children should feel in control Children should feel able to question Children should feel able to choose

> (Pen Green Centre 1986)

Since 1986, when a five-year-old child was abducted and murdered in Corby, we have further promoted these ideas by creating an assertiveness programme for young children called 'Learning to be Strong' (LTBS), which is embedded in our philosophy and way of working with the children and is emphasized in small-group work during the term before children leave Pen Green Nursery to start attending primary school. This programme stemmed from parents' concerns about their children going to school and possibly being bullied and helps children to: develop self-awareness, self-regulate, and engage in positive relationships. Staff access training each year prior to working with children. All parents/carers are encouraged to attend a LTBS workshop before giving their informed consent for their children to participate in the small-group work.

We stated that what we wanted for children also applied to staff and parents. This meant that continuing professional development was a priority for staff, and 'adult and community education' soon began to be on offer for parents. During the early years there were four main strands of activity:

- the community nursery
- family work
- health work
- adult and community education.

Our own staff team could not possibly carry out all of these strands of activity, so it was essential to work with other professionals—mainly from Health and Social Care. Whilst our Head of Centre had a background in teaching and community education, our deputy was a social worker. This mix of heritages proved to be extremely stimulating and beneficial. 'Family workers' (our term for what has more recently become known as 'key persons') in the nursery had access to various courses providing professional development from different perspectives, which, again, stimulated growth and development professionally (Elfer et al. 2012).

The journey

The original nursery space (now called the 'Den') was a large space with a high ceiling and high windows that, at first, did not lend itself to being a suitable space for young children. We consulted parents and made various adjustments in terms of creating: low windows so that children could see out; a large number of dividers at child height in order to create cosy, enclosed spaces; a horizontally hung Venetian blind to lower the ceiling in one corner of the room; and an intimate home corner in which the space was divided so that children could go upstairs—and we retained space so that we could have climbing equipment indoors as well as outdoors (Whalley 1994).

At first, only part of the original building was allocated for our use. Our priority was to create the nursery space, closely followed by a room we still call the Family Room, where parents can drop in at any time. Parents make use of the Family Room for a variety of reasons: it may be warm in winter; they may be early to pick up children; they may be feeling isolated and need some company; or they may regularly meet friends there. We do have a worker in the Family Room, but no particular demands are made of parents using the space, and this is important as not all parents are ready to engage in groups or study.

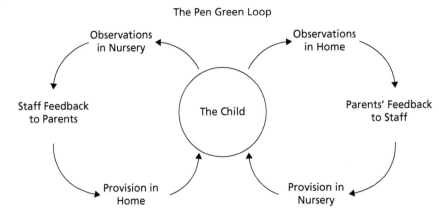

Figure 15.2 The Pen Green Loop.

Before long, parents' demands for further groups and services meant that we began to use other rooms in the building, and in 1990, part of the old building was knocked down and the remaining building was given over for our use. One of the first groups set up for adults was for the parents of children with special educational needs and/or disabilities.

Establishing our nursery practice

We knew from the very beginning that parents and members of the extended family (many still living 'up the road' in Scotland) were the most important people in children's lives. This was why we made regular home visits to all families using the nursery, whether referred through Health or Social Care or self-referred. We require parents, or at least an adult, close to the child to stay in the nursery to settle children in for the first two weeks after starting to attend the nursery. Some parents stay longer depending on their needs and the needs of their child. We see this as a great opportunity to get to know children's important adults and for them to get to know us. We also encouraged parents into the nursery for daily chats or to volunteer or to use groups.

We wanted children to 'feel in control' and to 'make choices', so gradually the nursery environment became a workshop where children could choose what and who to play with, and where we could observe them in order to learn, from the children themselves, about their interests and passions so that we could support these. We plan for each child's learning in dialogue with their parents. This is represented by the 'Pen Green Loop', which describes the process of listening and acting on what parents tell us about their child's interests at home, and vice versa (Figure 15.2).

It was not long before we were introduced to 'schemas' or 'repeated patterns of action' through which children learn (Athey 1990, 2007). Chris Athey came to Pen Green during the mid-1980s to talk with parents about schemas. Subsequently, we arranged for Tina Bruce to visit the nursery once a year to introduce ideas about schemas to parents. Tina would run three sessions in one day—morning, afternoon, and evening—so that the maximum number of parents could attend. A family worker who knew the parents accompanied Tina during these sessions. Most parents got really excited about their children's learning and began 'schema spotting' immediately. Conversations between workers and parents deepened when we began to share schema theory.

Another breakthrough occurred when we took part in the Effective Early Learning Project (EEL project) facilitated by Chris Pascal and Tony Bertram around 1994 (Pascal and Bertram 1997). As part of the EEL project we learned about the concept of 'involvement' as researched by Professor Ferre Laevers and his team in Belgium. Looking out for when children are 'deeply engaged' in an activity seemed to make sense. It was what we were doing a lot of the time anyway without the language to support the concept. So, learning about the Leuven Involvement Scale and signals, and sharing the concept with parents, deepened the dialogue we were able to engage in with parents (Laevers 1997).

The following year, a couple of staff members heard Professor Laevers speak, on this occasion, about the 'well-being scale and signs', and they excitedly relayed the information back to colleagues. We were beginning to realize that a framework of concepts shared with parents could help us, and the parents, to dialogue more effectively about the children's learning.

An important practice drawn from Social Care was monthly 'support and supervision' for all staff. Whalley (1994, p.141) explains:

> We all find it hard to get critical feedback from parents, or to be challenged by a colleague for a piece of bad practice. Supervision and support, on an individual basis, make it possible for us to hear what other people have to say about our work and to separate the personal from the professional.

Supervision and support provide guidance and can protect staff emotionally from some of the very difficult work they engage in with young children and families. We also realized that the 'well-being' signals and scale could be applied to ourselves as well as to children, and this is something we quickly incorporated into our weekly 'feelings' session (Laevers 1997). The signs helped some staff members to articulate their own feelings as well as understand the children's feelings. This sharing was always done in a small group where members had a level of trust in each other.

Establishing a research base

In 1994, Margy Whalley was seconded to The Open University for 18 months to write a course for parents entitled 'Confident Parents: Confident Children'. She agreed to go, on the understanding that staff could 'act up' in their professional roles, so that the secondment would benefit existing workers as well as Margy herself. This was agreed, and on her return, not wanting to 'demote' staff, who had continued to do a good job during the secondment, Margy came up with the idea of starting a small research base in the centre.

Over the years, many external researchers had carried out research within the centre, as the centre was increasingly recognized as promoting innovative practice, particularly with parents. By 1996, many of our own staff were doing graduate and postgraduate courses that involved researching our own practice and involving colleagues, parents, and children in that process. By then, we realized that small-action research projects were keeping our practice fresh and up to date and we had also been involved in a transnational project on 'Men as Carers' with the Reggio Emilia nurseries in northern Italy, so we were feeling more confident about adding a research strand to our activities.

'Involving Parents in their Children's Learning'—the pilot study

In 1996, with a £2,000 grant from the Teacher Training Agency, we embarked on our first funded piece of research work, entitled 'Parental Involvement in Education'. By now, we had been experimenting with using video with children and families and offering our video camera for parents to film at home. Our first attempts resulted in hours of parties and not a lot of useful data on which to base our planning for children's learning.

In our work with Pascal and Bertram, we had learned about the 'adult styles' used to analyze pedagogical approaches in the EEL project. These were drawn from the work of Carl Rogers on 'facilitative attitudes' and comprised 'sensitivity', 'stimulation', and 'allowing autonomy' (Rogers 1983). It seemed to us that understanding more about 'pedagogy' would be useful as a theory or framework to share with parents. We were interested in what we could learn from the parents about their pedagogical approaches that would help us work with their children more effectively.

With the £2,000 research grant, we embarked on a study that has been repeated many times since then with different groups of parents and workers (Whalley et al. 2001, 2007, 2017; Lawrence and Gallagher 2015). The parents were as keen as the workers to get involved in research. Eight families volunteered to take part in the study. Each of the eight children was filmed being settled in by their parent one morning, and filmed with their family worker later that same day. When all of the filming had been done, we had a nice lunch with the parents involved and viewed the filmed material together. Anyone could stop the film to engage in a discussion, but we decided together to limit discussions to five minutes. From the discussion, we drew up eight 'pedagogic strategies' that seemed useful when working with the children:

- **anticipation**—parents seem to intuitively know what to do next when a child needs something physically or emotionally;
- **recall**—the parents could share past experiences and relate them to what the children are doing or saying now while they play;
- **mirroring experience through language**—parents can verbally reflect back to the children what they are doing;
- **extending experiences and accompanying the child**—parents are quick to think about and show children new ways to approach things. They are also willing to follow their children's interest and give them the time and space to explore things;
- **asking the child's view**—parents are interested in what their children are thinking and feeling;
- **encouraging autonomy**—parents encourage their children to make choices and decisions;
- **boundary setting/encouraging risk taking**—parents seem to know when to step in and how to encourage their children to have a go;
- **judicious use of experience of failure/making mistakes**—parents support their children's right to experiment, to make mistakes and occasionally experience failure.

(cited in Whalley and the Pen Green Centre Team 1997, p. 13)

On the basis of this piece of research, we were able to secure funding from the Esmée Fairbairn Foundation to research 'Involving Parents in their Children's Learning' over the next three years, and by now we had established the concepts most useful to share with parents:

◆ schemas (Athey 1990)

◆ involvement (Laevers 1997)

◆ well-being (Laevers 1997)

◆ pedagogic strategies (Whalley and Arnold 1997).

'Involving Parents in their Children's Learning'—the three-year study

Our value base

We began by establishing our value base for thinking about being a parent. We came up with the following statements:

◆ parents and children both have rights;

◆ being a parent is a complex and difficult role;

◆ parenting is a key concern for both men and women;

◆ we believe that parents are deeply committed to their children;

◆ we need to create a culture of high expectations in early years centres.

(Pen Green 2001)

These values guided our approach to engaging with the parents of children attending the nursery over the three years from 1997 to 2000, and also took into account our context. At that time few people from Corby went on to further or higher education, partly because, historically, the steelworks had provided an education at so many levels, but also because courses were not always accessible to people in Corby. Many parents using our services had reported a poor experience of education, particularly at secondary level, and this was in contrast to the system many had experienced in Scotland before moving south.

Key concept sessions

We began by setting up 'key concept sessions' as parents were settling their children into nursery. During those sessions, we shared what had become our framework for understanding children's learning: schemas, involvement, well-being, and pedagogic strategies. We struggled at first with this idea of sharing theory with parents whilst sustaining an equal partnership. However, in 1992 Easen and collaborators had written about a 'developmental partnership' in which the professional shares their professional knowledge (the theory) with parents and the parent shares their intimate knowledge of their own child with the professional, resulting in a partnership that involves equality and trust, and this idea seemed to make sense to us (Easen et al. 1992).

Interviews with parents

Over the three years, we carried out an interview with each of the nursery parents, gathering data about their educational experiences as well as their hopes for their child. This interview usually lasted 90 minutes and was carried out in the home by their own family worker (key person) (Elfer et al. 2012). The process of conducting the interview deepened relationships and made us even more aware of the need for further and higher education to be more available locally as so many parents had not had opportunities to fulfil their potential.

Main findings

A major finding from the three-year study was that we needed many different ways for parents to become involved in their children's learning. No 'one way' could possibly suit all parents. Some parents had more time and could attend daytime groups. Others were working shifts, which was also a feature of the town and its history, and could only come in the evening every other week, depending on shift patterns. We also realized that each child's week could vary according to who was caring for them outside of nursery hours. As a consequence, we began to gather information about each child's week so that we could arrange meetings at times to suit parents and also understand each child's context and transitions.

Additionally, some parents were living separately and sharing the care of their child or children. We had to find out about 'parental responsibility'(PR) and the law and we also had to adapt our ways of inviting parents to meetings or groups. Most women seemed to prefer a 'soft' approach—for example, coming to meet someone who would illuminate their child's actions—whereas the feedback we had from fathers was that they preferred to be invited to a 'meeting' with someone qualified to tell them about some of the most recent research findings. We also realized how important it was to invite each parent personally so that they knew we really wanted them to be involved.

The introduction of study groups

One innovation which has continued to this day was the introduction of what the parents refer to as PICL ('Parents Involved in their Children's Learning') study groups, which run weekly, following on from the key concept sessions. The study groups run, one morning, one afternoon, and one evening each week and usually have a regular membership of eight to ten parents and two family workers. The parents observe their children at home and the workers observe the children at nursery. They view video footage and discuss the learning using the key concepts to analyze the children's play. Obviously, not all parents can commit to a weekly group, but those that attend contribute a great deal to our practice.

Case study: Sarah and Sofia

Sarah's daughter Sofia attended the 'Snug' nursery and was in Leanne's family group. Leanne explained the PICL study group to Sarah. Leanne ran the group each week and thought this would be something Sarah would be interested in attending. Sarah started to attend the weekly group and found it beneficial having Leanne there. Sarah had a relationship with Leanne and found her easy to talk to.

Each week, in the PICL study group, video footage was shared of the children in the nursery. Sarah found it really interesting watching the video of Sofia as she played. She was fascinated with seeing the experiences Sofia was having and what she enjoyed doing when Sarah wasn't there to see her. Sarah was also really pleased to see Sofia so happy in nursery and interacting with her friends.

Sarah quite quickly noticed some similarities in the experiences Sofia was engaging with in nursery to those she was interested in at home. Sarah explained that after watching the video footage she found the discussions with the workers and the other parents really helpful. She went on to say that she would often get different ideas for experiences for Sofia from the parents in the groups—things that she hadn't necessarily thought of herself.

Through watching the video footage in the study group, Sarah noticed that when Sofia was in nursery she also had a strong interest in 'covering' herself (*a 'repeated pattern' or schema*). Sarah explained she would cover herself in paint, mud, sand, a whole variety of different materials. Sarah talked with the workers and parents about Sofia's strong 'enveloping' schema. Watching the video footage of Sofia 'enveloping' herself with lots of different resources and talking about it in the group helped Sarah to see how much Sofia loved doing it and what she was learning. With Sarah's increased knowledge of Sofia's interest in nursery, Sarah was able to buy resources and set up experiences for Sofia at home, knowing they would be things she liked to do.

Sarah reflected that the discussions in the PICL group had helped her to understand Sofia's interest in 'enveloping' and gave her ideas for how she could further support her. Sarah realized this was not something she would have necessarily encouraged otherwise. She was clearly able to see the benefit for Sofia, and she then not only allowed her to do it at home, but provided different resources that encouraged her to 'envelop' herself.

Sarah also took photos and filmed Sofia when she was deeply involved with an activity at home, and shared these with Leanne. Sarah could then see that Leanne would use this information from home to think about new experiences for Sofia in nursery. Leanne was using the rich information from Sarah to plan new opportunities for Sofia and think about what new things Sofia may be interested in doing when she is in nursery.

Leanne then documented Sofia's experiences, including observations from nursery and Sarah's observations from home, in a 'celebration of achievement' file. Sarah has valued seeing how Leanne uses her video footage and photos from home to document Sofia's development and learning and provide ideas for future planning.

The ways parents became involved

During the three years of the study, parents demonstrated their interest and commitment to their children's learning in many ways:

- through daily chats with their family worker or other staff when dropping off or picking up their child from nursery
- by attending 'key concept' sessions
- by attending nursery open evenings
- by keeping a diary of what their child became involved in at home
- by borrowing the nursery video camera to film their child at home
- by receiving video footage of their child filmed at nursery
- by attending a weekly study group during the day or in the evening
- by attending a family group meeting (with their own 'key person')
- by going on a trip to the Science Museum in London with their own child, two members of staff, and other parents and children (this proved popular with many fathers)

- by attending issue-specific workshops, e.g. on science and technology
- by attending individual sessions
- by contributing to a home/school book.

(Pen Green 2001)

As a result of the three-year study, we gathered video footage and put together training materials to facilitate a three-day course for early years practitioners. These materials are currently being updated for the second time since then.

Continuing to involve more parents in their children's learning: 'Growing Together' for parents and children (birth to three years)

Although the three-year project was highly successful in engaging 84% of parents using the nursery, it was confined to those parents whose children were currently attending the nursery. Other parents of younger children expressed a wish to take part. We thought very carefully about how this may look for the younger children and their families. We were already running a number of groups for parents to attend with their children (e.g. 'Messy Play'), but parents seemed to be asking for something different. (Figure 15.3) Colette Tait (2007a, p. 141) explains:

> 'We wanted to provide a forum in which parents and workers could study the younger children's development, once again using video material and the four key concepts that we had successfully used in the PICL project:
>
> - involvement (Laevers 1997)
> - well-being (Laevers 1997)
> - schemas (Athey 1990)
> - pedagogical strategies.'

(Whalley and Arnold 1997)

And so, 'Growing Together' was set up. However, there were some differences. Parents were going to attend a weekly group lasting 90 minutes *with* their children. The group needed to be well staffed so that one member of staff could spend time solely with one family filming, viewing the film, and discussing the child's development and learning. The staff team includes a psychotherapist, and a great deal of attention is given to planning, setting up a predictable environment and reflecting on what has happened after the session.

Our aims for the group are:

- to give parents an opportunity to play with their child (we provide a crèche so that parents with more than one child can focus on one child at a time while other children are attended to separately)
- to help parents understand more about their relationship with their child
- to dialogue with parents about their child's development
- to encourage reflective parenting (through reflecting on video material)
- to facilitate parent-to-parent support
- to validate the feelings women are experiencing when they have postnatal depression (PND)

Figure 15.3 A father and daughter using the centre.

 ◆ to encourage helpful attachment experiences through video feedback and discussions.

(Benford and Tait 2017, p. 225)

We soon realized that other theories were important to draw on to develop an understanding of what was happening for the children, their families, and ourselves:

 ◆ *holding* (Winnicott 1960)—the 'emotional holding that parents can give their baby by holding him or her in mind'

 ◆ *containment* (Bion 1962)—'the concept of containment describes the parent taking in the baby's distress, understanding it and responding so that the baby feels emotionally looked after and contained'

 ◆ *attachment* (Bowlby 1969)—'how adults and children form and develop reciprocal relationships' that provide security

♦ *companionship* (Trevarthen 2002)—attachment for companionship within 'an effective parent-infant exchange can have the quality of a conversation between equals'.

(Tait 2007a, pp. 142–44)

The family who is filmed leaves the group after 90 minutes, having been filmed for about 5 minutes, views and discusses what has occurred on film, possibly being introduced to whichever theories are most appropriate, and puts together a one-page portfolio about their child's development and/or relationships consisting of a sequence of photos and words as a commentary. Originally, we set up a computer in the corner of the room to facilitate this, but with recent technological advances, we now use an iPad.

Case study: Kinga and Hugo at the 'Growing Together' group

Kinga comes to the Growing Together group at the centre on a Friday afternoon with her son Hugo. Growing Together is a weekly group for parents and carers with infants and toddlers; children can attend the group from birth up until their third birthday.

In the group, workers share child development theory and psychodynamic theory with parents and discuss their children's development and learning. Together, parents and workers consider the children's experiences at home and their interests in the group, and make links with child development theory.

Hugo was 11 months old and was filmed in the group by Tracy (group leader in the Growing Together group), as he played with his mum. Hugo was excitedly exploring the resources in the sand tray; this was the first time he had played with the sand in the group despite this being available every week. Kinga quickly noticed that Hugo was particularly interested in using the rake in the sand tray.

After the filming had finished, Kinga and Tracy sat together and looked back at the video footage of Hugo playing in the sand. They discussed Hugo's experiences and how interested he was in the pointed shape of the prongs on the rake. Kinga made links with Hugo's experiences at home and explained that he was able to recognise stars, and this was something he had been able to do for some time. Kinga said how surprised she had been in Hugo's ability to recognize the shape of a star from a very young age.

As Kinga and Tracy discussed this further, they considered Hugo's interest in the pointed shape of the stars and the similarity of the pointed prongs on the rake. Kinga reflected on Hugo's experiences at home and considered whether Hugo's interest in pointed shapes came from his familiarity with their dog and his pointed teeth. Kinga explained that they have a big dog at home and he often lays on his back with his mouth open. As he lays down, he shows off his large pointed teeth. Kinga hadn't previously made the connection that Hugo's interest in the stars could have developed with his repeated experience at home of seeing the dog's teeth and the shapes being similar.

Kinga explained that coming to the group and thinking about Hugo's play had been useful for her. She had found it particularly helpful having the opportunity to watch the footage of Hugo at play and discuss it together with Tracy. The reflection had helped Kinga make the connection with Hugo's interests at home and his interests in the group.

Kinga went on to discuss Hugo's impending transition to the 'Nest', as Kinga was due to return to work following her maternity leave. Kinga and Tracy talked about the importance of sharing—with Hugo's family worker in the Nest—her insight into Hugo's interest in pointed shapes as *this would help with their planning for his experiences.*

Three 'Growing Together' groups run each week (two at the Pen Green Centre and one at the Kingswood Centre). The same provision is set up for the children, consisting of sand, water, dough, dressing up, a doll's house with furniture and play people, trucks, a train set, and treasure baskets for the babies. About ten minutes before the end of the group, the older children and adults blow bubbles to signify to even the youngest children that the time together in the group is coming to an end.

Recent developments

The Nursery

Over the last 10–15 years, the nursery has expanded. There are now three nursery spaces for two- to five-year-olds: the 'Den', the 'Snug', and the 'Studio'. Each space is different but contains features we have found to be important, such as a rocking horse, a workshop environment, and wide opportunities to experience the whole curriculum both indoors and out of doors.

In 2004, the 'Baby Nest' opened—a smaller, more intimate space for children aged from nine months to three years. The Nest contains climbing equipment, a sunken sandpit, a 'Belfast' sink at child level, and a sleep area containing sleep baskets that children can access when it is right for them, as well as an outdoor area. The 'Nest' adjoins the 'Den' so children can move into the bigger space when *they* are ready.

The Couthie

One of our more recent developments has been setting up a second provision for children to attend from nine months of age. We planned the second provision after consulting with parents; we had a huge demand for places in our existing provision and there was proposed change in the government's agenda around providing funding for eligible two-year-olds. We set up a 'steering group', as we had done previously when developing our first infant and toddler provision (the Baby Nest), and once again the parents were involved in all aspects of planning and designing the new provision.

The parents from the 'steering group' held an event at which they asked other parents in the centre to name the new pedagogical space. We wanted a name that reflected the containing and nurturing environment we were creating. Many names were suggested and were then made available for voting. Parents eagerly voted for their favourite and the chosen name was the 'Couthie'. The parents were keen to use a Scottish word as they felt it honoured the Scottish population who lived in the town and represented the cosy and comfortable environment we were creating. The 'Couthie' adjoins the 'Studio' so that children can move into the bigger space when *they* are ready.

Pen Green Research, Development and Training Base

The Pen Green Research Base has expanded since its inception 21 years ago. We are self-financing and offer a range of professional development opportunities. Pen Green Research, Development and Training Base has become an early years research and higher education organization that adjoins the Centre for Under Fives and their Families located in Corby, Northants. We believe that developing knowledge and understanding through practitioner reflection and action research is a central feature of successful service provision. We offer practitioners in the early years, health, and social sectors a comprehensive range of professional development opportunities, including a full early years degree programme (Foundation Degree, BA and MA), teacher training (EYITT and QTS), short courses, conferences, seminars, and bespoke training (for further information, visit https://www.pengreen.org).

The research base is an extension of our centre for children and families. Our daily practice is informed by our research, and our research is generated from our work with children and families. Parents and practitioners collaborate as co-researchers, and many have presented their work at national and international early years research conferences and symposia.

Recent thinking about the PICL project

A Polish study group

Originally, as explained, Corby was mainly populated by white British— mainly from Scotland—and a few Eastern Europeans, as well as people from other parts of the UK.

This demographic has radically changed over the last few years and our current nursery population is much more diverse. The second language used most frequently in the centre is Polish, and over the last two years we have set up a study group for parents to discuss their children's development and learning in which the Polish language is used. This has proved to be popular with parents, enabling them to discuss our whole education system in a small group using their home language as well as discuss their own children's development and learning with other group members.

Fathers have been more included by using the same techniques of filming and reflecting on the filmed material at groups that run at the weekend.

A 'knowledge-sharing' approach

Our thinking has moved on too, in the sense that we are describing PICL as an 'approach' rather than a 'programme'. It is about 'knowledge-sharing', so the title of our most recent book includes that term in the title: *Involving Parents in their Children's Learning: A Knowledge-Sharing Approach*. We want to be absolutely clear that the approach is about a two-way exchange of knowledge. Early years practitioners, who attend our 3-day professional development opportunity, do not have to do exactly as we do, but can make the approach their own. According to Easen et al. (1992), the emphasis is on the 'two way exchange of knowledge' or the 'developmental partnership' (Figure 15.4).

The introduction of an online learning journal

Another recent innovation is the use of an online learning journal (OLJ) for each child that attends the nursery. We are still experimenting with using this technique and do not find the 'assessment' part of the software useful, but in terms of engaging in a 'dialogue' with families, including families that live in other parts of the world, the OLJ is extremely useful (Freire 1970).

We do not use the 'assessment tool' as it seems a computer can only predict 'next steps' using a kind of 'deficit' model, and we do not work in this way with children. We try to build on children's interests and celebrate their learning rather than filling gaps in their knowledge.

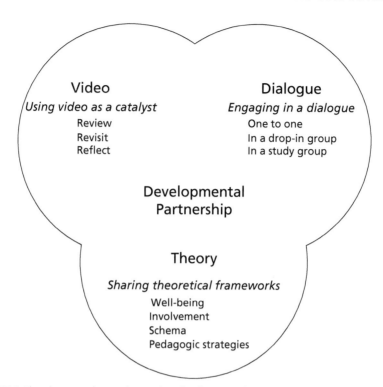

Figure 15.4 The elements that make up the 'developmental partnership'.
Reproduced from C. Tait, 'Thinking About Feeling: Facilitating reflection', Masters Dissertation, Pen Green Research Base, 2007.

Case study: Sarah, Steven, and Lara using the online learning journal

Sarah and Steven's daughter Lara started to attend the Couthie when she was 12 months old. Sarah and Steven were immediately interested in sharing information with Jo, Lara's family worker. Sarah and Steven engaged in using the online learning journal for sharing information with Jo.

Sarah and Steven have found the OLJ useful for sharing information about Lara's experiences and interests at home, but also for letting Jo know about family events, outings, and special moments. They both also found it useful to hear from Jo about all the experiences Lara was having in the Couthie. They found using the OLJ a good link between Lara's learning at home and her learning in the Couthie.

Sarah and Steven have been able to think about Lara's interests in the Couthie and plan for this at home. They were able to see how much Lara enjoyed the bikes when in the Couthie garden. As a result of this, Sarah and Steven agreed it was time to buy Lara her first bike for her to have at home. Sarah and Steven knew she had expertly used the bikes in the Couthie, so they were confident to let her ride her new bike and even face the challenge of going down a big hill. Lara absolutely loved it. Sarah and Steven were able to document this and share it instantly with Jo through the online journal. Jo was immediately aware of Lara's new achievement, going down the big hill on her bike. (In Figure 15.5, we see Lara on her bike accompanied by her father. This is an example of photographic information shared by the parents with Lara's family worker through the online learning journal.) Sarah and Steven explained they had found the online journal a really useful method of creating a dialogue between Jo and themselves.

Figure 15.5 Lara on her bike.

Sarah and Steven were able to use the OLJ to update Jo when they moved house, showing Jo their new home and acknowledging how well Lara had coped with the transition. Making Jo aware of this helped Jo to effectively support Lara when she was in the Couthie, knowing the major transition she had just experienced.

Another recent observation Jo shared with Sarah and Steven using the online journal was Lara climbing onto the hollow blocks in the Couthie. Steven saw this and built a balancing beam for Lara in the garden at home. Steven used bricks and a plank of wood. Lara was then able to continue her interest in climbing when she was at home.

Sarah and Steven have found the use of the OLJ particularly useful as it is something they can both be involved in and they can upload photos and observations at a time that suits them. This is often in the evening, when Lara is in bed and they have a few spare minutes. They also find it useful as they can use their phones or iPad to send information, which makes it really convenient wherever they are. Jo is able to read the observations of Lara from Sarah and Steven and plan interesting experiences for Lara when she is next in the Couthie. The online journal makes the exchange of information easy and quick for Sarah and Steven, and therefore Jo, with regular information from home, is able to be responsive and plan for Lara, holding in mind her current curiosities.

Sarah and Steven exchanged information with Jo, sharing Lara's interest in watches, wristbands, and bracelets. They described Lara playing at home with Sarah's jewellery holder, putting the bracelets firstly on her wrists and then on the branches of the jewellery tree. Jo was able to think about Lara's explorations and consider possible experiences for Lara when she was next in the Couthie. Jo planned to set up the dressing-up table with resources and the wooden mug tree with wooden rings. Jo reflected on the experiences Lara was having at home and planned opportunities to further extend her explorations of 'going through'. As Jo had received the information from home from Sarah and Steven she was able to respond immediately, so when Lara was next in the Couthie, Jo had already set up the resources to support Lara's schematic interests.

Sarah and Steven describe another benefit of the online journal as when, at home, they show Lara photos from her time in the Couthie. Sarah and Steven talk with Lara about what she has been doing. Jo also does this with Lara when she is in the Couthie, sharing the journal entries from home. Sarah and Steven both feel that the exchange of images and video footage helps Lara to have a voice and supports her communication with Jo. They also recognize that involving Lara in looking back at the journal entries at home and in the Couthie helps Lara to reflect on her experiences. Sarah and Steven have noticed that Lara loves to look back at the places they have been and the things they have done. With the journal entries they can do this, sharing their family experiences and Lara's experiences in the Couthie.

Looking to the future

As an organization we have worked with other organizations such as the Anna Freud Centre, the Tavistock Clinic, and the Northern School of Psychotherapy. These organizations have provided professional development opportunities for our staff team. The learning from these opportunities has enabled staff to develop their skills in reflecting on the relational aspects of our work with parents, children, and each other. Since 2002, we have had a consultant child and adolescent psychiatrist support practitioners in thinking about the complexities of their work with vulnerable families, and in processing their emotions. Additionally, from 2008 a psychologist and expert in group relations and organizational consultant has helped the centre leadership team to develop their ability to understand and make use of organizational dynamics in identifying new approaches to challenges that we and the organization are facing. As part of our focus on the emotional worlds of young children, we have introduced what we are calling 'consultancy observations', whereby if workers in the nursery are struggling to understand a child, someone from our team trained in the 'Tavistock Method' of observation (Rustin 2003), who does not know the child, can come in and make an observation of the child which they then feed back to staff in a meeting. We are finding that this method of observation, along with the opportunity to come together for group reflection, is really useful as it often results in a changed view of the child.

We are currently engaging in a transnational project on 'transitions' called Better Start, with local settings and with colleagues in Slovenia, Italy, and Belgium. Our focus is on those children at risk of social exclusion.

We have recently opened a nursery in another part of the town, Kingswood Community Nursery, which gives us a new opportunity to engage with parents about their children's learning, utilizing everything learned up to now.

A 'locality' model of working has recently been introduced, and we have great hopes of once again working in a multidisciplinary way with other professionals. We are having regular multi-agency meetings, which bodes well for families.

Another policy decision has been the introduction of 'Teaching Schools'. Pen Green Centre has been designated as a Teaching School, and again, this is a great opportunity to interact with other professionals, to discuss practice, and to offer the best possible service to families. We hope that our view of parents and their knowledge about their own children will filter through to schools in the near future. As Paolo Freire said:

Be humble, have faith in others and believe in their strengths

(Freire 1970, p. 71)

References

Athey, C. (1990). *Extending Thought in Young Children: A Parent-Teacher Partnership*. London: Paul Chapman.

Athey, C. (2007). *Extending Thought in Young Children: a Parent-Teacher Partnership*, 2nd edn. London: Sage.

Benford, J. and Tait C. (2017). Working in groups with parents of young children: Growing together at the Pen Green Centre. In: M. Whalley and the Pen Green Centre Team (eds.) *Involving Parents in their Children's Learning: A Knowledge-Sharing Approach*, 3rd edn. London: Sage, pp. 222–38.

Bion, W. (1962). *Learning from Experience*. London: Heinemann.

Bowlby, J. (1969) [published 1991]. *Attachment and Loss*, vol. 1. London: Penguin.

Easen, P., Kendall, P., and Shaw, J. (1992). Parents and educators: Dialogue and development through partnership. *Children and Society*, 6(4), 282–96.

Elfer, P., Goldschmied, E., and Selleck, D. (2012). *Key Persons in the Nursery: Building Relationships for Quality Provision*. London: David Fulton.

Freire, P. (1970). *Pedagogy of the Oppressed*. London: Penguin.

Laevers, F. (1997). *A Process-Oriented Child Monitoring System for Young Children* (Experiential education series). Leuven, Belgium: Centre for Experiential Education.

Lawrence, P., Gallagher, T., and the Pen Green Team (2015). 'Pedagogic Strategies': A conceptual framework for effective parent and practitioner strategies when working with children under five. *Early Child Development and Care*, 185(11-12), 1978–94.

Pascal, C. and Bertram, A.D. (1997). *Effective Early Learning*. London: Hodder & Stoughton.

Pen Green Centre (1986). Pen Green Curriculum Document, Corby, unpublished document for parents.

Pen Green Centre (2001). Involving Parents in their Children's Learning Training Pack. Corby, UK: Pen Green Research Base.

Rogers, C.R. (1983). *Freedom to Learn for the 80s*. London: Merrill.

Rustin, M. (2003). Learning about emotions: The Tavistock approach. *European Journal of Psychotherapy & Counselling*, **6**(3), Special Issue: 'Emotional Learning'.

Tait, C. (2007a). Growing Together Groups: Working with parents and children from birth to three years of age. In: M. Whalley and **the Pen Green Centre Team** (eds.) *Involving Parents in their Children's Learning*, 2nd edn. London: Paul Chapman, pp. 141–55.

Tait, C. (2007b). *Thinking About Feeling: Facilitating Reflection*, Leicester University, unpublished masters dissertation (available at the Pen Green Research Base).

Trevarthen, C. (2002). Learning in companionship. *Education in the North: the Journal of Scottish Education*, New Series, **10**, 16–25.

Whalley, M. (1994). *Learning to be Strong: Setting Up a Neighbourhood Service for Under-Fives and Their Families* (0-8 Years Series). London: Hodder Education.

Whalley, M. and Arnold, C. (1997). *Effective Pedagogic Strategies, TTA Summary of Research Findings*. London: Teacher Training Agency.

Whalley, M. and **the Pen Green Centre Team** (1997). *Working with Parents*. London: Hodder Education.

Whalley, M. and **the Pen Green Centre Team** (2001). *Involving Parents in their Children's Learning*. London: Paul Chapman.

Whalley, M. and **the Pen Green Centre Team** (2007). *Involving Parents in Their Children's Learning*, 2nd edn. London: Paul Chapman.

Whalley, M. and **the Pen Green Centre Team** (2017). *Involving Parents in their Children's Learning: A Knowledge-Sharing Approach*, 3rd edn. London: Sage.

Winnicott, D.W. (1960). The theory of the infant-parent relationship. In: Caldwell, L. and Joyce, A. (2011) (eds.) *Reading Winnicott*. East Sussex, UK: Routledge, pp. 152–69.

Chapter 16

Children's 'working theories' as curriculum outcomes

Sally Peters, Keryn Davis, and Ruta McKenzie

Children making sense of their worlds

Young children are active explorers of their physical and social worlds. This chapter draws on research in early childhood settings in Aotearoa (the Māori name for New Zealand) to argue for an approach to curriculum that fosters children's curiosity and inquiry as they make sense of their worlds. We consider pedagogical approaches that are attuned and sensitive to the child, where adults prioritize particular ways of being and interacting with children to achieve intersubjectivity and the mutual understanding necessary for the co-construction of learning (Rogoff 1990) and the development of 'working theories'. With a solid research base pointing to the value of approaches in early education that support critical thinking and promoting later-life learning and engagement (OECD 2002; Rychen 2003; Heckman and Kautz 2013; Heckman 2014), building teacher confidence and competence to work in these ways is an important step in addressing this aim. Working in these ways to develop and foster children's learning presents an exciting and challenging endeavour for early years educators. We discuss some of the dilemmas and challenges involved.

Ultrasound video footage recorded during pregnancy indicate evidence of the exploratory sensation-testing nature of fetal action in the womb, with increasing prospective control and sensorimotor anticipation (Delafield-Butt and Gangopadhyay 2013). Once babies are born, their sensorimotor exploration is well documented (see, for example, Piaget 1953). Claxton (2015) overviews how the genetic predisposition for learning unfolds in the early years, through what he calls a learning operating system (LOS), which initially involves attention control and exploration—picking things up, stroking, dropping, shaking, throwing, and sucking—tests which increase as the child becomes mobile and able to explore more widely. Later, the LOS includes strategies such as good guesses, imitation, imagination, and reverie. The advent of language allows children to ask questions and to generate or apply explanatory frameworks for puzzling phenomena that, in turn, can generate ideas for action and experimentation. Babies and young children are therefore equipped with a maturational potential for learning, which Claxton (2015) notes is 'cumulatively strengthened (or undermined)' by cultural messages from those surrounding the child and by environmental experiences (p. 369).

The interaction of the child's characteristics with the messages and experiences from the environment can be thought of in terms of *proximal processes*, which Bronfenbrenner argued are the primary mechanisms of development (Bronfenbrenner and Morris 2006). To be effective, the interactions need to take place regularly over extended periods of time. The power of proximal processes to influence development varies as a function of the characteristics of the developing person (including dispositions, and resources such as knowledge, experiences, and skills), the immediate and more remote contexts, and the time periods in which the processes take place. The person's characteristics interact with features of the environment that invite or inhibit engagement. These progressively more complex reciprocal interactions between a child and the people, objects, and symbols in the immediate environment are at the core of the bioecological model, which locates the child within the nested contexts and relationships of their family, community, and wider social and political environments (Bronfenbrenner and Morris 2006).

Taking a socio-cultural view, it is through engagement in cultural activities, using the tools provided by culture, and through interactions with more skilled partners in their zone of proximal development, that children develop (Vygotsky 1978).

Working theories

As children interact with the people, places, and things in their environment, utilizing aspects of the LOS described above, they develop theories about the world. Claxton (1990) explained: 'Learning at its most general is the business of improving our theories, elaborating and tuning them …' (p. 23). Claxton (1990) proposed that knowledge consists of a large number of situation-specific packages he called 'mini theories'. Over time, the theories are edited so that they contain better-quality knowledge and skill and are better located with respect to the area of experience where they are suitable.

Claxton's (1990) description of mini theories was influential in the approach to learning in Aotearoa New Zealand's early childhood curriculum *Te Whāriki* (Ministry of Education 1993). In the 1996 document, the authors described 'mini theories' as 'working theories', and working theories and learning dispositions were key outcomes:

> The outcomes of a curriculum are knowledge, skills, and attitudes.… These three aspects combine together to form a child's 'working theory' and help the child develop dispositions that encourage learning.

> (Ministry of Education 1996, p. 44)

While there was a body of literature about learning dispositions, which continued to grow, working theories were largely defined by the curriculum. Meade (2008) identified this imbalance, suggesting the study of working theories was an important area for future research. In our own work we responded to this call (Davis and Peters 2011) and found Claxton's (1990) analogy of mini theories as 'islands' a useful starting place. This analogy describes what we feel we understand as being like islands in a sea of what we do not know. When we experience something new, we are either 'on firm ground', because we relate it easily to what we know, or we are 'at sea', uncertain and unsure how to interpret this experience or how to behave. Other things are 'in the shallows', unfamiliar but close to the borders of our competence so we can explore relatively easily. Being on firm ground or at sea connects to Piaget's descriptions of equilibration. Experiences that create a state of conflict disrupt and contradict an initial view. The processes of 'assimilation' and 'accommodation' bring a return to equilibrium (Piaget 1964).

Working theories therefore may become certain and on firm ground at a given point in time, or remain fluid and uncertain. Even those that currently seem on firm ground might later be revised or elaborated, meaning some islands of understanding may eventually connect as we come to realize they are not dissimilar. Likewise, what was once thought of as one island could, with greater experience, become two (Claxton 1990). The focus of working theories is about *how* we learn rather than the specifics of what is being learnt.

Later authors have continued to explore and define working theories. For example, Hedges offered the following definition:

> Working theories ... can be considered as evidence of inquiry acts, ways children process intuitive, everyday, spontaneous knowledge and use this creatively to interpret new information, and think, reason and problem-solve in wider contexts. Working theories may represent children's intellectual curiosity and thinking as they attempt to make connections between current and desired understandings and experiences in matters of interest to them.
>
> (Hedges 2014, p. 40)

A key element across definitions is the notion of 'working': keeping open the potential for theories to be reviewed and expanded. Hargreaves described the value of knowledge being treated as a source of ambiguity: ' 'It could be' opens up possibilities and provokes imagination, as opposed to 'yes it is' or 'no it isn't', which can shut down a train of ideas' (Hargreaves 2013, p. 37).

Although working theories may appear to align with aspects of schema, Hargreaves (2014) explained that they should not be viewed as the same thing. Schema, a mechanism for coordinating and integrating development and learning (Bruce and Halder 2015, p. 84), while able to be modified, are often related to repeated patterns of action (Arnold 2010). In contrast, Hargreaves (2014) noted that working theories are not necessarily linear and coherent, and many will be more intuitive and piecemeal than schema. Also, the 'concept of theory suggests a more complex and multi-faceted knowledge structure' (p. 320), and coming from a socio-cultural perspective, working theories are developed to serve particular functions and may be partial, local, and situated.

Working theories as a curriculum outcome

The Aotearoa New Zealand updated early childhood curriculum *Te Whāriki* (Ministry of Education 2017) retained the same principles and strands as its predecessor (Ministry of Education 1996). As in many countries, there is a focus on a responsive, child-centred curriculum and the aspiration for 'competent and confident learners and communicators, healthy in mind, body and spirit, secure in their sense of belonging and in the knowledge that they make a valued contribution to society' (Ministry of Education 2017, p. 5).

The curriculum sees learning dispositions and working theories as the combination of knowledge skills and attitudes, with the two being closely interwoven. 'For example, the disposition to be curious involves having the inclination and skills to inquire into and puzzle over ideas and events. These inquiries will often lead to the development of working theories' (Ministry of Education 2017, p. 23). Working theories in the curriculum are described as 'the evolving ideas and understandings that children develop as they use their existing knowledge to try to make sense of new experiences' (Ministry of Education 2017, p. 23). Environments where uncertainty is valued, inquiry is modelled, and meaning-making is the goal are noted as conducive to the development of working theories.

Beyond Aotearoa New Zealand, the term 'working theories' may be unfamiliar, although the ideas embodied in *Te Whāriki* in relation to this concept do connect with other international early years curricula. Work in progress (Dunlop and Mark 2016) has begun exploring working theories from *Te Whāriki* as a pedagogical lens in the Scottish early-level curriculum.

Research about working theories: Two collaborative practitioner research projects

In the following sections we will explore aspects of the pedagogies that foster children's working theories. The findings are drawn from two Teaching and Learning Research Initiative (TLRI) projects. The first two-year project, 'Moments of wonder, everyday events: Children's working theories in action', was undertaken in five parent-led early childhood education settings in Canterbury, Aotearoa New Zealand. That project highlighted ways in which children express and develop working theories, and how practitioners understood these, and explored how best to respond to this learning (Davis and Peters 2011). We found that the conceptual framework of working theories offered educators a powerful way to both see and understand children's learning about the social and physical world. The project also highlighted some of the challenges and dilemmas for teachers in this process (Peters and Davis 2011).

The second project, 'Nurturing and encouraging young children's identity, language and culture in the early years' (Davis and McKenzie, 2018), builds on the first project, but this time focuses on developing young children's working theories about identity, language, and culture—about their own identity, language, and culture, as well as those of others. The study explored the ways in which teachers can help children to make sense of 'self' and the social world, and of difference and similarities, issues which are frequently silenced in young children and in learning communities (Copenhaver-Johnson 2006; Brooker and Woodhead 2008). In so doing, the project aimed to enable learners to embrace cultures and languages other than their own, in turn to ensure that ECE (early childhood education) settings are more able to support learners of diverse identities.

The Davis and McKenzie project was based in two community early childhood education centres in Christchurch, Aotearoa New Zealand. These two research sites acted as 'sister' centres, both collaborating and supporting one another throughout the project.

The sister centres contrast in that one is a full Samoan-immersion environment where the language and culture of the centre is deeply rooted to Samoan ways of being, knowing, and doing, while the other is English-medium. While the English-medium environment has teachers and families from diverse cultures, the dominant culture is *Pākehā* or Palagi (Aotearoa New Zealanders of European descent), and therefore the centre is shaped strongly by western world views.

In each project the method involved working collaboratively with practitioner researchers in the settings, in a process of problem posing, data gathering, analysis, and action around teaching and learning (Cochran-Smith and Donnell 2006). The design was informed by Kemmis and McTaggart's (2000) criterion for action research, in which participants develop a stronger sense of understanding and development in their practices, and the situations in which they practise.

Working theories in action

Our ideas and understandings about working theories in these two projects have not been limited to any particular domain, such as scientific thought; rather, we were interested in children's creativity, imaginings, problem seeking and solving, theorizing, acting, and interactions as they engage in everyday inquiries and conversations with others (Davis and Peters 2012). The following sections consider getting started with a working theories approach, the complexity of a child-initiated curriculum that is co-constructed with interested adults to create a climate of curiosity and working theories about identity, language, and culture.

Getting started

In the first project, when adults started to look for and listen for children's working theories, it initially became a little overwhelming. Firstly, there were the many actions that indicated children were developing their working theories about the world. For example:

> "As a baby, Felix enjoyed taking objects in and out of containers and he was amazed when he discovered that when objects were placed in a tube, they fell out the other end".

> "Tim loves to play with water at home. He has just realized that if he takes a chair to the bathroom he can stand on it and turn the tap on. Then he stands there watching it with fascination".

As adults became attuned to observing children, they began to wonder about the working theories babies and young children might have, and found themselves responding very differently to an observed behaviour if they stopped to consider what a child might be thinking. The adoption of a pedagogical approach that included trying to recognize unspoken theories had the potential to shift the ways the youngest members of learning communities are seen and understood as learners. More attention and respect were offered to what the youngest children might be engaged with, and thinking about.

In addition to the unspoken theories, so many of the statements children made implied theorizing, as the following examples show:

> 'Girls can't be bullies.'

'Don't touch the spider, they pinch.'

'Babies can't be naughty. They start being naughty when they're one.'

Then there were the direct questions that children were thinking about:

'Why do we have Christmas?'

'Do you know how you can die?'

At an early team meeting for the project the practitioner researchers shared that, with so many rich opportunities, they had dilemmas about which potential working theories they should respond to. Some interests were fleeting, while others were more connected or revisited more frequently by children. We adapted Claxton's (1990) island analogy to create a metaphor for working theories that reflected sustained interest, and called these 'islands of interest'. As a getting-started strategy, when adults could identify a child's island of interest or expertise, they felt better able to delve into the possible working theories within these interests.

The complexity of a child-initiated curriculum

Over time, as the adults engaged more closely with the children's ideas, it was clear that the children were engaging in trying to make sense of, and understand, the world, and that their interests were often challenging and complex. Self-initiated topics included fantasy creatures such as a 'tuatara expansion lizard' (the 'tuatara' is a spiny reptile of Aotearoa New Zealand) and 'earthquake rescue lizards', the good and evil themes of Harry Potter, how water travels, and whether volcanoes have conscious will and 'decide' when to erupt (Peters and Davis 2015). Overall, it was clear that the child's curriculum was much more complex than adults might perhaps plan for young children. In fact, the depth of children's ideas and designs often pushed the adults' thinking or challenged the adults to keep up.

For example, Sarah-Kate's knowledge of animals led to a rich library of stories told by Sarah-Kate and recorded by adults (Peters and Davis 2015). In the example below, where two boys were drawing designs for water runs, Jack was keen to explore how to make water go up, and used the example of a coffee pot to convince the adult (who was focused on water going down) that this could happen.

ADULT [LOOKING AT JACK'S DRAWING]   So, Jack, tell me about your design.

JACK   It's about a waterfall.

ADULT   It's about a waterfall … and this bit is?

JACK [DRAWING]   The water goes through there, down there …

ADULT   Hmm

JACK   … and the water goes up … and it goes in here … and it goes out, then around … and into that big box.

ADULT   And into that big box. So it's going to go *down* the pipe, and then it's going to go *up* here?

JACK   Yeah. Then it goes all the way down there.

ADULT   Ahmmm. Do you remember when we were watching the movie before [of a water run the children had made previously] and the water was going *down, down, down* and the pipes going into the drain were going *down, down, down*?

JACK [INTERRUPTS]   I'm going to make something, we need to make a good, good river and a big, big, big hole and we could find a waterfall ...

JACK [CONTINUES WITH HIS THEME]   And do you know what? We could find a coffee-making machine, that doesn't work any more, could push it and now go *up, up*

ADULT   Ahh, because water can go *up, up, up* if it's in a coffee machine?

The conversation moved on and the idea of making water travel up was not pursued at the time, but the adult later reflected that Jack's ideas about getting water to go up and relating this to what happens in a coffee pot extended her own thinking. In the same centre the adults were surprised when during a group of children's exploration of floating and sinking, a large cardboard 'boat' (a big box) did not sink, even when the children made holes in it, eventually having to be hammered down before it leaked (Figure 16.1).

The adults found that when they began exploring the children's interests, they were learning too. As one practitioner commented, 'Since starting this research project I am noticing how many of my theories are flawed and that I need to refine them. It is interesting to do this with the children and I am looking forward to much more of it'. This open-mindedness was an important outcome from the pedagogical approach that was being explored. There seemed to be a reluctance from many adults to be 'at sea' in their own thinking and a number of examples where well-meaning adults 'hijacked' the children's thinking, steering it back to the safer ground of the adult view of curriculum (e.g. how many bees?) rather than the child's interests (how do bees make honey?) (Peters and Davis 2011). We found that when adults became interested in exploring with children and challenging their own theories, a climate of curiosity and creativity was more likely to be developed, which led to greater complexity for everyone's thinking.

Nurturing ideas about identity, language, and culture

The second project 'Nurturing and encouraging young children's identity, language and culture in the early years' project (Davis and McKenzie, 2018) built on the findings of the first. It was committed to the view that curiosity and creativity are important, and in addition, that quality learning happens when it is personalized and contextualized and

Figure 16.1 Floating and sinking the cardboard boat.

when learners see themselves reflected in their learning. Powerful learning leverages participation, engagement, and collaboration (Claxton 2002; Ministry of Education 2007). However, problematic working theories about identities, languages, and cultures that de-legitimate learners' identities, languages, and cultures prevent productive participation, diminish opportunities for respectful collaboration, and thwart learning opportunities for all parties (Derman-Sparks 1989). There are benefits, therefore, in working with young children in ways that help them to recognize similarities, and seeing differences as 'normal' contributes to understanding diversity and addressing inequalities (Siraj-Blatchford and Clarke 2000). Perspective-taking is a feature mandatory to the analysis and critical thinking we seek to develop in lifelong learners (Claxton 2002).

The first dataset from this project revealed ways in which the children in the study were making sense of cultural values and practices—of others (in terms of difference and sameness) and of their cultural selves—and how they were making connections (and making sense of these connections) between their worlds, and with and between people. At the same time these expressions by children revealed new understandings for teachers not only about their own pedagogy, but also about the cultural nature of children's learning.

One of the examples presented by the Samoan teacher researchers in the study illustrates the ways in which they noticed a three-year-old child taking responsibility for the care of her cousin at the centre. Laumata (the child) demonstrated her ability to care for her cousin by putting on his socks, assisting him to go inside 'because it is cold', pushing him on the ride-on toy, and inviting a friend to come along too. Later, Laumata used a doll in a similarly caring way. This time she pushed the doll on the swing and gave the doll a ride on the trike, saying in Samoan, 'I'm very careful here so that he doesn't fall down'. On another occasion Laumata washed a doll 'because she is all dirty', being careful to wash the face, head, and body of the baby, before resting the doll on a table, drying it, and putting on a nappy. After dressing the doll, Laumata wrapped it in a sheet and announced, 'I'm going to put her to bed'. Laumata checked on her 'sleeping' doll a number of times to see if it was okay.

From a Samoan cultural perspective, Laumata demonstrated the values of caring and taking responsibility for siblings and cousins in action. These practices represent the ways respect, love, family, and inclusiveness are lived out in a Pasifika context (Ministry of Education 2013). For the Samoan members of the research team, Laumata's actions and words represented the development of working theories that are steeped in identity, language, and culture. In contrast, the demonstration of Laumata's understanding of these cultural practices and values was not initially clear to other members of the research team. Instead, this play was seen through their own cultural lens—that is, that Laumata was 'playing mums and dads'—rather than 'being a cousin' or 'taking responsibility', which the Samoan teachers recognized in the play. While 'playing mums and dads' represents the development of working theories that relate to cultural values and practices too, seeing Laumata's behaviour from a Samoan cultural perspective meant seeing Laumata's cultural competence and possible ideas and understandings of her world, and self, through new eyes.

Teacher-researchers began playing with strategies for prompting and encouraging children's thinking using the cross-cultural experience of visits by children and teacher-researchers to each other's centre. One of the goals of these visits was to see what children 'pick up' from each centre in the hope of growing new or mutually interesting ideas between the children of the two centres.

When a group of children and teacher-researchers from the English-medium centre visited the Samoan-immersion centre during Samoan Language Week, the Samoan teacher-researchers had prepared a number of experiences for their visitors. One of these experiences was a demonstration by Mara (a teacher-researcher) of how to open a coconut. Speaking only in Samoan, Mara held the coconut in her left hand at an angle, and using a large knife, she hit the coconut several times in order to split it. Tipping the coconut upright, she prised apart the coconut with the knife to reveal the flesh and milk to the children (Figure 16.2).

On returning to their own centre, one of the Palagi children (Angus) opted to instruct Hannah (one of the Palagi teacher-researchers who didn't go on the trip, and had no experience of the task at hand) on how to open a coconut. Hannah worked hard to listen to and follow Angus' theory that to open the coconut it should be placed on its side on a chopping board and be sawn quickly with a knife (Figure 16.2). While other children offered a range of conflicting theories, including those who described and demonstrated Mara's method, Angus persisted with his view despite a lack of progress. Repeatedly watching a video of Mara opening the coconut did not shift Angus' thinking. While Angus' theory surprised the adults involved in the coconut opening, it did not surprise Angus' mum, who immediately recognized where this had come from: 'Oh, that's because he cuts all the vegetables at home like that. He helps prepare dinner every night. It's what he does at home'.

And with this, she produced two photos of Angus on her phone: one of him at the kitchen bench cutting vegetables with a knife and chopping board, and the other of him cutting up a fish his dad had caught (Figure 16.3).

Claxton (1990) noted that, even as adults, many of our implicit theories are treated by us as reality rather than hypothesis and are 'remarkably resistant to change even in the face of good evidence' (p. 24). Other theories we know to be conjectures and are willing to revise them (Claxton 1990, p. 26). In Angus' case the teachers focused on understanding his theory when attempts to disrupt it were ineffective, and thereby gained new insights into his thinking.

Supporting working theories

Using video footage was helpful for the research team as a means of revisiting children's words and actions more carefully than would have been possible when learning and teaching were 'in flight'. It also proved to be a powerful tool in assisting the team to analyze teachers' strategies and responses. Hannah and Hayley were two teacher-researchers who made good use of what they saw of their practice from the video footage of the coconut opening.

While Hannah and Hayley were determined to develop a broader repertoire of strategies to foster children's working theories, which included talking less and listening more, this did feel awkward initially:

Figure 16.2 *Above*: A Samoan-speaking teacher-researcher demonstrates to English-speaking teacher-researchers and children how to open a coconut. *Below*: A Pelagi boy, Angus, explains to a Pelagi teacher-researcher who did not attend the demonstration what he thought he had learned about how to open the coconut, using ideas from experience at home.

HANNAH: I've really been aware of how much I talk. And ... how many questions I ask. But instead of questioning I get a wee bit stuck on what to say, and I feel like I say the same thing quite a bit. So, I think just playing around with ... just different ways of wording things, ... and I guess the more that we do it, the easier it will become. But it feels a lot like it's 'Oh, I wonder.... Hmm.

HAYLEY: We feel quite dorky. We were almost laughing at each other the other day.

HANNAH: It doesn't flow very naturally at the moment.

Figure 16.3 Angus cutting vegetables, and a fish, at home.

HAYLEY: I think one of the children actually looked at me like [laughing], 'What are you talking about?' Like, 'This isn't the normal you!'

While they may have felt 'dorky', Hannah and Hayley could see a difference for children's learning the very first time they intentionally chose to use these strategies around an authentic opportunity for problem-solving:

HANNAH: But even though it was a bit awkward at times, what we got from that situation was *so* much more; there was *so much* richness.

HAYLEY: It's totally different to what we would have done a day earlier!

The work for adults was engaging and rewarding, but did take time and practice to develop. Three key points emerged that are relevant to both teachers and parents:

1   To learn to listen carefully to the ways young children think, and can think, about the world around them

2   To intentionally form a repertoire of strategies that help, rather than hinder, the development of thinking

3   To create authentic learning opportunities for young children that are highly motivating and interest-focused which build on existing interests and expertise and which grow new ones.

Risk and power in the proximal processes

Bronfenbrenner and Morris' (2006) 'proximal processes'—the reciprocal engagement of the individual with the immediate environment of persons, objects, and symbols, or uses and meanings—and Claxton's (2015) description of the interaction of the child's characteristics with the messages and experiences from the environment, are important reminders when reflecting on what learning may be strengthened or undermined.

Overall, the findings from our two projects suggest the value of strategies such as adults asking questions, wondering with children, offering provocations (such as evidence that might disrupt a current theory), and allowing sufficient wait time and spaces for children's ideas to emerge. These approaches did not always come easily and were not always equally applied. Some children's ideas seemed to invite more adult attention, and power relationships were also influential. Like Areljung and Kelly-Ware (2016), we found some working theories to be riskier than others, because they perhaps place the adult 'at sea' or because the topics were ones the adults felt uncomfortable pursuing because they may put at stake the children's well-being (for example, if they are about the behaviour of other children in the centre). Areljung and Kelly-Ware (2016) note that less risky theories are likely to be the ones that are voiced and reified by teachers. Overall, it was important to consider whose voices were heard and encouraged and which adult–child interactions enhanced or inhibited a sense of wonder and curiosity.

Conclusion

The idea of 'working theories' as a curriculum outcome was initially defined by the 1996 *Te Whāriki* curriculum (Ministry of Education 1996). In the intervening years a number of projects have sought to give greater clarity to this aspect of learning and also examine pedagogies to support the development of children's working theories. We have focused here on the building, editing, and refining of working theories as a key approach to learning, but in practice working theories are not separated from the development of learning dispositions. Working theories and learning dispositions can be thought of as two sides of the same coin, both being about the *what* and the *how* of learning, and they are relevant to learning in the early years and beyond. Heckman and Kautz (2013) concluded that building an early base of skills that promote later-life learning and engagement is important, and early childhood programmes that do this successfully are more effective than remedial programmes that try to address this later.

This chapter proposes that when planning the child's curriculum, we might start with the children's curiosity and desire to make sense of the world. For young children, what they find interesting is often a powerful motivator for learning (Ryan and Deci 2000). Fostering young children's interests is a means of enhancing the 'worthwhileness' (Drummond 1993) of their learning experiences. In Aotearoa New Zealand, we are fortunate to have a curriculum, *Te Whāriki* (Ministry of Education 2017), that supports such an approach. It recognizes that each child comes into the world eager to learn, that each child is on a unique journey, and that:

> As global citizens in a rapidly changing and increasingly connected world, children need to be adaptive, creative and resilient. They need to 'learn how to learn' so that they can engage with new contexts, opportunities and challenges with optimism and resourcefulness.
>
> (Ministry of Education 2017, p. 7)

By setting out the goals for the environment alongside the outcomes for children, each strand of *Te Whāriki* highlights the responsibilities educators have in creating these environments and for paying attention to the affordances of those environments for each child and the nature of the children's experiences within them. This approach recognizes the proximal processes that lead to outcomes and also that the child's curriculum is formed by the nature of the interactions between the child and people, places, and things.

In this chapter we have outlined some research findings from two projects where ECE practitioners and teachers explored pedagogical strategies to foster a working-theory approach to learning. They chose to prioritize the children's interests as they made sense of the world and adopted a co-construction approach to foster deep and complex learning. Many of the child-initiated topics were sophisticated, complex, and creative. Adults did not see themselves as the holders of all knowledge, but rather engaged in the explorations, deliberately trying—through their interactions—to keep the thinking open and strengthen the children's learning, rather than inhibiting inquiry and closing down a train of thought by moving things to 'firm ground'. This work is interesting and challenging. It requires skilled adults who can respond appropriately, and a context that supports the complexity of teachers' work and encourages a sense of wonder and curiosity for all.

Acknowledgement

We acknowledge with thanks funding from the Teaching and Learning Research Initiative (TLRI) for the two projects discussed in this chapter (http://www.tlri.org.nz/home). We are also very grateful to our practitioner-researcher colleagues who have been central to the work of this project, and to the children and families who have allowed their experiences to be shared.

References

Areljung, S. and Kelly-Ware, J. (2016). Navigating the risky terrain of children's working theories. *Early Years: An International Research Journal*, 37(4), 370–85. doi: 10.1080/09575146.2016.1191441

Arnold, C. (2010). *Understanding Schemas and Emotion in Early Childhood*. Thousand Oaks, CA: Sage.

Bronfenbrenner, U. and Morris, P.A. (2006). The bioecological model of human development. In: R.M. Lerner (ed.) *Handbook of Child Psychology*, vol. 1: *Theoretical Models of Human Development*, 6th edn. Hoboken, NJ: John Wiley, pp. 793–828.

Brooker, L. and Woodhead, M. (eds.) (2008). *Developing Positive Identities: Diversity and Young Children* (Early Childhood in Focus 3). Milton Keynes: Open University.

Bruce, T. and Halder, S. (2015). *Early Childhood Education*. London: Hodder Education.

Claxton, G. (1990). *Teaching to Learn a Direction for Education*. London: Cassell.

Claxton, G. (2002). *Building Learning Power: Helping Young People Become Better Learners*. Bristol, UK: TLO.

Claxton, G. (2015). The development of learning power: A new perspective on child development and early education. In: S. Robson and S. Quinn (eds.). *International Handbook of Young Children's Thinking and Understanding*. UK: Routledge, pp. 367–76.

Cochran-Smith, M. and Donnell, K. (2006). Practitioner inquiry: Blurring the boundaries of research and practice. In: J.L. Green, G. Camilli, P.B. Elmore, A. Skukauskaité, and P. Grace (eds.) *Handbook of Complementary Methods in Education Research*. Mahwah, NJ: Erlbaum (for the American Educational Research Association), pp. 503–18.

Copenhaver-Johnson, J. (2006). Talking to children about race: The importance of inviting difficult conversations. *Childhood Education*, **83**(1), 12–22.

Davis, K. and **McKenzie, R.** (2018). *Children's working theories about identity, language and culture: O faugamanatu a fanau e sa'ili ai o latou fa'asinomaga, gagana ma aganu'u*, Final Report. Wellington, New Zealand: Teaching and Learning Research Initiative.

Davis, K. and **Peters, S.** (2011). *Moments of wonder, everyday events: Children's working theories in action*, Teaching and Learning Research Initiative, Final Report, http://www.tlri.org.nz/tlri-research/research-completed/ece-sector/moments-wonder-everyday-events-children%E2%80%99s-working, accessed 29 Mar 2018.

Davis, K. and **Peters, S.** (2012). Exploring learning in the early years: Working theories, learning dispositions and key competencies. In B. Kaur (ed.) *Understanding Teaching and Learning in the Classroom: Classroom Research Revisited*. Rotterdam, The Netherlands: Sense Publishers.

Delafield-Butt, J. and **Gangopadhyay, N.** (2013). Sensorimotor intentionality: The origins of intentionality in prospective agent action. *Developmental Review*, **33**(4), 399–425.

Derman-Sparks, L. (1989). *Anti-Bias Curriculum: Tools for Empowering Young Children*. Washington, DC: National Association for the Education of Young Children.

Drummond, M.J. (1993). *Assessing Children's Learning*. London: David Fulton.

Dunlop, A.-W. and **Mark, R.** (2016). *Taking Learning to School: Children's working theories and transition to school*, unpublished report of a pilot project.

Hargreaves, V. (2013). What are working theories? What should we do to support them? *Early Education*, **54**, 34–7.

Hargreaves, V. (2014). Complex possibilities: 'Working theories' as an outcome for the early childhood curriculum. *Contemporary Issues in Early Childhood*, **15**(4), 319–28.

Heckman, J. (2014, October 22). 'Skills and scaffolding', Brookings Institution, http://www.brookings.edu/research/papers/2014/10/22-skills-scaffolding-heckman, accessed 29 Mar 2018.

Heckman, J.J. and **Kautz, T.** (2013). *Fostering and Measuring Skills: Interventions That Improve Character and Cognition*, Working paper no. 19656, National Bureau of Economic Research, http://www.nber.org/papers/w19656, accessed 29 Mar 2018.

Hedges, H. (2014). Young children's 'working theories': Building and connecting understandings. *Journal of Early Childhood Research*, **12**(1), 35–49.

Kemmis, S. and **McTaggart, R.** (2000). Participatory action research. In: N.K. Denzin and Y.S. Lincoln (eds.) *Handbook of Qualitative Research*, 2nd edn. London: Sage, pp. 567–605.

Meade, A. (2008). *Research Needs in the Early Childhood Sector*. Wellington, New Zealand: Teaching and Learning Research Initiative.

Ministry of Education (1993) *Te Whāriki: He whāriki mātauranga mō ngā mokopuna o Aotearoa, Draft Guidelines for Developmentally Appropriate Programs in Early Childhood Services*. Wellington, New Zealand: Learning Media.

Ministry of Education (1996). *Te Whāriki He whāriki mātauranga mō ngā mokopuna o Aotearoa, Early Childhood Curriculum*. Wellington, New Zealand: Learning Media.

Ministry of Education (2007). *The New Zealand Curriculum: The English-medium teaching and learning in years 1-13*. Wellington, New Zealand: Learning Media.

Ministry of Education (2013). *Pasifika Education Plan 2013-2017*. Wellington, New Zealand: Learning Media.

Ministry of Education (2017). *Te Whāriki He whāriki mātauranga mō ngā mokopuna o Aotearoa, Early Childhood Curriculum* (update). Wellington, New Zealand: Ministry of Education.

OECD (2002). *Definition and Selection of Key Competencies (DeSeCo): Theoretical and Conceptual Foundations*, Strategy Paper, http://deseco.ch/bfs/deseco/en/index/02.html, accessed 29 Mar 2018.

Peters, S. and Davis, K. (2011). Fostering children's working theories—pedagogical issues and dilemmas in New Zealand. *Early Years: An International Journal of Research and Development*, **31**(1), 5–17.

Peters, S. and Davis, K. (2015). Babies, boys, boats and beyond: Children's working theories in the early years. In: S. Robson and S. Quinn (eds.) *International Handbook of Young Children's Thinking and Understanding*. London: Routledge, pp. 251–61.

Piaget, J. (1953). *The Origin of Intelligence in the Child*. London: Routledge.

Piaget, J. (1964). Development and learning. In: R. Ripple and V. Rockcastle (eds.) *Piaget Rediscovered*. Ithaca, NY: Cornell University Press, pp. 7–19.

Rogoff, B. (1990). *Apprenticeship in Thinking: Cognitive Development in Social Context*. New York: Oxford University Press.

Rogoff, B. (2003). *The Cultural Nature of Human Development*. Oxford/ New York: Oxford University Press.

Ryan, R.M. and Deci, E.L. (2000). Intrinsic and extrinsic motivations: Classic definitions and new directions. *Contemporary Educational Psychology*, **25**, 54–67.

Rychen, D.S. (2003). Key competencies: Meeting important challenges in life. In: D.S. Rychen and L.H. Salganik (eds.) *Key Competencies for a Successful Life and a Well-functioning Society*. Göttingen, Germany: Hogrefe & Huber, pp. 63–107.

Siraj-Blatchford, I. and Clarke, P. (2000). *Supporting Identity, Diversity, and Language in the Early Years*. Philadelphia, PA/ Buckingham, UK: Open University Press.

Vygotsky, L.S. (1978). Interaction between learning and development. In: M. Cole, V. John-Steiner, S. Scribner, and E. Souberman (eds.) *Mind in Society: The Development of Higher Psychological Processes*. Cambridge, MA: Harvard University Press, pp. 79–91.

Chapter 17

The spirit of the child inspires learning in the community: How can we balance this promise with the politics and practice of education?

Colwyn Trevarthen, Aline-Wendy Dunlop, and Jonathan Delafield-Butt

Motives of child development and learning

Early conviviality, acquiring common sense in intimate play, with mutual trust

> Against the assumption that the Self is at least primarily a 'knowing subject', I have maintained that its subjecthood is a derivative and negative aspect of its agency. This corresponds to the fact that most of our knowledge, and all our primary knowledge, arises as an aspect of activities which have practical, not theoretical objectives; and that it is this knowledge, itself an aspect of action, to which all reflective theory must refer. Against the assumption that the Self is an isolated individual, I have set the view that the Self is a *person,* and that personal existence is *constituted* by the relation of persons.

> (Macmurray 1959, pp. 11–12)

All a clever human mind contributes to human culture is founded on the readiness of the child for convivial activity—an innate capacity for imitation of purposes with feelings and for learning in companionship with others. A newborn infant searches for eye-to-eye contact with a person who offers attention to them, and the baby can imitate many expressions, and then repeat them to evoke a confirming response. We are born to learn in dialogue.

This foundation for companionship of states of life, in movement, imaging, or 'mirroring' the correspondence of body parts, is the inborn power of our animate self. It requires no learned explanation or 'theory of mind'. It is not acquired by a process of conditioning of appetitive reflexes. It is an 'innate sympathy', a creative feeling for relating that seeks to complement and contribute to what other human beings experience. Its vitality has an acute sense of time for the universal rhythms that guide human body movement—a pulse of excitation which originates in the brain, many months before a child is born. At birth, the child, if alert and contented, is willing to share small projects of imaginative action, which require serial ordering of movements in compositions with narrative form. They are projects to be carried out with feeling, and stories to be told.

A rapid maturation of visual awareness in the first few weeks after birth transforms the first efforts at dialogue into well-formed cooperative 'proto-conversations' with phases animated as 'introduction', 'development', 'climax', and 'resolution' (Bateson 1979, Malloch and Trevarthen 2010; Delafield-Butt and Trevarthen, 2015). Now the baby is capable of sharing a mother's story of their mutual interest, and can tell his or her own version of what is happening. As Jerome Bruner discovered, that is the way each of us claim and defend our place in society, by telling our personal life story (Bruner 2003). A young child at school, or a postgraduate student at university, wants teachers that understand this ambition to take an honourable role or place in a meaningful world. Learning facts and symbols to recall them is part of the method of doing well with 'common sense', the product of a rich communication before language. As von Bonsdorff and Nye explain, the impulses and feelings of the child expressed in imaginative ways have the essential qualities of artful and spiritual creativity for a lifetime of achievement.

Everything that happens in affectionate life, in play with siblings or peers, and in class with a teacher may be conceived as a 'communicative musicality' shared in the dynamics of human vitality (Erickson 2010). This instinctive rhythm of relating is enriched and preserved by assimilating conventional forms of art, reasoning, or technique. It does not begin with them. The childish language of this talent is expressed in spontaneous activities of play.

The realm of shared invention of possible actions with the feelings they inspire remains the place where great achievements are made in literature, science, and mathematics. As an example we quote Einstein, who confessed that his experience of mathematical invention was in sensations of bodily movement, which is a way of saying that, for him, making advances in mathematics was play.

> The words of language, as they are written or spoken, do not seem to play any role in my mechanism of thought. The psychical entities which seem to serve as elements of thought are certain signs and more or less clear images which can be 'voluntarily' reproduced and combined....
>
> The above-mentioned elements are, in my case, of visual and some of muscular type. Conventional words or other signs have to be sought for laboriously only in a secondary stage, when the mentioned associative play is sufficiently established and can be reproduced at will.
>
> According to what has been said, the play with the mentioned elements is aimed to be analogous to certain logical connections one is searching for.
>
> ... In a stage when words intervene at all, they are, in my case, purely auditive, but they interfere only in a secondary stage as already mentioned.
>
> (Hadamard 1945, Appendix II, pp. 142–3)

This can be read as a concise description of the life of an infant, with an 'unspeakable' consciousness of life in movement, including impulses and pleasures that are shared with companions of all ages. We are not only born with communicative musicality; we feel mathematical forms that can be discovered in our moving.

Moral foundations of human culture in infant care and education

Kurth and Narvaez describe how protection and education of early life in an 'evolved developmental niche' of intelligent group care support the growth of the human brain and mind born in an early stage of its long development. Adaptations of a child born so immature, and of adults, especially loving parents, who give essential protection and support, show the way to a life of sympathetic relationships and shared responsibility in a whole society, and build strength of character in individuals. The need for intimate attention and care and the benefits of an established and stable parenting, as well as creative participation in a familiar community with its cultivated environment and habits, has evolved to transmit cultural understanding through countless generations. It needs a long period of social play in a protected habitat with intimate communication of inner needs and shared creation of knowledge and skills.

Group care in the modern world is changing. Family life is transformed and new artificial competences are required early in the life of children, to fit the regulations of mobility, of access to the natural world, and for the use of processed habitations and food, and methods of sanitation and healthcare. Exaggeration of these regulations and restrictions in relationships and experience can lead to serious disorders of behaviour and self-regulation, which require special compensation to recover the inherent talents for a shared life.

Policies for education that respond to the spirit of the child

Humanizing the curriculum of symbolic and industrial education, and its testing

As described in Chapter 2, throughout the recorded history of Europe and the colonial world it has created, there has been a conflict of purposes in early child education. On the one hand, there were those eager to formulate a curriculum of instruction that will lead an impressionable young mind to mastery of what the Romans called the 'trivium' of formal knowledge—'grammar, logic, and rhetoric', as training for the literary and mathematical skills of a 'free man' in a rich industrial culture. On the other hand are the 'educational reformers' who have strived to liberate the impulses of the young person to share a life of discovery and mastery of skills (Quick 1894). In the past 300 years, since the industrial revolution, this battle has led defenders of the early years to pronounce humanistic rules for rich and productive teaching practice that strengthens the community.

The crucible of our thinking about education and care for early years is the small northern nation of Scotland. The origins of this book lie in a struggle to combat local policy which has sought to make swingeing cuts in the face of the top-down austerity policies of recent years, choosing the non-mandatory elements of the child's early learning journey to make savings.

Now, Scottish Government seeks to increase the offer of early learning and childcare to hours equivalent to the primary school day, and is making budget available to do this. Scotland's child-garden tradition, combined with its contemporary guidance on pre-birth to three years and its Early Level 3-6 of the Curriculum for Excellence 3-18 (Scottish Government 2007), embraces both early learning and care, in the years before school and the first years of primary school, by espousing responsive, play-based child-led approaches supported by well-qualified staff through their relationships with children and their families. The policy promise of early years curriculum transformation has, however, proved to be fragile, especially in the early years of primary education, and in need of stronger articulation. 'Building the Ambition' (Scottish Government 2014) and 'Getting it Right for Every Child' (Scottish Government 2017) are each strong policy initiatives which, along with the *Early Level of the Curriculum for Excellence* (Scottish Government 2007), could achieve this transformation with the right mix of staffing and appropriate pedagogies. We believe that the principles we seek to promote in Scotland have international relevance for contemporary changes in early childhood policy and practice.

The collective endeavour of our authors leads to the principles put forward in this book and summarized in Box 17.1. They place the child at the centre of discovery, appreciated as a non-verbal actor rich with a zest for learning who can, with the right attention and attuned interest and support, energize learning and bring together a community in shared interest and love of companionship. Recognition of the natural, psychobiological zest for a life of knowledge in all children helps steer our professional practice and policy in governance of education and care for early childhood. We must attend intimately and sensitively to individual feelings of confidence or fear, giving reassurance in insecurity and guiding the impulse to rise to a challenge. It is only by responding at this fundamental inter-personal level in trusted relationships that policy can make a difference so our aspirations for the well-being of children become realized in ways from which we will all benefit.

Box 17.1 Principles of early childhood education and care advanced in the child's curriculum

1   Professional and expert attention to children's agency and interest

2   Guided pedagogy that supports this interest and curiosity for learning and for establishing meaningful social relations, through art and companionship in play

3   Recognition of the value of parents and community in the child's development, and intellectual and policy tools to do this work

4   Recognition of the importance in our society of sensitive and protected support for children's feelings for each other, for family, and in community, as well as a course of guided learning that brings long-term economic and health benefits

We have strived in this volume to articulate what matters for children and their families and why it matters, aware that levels of subjective well-being of the children and those of their parents are linked significantly to each other (Children's Society 2014).

The ways in which children are perceived politically will inevitably influence how states provide for them. In the worlds represented here in 'the child's curriculum', most children experience a more protected childhood than do many children globally. The intention is not to homogenize childhood experience as if it is uniform—diversities are many—but perhaps a more generalized comparison can be accepted. For many children worldwide, 'work' is prioritized over 'play', whereas in the childhoods of our book, children are privileged in their opportunities to play, and their society benefits.

Punch (2003) writes compellingly about the integration of work, play, and school among Bolivian children. She shows, through lively examples, how children move easily between child and adult worlds, and although their domestic and agricultural tasks become more complex and demanding as they grow older, 'they combine their play with both work and school, by negotiating their own time and space to unite these different activities' (Punch 2003, p. 288), rather than—as may be argued in western culture—residing firmly in the protected spaces we make for children. In our worlds governments focus on investing in early childhood and school education as part of raising a productive future workforce, and these investment arguments are predicated on what Vandenbroeck calls 'the Heckmanisation of early childhood' (Vandenbroeck, 2017): the curve that shows the route to return for investment is in human capital. We need a critical pedagogy which promotes a dialectical connection or relation between principles, policy, and practice.

We need to avoid taking for granted universalizing assumptions about early childhood, to consider what images of the child prevail locally and nationally, keeping in touch with the diversity of childhood, as well as with the variety of perceptions held by different people about any single child. The political desire for investment in early childhood seeks to remedy current inefficiencies and inequalities in our society, in order to prevent intergenerational transmission of worklessness and poverty.

> Ideas about children, as well as about parenthood, are changing too. Constructions of children as knowledge reproducers and redemptive agents, who require shaping and processing by technicians, do not sit comfortably with constructions of the child as an active subject, citizen with rights and co-constructor of knowledge, identity and values.

(Moss, 2006, p. 39)

We now require a different language, as we have strived to achieve in this book, to accept and support the benefits and hopes of human nature, rather than simply the economic imperative. Dahlberg, Moss, and Pence (2013) and Moss (2016) reject the scripts of 'quality', 'high returns', and 'markets', preferring to talk about early childhood education with a different story and vocabulary using words such as: 'projects', 'potentialities', 'possibilities', 'uncertainty', 'wonder', 'surprise', 'lines of flight', 'images', 'interpretations', 'democracy', 'experimentation'—and 'meaning-making'. With such a language, the strictures placed on practitioners and children through policy technologies are more visible and may be challenged.

This book carries many ideals and strong ideas of children's rights and what is right for children in the family, in the community, and in the early childhood settings they occupy. The child's curriculum aims to celebrate the tradition of excellent early childhood provision in Scotland, advancing principles of child learning and development for excellent education and care in which the child leads the way. With leaders of reform for early education such as Froebel, we embrace the life of the child within family, community, and culture, and promote children's natural growth and children's rights as inseparable in good practice.

As we have demonstrated in this book, now, because of major changes in society and advances in the science of human psychological development, it is again necessary to put a rich theory of the human spirit into an improved policy for pedagogy, to strengthen a practice that recognizes the powers of human nature—the innate dispositions for culture evident in the young of every human community. The community, however developed in cultivation of literacy and technology, has to understand that its youngest members are human beings seeking enjoyment of a lifetime of learning in affectionate company (Trevarthen, Gratier, and Osborne 2014).

Science of the young child's mind has advanced significantly in the past century to bring us to a position where we must understand how the biology and health of every developing boy or girl, and the development of their intelligence, are inseparable from their feelings of psychosocial health and well-being. His or her success in learning what we want them to know, and the skills we want them to use, is inseparable from their community of affectionate relations with parents and professionals.

In Alfred North Whitehead's words, 'Ideas won't keep, something must be done about them' (Price 1954, p. 100). With this in mind, the Child's Curriculum Group will strive to help our government give support for the enthusiasm of early years teachers in their dedicated work to help children, families, and the community. This book is intended to clarify what young children need and must receive for confident development, and we hope it will be of benefit to you in your work and understanding. We invite you to join us in the effort to put these ideas into a practice that seeks to follow, and enjoy, the creativity and zest for learning in every child.

References

Bateson, M.C. (1979). The epigenesis of conversational interaction: A personal account of research development. In: M. Bullowa (ed.) *Before Speech: The Beginning of Human Communication*. London: Cambridge University Press, pp. 63–77.

Bruner, J.S. (2003). *Making Stories: Law, Literature, Life*. Cambridge, MA: Harvard University Press.

Children's Society (2014). *The Good Childhood Report 2014*, The Children's Society, London, https://www.childrenssociety.org.uk/sites/default/files/publications/the_good_childhood_report_2014_-_final.pdf, accessed 30 Mar 2018.

Dahlberg, G., Moss, P., and Pence, A. (2013). *Beyond Quality in Early Childhood Education and Care: Languages of Evaluation*, 3rd edn. London: Routledge.

Delafield-Butt, J. T. and Trevarthen, C. (2015). The ontogenesis of narrative: From moving to meaning. *Frontiers in Psychology*, 6. doi:10.3389/fpsyg.2015.01157

Erickson, F. (2010). Musicality in talk and listening: A key element in classroom discourse as an environment for learning. In: S. Malloch and C. Trevarthen (eds.) *Communicative Musicality: Exploring the Basis of Human Companionship*. Oxford: Oxford University Press, pp. 449–64.

Hadamard, J. (1945). *The Psychology of Invention in the Mathematical Field*. Princeton, NJ: Princeton University Press.

Macmurray, J. (1959) *The Self as Agent*. London: Faber and Faber.

Malloch, S. and Trevarthen, C. (eds.) (2010). *Communicative Musicality: Exploring the Basis of Human Companionship*. Oxford: Oxford University Press.

Moss, P. (2006). Structures, understandings and discourses: Possibilities for re-envisioning the early childhood worker. *Contemporary Issues in Early Childhood*, 7(1), 30–41.

Moss, P (2016). Why can't we get beyond quality? *Contemporary Issues in Early Childhood* 17(1), 8–15.

Price, L. (1954). *Dialogues of A.N. Whitehead—As Recorded by Lucien Price*. London: Max Reinhardt.

Punch, S. (2003). Childhoods in the majority world: Miniature adults or tribal children? *Sociology*, 37(2), 277–95.

Quick, R.H. (1894). *Essays on Educational Reformers*. London: Longmans, Green and Co.

Scottish Government (2007). 'Building the Curriculum 2: Active Learning in the Early Years', https://www.education.gov.scot/Documents/btc2.pdf, accessed 30 Mar 2018.

Scottish Government (2014). *Building the Ambition: National Practice Guidance on Early Learning and Childcare (Children and Young People Scotland Act)*, http://www.gov.scot/Resource/0045/00458455.pdf, accessed 30 Mar 2018.

Scottish Government (2017). 'Getting it Right for Every Child', http://www.gov.scot/Topics/People/Young-People/gettingitright/what-is-girfec, accessed 30 Mar 2018.

Trevarthen, C., Gratier, M., and Osborne, N. (2014). The human nature of culture and education. *Wiley Interdisciplinary Reviews: Cognitive Science*, 5 (Mar/Apr), 173–92. doi: 10.1002/wcs.1276

Vandenbroeck, M. (2017). 'Facts matter. And so do opinions: A plea for the repoliticisation of early childhood education', keynote address, European Early Childhood Education Research Association, 27th Annual Conference, Bologna, Italy, 29 August–1 September.

Index

Tables, figures, and boxes are indicated by an italic *t*, *f*, and *b* following the page number. Footnotes are indicated by the letter 'n' following the page number.

Israel 93
Italy 244, 277
   see also Reggio Emilia
I–Thou awareness 19, 34, 61

J

Jain, J. 47
James, Alison 129
James, William 17, 142, 147
Japan 72, 244
Jasper, H.H. 62
Jesuits 16
Johnstone, B. 142
Jones, C. 185
Joseph, Marilyn 265
joy
   in companionship 4, 11*f*, 218
   in sharing 86

K

Kaiser Permanente 163, 172
kangaroo care of premature baby 22*f*
Kant, Immanuel 40, 41
Kautz, T. 307
Kegan, R. 144
Kelly-Ware, J. 307
Kemmis, S. 300
Kennedy, John F. 59
Key, Ellen 235 n
kindergartens, *see* nursery schools
Kingswood Community Nursery, Corby 294
Kinney, P. 47, 51–2
Klein, Melanie 44
knowledge-based economies 241
Kohlberg, L. 146
Komensky, John Amos (Comenius) 15, 16
Kraamzorg 174
Kugiumutzakis, Giannis 21

L

Laevers, Ferre 281
Lancy, D. 106
Langer, Susan 17, 27
language development
   from proto-language musicality to language-specific vowels 25, 29, 30*f*
   language readiness at the end of infancy 162, 163*f*
   with assistance in the Harlem Project 265
Lashley, Karl, serial ordering of movements 67
Latvia 170
Leadsom, Andrea 184
Learner, S. 185
learning
   anthropology, insights from 32–3
   barriers to 10, 13
   in community 2–3, 4–5, 316
      education of understanding 313–16
      enthusiasm for 3
      initiative of children 311–13
      moral foundations 313

      politics and practice 10, 313–16
      respect for 'common sense' 311–12
      traditional practices 2
   dispositions 297, 299, 307
   home 8
   in nature (*see* natural environment)
   lifelong 44, 214, 223, 241, 303
   motives 10, 14, 311–16
   playful 3, 8–9, 312
   principles 197–8
   resources 87–90, 93–9, 102
   socio-cultural 212
   summary of practices 116
   vitality for learning 10, 13
   see also collaborative learning; our learning
learning operating system (LOS) 296, 297
Learning to be Strong (LTBS) programme 278
Leuven Involvement Scale 281
Lewis, Tyson E. 136
lifelong learning 44, 214, 223, 241, 303
   working theories 303
life skills 166, 167
Lindgren, Astrid, *Pippi Longstocking* 131–2, 135, 136
Linnæus, Carl 193
listening, pedagogy of 196, 198, 199, 209, 210
literacy
   enriching environments 102–3
   home life 97
Lithuania 170
logico-scientific intelligence 77–8
Lothian Region 7–8
   A Curriculum for the Early Years 3–8: 221, 221*b*
lying 126, 131–3, 135, 136–7

M

Mackenzie, A.F. 217
MacKinnon, Gill 7
Macmurray, John 1, 311
MacNaughton, G. 183
Magnússon, Snorri 18*f*, 19
make-believe 133–5, 137
   and lying with imagination, for well-being and fun in relationships, 126
making sense together 296–9, 307
Malaguzzi, Loris
   community-affirming education 5
   courage of utopia 198, 201, 210
   essence of Reggio approach 115, 196–8, 200–1, 210
   one child's creativity 197*f*
   hundred languages of childhood 17
   moral development 119
   'No way. The hundred is there' 194–5
   vision 238
male role models 179, 180, 181, 183, 184
Malloch, Stephen 22, 27–8, 28*f*, 128, 142
Manning-Morton, J. 52
Maoris 4, 33, 248
Marshall, Ros 8
Martlew, J. 201
maternal employment 238–40, 242, 246

Saint-Exupéry, Antoine de 86, 103
salaries, childcare workforce 120, 182, 183, 185
Samoan culture 300, 303–4, 305*f*
Sander, Louis 20, 66
Scarlett, W. 40, 45
schemas
 Pen Green Centre, Corby 280–1, 285
 social
  co-created narratives 72–3
  that enable learning 16, 73–7
 of thought, feeling, and action, with
  ambition 59, 60–1
 and working theories 298
Schleicher, Andreas 223
Schutz, A. 145
Schooling
 curriculum of instruction with tests 13
 transition from early education and care 13
Scotland
 Achieving Our Potential 222
 attitude towards children 172, 175
 Building the Ambition 223, 224, 314
 *Building the Curriculum 2—The Early Level
  3–6*: 224
 *Building the Curriculum 3–18—Active Learning in
  the Early Years 3–6*: 222
 Child Poverty Bill 171
 Children and Young People Scotland Act
  (2014) 223
 children's rights 160, 162, 165–6, 170
 children's varied lifestyles 160
 Child's Curriculum group 2, 7–10
 and Corby, England 277, 280, 283, 289
 Curriculum for Excellence 3–18 (CfE) 215, 222,
  223, 314, 314*b*
 Curriculum Framework 3–5: 222
 *Curriculum Framework for the Pre-School
  Year* 222
 early-level curriculum 212–32, 313–14, 316
  play 49
  working theories 299
 Early Level Curriculum 3–6: 224–5, 227, 228,
  232, 314
 early years care and parenting 173–4, 176–7
  developmental disorders, care and parental
   work 174–7
 Early Years Framework 222
 Education Act (1633) 214
 Enlightenment 2, 214, 221, 231–2
 Equally Well 222
 Futureskills Scotland 166
 gender balance in childcare workforce 182, 183,
  185, 187, 188
 Getting it Right for Every Child 222, 314
 history of education 214–22
 humanism 2, 213, 214
 Independent Review of the Scottish Early
  Learning and Childcare Workforce and out
  of School Care 2015 201
 Men in Childcare (MIC) 185–6, 188
 National Practice Guidance 39

needs of children and their parents, attention
 to 170–1
overall well-being of children 170
play 49
Pre-birth to Three 224
primary schools 8–9, 217, 221, 224–5, 231, 314
proto-conversations 72
public spending 172–3, 176–7
secondary schools 223
smoking ban 173–4
working theories 299
Scottish Enterprise 166
secondary schools
 male teachers 183
 Scotland 223
 struggling teenagers 230
 transition to 223
security, and environmental well-being 109
Seldin, T. 114
self
 animate 311
 development in companionship 311–12
 Macmurray on 311
 as purposeful agent 1
self-confidence 2
 communicative musicality 28
 enriching environments 85, 86, 88
 gender balance in childcare workforce 181
 Montessori method 114
 nurture groups 73, 77
 Scottish early-level curriculum 223
 shared narratives 80
 transition from ECEC to primary school 230
  risks for spontaneous learning 13
 whole child 103, 247
self-creation 103, 133
self-generated movements, *see* movement
self-regulation
 evolved developmental niche 105–6
  child well-being framework 110
  developmentally appropriate practice 108
  Reggio Emilia method 116
  RIE* 112
 moral development 117
 self-realization 86, 100–1
 shame inhibits learning 13
self-reliance 85, 86, 88, 91–2
self-respect 110
Selleck, D. 52
sense-making 296–9, 307
 aesthetic agency 129–30
 embodied projects of organised
  movement 60, 80
 planning actions as rituals 64
 practical and reasoned agency 79–80
 shared plans of action for
  meaning-making 59–80
sensorimotor intelligence 18*f*, 60
sensory development 162, 163*f*
serendipity 89–90
serotonin 120